Studies in International Investment Law
Studien zum Internationalen Investitionsrecht

edited by
Prof. Dr. Marc Bungenberg, LL.M., Universität des Saarlandes
Prof. Dr. Dr. h.c. Dr. h.c. Stephan Hobe, LL.M., Universität zu Köln
Prof. Dr. August Reinisch, LL.M., Universität Wien
Prof. Dr. Andreas R. Ziegler, LL.M., Universität Lausanne

in cooperation with
International Investment Law Centre Cologne (IILCC)
Prof. Dr. Dr. h.c. Dr. h.c. Stephan Hobe, LL.M.
Prof. Dr. Bernhard Kempen
Prof. Dr. Heinz-Peter Mansel
Prof. Dr. Burkhard Schöbener

Volume 43
and Volume 20 of the series
International Investment Law Centre Cologne (IILCC)

Julian Scheu (Ed.)

Creation and Implementation of a Multilateral Investment Court

Assistant Editor
Lisa Schöttmer

HART
PUBLISHING

Nomos

facultas

DIKE

The Deutsche Nationalbibliothek lists this publication in the Deutsche Nationalbibliografie; detailed bibliographic data are available on the Internet at http://dnb.d-nb.de

ISBN:	HB (Nomos)	978-3-8487-8386-1
	ePDF (Nomos)	978-3-7489-2776-1

ISBN	978-3-7089-2285-0	(facultas Verlag, Wien)
ISBN	978-3-03891-473-0	(Dike Verlag, Zürich/St. Gallen)

British Library Cataloguing-in-Publication Data
A catalogue record for this book is available from the British Library.

ISBN:	HB (Hart)	978-1-5099-6436-9

Library of Congress Cataloging-in-Publication Data
Scheu, Julian
Creation and Implementation of a Multilateral Investment Court
Julian Scheu (Ed.)
331 pp.
Includes bibliographic references.

ISBN	978-1-5099-6436-9	(hardcover Hart)

1st Edition 2022

Foreword

Intensive discussions have been taking place over recent years on the future of the dispute settlement mechanism in international investment law. Whereas, on the one hand, advocates of the traditional system of international adjudication point to the undisputed success of ad hoc investment arbitration, advocates of substantial reforms favor a more permanent system such as the establishment of a Multilateral Investment Court (MIC).

This was the background against which a group of young lawyers involved with the International Investment Law Centre Cologne (IILCC) assembled and discussed the various alternatives and problems of an MIC, thereby taking stock of the current discussion held at UNCITRAL Working Group III.

Under the guidance of the institute's General Manager, Junior Professor Dr. Julian Scheu, the various aspects were discussed in detail before each of the participants laid down his and her ideas in writing. Many thanks are due to the IILCC staff members Lisa Schoettmer and Eva-Maria Wettstein who provided outstanding assistance in this process.

The result looks to me like a remarkable contribution to the current debate. Accordingly, the IILCC had no hesitation in incorporating this book into its publication series on international investment law.

Be the readers inspired and the book a welcome contribution to this ongoing debate!

Cologne, March 2022
Prof. Dr. Dr. h.c. Stephan Hobe
Executive Director
International Investment Law Centre Cologne

Table of Contents

Abbreviations

ACWL	Advisory Centre on World Trade Law
ACWLA	Agreement Establishing the Advisory Centre on WTO Law
ADR	Alternative Dispute Resolution
BEPS	Base Erosion and Profit Shifting
BIT	Bilateral Investment Treaty
CAS	Court of Arbitration for Sport
CCIAG	Counsel International Arbitration Group
CETA	Comprehensive Economic and Trade Agreement
cf	*confer*
Charter	Charter of Fundamental Rights of the European Union
CIDS	Geneva Centre for International Dispute Settlement
CJEU	Court of Justice of the European Union
COP	Conference of the Parties
CRCICA	Cairo Regional Centre for International Commercial Arbitration
DIS	Deutsche Institution für Schiedsgerichtsbarkeit
Doc(s)	Document(s)
DPA	Dispute Prevention and Avoidance
DPM	Dispute Prevention Mechanisms
DPP	Dispute Prevention Policies
DSU	Understanding on Rules and Procedures Governing the Settlement of Disputes
ECHR	European Convention of Human Rights
ECT	Energy Charter Treaty
ed(s)	editor(s)
edn	edition

EFILA	European Federation for Investment Law and Arbitration
eg	*exempli gratia*
et al	*et alia*
et seq(q)	*et sequentes/ et sequential*
etc	*et cetera*
EU	European Union
FDI	Foreign Direct Investment
FTA	Free Trade Agreement
FTC	Free Trade Commission
GATT	General Agreement on Tariffs and Trade
IASB	International Accounting Standards Board
IBA	International Bar Association
IBA Guidelines	IBA Guidelines on Conflicts of Interest in International Arbitration
ibid	*ibidem*
ICC	International Chamber of Commerce
ICJ	International Court of Justice
ICS	Investment Court System
ICSID	International Centre for Settlement of Investment Disputes
IDLO	International Development Law Organization
ie	*id est*
IIA	International Investment Agreement
IILCC	International Investment Law Centre Cologne
IIMS	International Investment Mediation Service
IPA	Investment Protection Agreements
ISDA	International Swaps and Derivatives Association
ISDS	Investor-State Dispute Settlement
ISP	Investment Support Programme
ITLOS	International Tribunal for the Law of the Sea
IUSCT	Iran-United States Claims Tribunal
JAC	Joint Administrative Commissions

KOTRA	Korea Trade-Investment Promotion Agency
LCIA	London Court of International Arbitration
LDC	Least Developed Countries
lit	*littera*
MAI	Multilateral Agreement on Investment
MFN	Most-favoured-nation
MIAM	Multilateral Investment Appeals Mechanism
MIC	Multilateral Investment Court
MIC Draft Statute	Draft Statute of the Multilateral Investment Court
MIDSI	Multilateral Institution for Dispute Settlement on Investment
MLI	Multilateral Convention to Implement Tax Treaty Related Measures to Prevent Base Erosion and Profit Shifting
MRI	Multilateral Reform Instrument
n	Footnote
NAFTA	North American Free Trade Agreement
NGO	Non-governmental Organisation
No	Number
OAS	Organization of American States
OECD	Organisation for Economic Cooperation and Development
OIO	Office of the Foreign Investment Ombudsman
para(s)	paragraph(s)
PCA	Permanent Court of Arbitration
QMUL	Queen Mary University of London
SCC	Arbitration Institute of the Stockholm Chamber of Commerce
SME	Small and Medium Enterprises
SSDS	State-to-State Dispute Settlement
TEU	Treaty on European Union
TFA	Task Force Argentina
TFEU	Treaty on the Functioning of the European Union

TPF	Third-Party Funding
TTIP	Transatlantic Trade and Investment Partnership
UN	United Nations
UNCITRAL	United Nations Commission on International Trade Law
UNCLOS	United Nations Convention on the Law of the Sea
UNCTAD	United Nations Conference on Trade and Development
UNFCCC	United Nations Framework Convention on Climate Change
UNTS	United Nations Treaty Series
US	United States
USD	United States Dollar
v	*versus*
VCLT	Vienna Convention on the Law of Treaties
WTO	World Trade Organization

UNCITRAL Working Group III – Working Paper Documents

All documents accessed online on 13 January 2022.

Full citation	Doc.-No.	Short Name	Date	Cited in this volume
UNCITRAL, Working Group III, 'Possible Reform of Investor-State Dispute Settlement (ISDS) - Note by the Secretariat' (18 September 2017), A/CN.9/WG.III/WP.142, available at https://undocs.org/en/A/CN.9/WG.III/WP.142	A/CN.9/WG.III/WP.142	UNCITRAL WG III, Possible Reform of ISDS, WP 142 (2017)	2017-09-18	Chap. 02, Fn 42, 84.
UNCITRAL, Working Group III, 'Possible reform of investor-State dispute settlement (ISDS): Submission from the European Union and its Member States' (12 December 2017), A/CN.9/WG.III/WP.145, available at https://undocs.org/en/A/CN.9/WG.III/WP.145	A/CN.9/WG.III/WP.145	UNCITRAL WG III, Submission European Union and its Member States, WP 145 (2017)	2017-12-12	Chap. 06, Fn 50, 54, 63, 187, 188. Chap. 11, Fn 03, 55, 79.
UNCITRAL, Working Group III, 'Possible reform of investor-State dispute settlement (ISDS)' (5 September 2018), A/CN.9/WG.III/WP.149, available at https://undocs.org/en/A/CN.9/WG.III/WP.149	A/CN.9/WG.III/WP.149	UNCITRAL WG III, Possible Reform of ISDS, WP 149 (2020)	2020-11-12	Chap. 03, Fn 42. Chap. 05, Fn 110. Chap. 07, Fn 03.
UNCITRAL, Working Group III, 'Possible reform of investor-State dispute settlement (ISDS) - Consistency and related matters - Note by the Secretariat' (28 August 2018), A/CN.9/WG.III/WP.150, available at https://undocs.org/en/A/CN.9/WG.III/WP.150	A/CN.9/WG.III/WP.150	UNCITRAL WG III, Consistency, WP 150 (2018)	2018-08-28	Chap. 04, Fn 04, 19, 25, 40, 44, 76.
UNCITRAL, Working Group III, 'Cost and Duration - Note by the Secretariat" (31 August 2018), A/CN.9/WG.III/WP.153, avail-	A/CN.9/WG.III/WP.153	UNCITRAL WG III, Cost and Duration, WP 153 (2018)	2018-08-31	Chap. 02, Fn 45. Chap. 03, Fn 42.

Full citation	Doc.-No.	Short Name	Date	Cited in this volume
able at https://undocs.org/en/A/CN.9/WG.III/WP.153				
UNCITRAL, Working Group III, 'Possible reform of investor-State dispute settlement (ISDS) Submission from the European Union and its Member States' (24 January 2019), A/CN.9/WG.III/WP.159/Add.1, available at https://undocs.org/en/A/CN.9/WG.III/WP.159/Add.1	A/CN.9/WG.III/WP.159/Add.1	UNCITRAL WG III, Submission European Union and its Member States, WP 159 (2019)	2019-01-24	Chap. 05, Fn 131. Chap. 06, Fn 50, 63, 188. Chap. 08, Fn 29, 30, 93. Chap. 10, Fn 02, 22, 25, 28. Chap. 11, Fn 03, 56, 58, 59, 71, 72, 82.
UNCITRAL, Working Group III, 'Submission from the Government of Morocco' (4 March 2019), A/CN.9/WG.III/WP.161, available at https://undocs.org/en/A/CN.9/WG.III/WP.161	A/CN.9/WG.III/WP.161	UNCITRAL WG III, Submission Morocco, WP 161 (2019)	2019-03-04	Chap. 03, Fn 109.
UNCITRAL, Working Group III, 'Submission from the Government of Thailand' (8 March 2019) A/CN.9/WG.III/WP.162, available at https://undocs.org/en/A/CN.9/WG.III/WP.162	A/CN.9/WG.III/WP.162	UNCITRAL WG III, Submission Thailand, WP 162 (2019)	2019-03-08	Chap. 02, Fn 61. Chap. 03, Fn 39, 44, 47.
UNCITRAL, Working Group III, 'Submission from the Governments of Chile, Israel and Japan' (15 March 2019), A/CN.9/WG.III/WP.163, available at https://undocs.org/en/A/CN.9/WG.III/WP.163	A/CN.9/WG.III/WP.163	UNCITRAL WG III, Submission Chile, Israel and Japan, WP 163 (2019)	2019-03-15	Chap. 02, Fn 61.
UNCITRAL, Working Group III, 'Submission from the Government of Costa Rica' (22 March 2019), A/CN.9/WG.III/WP.164, available at https://undocs.org/en/A/CN.9/WG.III/WP.164	A/CN.9/WG.III/WP.164	UNCITRAL WG III, Submission Costa Rica, WP 164 (2019)	2019-03-22	Chap. 02, Fn 61. Chap. 03, Fn 39.
UNCITRAL, Working Group III, 'Possible reform of investor-State dispute settlement (ISDS), Note by the Secretariat' (15 Jan-	A/CN.9/WG.III/WP.166	UNCITRAL WG III, Possible Reform of	2020-01-15	Chap. 02, Fn 47.

Full citation	Doc.-No.	Short Name	Date	Cited in this volume
uary 2020), A/CN.9/WG.III/ WP.166, available at https://undocs.org/en/A/CN.9/WG.III/WP.166		ISDS, WP 166 (2020)		
UNCITRAL, Working Group III, 'Possible Reform of Investor-State Dispute Settlement' (30 July 2019), A/CN.9/WG.III/ WP.166/Add.1, available at https://undocs.org/en/A/CN.9/WG.III/WP.166/Add.1	A/CN.9/ WG.III/ WP.166/Add.1	UNCITRAL WG III, Reform Options Table, WP 166/Add.1 (2019)	2019-07-30	Chap. 02, Fn 43.
UNCITRAL, Working Group III, 'Possible reform of investor-State dispute settlement (ISDS) Advisory Centre' (25 July 2019), A/CN.9/WG.III/WP.168, available at https://undocs.org/en/A/CN.9/WG.III/WP.168	A/CN.9/ WG.III/ WP.168	UNCITRAL WG III, Advisory Centre, WP 168 (2019)	2019-07-25	Chap. 03, Fn 45, 46, 51, 53,118.
UNCITRAL, Working Group III, 'Possible reform of investor-State dispute settlement (ISDS), Note by the Secretariat, Selection and appointment of ISDS tribunal members' (31 July 2019), A/CN.9/WG.III/ WP.169, available at https://undocs.org/en/A/CN.9/WG.III/WP.169	A/CN.9/ WG.III/ WP.169	UNCITRAL WG III, Selection and appointment of ISDS tribunal members, WP 169 (2019)	2019-07-31	Chap. 06, Fn 02, 06, 12, 13, 27, 36.
UNCITRAL, Working Group III, 'Possible reform of investor-State dispute settlement (ISDS), Shareholders claims and reflective loss' (9 August 2019), A/CN.9/ WG.III/WP.170, available at https://undocs.org/en/A/CN.9/WG.III/WP.170	A/CN.9/ WG.III/ WP.170	UNCITRAL WG III, Shareholder claims and reflective loss, WP 170 (2019)	2019-08-09	Chap. 05, Fn 108.
UNCITRAL, Working Group III, 'Possible reform of investor-State dispute settlement (ISDS) Third-party funding – Possible solutions' (2 August 2019), A/CN.9/WG.III/WP.172, available at https://undocs.org/en/A/CN.9/WG.III/WP.172	A/CN.9/ WG.III/ WP.172	UNCITRAL WG III, Third-party funding – Possible solutions, WP 172 (2019)	2019-08-02	Chap. 03, Fn 48, 114, 115.

Full citation	Doc.-No.	Short Name	Date	Cited in this volume
UNCITRAL, Working Group III, 'Possible reform of investor-State dispute settlement (ISDS), Submission from the Government of Colombia' (14 June 2019), A/CN.9/WG.III/WP.173, available at https://undocs.org/en/A/CN.9/WG.III/WP.173	A/CN.9/WG.III/WP.173	UNCITRAL WG III, Submission Colombia, WP 173 (2019)	2019-06-14	Chap. 08, Fn 30, 58.
UNCITRAL, Working Group III, 'Submission from the Government of Turkey' (11 July 2019), A/CN.9/WG.III/WP.174, available at https://undocs.org/en/A/CN.9/WG.III/WP.174	A/CN.9/WG.III/WP.174	UNCITRAL WG III, Submission Turkey, WP 174 (2019)	2019-07-11	Chap. 03, Fn 43, 47.
UNCITRAL, Working Group III, 'Possible reform of investor-State dispute settlement (ISDS), Submission from the Government of Ecuador' (17 July 2019), A/CN.9/WG.III/WP.175, available at https://undocs.org/en/A/CN.9/WG.III/WP.175	A/CN.9/WG.III/WP.175	UNCITRAL WG III, Submission Ecuador, WP 175 (2019)	2019-07-17	Chap. 08, Fn 29, 30.
UNCITRAL, Working Group III, 'Submission by the Government of China' (19 July 2019), A/CN.9/WG.III/WP.177, available at https://undocs.org/en/A/CN.9/WG.III/WP.177	A/CN.9/WG.III/WP.177	UNCITRAL WG III, Submission China, WP 177 (2019)	2019-07-19	Chap. 02, Fn 09.
UNCITRAL, Working Group III, 'Submission from the Government of Costa Rica' (31 July 2019), A/CN.9/WG.III/WP.178, available at https://undocs.org/en/A/CN.9/WG.III/WP.178	A/CN.9/WG.III/WP.178	UNCITRAL WG III, Submission Costa Rica, WP 178 (2019)	2019-07-31	Chap. 02, Fn 61.
UNCITRAL, Working Group III, 'Submission from the Government of the Republic of Korea' (31 July 2019), A/CN.9/WG.III/WP.179, available at https://undocs.org/A/CN.9/WG.III/WP.179	A/CN.9/WG.III/WP.179	UNCITRAL WG III, Submission Korea, WP 179 (2019)	2019-07-31	Chap. 02, Fn 115. Chap. 03, Fn 41, 44, 47, 55, 89, 90.

Full citation	Doc.-No.	Short Name	Date	Cited in this volume
UNCITRAL, Working Group III, 'Submission from the Government of Bahrain' (29 August 2019), A/CN.9/WG.III/WP.180, available at https://undocs.org/A/CN.9/WG.III/WP.180	A/CN.9/WG.III/WP.180	UNCITRAL WG III, Submission Bahrain, WP 180 (2019)	2019-08-29	Chap. 02, Fn 44, 61.
UNCITRAL, Working Group III, 'Possible reform of investor-State dispute settlement (ISDS), Submission from the Governments of Chile, Israel, Japan, Mexico and Peru' (2 October 2019), A/CN.9/WG.III/WP.182, available at https://undocs.org/en/A/CN.9/WG.III/WP.182	A/CN.9/WG.III/WP.182	UNCITRAL WG III, Submission Chile, Israel, Japan, Mexico and Peru, WP 182 (2019)	2019-10-02	Chap. 08, Fn 29, 30.
UNCITRAL, Working Group III, 'Possible reform of investor-State dispute settlement (ISDS) - Appellate and multilateral court mechanisms, Note by the Secretariat' (29 November 2019), A/CN.9/WG.III/WP.185, available at https://undocs.org/en/A/CN.9/WG.III/WP.185	A/CN.9/WG.III/WP.185	UNCITRAL WG III, Appellate and multilateral court mechanisms, WP 185 (2019)	2019-11-29	Chap. 02, Fn 04, 09, 39. Chap. 04, Fn 111, 112, 121, 144, 147, 154, 155, 164, 166.
UNCITRAL, Working Group III, 'Submission from the Government of the Russian Federation' (30 December 2019), A/CN.9/WG.III/WP.188, available at https://undocs.org/en/A/CN.9/WG.III/WP.188/Add.1	A/CN.9/WG.III/WP.188	UNCITRAL WG III, Submission Russian Federation, WP 188 (2019)	2019-12-30	Chap. 02, Fn 44, 61. Chap. 03, Fn 43, 47.
UNCITRAL, Working Group III, 'Possible reform of investor-State dispute settlement (ISDS), Dispute prevention and mitigation - Means of alternative dispute resolution, Note by the Secretariat' (15 January 2020), A/CN.9/WG.III/WP.190, available at https://undocs.org/en/A/CN.9/WG.III/WP.190	A/CN.9/WG.III/WP.190	UNCITRAL WG III, Dispute prevention and mitigation, WP 190 (2020)	2020-01-15	Chap. 02, Fn 96, 112, 121, 126, 130, 152, 153. Chap. 03, Fn 45, 51, 109.

Full citation	Doc.-No.	Short Name	Date	Cited in this volume
UNCITRAL, Working Group III, 'Possible Reform of Investor-State Dispute Settlement (ISDS) – Interpretation of Investment Treaties by Treaty Parties' (17 January 2020), A/CN.9/WG.III/WP.191, available at https://undocs.org/en/A/CN.9/WG.III/WP.191	A/CN.9/WG.III/WP.191	UNCITRAL WG III, Interpretation of Treaties, WP 191 (2020)	2020-01-17	Chap. 02, Fn 83. Chap. 03, Fn 50.
UNCITRAL, Working Group III, 'Possible reform of investor-State dispute settlement (ISDS), Multiple proceedings and counterclaims' (22 January 2020), A/CN.9/WG.III/WP.193, available at https://undocs.org/en/A/CN.9/WG.III/WP.193	A/CN.9/WG.III/WP.193	UNCITRAL WG III, Multiple proceedings and counterclaims, WP 193 (2020)	2020-01-22	Chap. 05, Fn 109, 142.
UNCITRAL, Working Group III, 'Possible reform of investor-State dispute settlement (ISDS) – Multilateral instrument on ISDS Reform' (16 January 2020), A/CN.9/WG.III/WP.194, available at https://undocs.org/en/A/CN.9/WG.III/WP.194	A/CN.9/WG.III/WP.194	UNCITRAL WG III, Multilateral instrument on ISDS reform, WP 194 (2020)	2020-01-16	Chap. 02, Fn 175. Chap. 04, Fn 51. Chap. 05, Fn 10. Chap. 08, Fn 03, 04, 12, 16, 23, 28, 29, 30, 47, 54, 58, 60, 84, 86, 96, 107, 116.
UNCITRAL, Working Group III, 'Possible reform of investor-State dispute settlement (ISDS), Draft code of conduct, Note by the Secretariat' (9 November 2020), A/CN.9/WG.III/WP.201, available at https://undocs.org/en/A/CN.9/WG.III/WP.201	A/CN.9/WG.III/WP.201	UNCITRAL WG III, Draft code of conduct, WP 201 (2020)	2020-11-09	Chap. 08, Fn 90.
UNCITRAL, Working Group III, 'Appellate mechanism and enforcement issues, Draft Note by the Secretariat' (12 November 2020), A/CN.9/WG.III/WP.202, available at https://undocs.org/en/A/CN.9/WG.III/WP.202	A/CN.9/WG.III/WP.202	UNCITRAL WG III, Appellate mechanism and enforcement issues, WP 202 (2020)	2020-11-12	Chap. 02, Fn 09. Chap. 09, Fn 17, 31, 71, 94, 95, 111, 138.

Full citation	**Doc.-No.**	**Short Name**	**Date**	**Cited in this volume**
UNCITRAL, Working Group III, 'Possible reform of investor-State dispute settlement (ISDS) Selection and appointment of ISDS tribunal members' (16 November 2020), A/CN.9/WG.III/WP.203, available at https://documents-dds-ny.un.org/doc/UNDOC/LTD/V20/065/89/PDF/V2006589.pdf?OpenElement	A/CN.9/WG.III/WP.203	UNCITRAL WG III, Selection and appointment of tribunal members, WP 203 (2020)	2020-11-16	Chap. 11, Fn 61.
UNCITRAL, Working Group III, 'Possible reform of investor-State dispute settlement (ISDS) Standing multilateral mechanism: Selection and appointment of ISDS tribunal members and related matters, Note by the Secretariat' (8 December 2021), A/CN.9/WG.III/WP.213 (advance copy) available at https://uncitral.un.org/sites/uncitral.un.org/files/media-documents/uncitral/en/acwp_213_for_submission.pdf	A/CN.9/WG.III/WP.213	UNCITRAL WG III, Selection and appointment of ISDS tribunal members and related matters, WP 213 (2021)	2021-12-08	Chap. 1, Fn 78. Chap. 2, Fn 12. Chap. 6, Fn 6, 13, 25, 165, 173. Chap. 7, Fn 75.
UNCITRAL, Working Group III, 'Annotated comments from the European Union and its Member States to the UNCITRAL Secretariat*' (19 October 2020), A/CN.9/WG.III/WP., available at https://trade.ec.europa.eu/doclib/docs/2020/november/tradoc_159043.pdf	A/CN.9/WG.III/WP.	UNCITRAL WG III, Comments EU and Member States, WP. (2020)	2020-10-19	Chap. 09, Fn 96.
UNCITRAL Working Group III, 'Possible reform of investor-State dispute settlement (ISDS) Mediation and other forms of alternative dispute resolution (ADR), Note by the Secretariat' (2021), available at https://uncitral.un.org/sites/uncitral.un.org/files/media-documents/uncitral/en/draft_clauses_on_mediation.pdf		UNCITRAL WG III, Mediation and other forms of ADR (2021)		Chap. 2, Fn 126, 152, 160.

UNCITRAL Session Reports and other UNCITRAL Documents

All documents accessed online on 13 January 2022.

Full citation	Doc.-No.	Short Name	Date	Cited in this volume
UNCITRAL, 'Report of the United Nations Commission on International Trade Law on the work of its eighteenth session' (3-21 June 1985), A/40/17, available at https://undocs.org/en/a/40/17(supp)	A/40/17	UNCITRAL, Report Trade Law, Session 18, A/40/17 (1985)	1985-06-03	Chap. 09, Fn 106.
UNCITRAL, 'Report of the United Nations Commission on International Trade Law on the work of its thirty-ninth session' (19 June-7July 2006), A/61/17, available at https://undocs.org/en/A/61/17(SUPP)	A/61/17	UNCITRAL, Report Trade Law, Session 39, A/61/17 (2006)	2006-06-19	Chap. 09, Fn 72, 106.
UNCITRAL, 'Report of the United Nations Commission on International Trade Law, Forty-sixth session' (8-26 July 2013), A/68/17, available at https://undocs.org/A/68/17	A/68/17	UNCITRAL, Report Trade Law, Session 46, A/68/17 (2013)	2013-07-8	Chap. 08, Fn 35.
UNCITRAL, 'Report of the United Nations Commission on International Trade Law, Forty-ninth session (27 June-15 July 2016)', A/71/17, available at https://documents-dds-ny.un.org/doc/UNDOC/GEN/V16/048/29/PDF/V1604829.pdf?OpenElement	A/71/17	UNCITRAL, Report Trade Law, Session 49, A/71/17 (2016)	2016-06-27	Chap. 01, Fn 58.
UNCITRAL, 'Report of Working Group II (Arbitration and Conciliation) on the work of its fifty-fifth session (Vienna, 3-7 October 2011)' (17 October 2011), A/CN.9/736, available at https://undocs.org/en/A/CN.9/736	A/CN.9/736	UNCITRAL, Report WG II, Session 55, A/CN.9/736 (2011)	2011-10-17	Chap. 08, Fn 88.
UNCITRAL, 'Possible future work in the field of dispute settlement: Reforms of investor	A/CN.9/917	UNCITRAL, Possible future work in the	2017-04-20	Chap. 03, Fn 38.

Full citation	Doc.-No.	Short Name	Date	Cited in this volume
State dispute settlement (ISDS)' (20 April 2017), A/CN.9/917, available at https://undocs.org/A/CN.9/917		field of dispute settlement, A/CN.9/917 (2017)		
UNCITRAL, 'Report of Working Group III (Investor-State Dispute Settlement Reform) on the work of its thirty-fourth session (Vienna, 27 November-1 December 2017), Part I' (19 December 2017), A/CN.9/930/Rev. 1, available at https://undocs.org/en/A/CN.9/930/Rev.1	A/CN.9/930/Rev. 1	UNCITRAL, Report WG III, Session 34, A/CN.9/930/Rev. 1 (2017)	2017-12-19	Chap. 01, Fn 59. Chap. 03, Fn 39. Chap. 05, Fn 122. Chap. 10, Fn 23.
UNCITRAL, 'Report of the Working Group III (Investor-State Dispute Settlement Reform) on the work of its Thirty-Fourth Session (Vienna, 27 Nobember-1 December 2017) Part II' (26 February 2018), available at https://documents-dds-ny.un.org/doc/UNDOC/GEN/V18/029/89/PDF/V1802989.pdf?OpenElement	A/CN.9/930/Add.1/Rev.	UNCITRAL, Report WG III, Session 34, A/CN.9/930/Add.1/Rev. (2018)	2018-02-26	Chap. 02, Fn 42.
UNCITRAL, 'Report of Working Group III on the work of its thirty-fifth session' (14 May 2018), A/CN.9/935, available at https://undocs.org/en/A/CN.9/935	A/CN.9/935	UNCITRAL, Report WG III, Session 35, A/CN.9/935 (2018)	2018-05-14	Chap. 01, Fn 92. Chap. 05, Fn 109, 112.
UNCITRAL, 'Report of Working Group III on the work of its thirty-sixth session (Vienna, 29 October–2 November 2018)', (6 November 2018), A/CN.9/964, available at https://undocs.org/en/A/CN.9/964	A/CN.9/964	UNCITRAL, Report WG III, Session 36, A/CN.9/964 (2018)	2018-11-06	Chap. 03, Fn 39. Chap. 06, Fn 165. Chap. 07, Fn 07.
UNCITRAL, 'Report of Working Group III (Investor-State Dispute Settlement Reform) on the work of its thirty-seventh session (New York, 1–5 April 2019)', (9 April 2019), A/CN.9/970, available at https://documents-dds-ny.un.org/doc/UNDOC/GEN/V19/024/04/PDF/V1902404.pdf?OpenElement	A/CN.9/970	UNCITRAL, Report WG III, Session 52, A/CN.9/970 (2019)	2019-04-09	Chap. 01, Fn 92.
UNCITRAL, 'Report of Working Group III (Investor-State	A/CN.9/1004*	UNCITRAL, Report WG	2019-10-23	Chap. 03, Fn 40, 41, 49, 52, 54, 56,

Full citation	**Doc.-No.**	**Short Name**	**Date**	**Cited in this volume**
Dispute Settlement Reform) on the work of its thirty-eighth session (Vienna, 14–18 October 2019)' (23 October 2019), A/CN.9/1004*, available at https://undocs.org/en/A/CN.9/1004		III, Session 38, A/CN.9/1004* (2019)		87, 88, 92, 93, 96, 98, 102, 128. Chap. 08, Fn 03, 29.
UNCITRAL, 'Report of Working Group III (Investor-State Dispute Settlement Reform) on the work of its resumed thirty-eighth session' (28 January 2020), A/CN.9/1004/Add.1, available at https://undocs.org/en/A/CN.9/1004/Add.1	A/CN.9/1004/Add.1	UNCITRAL, Report WG III, Resumed Session 38, A/CN.9/1004/Add.1 (2020)	2020-01-28	Chap. 01, Fn 60. Chap. 04, Fn 161, 162, 164, 169, 197. Chap. 06, Fn 03, 25, 29, 40, 43, 153. Chap. 10, Fn 24.
UNCITRAL, 'Report of Working Group III (Investor-State Dispute Settlement Reform) on the work of its thirty-ninth session (Vienna, 5-9 October 2020)' (10 November 2020), A/CN.9/1044, available at https://undocs.org/en/A/CN.9/1044	A/CN.9/1044	UNCITRAL, Report WG III, Session 39, A/CN.9/1044 (2020)	2020-11-10	Chap. 04, Fn 49. Chap. 08, Fn 02, 03, 19, 56, 58, 97.
UNCITRAL, Working Group II (Arbitration and Conciliation), 'Settlement of commercial disputes, Preparation of a legal standard on transparency in treaty-based investor-State arbitration, Comments of arbitral institutions on the interplay between the draft rules on transparency and their institutional rules, Note by the Secretariat' (19 July 2012), A/CN.9/WG.II/WP.173, available at https://undocs.org/en/A/cn.9/WG.II/WP.173	A/CN.9/WG.II/WP.173	UNCITRAL WG II, Settlement of commercial disputes, WP 173 (2012)	2012-07-19	Chap. 08, Fn 89.
ICSID, UNCITRAL, 'Draft Code of Conduct for Adjudicators in International Investment Disputes, Version Two' (19 April 2021), available at https://icsid.worldbank.org/sites/default/files/draft_code_of_conduct_v2_en_final.pdf		ICSID, UNCITRAL, 'Draft Code of Conduct for Adjudicators in International Investment Disputes, Version Two' (19 April 2021)	2021-04-19	Chap. 07 Fn 8, 40, 58, 82, 88, 90.

Full citation	Doc.-No.	Short Name	Date	Cited in this volume
UNCITRAL, ICSID, 'Draft Code of Conduct, Comments by State/Commenter as of January 14, 2021' (14 January 2021), available at https://uncitral.un.org/sites/uncitral.un.org/files/media-documents/uncitral/en/code_of_conduct_-_comments_by_state-commenter_-_updated_01.14.21.pdf		UNCITRAL, ICSID, 'Draft Code of Conduct, Comments by State/Commenter' (14 January 2021)	2021-01-14	Chap. 06 Fn 81. Chap. 07 Fn 88, 90.

Contributors (in alphabetical order)

Johanna Braun *studied law at Humboldt University in Berlin and the University of Padua. She is currently a doctoral candidate at the University of Cologne where she focuses on standards of investment protection. In addition, she works as a researcher at Investment Arbitration Reporter. She previously worked as a research assistant in different law firms, focusing on various areas of public and European Union law.*

Ingo Borgdorf *works as a lawyer in an international law firm and is specialised on international arbitration and court proceedings with a focus on Investor-State Dispute Settlement. He completed his legal education at the University of Münster, University of Lyon and McGill University (Canada), where he was awarded a Master of Laws degree (LLM).*

Alexander Dünkelsbühler *is a doctoral candidate in public international law at the University of Cologne, where he focusses on international investment arbitration and economic sanctions, and a judicial clerk (Referendar) at the Higher Regional Court of Frankfurt. He studied law in Mainz (First State Examination), Beijing, and at Panthéon-Sorbonne University in Paris (Master's degree in international economic law). He previously was a visiting scholar at the Lauterpacht Centre for International Law in Cambridge and at Georgetown University Law Center in Washington, D.C.*

Leonard Funk *is a doctoral candidate at the University of Cologne and works as a research assistant at the International Investment Law Centre Cologne. He is the recipient of a PhD scholarship from the German Economy Foundation (Stiftung der Deutschen Wirtschaft). He studied law in Cologne (University of Cologne) and London (UCL).*

Moritz Keller *is a Partner in the International Arbitration team of Clifford Chance, Frankfurt, where he leads a renowned commercial and investment treaty arbitration team. Moritz has practiced arbitration out of Vienna, London and New York as well as now out of Frankfurt, acting regularly for both investors and States in investment treaty matters. He teaches investment arbitration and EU law at the University of Passau and international arbitration at the University of Frankfurt. He regularly publishes and lectures on issues of public international law and investment arbitration and is also involved in the training of government officials.*

Caroline Kittelmann *is a Senior Foreign Lawyer in the International Arbitration team of Clifford Chance, Frankfurt, where she specialises in commercial and investment treaty arbitration. Caroline is qualified as a lawyer in England and Wales and also in Ireland. She holds a first-class Bachelor degree in law from the University of Keele, as well as a Masters degree and a PhD in law from the University of Lancaster. Prior to joining Clifford Chance, Caroline worked for another Magic Circle law firm in London* *and Frankfurt and undertook a Research Fellowship at the Department of Law at the University of Oxford.*

Niclas Landmann *is a doctoral candidate at Cologne University. He studied German law at Frankfurt University, Germany and Investment Treaty Arbitration at Uppsala University, Sweden. Currently, he works as a legal clerk at the Regional Court of Hanau and as a research assistant in the dispute resolution team of a corporate law firm in Frankfurt.*

Carla Müller *is a legal trainee at the Higher Regional Court of Cologne and a PhD candidate in international investment law at the University of Cologne. She studied law at the University of Cologne and the Université Paris I-Panthéon Sorbonne and graduated with an LL.B (Köln/Paris I), a Maîtrise en Droit and the first State Examination. Whilst writing her PhD thesis she worked as a legal trainee in the dispute resolution practice of an international law firm in Frankfort and completed an internship at ICSID.*

Petyo Nikolov *is a doctoral candidate at the University of Cologne, where he works as a research fellow at the International Investment Law Centre Cologne (IILCC). His research focuses on international investment law, European law, international dispute settlement, and energy law. Petyo holds an LL.M. degree in Business Law from the University of Cologne. Prior to joining the IILCC, he worked as a legal assistant with the Federal Network Agency in Bonn, Germany, and the law firm Heuking Kühn Lüer Wojtek in Düsseldorf, Germany.*

Philipp Reinhold *studied law at Bonn University and the University of Lausanne. Currently, he is a doctoral candidate at Saarland University, where he also works as a research associate at the Chair of Public Law, Public International Law and European Law of Prof. Dr. Marc Bungenberg, LL.M. and the Europa-Institut. In addition, he serves as a trainee lawyer at the District Court in Limburg an der Lahn.*

Julian Scheu *is Junior Professor of Public Law, International Law, and International Investment Law at the University of Cologne and head of management at the International Investment Law Centre Cologne (IILCC). His research focuses on international economic law, European law, international dispute settlement, and comparative administrative law. Prior to joining the IILCC, he worked as legal assistant with the German Arbitration Institute (DIS).*

Chapter 1: The Idea of a Multilateral Investment Court in the Rise, Crisis, and Reform of International Investment Law

by Julian Scheu[*]

International investment law is a well-established subfield of international economic law which is, at the same time, in a state of constant change.[1] Reasons for this dynamic may be found in the need to adapt the legal framework to global investment flows and, in particular, the fact that the very concept of investment protection remains disputed and therefore subject to policy shifts.[2]

International investment law can be distinguished from other fields of international economic law, and even plays, in view of the importance it attributes to private individuals and corporations, a particular role within the international legal order.[3] Its unknowingly fast development triggered questions about the legitimacy of investment protection, the power of arbitral tribunals and the regime's impact on national sovereignty. These

---

* Julian Scheu is Junior Professor of Public Law, International Law, and International Investment Law at the University of Cologne and head of management at the International Investment Law Centre Cologne (IILCC).

1 Chester Brown and Kate Miles, *Evolution in Investment Treaty Law and Arbitration* (CUP 2011), 3; Marc Bungenberg et al, *General Introduction to International Investment Law* in Bungenberg et al (eds), *International Investment Law – A Handbook* (Beck/Hart/Nomos 2015), 1. See for an overview on latest developments: Stephan Hobe and Julian Scheu (eds), *Evolution, Evaluation and Future Developments in International Investment Law* (Nomos 2021).

2 Martins Paparinskis, *Basic Documents on International Investment Protection* (Bloomsbury Publishing 2019), 1. As Muthucumaraswamy Sornarajah observes, few areas of public international law excite as much controversy as international investment law. See Sornarajah, *The International Law on Foreign Investment* (CUP 2021), 1. Characterising investment law as a complex adaptive system: Joost Pauwelyn, 'At the Edge of Chaos? Foreign Investment Law as a Complex Adaptive System, How It Emerged and How It Can Be Reformed' (2014) 29.2 ICSID Review, 372-418.

3 Speaking of a 'quiet revolution' in international law: John Collier and Vaughan Lowe, *The Settlement of Disputes in International Law: Institutions and Procedures* (OUP 1999), 191; Anne Peters, *Beyond Human Rights: The Legal Status of the Individual in International Law* (CUP 2016), 282.

phenomena have sometimes been described as excesses or growing pains,[4] and ultimately opened up the path towards meaningful negotiations about systemic reforms. In the current discussions, the idea of creating a Multilateral Investment Court (MIC) plays a central role. Already debated in 1960,[5] the establishment of a permanent arbitral body or a world investment court does not seem to have lost much of its conceptional appeal. However, the complexity of such an endeavour cannot be underestimated.

To adequately situate the MIC reform project within the legal framework first requires acknowledging that investment law is characterized by systemic features which are based on two separate building blocks (A.). It is also vital to recall the systemic concerns which led to the backlash against investment arbitration. These concerns are at the same time guiding principles and benchmark for a future MIC (B.). It is against this background that the chapters in the present volume evaluate and analyse the options, merits, pitfalls, and potential consequences of creating and implementing a Multilateral Investment Court (C.). Regardless of its concrete institutional form, multiple challenges lay ahead for such a permanent body created to position itself within the international investment law regime (D.).

A. *Systemic Features of the International Investment Law Regime*

Since its creation during the second half of the twentieth century,[6] contemporary investment law consists of two building blocks: substantive

---

4 See, eg, David Schneiderman, 'Against Constitutional Excess: Tocquevillian Reflections on International Investment Law' (2018) 85.2 University of Chicago Law Review, 585-608; Silvia Constain, 'ISDS Growing Pains and Responsible Adulthood' in Kalicki and Joubin-Bret (eds), *Reshaping the Investor-State Dispute Settlement System* (Brill Nijhoff 2015), 344-350.

5 ILA, 'Juridical Aspects of Nationalization and Foreign Property' (1960) 49 International Law Association Reports of Conferences, 175 et seq.

6 Modern international investment law did not arise out of nowhere but can be traces back to the international law doctrine of State responsibility for injuries to aliens and earlier State practice of concluding treaties on Friendship, Commerce and Navigation. See, eg, Chester Brown, 'International Investment Agreements – History, Approaches, Schools' in Bungenberg et al (eds), *International Investment Law – A Handbook* (Beck/Hart/Nomos 2015), 153 et seq.; Wolfgang Alschner, 'Americanization of the bit universe: The influence of friendship, commerce and navigation (fcn) treaties on modern investment treaty law' (2013) 5.2 Goettingen Journal of International Law, 455-486; Muthucumaraswamy Sornarajah, 'The Cli-

investment protection standards and a procedural framework on investor-State dispute settlement (ISDS). In combination, both normative building blocks define the systemic features of today's international investment law regime.

I. Substantive Investment Protection

Substantive investment law is rooted in mostly bilateral international investment treaties (BITs) which have been concluded by the thousands since the 1960's.[7] Content and structure of the first BITs were influenced by academic discussions on multilateral draft conventions on investment protection such as the 1959 Abs-Shawcross Draft Convention on Investments Abroad.[8] Given that the international community of States could not agree on a common standard of protection in a multilateral treaty,[9]

---

mate of International Arbitration' (1991) 8.2 Journal of International Arbitration 47, 180. See also from an historical perspective: Stephan Schill, Christian Tams, and Rainer Hofmann (eds), *International Investment Law and History* (Edward Elgar Publishing 2018).

7 According to the UNCTAD Investment Agreements Navigator, 2258 BITs were worldwide in force as of November 2021, data available at <https://investmentpolicy.unctad.org/international-investment-agreements> 6 January 2022. See generally on the economic and policy motives for concluding BITs: Zachary Elkins, Andrew Guzman, and Beth Simmons, 'Competing for Capital: The Diffusion of Bilateral Investment Treaties, 1960-2000' (2006) 60.4 International Organization, 811-846.

8 The draft was published in: 9.1 Journal of Public Law (presently Emory Law Journal) (1960), 115-118. Other influential multilateral draft conventions were the International Convention for the Mutual Protection of Private Property Rights in Foreign Countries (1957), the Harvard Draft Convention on the International Responsibility of States for Injuries to Aliens (1961), and the OECD Draft Convention on the Protection of Foreign Property (1962). At the time of their publication, these draft conventions were subject of heated academic discussions. See, eg, Arthur S Miller, 'Protection of Private Foreign Investment by Multilateral Convention' (1959) 53.2 The American Journal of International Law, 371-378; Georg Schwarzenberger, 'The Abs-Shawcross Draft Convention on Investments Abroad: A Critical Commentary' (1960) 9.1 Journal of Public Law, 147-171; Ignaz Seidl-Hohenveldern, 'The Abs-Shawcross Draft Convention to Protect Private Foreign Investment: Comments on the Round Table' (1961) 10.1 Journal of Public Law, 100-112. See for an overview on multilateral approaches to investment protection: Brown (*n 6*), 14-59.

9 Pointing to the crucial role that the World Bank played in this process: Taylor St John, *The Rise of Investor-State Arbitration: Politics, Law, and Unintended Consequences* (OUP 2018), 97-99.

these draft conventions became an inspiration for many capital-exporting countries to conclude such treaties on a bilateral basis.[10] With decades of experience in negotiating and drafting BITs, some States published their own benchmark agreement, also known as model BIT. These instruments became de facto guidelines for the negotiation of investment treaties,[11] so State practice led to standardised treaty texts.[12] In view of these aligned practices which were influenced by multilateral approaches, one could indeed speak of a factual multilateralisation of international investment law.[13] But despite general trends of regional and substantive convergence,[14] the normative basis of today's substantive investment protection is still based on thousands of individual treaties. The substantive building block therefore remains characterised by bilateralism and fragmentation.[15]

In addition, substantive investment protection consists to a large extent of open-worded legal concepts such as fair and equitable treatment or the protection against unlawful indirect expropriation.[16] The vagueness of substantive legal concepts undeniably poses a major challenge for tribunals

---

10 Among the capital-exporting nations to first conclude bilateral investment treaties belong Germany (since 1958), Switzerland (since 1961), Netherlands (since 1963), France (since 1963), and Italy (since 1964).

11 Recalling that investment treaty negotiations are often driven by strategic foreign policy considerations: Lauge N. Skovgaard Poulsen, Emma Aisbett, 'Diplomats Want Treaties: Diplomatic Agendas and Perks in the Investment Regime' (2016) 7.1 Journal of International Dispute Settlement, 72-91.

12 Stephan W Schill, *The Multilateralization of International Investment Law* (CUP 2010), 89-91.

13 Stephan W Schill, 'The Multilateralization of International Investment Law: Emergence of a Multilateral System of Investment Protection on Bilateral Grounds' (2010) 2.1 Trade, Law and Development, 59. See for a critique of the multilateralisation argument: Aniruddha Rajput, 'The myth of a multilateral framework in international investment law' (2016) 56.3-4 Indian Journal of International Law, 427-461.

14 In this sense, arguing that mega-regional treaties such as CETA or RCEP provide a vehicle for future multilateral investment rules: Tania Voon, 'Consolidating International Investment Law: The Mega-Regionals as a Pathway towards Multilateral Rules' (2018) 17.1 World Trade Review, 33-63.

15 Recalling that the law 'largely consists of a collection of bilateral or plurilateral treaties with no systematic interconnectedness': Jörg Kammerhofer, *International Investment Law and Legal Theory: Expropriation and the Fragmentation of Sources* (CUP 2021), 3.

16 See, eg, addressing the dilemma of vagueness: Yves Fortier and Stephen Drymer, 'Indirect Expropriation in the Law of International Investment: I Know It When I See It, or Caveat Investor' (2004) 19.2 ICSID Review, 293-327.

in applying the law to the facts of a specific case.[17] The reluctance of the contracting States to specify the meaning of their investment treaty amounts to a delegation of substantial decision-making powers to the tribunal. This leads to the question who interprets and applies the law and on which legitimate grounds is the exercise of such wide-reaching powers based.

II. Procedural Framework on Dispute Settlement

From the very beginning, substantive investment protection standards were combined with a procedural framework on ISDS as the regime's second building block. When the Abs-Shawcross Draft Convention on Investments Abroad was published in 1960, Hermann J. Abs and Lord Shawcross argued that

> [t]here must, at the heart of any instrument dedicated to the creation of an atmosphere of confidence, always lie a provision for the effective adjudication by an impartial body of all disputes which may arise. Undertakings without the machinery for determining their content and application cannot achieve the desired end.[18]

Accordingly, in its annex relating to the arbitral tribunal, the Abs-Shawcross Draft Convention on Investments Abroad provided for ad hoc investment arbitration.[19] Since 1968, investment treaties systematically contained ISDS provisions which grant foreign investors direct access to international arbitration in case of a dispute with the host State.[20] Ad hoc investment arbitration, where tribunals are constituted on a case-by-case basis, became the global standard.[21] Today, the system of investment arbitration is characterized by its efficiency and attractiveness for foreign investors. There are four main reasons which explain the success of invest-

---

17 Marcela Klein Bronfman, 'Fair and Equitable Treatment: An Evolving Standard' in von Bogdandy and Wolfrum (eds) (2006) 10 Max Planck Yearbook of United Nations Law, 631.

18 Hermann J Abs and Lord Shawcross, 'Comment on the Draft Convention by its Authors' (1960) 9.1 Journal of Public Law [presently Emory Law Journal], 123.

19 'The Proposed Convention to Protect Private Foreign Investment' (1960) 9.1 Journal of Public Law [presently Emory Law Journal], 118.

20 The first bilateral investment treaty providing for modern ISDS was the Netherlands-Indonesia BIT (1968).

21 See for an analysis from a policy perspective: St John (*n 9*).

ment treaty arbitration: direct accessibility to an international forum (1.), participation in the constitution of the arbitral tribunal (2.), finality of the decision-making (3.), and enforceability of the award (4.).

1. *Direct Accessibility to International Arbitration*

First, the ISDS clauses contained in most investment treaties grant foreign investors direct access to international arbitration without having to exhaust local remedies before national courts of the host State.[22] This waiver speeds up the process of dispute resolution significantly since national court proceedings may require years, if not decades of litigation. Direct access to international arbitration is a unique feature which distinguishes ISDS from other international law fora where private parties have standing such as human rights courts.[23]

2. *Participation in the Composition of the Arbitral Tribunal*

Second, all main arbitration rules used in ISDS provide for the right of disputing parties to appoint a member of the arbitral tribunal.[24] Subject to its impartiality and independence, any individual appointed by a disputing party is in principle capable of serving as arbitrator.[25] In contrast to courts and tribunals where all adjudicators have been appointed by States, investors have an equally significant influence on the constitution of the arbitral tribunal. This active participation of the private party is based on

22 No exhaust local remedies in ISDS (generally).

23 See, eg, Chittbaranjan F Amerasingbe, 'The Rule of Exhaustion of Domestic Remedies in the Framework of International Systems for the Protection of Human Rights' (1968) 28 Heidelberg Journal of International Law, 257-300; Cesare P R Romano, 'The Rule of Prior Exhaustion of Domestic Remedies: Theory and Practice in International Human Rights Procedures' in Boschiero et al (eds), *International Courts and the Development of International Law* (Springer 2013), 561-572.

24 Article 37 ICSID Convention, Article 9 UNCITRAL Arbitration Rules, Article 17 SCC Arbitration Rules.

25 Should reasonable doubts with respect the individual's impartiality or independence arise at any point in time, the arbitrator must step down. See for a detailed analysis of the process: Chiara Giorgetti, 'Selecting and Removing Arbitrators in International Investment Arbitration' (2018) 2 Brill Research Perspectives in International Investment Law and Arbitration <https://doi.org/10.1163/24055778-12340007> accessed 13 January 2022.

the consensual nature of arbitration and inspired by the idea of equality of arms.[26] In addition, the appointment is an act of direct delegation of interpretative powers from the treaty parties to the tribunal.[27] By proactively integrating the disputing parties, the legitimacy of the decision-making process is increased and incites the losing party to accept an award rendered not in her favour.

3. *Finality of the Decision-Making*

Third, arbitral awards rendered by ISDS tribunals are final. Finality means that the procedure before an ISDS tribunal is the first and last forum to settle the case.[28] Accordingly, in addition to not having to exhaust local remedies, investors must only go through a single ISDS procedure to obtain a final decision. This feature reflects arbitration's focus on effective dispute settlement. In the trade-off between efficiency and correctness of decisions, investment arbitration traditionally prioritises the former.[29]

---

26 Recalling that the right of disputing parties to appoint the members of the arbitral tribunal holds in balance party autonomy and the equality of the parties as two inter-linked principles of international adjudication: Campbell McLachlan, *The Institute of International Law's Resolution on the Equality of Parties Before International Investment Tribunals: Introduction, Text and Commentaries* (CUP 2021), para 163.

27 Anthea Roberts, 'Power and Persuasion in Investment Treaty Interpretation – The Dual Role of States' (2010) 104.2 American Journal of International Law, 180.

28 The finality of arbitral awards is a general principle which does not apply to full extent. Accordingly, no arbitration system goes so far as to deprive the parties of remedies against arbitrariness and the departure from fundamental principles of justice. See Georges R Delaume, 'The Finality of Arbitration Involving States: Recent Developments' (1989) 5.1 Arbitration International, 34.

29 Jason Clapham, 'Finality of Investor-State Arbitral Awards: Has the Tide Turned and is there a Need for Reform?' (2009) 26.3 Journal of International Arbitration, 440 et seq. Pointing out that the relationship between final and correct decisions in arbitration is adaptable and the result of party autonomy: Rowan Platt, 'The Appeal of Appeal Mechanisms in International Arbitration: Fairness over Finality?' (2013) 30.5 Journal of International Arbitration, 531-560. In this context pointing to the difference between consistent and accurate decisions: Mark Feldman, 'Investment Arbitration Appellate Mechanism Options: Consistency, Accuracy, and Balance of Power' (2017) 32.3 ICSID Review, 531-534.

4. *Enforceability of Awards*

But whether a final award is effective in practice largely depends on its enforceability against the losing party.[30] Two multilateral conventions guarantee the international enforceability of investment arbitration awards. The Convention on the Recognition and Enforcement of Foreign Arbitral Awards signed 1958 in New York (New York Convention, NYC)[31] is considered as the legal foundation of a global system of arbitral dispute resolution.[32] The NYC applies to commercial and investment arbitration awards and significantly limits judicial review of the award by national courts.[33] In addition, the Convention on the Settlement of Investment Disputes between States and Nationals of Other States signed 1965 in Washington (ICSID Convention) provides for a procedural framework specifically designed for ISDS proceedings and awards. The self-contained enforcement regime pursuant to Art. 54 ICSID Convention goes even further than the NYC and provides for automatic enforceability of ICSID arbitration awards.[34] In view of the high ratification rate of both conventions,[35] investment arbitration awards are almost globally enforceable.

Together, these four distinct features create the above-mentioned 'atmosphere of confidence' and are the main reasons why contemporary investment arbitration is widely accepted and commonly used by foreign investors.

---

30 Albert-Jan van den Berg, 'Recent enforcement problems under the New York and ICSID conventions' (1989) 5.1 Arbitration International, 2.

31 As of December 2021, the New York Convention has been ratified by 169 States. The ratification status is available at <https://uncitral.un.org/en/texts/arbitration/conventions/foreign_arbitral_awards/ status2> accessed 13 January 2022.

32 In this context, arguing for the existence of an authentic and autonomous arbitral legal order: Emmanuel Gaillard, 'The Arbitral Legal Order: Evolution and recognition' in Schultz and Ortino (eds), *The Oxford Handbook of International Arbitration* (OUP 2020), 555 et seq.

33 van den Berg (*n 30*), 3 et seq.

34 Aron Broches, 'Awards Rendered Pursuant to the ICSID Convention: Binding Force, Finality, Recognition, Enforcement, Execution' (1987) 2.2 ICSID Review, 287-334. As of December 2021, the ICSID Convention has been ratified by 156 States. The ratification status is available at <https://icsid.worldbank.org/en/Pages/about/Database-of-Member-States.aspx> accessed 13 January 2022.

35 See Voon (*n 14*) and Klein Bronfman (*n 17*).

III. Combining Substantive and Procedural Building Blocks

Unlike substantive investment protection, ISDS is characterised by norms of global reach such as the multilateral ICSID Convention or the NYC. The procedural framework therefore seems to be in stark contrast to the fragmented web of treaties containing the substantive norms. However, the direct consequences for a State of joining a multilateral procedural framework such as the ICSID Convention are fairly limited,[36] as the Convention does neither contain substantive investment protection nor serve as single legal basis for investment claims. Each arbitration conducted under the ICSID system requires the specific consent of the disputing parties.[37] Therefore, even after joining ICSID, States remain in control of the applicable substantive law and get to decide which investment disputes should be arbitrable under the ICSID Convention.[38] In this sense, the procedural building block is separate from substantive investment obligations. The combination of substantive and procedural rules is done on a case-by-case basis through the ISDS clause in individually negotiated investment treaties or contracts and represents the starting point of modern investment law.[39]

Separating procedural from substantive commitments turned out to be a very successful implementation strategy and explains why 156 States have so far joined the multilateral system established by the ICSID Conven-

36 See for list of attributes to ICSID membership: ICSID (ed), 'Guide to Membership in the ICSID Convention' (2020), 3, <https://icsid.worldbank.org/sites/default/files/Guide_to_Membership_in_the_ ICSID_Convention_2020.pdf> accessed 13 January 2022.

37 Article 25 ICSID Convention.

38 That States would require sufficient control in that regard was already mentioned in 1960 at the discussions of the ILA Committee on The Juridical Aspects of Nationalization and Foreign Property. Accordingly, Committee member Günther Jaenicke pointed out that 'no State can be expected to accept the jurisdiction of a Court if it does not know what are the rules of substantive law the Court will probably apply'. See ILA 1960 (*n 5*), 194.

39 The emergence of modern investment law is associated with the Germany-Pakistan BIT from 1959 which is seen as the first modern BIT. In procedural terms, however, the treaty was limited to inter-State dispute settlement. Substantive investment protection and treaty-based ISDS were first combined by the Indonesia-Netherlands BIT from 1968. Since then, States started to grant private investors direct access to international arbitration through the inclusion of ISDS clauses in their BITs.

tion.[40] In light of the above, investment law's remarkable development has not taken place despite, but due to the deeply fragmented legal landscape of investment treaties.

B. Systemic Concerns as Guidelines for the Multilateral Investment Court

I. From Backlash to Reforming ISDS

Obligations under international investment treaties entered into by States are supposed to be meaningful.[41] Accordingly, the conclusion of investment agreements has the potential to trigger practical consequences for host States such as investment arbitration claims brought by foreign investors. This, however, occurred for a long time only in rare circumstances.[42] Substantial criticism against ISDS first appeared in the mid-1990s in the wake of anti-globalisation movements.[43] It gained significant momentum with the exponential rise of cases at the beginning of the 21st century.[44] Especially in reaction to politically sensitive investment claims such as Philip Morris v Australia,[45] the legitimacy of investment law was

---

40 In contrast, joining a multilateral treaty with substantive investment obligations was perceived as politically sensitive and explains why all multilateral investment conventions from the 1960's remained drafts.

41 Jan Paulsson, 'The Power of States to Make Meaningful Promises to Foreigners' (2010) 1.2 Journal of International Dispute Settlement, 341-352.

42 Between 1966 and 1991, ICSID registered only 26 cases. See for the ICSID caseload between 1966-2020: ICSID, 'The ICSID Caseload-Statistics', Issue 2021-1, 7.

43 Gabrielle Kaufmann-Kohler and Michele Potestà, 'Can the Mauritius Convention serve as a model for the reform of a permanent investment tribunal or an appeal mechanism? Analysis and roadmap', CIDS 2016, <https://uncitral.un.org/sites/uncitral.un.org/files/media-documents/uncitral/en/cids_researc h_paper_mauritius.pdf> accessed 13 January 2022, para 15.

44 St John (*n 9*), 5 (noting that an explosion in the investor–state caseload occurred largely after 2000). By the end of 2020, the total number of known ISDS cases reached over 1100 arbitrations with ICSID having registered 803 cases. See UNCTAD, 'IIA Issue Note – Investor-State Dispute Settlement Cases: Facts and Figures 2020' (September 2021) Issue 4, 1; ICSID (*n 42*), 7.

45 *Philip Morris Asia Limited v Australia* PCA Case No 2012-12. Notably, it was the very existence of a claim that fuelled academic and the public debates. The difference between the existence of a claim and its actual outcome did not play a decisive role. See, eg, Pauwelyn (*n 2*), 373 ('How did [foreign investment law] get to the stage where Philip Morris, the tobacco giant, gets to challenge Australian tobacco control measures, [...]?'). Noting that a few controversial cases are not

systematically called into question.[46] The criticism concerns investment law as a whole, but addresses both its substantive and procedural dimension.

From a substantive perspective, it is asked whether investment protection hinders the promotion of public values such as democracy, human rights, public health, or climate change policy.[47] And more generally, why did States ever agree to limit their sovereignty over foreign investors so substantially?[48] In addition, critics argue that the lack of legal predictability caused by vague standards of protection undermines domestic policy choices by imposing a chilling effect on host State regulation.[49] Due to legal insecurity,[50] foreign investors can threaten host States with the prospect of investment claims. As a result, costs related to environmental, human rights and other types of public interest compliance can be shifted away from investors at the expense of host State societies.[51]

---

necessarily representative of the regime as a whole: Kaufmann-Kohler, Potestà (*n 43*).

46 See, eg, David Schneidermann, 'Resisting Economic Globalization: Critical Theory and International Investment Law' (2013) 12.3 International Journal of Constitutional Law, 827; Gus Van Harten et al, 'Public Statement on the International Investment Regime' (31 August 2010), <https://www.osgoode. yorku.ca/public-statement-international-investment-regime-31-august-2010/> accessed 13 January 2022.

47 See, eg, Barnali Choudhury, 'Democratic Implications Arising from the Intersection of Investment Arbitration and Human Rights' (August 2009) 46.4 Alberta Law Review, 983-1008; Kyla Tienhaara, 'Regulatory Chill in a Warming World: The Threat to Climate Policy Posed by Investor-State Dispute Settlement' (2018) 7.2 Transnational Environmental Law, 229-250; Matthew Rimmer, 'The Chilling Effect: Investor-State Dispute Settlement, Graphic Heath Warnings, the Plain Packaging of Tobacco Products, and the Trans-Pacific Partnership' (2017) 7 Victoria University Law and Justice Journal, 76-93.

48 Pauwelyn (*n 2*), 373.

49 Gus van Harten, Jane Kelsey, and David Schneiderman, 'Phase 2 of the UNCITRAL ISDS Review: Why 'Other Matters' Really Matter' (2019) 328 All Papers, 10-13.

50 Emphasizing that foreseeability and predictability of the law and dispute settlement belong to the core elements of legal certainty and the rule of law: Peter-Tobias Stoll, 'International Investment Law and the Rule of Law' in Holterhus (ed), *The Law Behind Rule of Law Transfers - On Rule Based Interactions of Legal Orders in a Globalized World* (Nomos 2019), 285 et seq.

51 James Thuo Gathii, 'Reform and Retrenchment in International Investment Law', Keynote speech held at the Santander Roundtable Discussions on International Economic Law, co-hosted by Kenyatta University School of Law (Nairobi) and the International Investment Law Centre Cologne, 13 January 2021, <https://ssrn.com/abstract=3765169> accessed 13 January 2022.

With an emphasis on investment law's procedural dimension, it is asked why States opened themselves up to direct claims by private investors in investor–State arbitration?[52] Critics argue that ISDS tribunals are not fit for neutral dispute resolution as they would suffer from a lack of deference to the host State's right to regulate and were systemically biased in favour of foreign investors.[53]

This legitimacy crisis of or backlash against investment arbitration[54] created a dynamic which fundamentally changed the political environment for ISDS in many parts of the world, especially in Europe.[55] As a result of the political shift in relation to ISDS, the European Union (EU) implemented a permanent dispute settlement mechanism in its new free trade and investment agreements with Canada, Singapore and Vietnam, thereby creating an alternative to the existing model of ad hoc investment arbitration.[56] These developments ultimately led to the reform process currently conducted under the auspices of the United Nations Commission On International Trade Law (UNCITRAL).[57] In 2016, the Commission noted that

---

52 Pauwelyn (*n 2*), 373; Andrew T Guzman, 'Why LDCs Sign Treaties That Hurt Them: Explaining the Popularity of Bilateral Investment Treaties' (1998) 38 Virginia Journal of International Law, 639-688.

53 Emphasising the relationship between deference granted to States and the legitimacy of arbitral tribunals: Esmé Shirlow, 'Deference and Indirect Expropriation Analysis in International Investment Law. Observations on Current Approaches and Frameworks for Future Analysis' 2014 29.3 ICSID Review, 595. Summarising critical voices: Daniel Behn, 'Legitimacy, Evolution, and Growth in Investment Treaty Arbitration: Empirically Evaluating the State-of-the-Art' (2015) 46.2 Georgetown Journal of International Law 363, 366-368; Brown (*n 2*), 675.

54 See, eg, Susan Franck, 'The Legitimacy Crisis in Investment Treaty Arbitration: Privatizing Public International Law through Inconsistent Decisions' (2005) 73 Fordham Law Review, 1521-1626; Waibel et al (eds), *The Backlash Against Investment Arbitration* (Kluwer Law Arbitration 2010).

55 In this sense quoting the EU Trade Commissioner Malmström: Paul Ames, 'ISDS: The most toxic acronym in Europe, Politico', (17 September 2015) <https://www.politico.eu/article/isds-the-most-toxic-acronym-in-europe/> accessed 13 January 2022.

56 See, eg, for an overview on the EU Investment Court System: Freya Baetens, 'The European Union's Proposed Investment Court System: Addressing Criticisms of Investor-State Arbitration While Raising New Challenges' (2016) 43 Legal Issues of Economic Integration, 367-384.

57 Describing the origin of UNCITRAL's work on ISDS and the Commission's involvement as main forum for discussing reform options: Corinne Montineri, 'UNCITRAL Reform Process on ISDS' in Hobe and Scheu (eds), *Evolution, Eval-*

> criticism had developed towards investor-State arbitration in general, which included the alleged lack of impartiality and accountability of the arbitrators, the lack of transparency of the procedure, and the absence of consistency of the jurisprudence, all of which had triggered a growing demand for changes from a number of States, international organizations and civil society groups. It was further said that reforms had been undertaken to address those criticisms, and it would therefore be timely to consider the matter at a multilateral level to avoid the development of a fragmented system.[58]

Against this background, UNCITRAL Working Group III (WGIII) was entrusted with a broad mandate to discuss the possible reform of ISDS. The mandate should be exercised in three consecutive phases:

> (i) first, identify and consider concerns regarding ISDS; (ii) second, consider whether reform was desirable in light of any identified concerns; and (iii) third, if the Working Group were to conclude that reform was desirable, develop any relevant solutions to be recommended to the Commission.[59]

After concerns were registered and a reform was characterized as desirable, the Working Group started, as of its resumed 38th session in 2020, to consider concrete reform options, including the establishment of a standing multilateral investment court.[60]

II. Idea of a Multilateral Investment Court

The idea of establishing a permanent body for the settlement of international investment disputes is not new. In 1960, the International Law Association's Committee on The Juridical Aspects of Nationalization and

---

uation and Future Developments in International Investment Law (Nomos 2021), 157-172.

58 UNCITRAL, 'Report of the United Nations Commission on International Trade Law, Forty-ninth session (27 June-15 July 2016)', (A/71/17), para 190.

59 UNCITRAL, 'Report of Working Group III (Investor-State Dispute Settlement Reform) on the work of its thirty-fourth session (Vienna, 27 November-1 December 2017), Part I' (19 December 2017), A/CN.9/930/Rev.1, para 6.

60 UNCITRAL, 'Report of Working Group III (Investor-State Dispute Settlement Reform) on the work of its resumed thirty-eighth session' (28 January 2020), A/CN.9/1004/Add.1, paras 14 et seq.

Foreign Property was asked to discuss 'the establishment of international machinery for settling disputes arising from State takings of property'[61].

The rapporteur of the Committee, Ignaz Seidl-Hohenveldern recalled that 'many people and organizations nowadays stress the necessity for granting private individuals direct access to international instances in disputes involving foreign investments'[62]. Against this background, the Committee submitted a Draft Statute for an Arbitral Tribunal and, alternatively, to crystallise the discussion, for a Foreign Investment Court.[63]

Like today, the two models focused on dispute settlement and did not address the question of substantive law. This separation between the procedural and substantive building block was subject to discussion. Especially the German Branch criticised that the proposed drafts do not contain any substantive rules of law concerning foreign investments which the Tribunal or Court would have to apply.[64]

With a notable degree of farsightedness, it was also noted that putting in place a dispute settlement body without clarifying the substantive standards would require 'trust in the wisdom and the impartiality of the arbitrators or judges'[65]. This observation makes clear why investment adjudicators must meet the highest standards in order to claim legitimacy of their mandate.

Even though the permanent investment court did not see the light of day, the work of the Committee turned out to be influential. Not only because the discussions of the Committee foreshadowed the architecture of the current ISDS regime. As an alternative to a multilateral approach, it was suggested that arbitral procedures could 'be incorporated into bilateral treaties guaranteeing the security of certain investments to be defined in

---

61 ILA 1960 (*n 5*), 175.

62 ibid. This position, however, was not shared by all members of the Committee. Other members considered the existing institutions to be sufficient or argued that direct access for private parties to international arbitration would be contrary to the basic principles of international law. See ILA 1960 (*n 5*), 183 (Member Kalensky), 187 (Member Khalfinn).

63 ILA 1960 (*n 5*), 225-234 (Annex I - Draft Statutes of the Arbitral Tribunal for Foreign Investment); 235-240 (Annex II – Foreign Investment Court).

64 ILA 1960 (*n 5*), 176, 194 (Günther Jaenicke from the German branch doubted whether a multilateral convention would be a useful approach 'as long as there is no agreement between capital-exporting and capital-importing States as to the substantive law to be applied.').

65 ILA 1960 (*n 5*), 176.

the treaty'[66]. In addition, many issues in 1960 such as costs,[67] (professional) diversity of arbitrators,[68] counterclaims,[69] sovereignty of the host State,[70] or the influence of the home State[71] also play a role at UNCITRAL today.[72]

As the creation of a permanent ISDS body is once again on the agenda, the WG III can base its discussions on a rich and ongoing academic debate. Academic contributions have analysed the merits and insufficiencies of a permanent investment court and commentators have been taking account of historical, regional, institutional, and policy perspectives.[73] The pos-

---

66 ILA 1960 (*n 5*), 195; ILA, 'Juridical Aspects of Nationalization and Foreign Property' (1962) 50 International Law Association Reports of Conferences, 121 (the Dutch Member Jansma considered it 'extremely likely that provision for some kind of arbitration agreement would be made [...]' and that '[...] the present document will certainly be very useful in the drafting of such agreements.').

67 ILA 1960 (*n 5*), 176-177.

68 ILA 1960 (*n 5*), 177.

69 ILA 1962 (*n 66*), 119.

70 ILA 1962 (*n 66*), 118.

71 ILA 1960 (*n 5*), 177.

72 See also for a comparison: Taylor St John and Yuliya Chernykh, 'Deja vu? Investment Court Proposals from 1960 and today' (EJIL Talk: Blog of the European Journal of International Law, 2018), <https://www.ejiltalk.org/deja-vu-investment-court-proposals-from-1960-and-today/> accessed 13 January 2022.

73 See, eg, David M Howard, 'Creating Consistency through a World Investment Court' (November 2017) 41.1 Fordham International Law Journal, 1-52; Facundo Calvo, 'The Most Feasible Way Towards a Multilateral Investment Treaty' (November 2018) 3.1 European Investment Law and Arbitration Review, 61-76; Jansen Calamita, 'The Challenge of Establishing a Multilateral Investment Tribunal at ICSID' (2017) 32.3 ICSID Review, 611-624; Charles N Brower and Jawad Ahmad, 'From the Two-Headed Nightingale to the Fifteen-Headed Hydra: The Many Follies of the Proposed International Investment Court' (2018) 41 Fordham International Law Journal, 791-820; Jeremy K Sharpe, 'The Future of International Claims Commissions: Conceptualizing the EU's Proposed Multilateral Investment Court as an International Claims Tribunal' (2017) 111 Proceedings of the ASIL Annual Meeting, 102-105; Céline Lévesque, 'Will Asia breathe life into a Multilateral Investment Court?' in Nakagawa (ed) *Asian Perspectives on International Investment Law* (Taylor and Francis 2019), 83-113; Rizky Banyualam Permana, 'Achieving Multilateral Investment Court through EU-ASEAN Expansion of Bilateral Investment 'Court': Is It Possible?' (2019) 16.4 Indonesian Journal of International Law, 453-472; Łukasz Kułaga, 'A Brave, New, International Investment Court in Context. Towards a Paradigm Shift of the ISDS' (2018) 38 Polish Yearbook of International Law, 115-139; European Parliament, Study by Steffen Hindelang and Teoman M Hagemeyer, 'In Pursuit of an International Investment Court', EP/EXPO/B/INTA/2017/02 (2017); Richard Happ and Sebastian Wuschka, 'From the Jay Treaty Commissions towards a Multilateral Investment Court: Addressing the Enforcement Dilemma' (2017), 6.1 Indian Journal of Arbi-

itions exchanged by UNCITRAL State delegations are also closely followed by the Academic Forum on ISDS, an international network of academics which publishes concept papers on a regular basis.[74]

Prominent voices in the contemporary debate include *Gabrielle Kaufmann-Kohler* and *Michele Potestà* who provided a detailed roadmap for creating a permanent ISDS body.[75] With the same intention and based on a comprehensive academic study,[76] *Marc Bungenberg* and *August Reinisch* published a Draft Statute of the Multilateral Investment Court.[77] Both studies reflect a wide range of design options and were taken into account by the WGIII.[78]

C. *What to Expect from the Chapters in this Volume*

Against this background, the aim of the present volume is to provide a comprehensive overview and understanding on the issues relevant to the creation and implementation of a Multilateral Investment Court. Accordingly, the main goal of this book is not to evaluate all reform options currently discussed at UNCITRAL. Instead, the aim is to focus on the

---

tration Law, 113-132; Güneş Ünüvar, Joanna Lam, and Shai Dothan (eds), *Permanent Investment Courts - The European Experiment* (Spinger 2020); Alexander M Heideman, 'Investment Law for Investors: A Case against Multilateral Investment Courts' (2018) 19 UC Davis Business Law Journal, 1-26

74 See Academic Forum on ISDS, administered by PluriCourts. Further information on the Forum is available at <https://www.jus.uio.no/pluricourts/english/projects/leginvest/academic-forum/> accessed 13 January 2022.

75 Kaufmann-Kohler, Potestà (*n 43*).

76 Marc Bungenberg and August Reinisch, *From Bilateral Arbitral Tribunals and Investment Courts to a Multilateral Investment Court - Options Regarding the Institutionalization of Investor-State Dispute Settlement* (Springer Open 2020).

77 Marc Bungenberg and August Reinisch, *Draft Statute of the Multilateral Investment Court* (Nomos 2021).

78 See only recently: UNCITRAL, Working Group III, 'Possible reform of investor-State dispute settlement (ISDS) Standing multilateral mechanism: Selection and appointment of ISDS tribunal members and related matters, Note by the Secretariat' (8 December 2021), A/CN.9/WG.III/WP.213 (advance copy), para 1. See for a summary and comparison of the ideas suggested by Kaufmann-Kohler/Potestà on the one hand and Bungenberg/Reinisch on the other: IILCC, 'IILCC Comparative Report on the Creation and Implementation of a Multilateral Investment Court' (Research Paper Series of the International Investment Law Centre Cologne, 2020), <https://iilcc.uni-koeln.de/sites/iilcc/reports/IILCC_Study_Group_on_ISDS_Reform_-_MIC_Report_-01-2020.pdf> accessed 13 January 2022.

MIC as the most complex and comprehensive reform option. The added value all authors hope to provide is to analyse the multifaceted and interconnected issues related to the creation of an MIC. The analysis follows closely current developments at UNCITRAL while taking due account of the bigger picture drawn by more general considerations.

The book is based on the hypothesis that the international community of States is seriously considering the establishment and implementation of an MIC. How could such an institution look like? What are the most suitable design options to remedy the concerns of ad hoc ISDS? Do valuable alternatives to an MIC exist? Which reforms need to accompany the creation of an MIC? What would the impact on the current ISDS system be? Would creating an MIC come along with new concerns already on the horizon? And which practical hurdles need to be overcome before such a permanent court would be operable? These complex and often interconnected questions are addressed in each chapter with an issue-specific focus.

As a starting point, *Johanna Braun* and *Philipp Reinhold* discuss the fundamental question on which institutional structure an MIC could be based.[79] It contrasts the MIC with other reform approaches which focus on increasing State control, dispute prevention and alternative dispute resolution. It is recalled that a permanent court operating on the basis of a multilateral institutional structure would effectively address the fragmentation of the current system. Once established, it would be possible to complement the MIC by incorporating existing as well as new elements of dispute settlement. Turning away from ad hoc arbitration towards a permanent institutional structure therefore is considered as a key milestone.

A prominent example of an additional institutional element is the idea of an Advisory Centre on international investment law addressed in Chapter 3.[80] In view of its relevance to the legitimacy debate, the authors analyse the potential of such an institution with respect to its structure, beneficiaries, scope of services, and financing. Whether an advisory centre would be compatible with an MIC mainly depends on whether both institutions are created in a coordinated process. Taken together, the MIC and the Advisory Centre could serve as main elements of a coherent institutional structure.

Another cornerstone of any reformed investment law regime is the establishment of an appeal mechanism. In view of investment law's fragmented nature, the lack of consistency is a root cause of the legitimacy

79 See, Braun/Reinhold, Chapter 2, 51-82.
80 See, Braun/Reinhold, Chapter 3, 83-104.

crisis. Consequentially, the trade-off between finality, correctness, and consistency of ISDS decision-making lays at the heart of ongoing reform discussions. In accordance with its holistic approach, an MIC would also contain an appeal mechanism. In contrast, a stand-alone appeal body which would complement the current ad hoc system is discussed as an alternative.

Taking the issue of consistency as a guiding principle, *Niclas Landmann* sheds light on the wide range of different institutional options for the creation of an appeal mechanism.[81] Chapter 4 also discusses proposed alternatives to an appeal such as a preliminary ruling procedure and assesses how these alternatives prove effective in comparison to an appeal. The analysis shows that implementing an appeal mechanism will have a considerable impact on the dynamic of the ISDS process, including costs and efficiency of the proceedings, and the enforcement of awards.

In Chapter 5, *Petyo Nikolov* addresses the settlement of mass claims in international investment law. His analysis shows that procedures to resolve mass investment claims concern both procedural efficiency and the rights of individuals and small and medium-sized enterprises (SMEs).[82] Accordingly, the implementation of such mechanisms will be vital to the legitimacy of any future ISDS system. The Chapter examines the status quo of mass investment claims and stresses the need and merits to implement such in the rules of procedure of an MIC. In this sense, the analysis addresses a blind spot of the UNCITRAL reform process as it has not yet put the rights of individuals and SMEs on the agenda. By referring to the jurisprudence of the Court of Justice of the European Union (CJEU), however, it is convincingly argued that mass claims procedures should be an element of a future MIC.

The institutional structure and the procedural rules under which a future MIC would exercise its dispute settlement function is beyond doubt essential. However, as Martin Domke already stressed in 1960 during the ILA discussions about the draft statute of a foreign investment court:

> What interests the parties is the person of the arbitrator, his competence, fairness and impartiality. [...] The basic feature is the arbitration itself, a human matter - which cannot be dealt with in rules of procedure.[83]

81 See, Landmann, Chapter 4, 105-138.
82 See, Nikolov, Chapter 5, 139-166.
83 ILA 1962 (*n 66*), 107.

As a direct response to this statement, Committee member Ottoarndt Glossner replied: 'If we want to deal with arbitration, we need rules.'[84] The disagreement among two eminent international lawyers indicates that the truth may lay somewhere in the middle. On the one hand, one can hardly deny the outstanding relevance of the human factor in any adjudicatory process. On the other hand, binding legal rules indeed seem indispensable to provide guidelines and set boundaries for the exercise of decision-making power by individuals. The rules which ensure that only suitable individuals are entrusted with the settlement of international investment disputes have therefore been and remain central to the legitimacy of ISDS.

Against this background, *Caroline Kittelmann* and *Alexander Dünkelsbühler* examine the selection and appointment of adjudicators in Chapter 6.[85] They show what the shift from ad hoc arbitration to a permanent body means for the selection procedure. Among the different design options available, they draw a comparison between different selection procedures advanced by the European Union and legal scholarship. The chapter identifies the diversity of arbitrators, the transparency of the selection process and the perception of greater independence and impartiality as key factors to remedy current legitimacy concerns. With respect to the appointment of MIC judges it is recalled that adequate representation of member States must be ensured. At the same time, interests of investors should not be kept out of sight as those actors are likely to lose their right to appoint an adjudicator. It is argued that a future MIC selection procedure will ia be judged on whether it increases diversity of decision-makers in comparison to the current system of ad hoc arbitration.

Once selected and appointed, MIC adjudicators must exercise their mandate in a way which promotes the institution's legitimacy instead of putting it into question. In light of this expectation, a code of conduct of adjudicators may serve as key control element. In Chapter 7, *Alexander Dünkelsbühler* studies the use of codes of conduct in international dispute settlement and sets up guidelines for such an instrument in the context of an MIC.[86] Considering the institutional specificities of a permanent investment court and existing draft codes such as the one jointly proposed by ICSID and UNCITRAL, he argues that the adoption of such a code will combine political accountability of adjudicators with judicial independence.

---

84 ILA 1962 (*n 66*), 108.

85 See, Kittelmann/Dünkelsbühler, Chapter 6, 167-206.

86 See, Dünkelsbühler, Chapter 7, 207-226.

Once the main conceptual questions about creating an MIC have been resolved, draft statues and procedures are ready to be adopted. At the latest at this stage, the question of implementation arises. In view of investment law's deeply fragmented nature, an effective institutional reform poses considerable challenges. *Leonard Funk* addresses this question in Chapter 8 and examines the implementation of an MIC through a multilateral opt-in treaty.[87] Taking account of the specific legal framework in which an MIC will have to operate, the Chapter examines the scope of application of such a framework and its relation to the thousands of existing investment treaties. In addition, an opt-in mechanism could provide flexibility to States and, most importantly, could facilitate the integration of existing institutions into the new MIC structure.

Up and running, a newly established MIC will ultimately be judged by the effect of its decisions. Therefore, the efficiency of MIC dispute settlement is decisive on its authority within the international legal order. This question to a large extent depends on the recognition and enforcement of MIC decisions. *Carla Müller* evaluates this practically relevant aspect of the reform in Chapter 9.[88] In view of probable institutional choices, the analysis shows that MIC decisions will most likely not be enforced under the ICSID framework. In the same sense, enforcement under the New York Convention could be difficult. The Chapter therefore recalls that an MIC inherent enforcement system would be the most preferable option. In turn, this sets the bar high as regards the support within the international community of States. Accordingly, any aspect of designing an MIC should also be considered through the lens of enforcement.

Whether a newly established MIC will make an actual difference ultimately depends on the number of States willing to accept the court's jurisdiction. The very reason why the MIC project is currently being prominently discussed at UNCITRAL is to a large extent related to the proactive role of the EU. Like no other actor, the EU supports the creation of an MIC. Certainly, whether or not the project is successful will depend on whether other States will join the EU in this endeavour. On the other hand, the support of the EU seems necessary for any kind of MIC. Therefore, *Ingo Borgdorf* sheds light on the mandatory EU law requirements for the establishment of an MIC.[89] With due consideration of CJEU jurisprudence, the Chapter recalls that an MIC project must ensure compliance

---

87 See, Funk, Chapter 8, 227-250.

88 See, Müller, Chapter 9, 251-280.

89 See, Borgdorf, Chapter 10, 281-306.

with EU constitutional principles, the protection of public interests, and provide the equal access to an independent tribunal. While those requirements do not seem to pose insurmountable hurdles, an MIC should not be seen as a European project. Instead, the MIC's institutional design must reflect the interests of all implied States across the globe.

But even if the MIC is supported by the international community of States, its success also depends on those seeking justice from the court. In this sense, the benchmark established by Abs and Shawcross also applies to a future MIC. The court therefore must, to fulfil its mandate, create an atmosphere of confidence by effective and impartial adjudication.[90] It is therefore vital that the MIC gains the trust of those legal practitioners who advise disputing parties and appear on their behalf in ISDS proceedings.

Against this background, *Moritz Keller* and *Caroline Kittelmann* provide an outlook from practitioner perspective on the creation and implementation of an MIC in Chapter 11.[91] Their observations focus on the appointment of arbitrators and the proposals on an appeal mechanism. As arbitration practitioners, they argue that the widely criticised process of arbitrator appointment is in fact a well-functioning and balanced system that already ensures impartiality. In this context, it is asked whether moving away from the current system of party appointment towards State-appointed adjudicators is based on empirical evidence or mere perception. In the same sense, it is called into question whether the current system of ad hoc arbitration really suffers from inconsistent outcomes. Accordingly, the necessity to implement an appeal is challenged.

This critical approach to an MIC is unsurprising, given that regardless of its concrete shape, the establishment of such a court would have fundamental consequences for the systemic features for which ad hoc investment arbitration is appreciated by its users. It seems plausible that investors could still have direct access to an MIC without having to exhaust local remedies.[92] However, if the permanent court would be composed of judges appointed by States in their capacity as treaty parties, investors

90 Abs, Shawcross (*n 18*), 123.

91 See, Keller/Kittelmann, Chapter 11, 307-331.

92 This does exclude, as the UNCITRAL debates show, to combine the establishment of an MIC with the introduction of a requirement to exhaust local remedies. See UNCITRAL, 'Report of Working Group III (Investor-State Dispute Settlement Reform) on the work of its thirty-seventh session (New York, 1–5 April 2019)' (9 April 2019), A/CN.9/970, para 30; 'Report of Working Group III (Investor-State Dispute Settlement Reform) on the work of its thirty-fifth session' (14 May 2018), A/CN.9/935, para 97.

would lose their right to appoint an arbitrator.[93] The integration of an appeal mechanism would redefine the finality of the decision. And finally, an MIC would most likely not benefit from the existing enforcement regimes.

This outlook form practitioner perspective shows that the remarks of Martin Domke in 1960 remain relevant. He reminded the Committee that '[we] should not have the illusion that with adoption of the Draft Statues the job of arbitration is done.'[94] Instead, the process of creating and implementing an MIC is a long-term project. Setting up the institution, appointing judges, and rendering decisions are only the starting point.

D. Challenges Ahead for any Future Multilateral Investment Court

Gaining trust from multiple different stakeholders such as governments, civil society groups, public opinions and, last but not least, of investors will decide on whether an MIC can actually establish itself within the international investment law regime of the future. This challenge of persuasion requires endurance, since a newly created MIC would most likely not abruptly replace ad hoc investment arbitration. Instead, it seems likely that if an MIC is established, it will co-exist and to some extent compete with party-appointed investment tribunals for decades. 'Ad hoc' and 'bilateralism' on the one hand, 'permanent' and 'multilateral' on the other hand will characterise the two parallel universes of ISDS. The fact that both systems compete for the trust of investors and States as users should be good news to all stakeholders

In view of the current reform debate held at UNCITRAL, the idea of an MIC seems to be the most far-reaching one. However, the effects of a new investment court on the system as a whole should not be overstated either. The UNCITRAL reform process is characterised by its focus on ISDS. Thus, the effects will most likely be limited to investment law's procedural building block. All those systemic concerns related to substantive law will not be addressed. Especially from a developing countries perspective, limiting the scope of reform to ISDS raises questions as to the sufficiency and legitimacy of any reform project. If those legitimacy concerns related

93 In the case of an MIC, the principle of the equality of the parties does not require that each party retain the ability to appoint a judge. See, Article 4 (2) (b) of the Institute of International Law's Resolution on the Equality of Parties Before International Investment Tribunals. In the same sense: McLachlan (*n 26*) para 161.

94 ILA 1962 (*n 66*), 107.

to substantive issues such as the chilling effect of investment protection are put on the backseat, the current reform process could entrench systemic insufficiencies instead of providing true progress.[95]

In this sense, the legitimacy of an MIC also depends on the substantive law on which its decisions will be based. Even though the risk exists, there is a good chance that such an entrenchment will not materialize, given that investment law is in a state of constant transformation. That the UNCITRAL process focusses on procedure does not mean that investment protection standards such as FET remain unchanged. To the contrary, investment treaties keep being redrafted and new generations of treaties are inspired by the challenge of aligning investment protection with the host State's right to regulate and the promotion of public interests. Thus, the reform of investment law's two building blocks is going on in parallel. In comparison to ISDS, the renewal of substantive law takes place in bilateral negotiations and therefore follows a very different dynamic. As a consequence, the establishment of an MIC can only be the first meaningful step in reshaping the international investment law regime of the future.

95 See for a TWAIL perspective on the ISDS reform process, Gathii (*n 51*). See also, Makau Mutua and Antony Anghie, 'What Is TWAIL?' (2000) 94 Proceedings of the Annual Meeting of ASIL, 31-40.

Chapter 2: Institutional Elements for a Multilateral ISDS System

by Johanna Braun and Philipp Reinhold[*]

Selected Bibliography: Anne van Aaken, 'Delegating Interpretative Authority in Investment Treaties: The Case of Joint Administrative Commissions' in Jean E Kalicki and Anna Joubin-Bret (eds), Reshaping the Investor-State Dispute Settlement System: Journeys for the 21st Century (Koninklijke Brill 2015); Marc Bungenberg and August Reinisch, From Bilateral Arbitral Tribunals and Investment Courts to a Multilateral Investment Court (2nd edn, Springer Open 2019); Roberto Echandi, 'Towards a New Approach to Address Investor-State Conflict: Developing a Conceptual Framework for Dispute Prevention' (2011), NCCR Trade Working Paper No 2011/46; Anthea Roberts, 'State-to-State Investment Treaty Arbitration: A Hybrid Theory of Interdependent Rights and Shared Interpretive Authority' (2014) 55 Harv. Int'l L.J. 1, 29; Jeswald W Salacuse, 'Is There a Better Way? Alternative Methods of Treaty-Based, Investor-State Dispute Resolution' (2007) 31.1 FordhamIntlLJ 138; Stephan W Schill and Geraldo Vidigal, 'Designing Investment Dispute Settlement à la Carte: Insights from Comparative Institutional Analysis' (2019) 18 Law and Practice of International Courts and Tribunals 314.

A. *Introduction*

The idea of replacing the existing ad hoc investor-State dispute settlement (ISDS) system by a multilateral investment court (MIC) was already expressed some time ago.[1] Replacing the current ISDS system by a permanent mechanism is justified by the common criticism towards ad hoc arbitration, such as a lack of neutrality of party-appointed arbitrators, as

---

* Johanna Braun is a PhD candidate at the University of Cologne. Philipp Reinhold is a research associate at Saarland University.

1 See already Gus van Harten, 'A Case for an International Investment Court' (2008), Society of International Economic Law (SIEL) Inaugural Conference 2008 Paper.

well as high costs and long duration of the proceedings.[2] However, the overriding assumption seems to be of a more fundamental nature, namely that a system which is strongly influenced by commercial arbitration is not suitable for the public law nature of investment disputes, since it cannot take sufficient account of the specific nature of the public administrative procedure and, more generally, of the sovereignty of States.[3]

A number of reform proposals have been drawn up which are aimed at a permanent form of ISDS.[4] The most comprehensive and far-reaching proposal in this context was prepared by *Marc Bungenberg* and *August Reinisch* who published a study on this subject which has recently been complemented by a concrete proposal for a convention (MIC Draft Statute).[5]

This chapter aims at providing an introduction to the institutional framework of an MIC. In addition, the creation of an MIC will be put into the broader context of institutional reform proposals for a future ISDS regime. The provided overview on institutional reform proposals will set the stage for the following chapters which deal with specific features of the MIC approach. We will begin by presenting the institutional structure of the MIC as envisaged by *Bungenberg/Reinisch* (A.). Subsequently, the MIC structure will be compared with other institutional approaches to ISDS reform, introducing reform options focusing on enhancing State control (B.) and on dispute prevention and avoidance, as well as alternative dispute resolution (C.). We will finish with reform options emphasizing flexibility (D.) and a conclusion on institutional elements of a reformed ISDS (E.).

---

2 See eg Colin M Brown, 'A Multilateral Mechanism for the Settlement of Investment Disputes. Some Preliminary Sketches' (2017) 32.3 ICSID Review 673, 675-679; Marc Bungenberg and August Reinisch, *From Bilateral Arbitral Tribunals and Investment Courts to a Multilateral Investment Court* (2nd edn, Springer Open 2019), paras 59-63.

3 See Brown *(n 2)*, 675, 677-678.

4 For a selection of the existing literature see UNCITRAL, Working Group III, 'Possible reform of investor-State dispute settlement (ISDS) - Appellate and multilateral court mechanisms - Note by the Secretariat' (29 November 2019), A/CN.9/WG.III/WP.185, fn 3. Besides, there are a number of other proposals, see eg Rebecca L Katz, 'Modelling an International Investment Court after the World Trade Organization Dispute Settlement Body' (2016) 22 Harv Negotiation Law Rev 163, 163-188 or Umair H Ghori, 'The International Investment Court System: the way forward for Asia' (2018) 21 Int Trade Bus Law Rev 205, 205-229.

5 Bungenberg, Reinisch *(n 2)*. See in this context Marc Bungenberg and August Reinisch, *Draft Statute of the Multilateral Investment Court* (Nomos 2021).

B. Multilateral Investment Court Approach

Bungenberg/Reinisch propose the introduction of an MIC as an international organisation with a first instance and a court of appeal, each with full-time judges.[6] It is intended to have exclusive jurisdiction to adjudicate investment disputes submitted to it by consent of the members of the MIC.[7] In their study, the authors also propose the establishment of an independent 'Multilateral Investment Appeals Mechanism' (MIAM) as a possible alternative.[8] The MIAM represents only a single-tier appellate mechanism within a new international organisation, which would add to a first phase of ad hoc arbitration as practiced so far. An appeals mechanism is advocated for by a number of States in the ongoing negotiations of UNCITRAL Working Group III, in particular by China.[9] However, *Bungenberg/Reinisch* make it clear that they consider this to be only a second-best option because it would not represent a holistic and comprehensive reform and therefore would not be as well suited to counter the far-reaching criticism of the current ISDS regime.[10] Their proposed MIC Draft Statute, accordingly, refers to the MIC as a court with two instances.

The authors see considerable potential in an enhanced institutionalisation for greater consistency of decisions, reinforcement of the independence and neutrality of adjudicators, more expedient dispute settlement, limitation of costs for the parties involved, better accessibility for Small and Medium Enterprises (SMEs), and finally for greater transparency than in the current ISDS system operating on an ad hoc basis.[11] Arguably, within a multilateral and permanent ISDS system, States will in particular have greater control over the dispute settlement procedure because the institutional structure gives them more influence on its design.

---

6 Bungenberg, Reinisch *(n 2)*, 29-110; Articles 1 (2) and 3 MIC Draft Statute, Bungenberg, Reinisch *(n 5)*.

7 Bungenberg, Reinisch *(n 2)*, paras 247-261; Article 23 MIC Draft Statute, Bungenberg, Reinisch *(n 5)*.

8 Bungenberg, Reinisch *(n 2)*, 197-215. For further details on the MIAM see Landmann, Chapter 4.

9 UNCITRAL, Working Group III, 'Submission by the Government of China - Note by the Secretariat' (19 July 2019), A/CN.9/WG.III/WP.177, 4; UNCITRAL WG III, Appellate and multilateral court mechanisms, WP 185 (2019) *(n 4)*; UNCITRAL, Working Group III, 'Appellate mechanism and enforcement issues, Draft Note by the Secretariat' (12 November 2020), A/CN.9/WG.III/WP.202.

10 Bungenberg, Reinisch *(n 2)*, paras 64-69.

11 ibid, paras 50-63.

The MIC's institutional structure includes essentially a Plenary Body, a Court of First Instance, an Appellate Court, an Advisory Centre and a Secretariat.[12] The institutional structure of the MIAM would be almost identical to that of the MIC, except that the scope would be smaller, and an Advisory Centre would not be envisaged since the MIAM would only come into play at an advanced stage of the dispute settlement process.[13]

The Plenary Body consists of the representatives of all members and is considered the 'political organ' of the MIC.[14] It carries out all functions assigned to it by the MIC Statute, while retaining the power to interpret and amend the statue itself through consensus.[15] According to the MIC Draft Statute, the Plenary Body establishes its own rules of procedure and adopts or modifies the rules of procedure for all other organs.[16] Among these rules are a code of ethics and a code of conduct for the judges of the MIC, as well as rules of conduct and ethics for all staff members.[17] Moreover, the Plenary Body will adopt regulations on procedure to be followed for the registration, allocation and conduct of proceedings before the Court of First Instance and the Appellate Court and provisions on transparency, third-party funding, costs, and court fees.[18]

Furthermore, the Plenary Body selects the judges of the MIC, whereby it is supported by a sub-committee (Screening Committee).[19] It is also entitled to increase the number of MIC judges.[20] Initially, the MIC consists of 24 judges, nine of whom are assigned to the Appellate Court.[21]

---

12 Article 3 MIC Draft Statute, Bungenberg, Reinisch *(n 5)*; see also UNCITRAL, Working Group III, 'Possible reform of investor-State dispute settlement (ISDS) Standing multilateral mechanism: Selection and appointment of ISDS tribunal members and related matters, Note by the Secretariat' (8 December 2021), A/CN.9/WG.III/WP.213 (advance copy), para 62-64.

13 Bungenberg, Reinisch *(n 2)*, paras 609-615.

14 ibid, paras 80-108; Article 8 MIC Draft Statute, Bungenberg, Reinisch *(n 5)*.

15 ibid, paras 80, 108, 110; Articles 8 (2) and 8 (3) MIC Draft Statute, Bungenberg, Reinisch *(n 5)*. However, Article 63 (3) MIC Draft Statute, Bungenberg, Reinisch *(n 5)* reads: 'The adoption of an amendment on which consensus cannot be reached shall require a two-thirds majority of Members in the Plenary Body'.

16 ibid, paras 80, 106-107; Articles 8 (2), (4) and (5) MIC Draft Statute, Bungenberg, Reinisch *(n 5)*.

17 ibid, paras 80, 107; Article 8 (4) MIC Draft Statute, Bungenberg, Reinisch *(n 5)*. See for more details on the code of conduct Dünkelsbühler, Chapter 7.

18 ibid, Article 8 (4) MIC Draft Statute, Bungenberg, Reinisch *(n 5)*.

19 ibid, paras 84-95; Article 12 MIC Draft Statute, Bungenberg, Reinisch *(n 5)*.

20 ibid, paras 111-112; Article 9 (4) MIC Draft Statute, Bungenberg, Reinisch *(n 5)*.

21 ibid, para 86; Articles 9 (1), 12 (4) and (5) MIC Draft Statute, Bungenberg, Reinisch *(n 5)*.

They shall sit in chambers of an uneven number of at least three.[22] The assignment of judges as well as disputes to the Chambers is made by the President of the MIC, who is elected by all Members or by all judges of the Court.[23] The Chambers shall each elect a Vice-President.[24] The President may form together with all Vice-Presidents the Grand Chamber of the MIC.[25] In addition, all judges may meet in a plenary session for important questions.[26]

The Secretariat performs the administrative functions of the MIC which shall be specified by the Plenary Body.[27] It may have internal departments as required to perform its functions and is headed by the Director-General who shall also be appointed by the Plenary Body.[28] The Director-General shall appoint the members of the staff and determine their duties and conditions of service in accordance with the regulations adopted by the Plenary Body.[29] The Secretariat may provide administrative and legal support to the judges of the MIC.[30] At the same time, *Bungenberg/Reinisch* particularly emphasise that the Secretariat shall not seek or accept instructions from any government or any other authority external to the MIC and shall refrain from any action, which might adversely reflect on their position as officials of an international organisation.[31] The authors make clear that the Secretariat should by no means draft decisions for the judges or get involved with the parties.[32] The Secretariat of the WTO has been criticized in the past for unduly influencing negotiation positions or policies of members and in particular for exerting significant influence over the writing of WTO panel reports.[33] As this criticism has been one of the causes

22 ibid, paras 166-167; Articles 17 (1) and (3) MIC Draft Statute, Bungenberg, Reinisch *(n 5)*.

23 ibid, paras 163-164, 169-171; Articles 16 and 17 (2) MIC Draft Statute, Bungenberg, Reinisch *(n 5)*.

24 ibid, para 165; Article 17 (3) MIC Draft Statute, Bungenberg, Reinisch *(n 5)*.

25 ibid, Article 17 (4) MIC Draft Statute, Bungenberg, Reinisch *(n 5)*.

26 ibid, para 172; Article 17 (5) MIC Draft Statute, Bungenberg, Reinisch *(n 5)*. See for more details on the role of the judges Kittelmann/Dünkelsbühler, Chapter 6.

27 ibid, paras 177-187; Articles 11 (2) and (3) MIC Draft Statute, Bungenberg, Reinisch *(n 5)*.

28 ibid, paras 181-182, 184; Articles 11 (1) and (2) MIC Draft Statute, Bungenberg, Reinisch *(n 5)*.

29 ibid, para 182; Article 11 (2) MIC Draft Statute, Bungenberg, Reinisch *(n 5)*.

30 Article 11 (3) MIC Draft Statute, Bungenberg, Reinisch *(n 5)*.

31 Article 11 (4) MIC Draft Statute, Bungenberg, Reinisch *(n 5)*.

32 Bungenberg, Reinisch *(n 2)*, paras 179-180.

33 See eg Peter Sutherland et al, 'The Future of the WTO, Addressing institutional challenges in the new millenium – Report by the Consultative Board to the

of the current legitimacy crisis of the WTO system,[34] the responsibilities within the MIC should be clearly separated.

Finally, the authors propose the establishment of an Advisory Centre which shall have a separate budget and operate through staff members appointed by the Plenary Body.[35] It is intended to support developing countries and SMEs in MIC procedures.[36] It therefore does not offer any assistance to non-members. However, it shall cooperate with other international organisations as required to perform its functions.[37] Rules, specifying the role of the Advisory Centre, its duties, and provisions on confidentiality in the internal functioning and publication of information shall be adopted by the Plenary Body.[38]

Should the MIC be established as a centralised dispute settlement system, it may lead to more coherent and consistent decisions, as well as greater transparency and neutrality of adjudicators. The concrete financial burden on the individual States cannot be predicted precisely at present, partly because this will depend on the specific structure of the MIC.[39] However, the proponents of an MIC are convinced that there could be a cost benefit through economies of scale,[40] internal cost allocation and support mechanisms such as the Advisory Centre.[41] For the MIAM, no cost reduction can be expected through an Advisory Centre, but the financial volume would also be significantly lower.

Director-General Supachai Panitchpakdi' (WTO 2004), 73-78; Joost Pauwelyn and Krzysztof Pelc, 'Who Writes the Rulings of the World Trade Organization? A Critical Assessment of the Role of the Secretariat in WTO Dispute Settlement' (26 September 2019) <https://ssrn.com/abstract=3458872> accessed 13 January 2022.

34 See eg Manfred Elsig, 'The World Trade Organization's Legitimacy Crisis: What Does the Beast Look Like?' (2007) 41.1 J of World Trade 75; Michael Fakhri, 'Life Without the WTO – Part I: Stop all this Crisis-Talk' (2019) <https://www.ejiltalk.org/life-without-the-wto-part-i-stop-all-this-crisis-talk/> accessed 13 January 2022.

35 Bungenberg, Reinisch *(n 2)*, paras 188-192; Article 10 (1) MIC Draft Statute, Bungenberg, Reinisch *(n 5)*.

36 ibid, Article 10 (2) MIC Draft Statute, Bungenberg, Reinisch *(n 5)*.

37 ibid, para 191; Article 10 (5) MIC Draft Statute, Bungenberg, Reinisch *(n 5)*.

38 Article 10 (3) MIC Draft Statute, Bungenberg, Reinisch *(n 5)*. For a detailed account on an Advisory Centre see Braun/Reinhold, Chapter 3.

39 UNCITRAL WG III, Appellate and multilateral court mechanisms, WP 185 (2019) *(n 4)*, paras 62-66.

40 European Commission, 'Factsheet on the Multilateral Investment Court' (2017) <https://trade.ec. europa.eu/doclib/docs/2017/september/tradoc_156042.pdf> accessed 13 January 2022.

41 See Bungenberg, Reinisch *(n 2)*, paras 57-59, 188, 204, 206, 233, 306-315, 316-323, 603-605; Article 54 MIC Draft Statute, Bungenberg, Reinisch *(n 5)*.

C. Reform Options Focusing on Increasing States' Control

The ISDS reform process began with UNCITRAL's Working Group III identifying consistency, coherence, and predictability as pressing concerns.[42] However, not everyone agrees that a comprehensive reform is necessary to tackle these issues. Instead, the proponents of this group argue that the current system of ISDS can be adequately and sufficiently improved through specific and targeted reforms.[43] States have already submitted various of such targeted reforms.[44]

From a States' perspective, one way to achieve increased consistency, coherence and predictability in ISDS proceedings is to regain control in certain areas of investment law. This section will introduce two possibilities to achieve this objective: the reinforcement of State-to-State Dispute Settlement (SSDS) (I.) and the proliferation of Joint Administrative Commissions (JAC) (II.).

I. State-to-State Dispute Settlement (SSDS)

As an instrument for regaining control over the interpretation of investment protection standards and as an alternative to cost-intensive arbitration procedures, many governments advocate for a stronger role of SSDS.[45]

---

42 UNCITRAL, Working Group III, 'Report of the orking Group III (Investor-State Dispute Settlement Reform) on the work of its Thirty-Fourth Session' (Vienna, 27 Nobember-1 December 2017) Part II' (26 February 2018), A/CN.9/930/Add.1/Rev.1, paras 9-35; see also UNCITRAL, Working Group III, 'Possible Reform of Investor-State Dispute Settlement (ISDS)' (18 September 2017), A/CN.9/WG.III/WP.142.

43 For a tabular overview of all the reform proposals, their elements, main implications and the concerns addressed see UNCITRAL, Working Group III, 'Possible Reform of Investor-State Dispute Settlement' (30 July 2019), A/CN.9/WG.III/WP.166/Add.1.

44 See eg UNCITRAL, Working Group III, 'Submission from the Government of Bahrain' (29 August 2019), A/CN.9/WG.III/WP.180; UNCITRAL, Working Group III, 'Submission from the Government of the Russian Federation' (30 December 2019), A/CN.9/WG.III/WP.188.

45 David Gaukrodger, 'State-to-State dispute settlement and the interpretation of investment treaties' (2016) OECD Working Papers on International Investment 2016/03, 6-7. There seems to be no reliable data on the costs of SSDS so far, but it is pointed out that the length and complexity of the process can also lead to higher costs for SSDS and therefore general improvements should also be considered for them. See PCA, 'Duration and Cost of State-State Arbitration

At the same time, this could also help preserving States' sovereignty. In this context, SSDS is generally understood as a supplement to the existing ISDS system, with some exceptions, such as Brazil, wanting to replace ISDS with SSDS and have in part already done so in new international investment agreements.[46] Within the UNCITRAL Working Group III, the idea of a stronger role for SSDS is specifically taken up only as a supplement to investor-State arbitration.[47] So far, there has been no independent discussion of the possibilities of SSDS as a stand-alone reform instrument.

For historical reasons almost all international investment agreements (IIAs) already contain an SSDS clause.[48] However, SSDS has rarely been used in the past which is why the scope of application of these clauses as well as their relationship to ISDS clauses is not sufficiently clear.[49] Since the first SSDS cases occurred as an alternative to the preferred ISDS system, starting with a dispute between Italy and Cuba in 2005,[50] States and in particular the academic literature have shown an increasing interest in the functioning of the SSDS clauses and their interaction with ISDS.[51]

Proceedings' (24 October 2018) <https://uncitral.un.org/sites/uncitral.un.org/files/pca-_submission_-_duration_and_cost_-_20181024. pdf> accessed 13 January 2022; UNCITRAL, Working Group III, 'Cost and Duration' (31 August 2018), A/CN.9/WG.III/WP.153.

46 Gaukrodger *(n 45)*, 7. See eg the Investment Cooperation and Facilitation Treaty Between the Federative Republic of Brazil and the Republic of India (signed 25 January 2020). On the Brazilian approach see also Michel Roberto Oliveira de Souza, 'Changing Institutional Arrangements of International Dispute Resolution in a Global Order: Three Different Approaches' (2017) 3.2 Revista Estudos Institucionais 1246, 1271-1274.

47 UNCITRAL, Working Group III, 'Possible reform of investor-State dispute settlement (ISDS)' (15 January 2020), A/CN.9/WG.III/WP.166, para 10.

48 Michele Potestà, 'State-to-State Dispute Settlement Pursuant to Bilateral Investment Treaties: Is There Potential?' in Nerina Boschiero et al (eds), *International Courts and the Development of International Law – Essays in Honour of Tullio Treves* (The Hague 2013) 753, 754; Anthea Roberts, 'State-to-State Investment Treaty Arbitration: A Hybrid Theory of Interdependent Rights and Shared Interpretive Authority' (2014) 55.1 Harv Int'l LJ 1, 3.

49 See eg Potestà *(n 48)*, 753-768; Clovis J Trevino, 'State-to-State Investment Treaty Arbitration and the Interplay with Investor-State Arbitration Under the Same Treaty' (2014) 5.1 JIDS 199, 199-233; Roberts *(n 48)*, 1-70; Gaukrodger *(n 45)*.

50 See *Republic of Italy v Republic of Cuba* Interim Award, 15 March 2005; *Republic of Italy v Republic of Cuba* Final Award, 15 January 2008.

51 Potestà *(n 48)*, 753-768; Trevino *(n 49)*, 199-233; Roberts *(n 48)*, 1-70; Gaukrodger *(n 45)*; Rodrigo Polanco, *The Return of the Home State to Investor-State Disputes – Bringing Back Diplomatic Protection?* (CUP 2019), 212-273.

Within the current reform debate *Anthea Roberts* sees three possible applications for SSDS:[52] Firstly, the contracting States can clarify the meaning of an IIA provision in abstract terms. In addition, States can take action to recover own losses or those of their investors (diplomatic protection). In this context, *Roberts* argues that Article 27 of the Convention on the Settlement of Investment Disputes between States and Nationals of Other States (ICSID Convention)[53] gives home States the right to bring a diplomatic protection claim at any point before its national has submitted a claim or consented to arbitration under the convention or after the host State fails to pay the investor-State award.[54] According to *Roberts*, this 'sequencing' approach aims to prevent multiple legal claims arising from the same facts.[55] *Roberts* concludes that if the primary point of sequencing is to prevent multiple claims, a 'symmetrical approach' would be appropriate, with a State-to-State claim precluding a later investor-State claim and vice versa.[56] A third way of applying SSDS would be to seek a declaratory judgement on the compatibility of a certain measure or factual situation with the IIA.[57] *Roberts* supports the application of SSDS to all three scenarios, as this could balance not only the relationship between the rights of States and investors, but also the relationship between more powerful and weaker States.[58]

However, depending on the scope of application of such clauses, many complex questions arise regarding the interaction with ISDS which could at best be clearly regulated by the State parties within the treaty.[59] In this context, it may also be relevant whether or not reference is made to the ICSID Convention.[60]

---

52 Roberts *(n 48)*, 29-68.

53 Convention on the Settlement of Investment Disputes between States and Nationals of Other States (ICSID Convention) (1965), 575 UNTS 159.

54 Roberts *(n 48)*, 44-48.

55 ibid, 45-46.

56 ibid, 47.

57 As opposed to JACs' decisions, this form of SSDS is applied with regard to abstract legal questions independent of an individual investor, see ibid, 67: 'A home State could seek a declaration that the host State has violated the treaty, without identifying particular investors that have been harmed or seeking compensation on their behalf'.

58 ibid, 29-68.

59 See for further discussions Potestà *(n 48)*, 761-765; Trevino *(n 49)*, 212-231; Roberts *(n 48)*, 28-68; Gaukrodger *(n 45)*, 12-19; Polanco *(n 51)*, 212-273.

60 See Potestà *(n 48)*, 761-765; Trevino *(n 49)*, 212-231; Roberts *(n 48)*, 44-49 and 63-65; Gaukrodger *(n 45)*, 13; Polanco *(n 51)*, 215-221.

II. Joint Administrative Commissions (JACs)

Another recurring proposal in UNCITRAL Working Group III seeks to enhance States' control in the interpretation of IIAs.[61] There is already a number of possibilities for States to exercise control in IIA interpretation under the current ISDS system, from the drafting and conclusion of an investment agreement to subsequent interpretative agreements or practice.[62] *Anne van Aaken* takes up one of these existing, 'hitherto neglected' mechanisms – the so-called 'joint administrative commissions' – and advocates their proliferation.[63]

An analysis of recently concluded IIAs has shown that many agreements contain a clause which provides for joint interpretations by the contracting parties.[64] Usually, this task is performed by joint committees or commissions.[65] Probably the best-known institution of this kind is NAFTA's Free Trade Commission (FTC), established by Article 2001 North American Free Trade Agreement (NAFTA).[66] The FTC is staffed with cabinet-level representatives or their designees and issues binding interpretations of NAFTA Chapter 11 provisions.[67] Many States have included comparable bodies modelled after the FTC in their IIAs.[68]

---

61 See UNCITRAL, Working Group III, 'Submission from the Government of Thailand' (8 March 2019) A/CN.9/WG.III/WP.162, para 22; UNCITRAL, Working Group III, 'Submission from the Governments of Chile, Israel and Japan' (15 March 2019), A/CN.9/WG.III/WP.163, 8; UNCITRAL, Working Group III, 'Submission from the Government of Costa Rica' (22 March 2019), A/CN.9/WG.III/WP.164, 4; UNCITRAL, Working Group III, 'Submission from the Government of Costa Rica' (31 July 2019), A/CN.9/WG.III/WP.178, 5; UNCITRAL WG III, Submission Bahrain, WP 180 (2019) (*n 44*), para 62; UNCITRAL WG III, Submission Russian Federation, WP 188 (2019) (*n 44*), 3.

62 For an overview of the typologies of the different instruments of reassertion see Andreas Kulick, 'Reassertion of Control: An Introduction' in Andreas Kulick (ed), *Reassertion of Control over the Investment Treaty Regime* (CUP 2016) 3, 21-26; see also Anthea Roberts, 'Power and Persuasion in Investment Treaty Interpretation: The Dual Role of States' (2010) 104.2 AJIL 179, esp 207-215; UNCTAD, 'Interpretation of IIAs: What States Can Do' IIA Issues Note 3/2011.

63 Anne van Aaken, 'Delegating Interpretative Authority in Investment Treaties: The Case of Joint Administrative Commissions' in Jean E Kalicki and Anna Joubin-Bret (eds), *Reshaping the Investor-State Dispute Settlement System: Journeys for the 21st Century* (Koninklijke Brill 2015) 21.

64 Polanco (*n 51*), 106; see also Table 4.2 on 107.

65 ibid.

66 North American Free Trade Agreement (NAFTA) (1992).

67 Article 1131 (2) NAFTA.

68 See Polanco (*n 51*), 111-112 for numerous examples.

However, these institutions differ from JACs in a number of ways. Most importantly, joint interpretative commissions deliver abstract treaty interpretations outside arbitral proceedings whereas JACs interpret the agreement in a concrete case, namely apply the law to a specific case.[69] This affects, inter alia, the timeline: while the latter are usually bound by a strict time limit, the former are generally not.[70] Furthermore, extra-arbitral joint interpretative commissions are political bodies whereas the JACs endorsed by *van Aaken* are staffed with administrative personnel that is particularly knowledgeable in one area; for example financial regulation and taxation.[71]

Indeed, some BITs require a host State, which invokes 'prudential reasons' as a defence for a financial measure to submit the issue to the financial authorities of both host and home States for a joint and binding determination.[72] An arbitral tribunal will only decide on the issue if the authorities do not approve the defence within 120 days.[73] A number of Canadian BITs provide for a similar mechanism that applies to taxation measures. An investor claiming that a taxation measure constitutes an expropriation must, simultaneously to giving notice of intent to submit a claim, refer the matter to the home and host States' taxation authorities for a joint and binding decision. If the two authorities do not jointly conclude that the measure does not constitute an expropriation, the arbitral tribunal will deliver a decision.[74]

The underlying idea is that by delegating decision-making on specific measures to another body, States can, on the one hand, ensure expertise in complicated and highly regulated areas which otherwise can only be pro-

---

69 ibid, 106-107.

70 ibid, 108 with further references.

71 van Aaken *(n 63)*, 22.

72 Article 20 (3) Treaty between the United States of America and the Oriental Republic of Uruguay Concerning the Encouragement and Reciprocal Protection of Investment (US-Uruguay BIT) (2005); Article 20 (3) Treaty between the Government of the United States of America and the Government of the Republic of Rwanda Concerning the Encouragement and Reciprocal Protection of Investment (US-Rwanda BIT) (2008).

73 Article 20 (3) (c) and (d) US-Uruguay BIT; Article 20 (3) (c) and (d) US-Rwanda BIT.

74 Article 16 (3) Agreement between Canada and the Republic of Peru for the Promotion and Protection of Investments (Canada-Peru BIT) (2006); Article 14 (6) Agreement between Canada and the Republic of Moldova for the Promotion and Protection of Investments (Canada-Moldova BIT) (2018).

vided by expert arbitrators or tribunal appointed experts.[75] On the other hand, States can thereby prove that they are not acting for opportunistic, political reasons, as could be the case with joint committees which are dependent on their respective government.[76] However, as State authorities are, by their very nature, closely connected to governments, political dependencies can become an issue.[77]

Van Aaken submits that this mechanism could be expanded to other areas, for example to environmental measures.[78] It should, however, be ensured that the competent authorities are independent from political processes and not home biased.[79] This requires ensuring that the authorities in question are independent from governments, not only de jure but also de facto.[80] In case States come to the conclusion that they do not trust each other's agencies' independence, *van Aaken* suggests referring matters to international organisations which are experts in a specific subject matter, such as the International Monetary Fund, the Food and Agricultural Organization, the World Health Organization, or the United Nations Environmental Programme.[81] The advantage would be that international organisations are usually not home-biased and they are in principle considered politically independent.[82]

It remains to be seen whether this idea is taken up in the current reform process. While UNCITRAL's Working Group III seems to encourage using existing mechanisms to enhance contracting parties' control over treaty interpretation,[83] the proliferation of joint administrative commission has not played a role yet.

---

75 van Aaken *(n 63)*, 39-46.

76 ibid, 36-39.

77 See also below Section C.III.

78 cf van Aaken *(n 63)*, 45.

79 ibid.

80 ibid, 46.

81 ibid, 47.

82 ibid, 47. Recent discussions surrounding the independence of the World Health Organisation have, however, the potential to call this statement into question.

83 UNCITRAL, Working Group III, 'Possible Reform of Investor-State Dispute Settlement (ISDS) – Interpretation of Investment Treaties by Treaty Parties' (17 January 2020), A/CN.9/WG.III/WP.191, para 44.

III. State Control and the MIC

To a certain degree, both the MIC as well as the reform options focusing on States' control aim at limiting arbitrators' control while strengthening the States' position. However, they differ in the way this goal is pursued.

Most notably, while the MIC establishes a court system, the other two approaches provide new procedures within the existing arbitral dispute settlement mechanisms. Accordingly, the reform options require different institutional set-ups. While the MIC would be an entirely newly created international organisation comprising a statute, organs and a budget, SSDS and JACs are implemented in the current system and do not require comprehensive institutional reform. In fact, both mechanisms already exist but are, according to their proponents, not yet sufficiently used. Hence, the MIC has to be established from scratch, whereas SSDS and JACs must be made more popular.

The different institutionalisation might also reflect on their viability. In general, the more comprehensive a reform proposal is, the more difficult it will be to reach an agreement that all parties involved agree with. Smaller steps tackling individual problematic areas of concern may be easier to set on for a greater number of States. Such a gradual reform may thus be more realistic to carry out than a complete overhaul of the ISDS system which is, in addition, mainly driven by one group of (developed) countries including the EU.

On the other hand, a gradual reform can, by its very nature, only tackle a limited amount of issues. While consistency, coherence, and predictability may be improved by spreading approaches that enhance States' control, other concerns like the selection and appointment of arbitrators or the lack of a review mechanism will not be addressed.[84]

Finally, strengthening States' roles, as envisaged in SSDS and JACs, always entails the possibility of politicising investor-State disputes. Originally, however, one of the very objectives of the ISDS system as we know it today was to de-politicise these disputes.[85] Moving the resolution of investment disputes away from an independent third party towards the

---

84 See UNCITRAL WG III, Possible Reform of ISDS, WP 142 (2017) (*n 42)* for an overview of the concerns.

85 See eg Ibrahim F I Shihata, 'Towards a Greater Depoliticization of Investment Disputes: The Roles of ICSID and MIGA' (1986) 1.1 ICSID Review, 1; Christoph Schreuer, 'Do we need Investment Arbitration?' in Jean E Kalicki and Anna Joubin-Bret (eds), *Reshaping the Investor-State Dispute Settlement System* (Brill 2015), 879, 880; Ursula Kriebaum, 'Evaluating Social Benefits and Costs of In-

States to the detriment of investors can potentially have an overall negative impact on foreign investment States should certainly be aware of.

A distinct question pertains to the compatibility of SSDS and JAC with the establishment of an MIC as proposed by *Bungenberg/Reinisch*. Although the focus in designing the MIC lies on ISDS, the authors also consider the relationship between the MIC and SSDS.[86] In principle, *Bungenberg/Reinisch* recognise that SSDS based on existing IIAs could remain possible parallel to the MIC.[87] Then, however, it would have to be clarified how decisions of an inter-State panel would affect disputes within the jurisdiction of the MIC. On the one hand, the MIC Statute could or may have to recognise such decisions as binding.[88] On the other hand, the MIC Statute could also act as a modification of the bilateral investment agreement and remove any binding effect of the inter-State panel's decision on the MIC.[89] Conversely, the MIC Statute could order that a binding effect has to be presumed in case the IIA itself does not state such binding effect.[90] In any event, binding the MIC to intergovernmental decisions outside its jurisdiction could potentially have the effect of allowing individual member States to influence the subsequent jurisprudence of the MIC.[91]

Against this background, *Bungenberg/Reinisch* argue that the MIC should also be responsible for SSDS in order to create a coherent decision-making practice.[92] In principle, this would include all constellations of SSDS mentioned above.[93] Accordingly, Article 22 (1) MIC Draft Statute states that '[a]ny legal disputes between Members of the MIC regarding the interpretation or application of the Agreement listed under Annexes of this Statute may be resolved through recourse to the MIC' and paragraph 3 explains that

> [u]pon the parties' consent to MIC jurisdiction pursuant to paragraph 1, such jurisdiction shall be exercised to the exclusion of any other remedy provided in the specific International Investment Agreement between the disputing Members.

---

vestment Treaties: Depoliticization of Investment Disputes' (2018) 33.1 ICSID Review 14.

86 Bungenberg, Reinisch *(n 2)*, paras 256-261.

87 ibid, para 257.

88 ibid; see eg Article 36 (b) MIC Draft Statute, Bungenberg, Reinisch *(n 5)*.

89 ibid.

90 ibid, para 258.

91 ibid.

92 ibid, paras 259-260.

93 See above Section C.I.

Bungenberg/Reinisch point out that in such a case the relationship between SSDS and ISDS within the MIC would need further clarification, whereby the authors seem to envisage a binding effect of inter-State decisions on future cases.[94] With regard to diplomatic protection, Article 25 MIC Draft Statute contains a provision analogous to Article 27 ICSID Convention. This is likely to give rise to similar questions of interpretation as those relating to Article 27 ICSID Convention.[95]

It is not quite clear whether including JACs would be compatible with the proposed MIC in its current form. In their study, the authors point to a possible conflict between State interpretations and fundamental rule of law requirements. In addition, JACs specifically are not yet envisaged in the MIC Statute. This would, however, not prevent including them into the institutional structure of the MIC, for example according to Article 36 (b) MIC Statute, provided that they comply with fair trial requirements. In any case, the relationship between JACs' interpretation of the applicable investment agreement and the MIC should be clarified by procedural rules adopted under Article 8 (2) of MIC Statute.

D. *Reform Proposals Focusing on Dispute Prevention and Avoidance or Alternative Dispute Resolution*

A third category of reform proposals concentrates less on the establishment of a permanent dispute resolution mechanism or on increasing State control, but rather focuses on alternative types of proceedings that can make arbitration unnecessary, regardless of its form. While those mechanisms can replace arbitral proceedings, they are majorly intended as an additional option for the disputing parties, which means that the possibility of arbitration is not abandoned. Institutional alternatives in this sense include dispute prevention and avoidance (DPA) on the one hand (I.), as well as alternative dispute resolution (ADR) on the other hand (II.).

Both DPA and ADR represent a rather flexible alternative to the settlement of investor-State disputes by an arbitral tribunal, which is why both areas are regularly discussed together within the ISDS reform process.[96] However, they must be distinguished as independent spheres dealing

94 Bungenberg, Reinisch *(n 2)*, para 260.

95 See above Section C.I. notes 53-55.

96 UNCITRAL, Working Group III, 'Possible reform of investor-State dispute settlement (ISDS), Dispute prevention and mitigation - Means of alternative dispute resolution, Note by the Secretariat' (15 January 2020), A/CN.9/WG.III/WP.190.

with different levels of maturity of a conflict:[97] in conflict theory, the term 'conflict' is understood as 'the process of expressing dissatisfaction, disagreement, or unmet expectations with any organizational interchange', which is 'often ongoing, amorphous, and intangible'. In contrast, a 'dispute' is understood as 'one of the products of conflict' that is 'tangible and concrete – it has issues, positions, and expectations for relief'.

Against this background, DPA aims at reducing the number of conflicts that could transform into disputes by diminishing possible areas of dispute.[98] ADR follows DPA in time, and thus involves a different approach to dispute resolution, even if the boundaries are blurred.[99] A second possibility for differentiation lies in the one-sidedness of DPAs, in which State structures always form the starting point, whereas in ADR a neutral third party acts as the key to equal participation in the procedure.[100] The different approach does not mean, however, that both areas cannot have a common institutional framework. One institutional option discussed in UNCITRAL Working Group III, which could combine the two areas, would be an Advisory Centre, which is examined in more detail in *Braun/Reinhold* Chapter 3.

I. *Dispute Prevention and Avoidance*

The prevention of a dispute can be attempted in a variety of ways and at different levels. In order to be able to discuss the various approaches, they must first be categorized, in particular with regard to their institutional structure. The so far most detailed concept in this context can be found

---

See UNCTAD, *Investor-State Disputes: Prevention and Alternatives to Arbitration II* (United Nations 2011).

97 See on this Cathy A Constantino and Christian Sickles-Merchant, *Designing Conflict Management Systems* (San Francisco 1996), 5.

98 UNCTAD, *Investor-State Disputes: Prevention and Alternatives to Arbitration* (United Nations 2010), xiv. See also Roberto Echandi, 'Towards a New Approach to Address Investor-State Conflict: Developing a Conceptual Framework for Dispute Prevention' (2011) NCCR Trade Working Paper No 2011/46, 20: '(…) dispute prevention is conceptualized as the act of reducing the number of conflicts that escalate into formal conflicts'.

99 See on the conceptualization Echandi *(n 98)*, 20-26.

100 See eg Catharine Titi, 'Between Utopia and Realism: Mediation and the Settlement of Investment Disputes' in Catherine Titi and Katia Fach Gomez (eds), *Mediation in International Commercial and Investment Disputes* (OUP 2019) 21, 29-31.

in a paper written by *Echandi*. On this basis, the reform proposals will be assigned to regulatory levels. *Echandi* provides a framework for DPA that consists of dispute prevention policies (DPP) and dispute prevention mechanisms (DPM).[101]

DPPs can be adopted by one or more governments to avoid that conflicts between States and investors escalate into real disputes.[102] They can either be unilaterally designed and implemented at a domestic level (domestic DPPs) or be based on an international concerted approach (State-to-State DPPs).[103]

Domestic DPPs may include capacity building to government agencies,[104] communication and coordination protocols among State agencies, or the promotion of legal means such as the negotiation of investor-State contracts.[105] State-to-State DPPs may entail four different categories focusing on clarification and interpretation of the scope and content of provisions of IIAs, on promoting incentives to explore interest-based conflict management procedures before arbitration, on including joint State-to-State consultation mechanisms, or on promoting communication and coordination protocols between governments.[106]

DPMs are defined as concrete procedural mechanisms based on law or contract which facilitate early management of investor-State conflicts to prevent them from escalating.[107] *Echandi* proposes to distinguish between 'contractual DPMs' and 'institutional DPMs'.[108] The former are agreed to by the host State and the investor well before a conflict arises and may include problem-solving techniques that allow for third-party intervention.[109] The latter are embedded in the institutional structure of the host State and apply to all investments without a specific investment con-

101 Echandi *(n 98)*, 27-34.

102 ibid, 27.

103 ibid.

104 See eg the IDLO Investment Support Programme for Least Developed Countries (ISP/LDCs). For an overview of the Programme see <https://www.idlo.int/sites/default/files/documents/ISP%20LDCs% 20Programme%20doc%20%2022%20April%202019%20ver.pdf> accessed 13 January 2022.

105 Echandi *(n 98)*, 27.

106 Echandi *(n 98)*, 28-29.

107 ibid, 29.

108 ibid, 29-30.

109 ibid, 29.

tract being required.[110] Developing institutional DPMs entails the implementation of a comprehensive programme involving different aspects.[111]

In its note on dispute prevention and mitigation, the UNCITRAL Secretariat identified a great interest of States in promoting DPA on a national, bilateral, and international level.[112] Along these different levels, the Secretariat outlines existing examples for the establishment of a lead agency, information databases, monitoring and risk awareness systems, as well as initiatives that provide for State-to-State cooperation and capacity building.[113]

In this context, Peru, Colombia, and Korea stand out, which have created institutional DPMs that can serve as a point of reference for other States.[114] Korea has developed the Office of the Foreign Investment Ombudsman (OIO), a non-profit organization hosted by the Korea Trade-Investment Promotion Agency (KOTRA) whose main purpose is to support foreign investors facing difficulties in managing their business within Korea, identifying and solving investment related conflicts, as well as improving the overall investment environment.[115] Colombia has set up a lead agency that acts both as a focal point for all agencies involved in investment relations and as an intermediary between investors and the relevant government authorities.[116] Peru has established an institutional DPA mechanism for information sharing and early alerts which involves the Ministry of Economic and Finance as a 'Coordinator' to which information on IIAs and growing conflicts must be communicated, as well as a special committee, which deals with all aspects of the representation of the State in ISDS cases.[117] All these examples are suitable as orientation for other States to design their own DPA system based on existing experiences.

---

110 ibid, 30.

111 ibid, 32-33.

112 UNCITRAL WG III, Dispute prevention and mitigation, WP 190 (2020) *(n 96)*, paras 5-9.

113 ibid, paras 10-26.

114 For further details see UNCTAD, 'Investor-State Disputes: Prevention and Alternatives to Arbitration' (United Nations 2010) 68-92.

115 UNCITRAL, Working Group III, 'Submission from the Government of the Republic of Korea' (31 July 2019), A/CN.9/WG.III/WP.179, 5; UNCTAD *(n 114)*, 88-92.

116 UNCTAD *(n 114)*, 78-82.

117 ibid, 68-73. For a more detailed overview see Carlos José Valderrama, 'Investor-State Dispute Prevention: The Perspective of Peru' in Catherine Titi (ed), *Public Actors in International Investment Law* (Springer 2021), 117.

II. Alternative Dispute Resolution (ADR)

The term ADR involves the intervention of a third party who assists the parties in the settlement of their dispute.[118] Unlike in arbitration, the third party assists the parties to resolve their dispute amicably on their own.[119] The parties to the dispute have considerably more control than in court or arbitration proceedings, but less than in bilateral negotiations.[120] The most common types of procedures in the field of ADR are mediation and conciliation, even if other forms of amicable settlement of disputes are conceivable.[121] The distinction between mediation and conciliation is not always clear-cut: sometimes both terms are used synonymously for an amicable dispute resolution involving a third party.[122] However, most scholars distinguish the two concepts according to whether there is a formalised, rights-based (conciliation) or a more informal, interest-based procedure (mediation).[123]

---

118 Jeswald W Salacuse, 'Is There a Better Way? Alternative Methods of Treaty-Based, Investor-State Dispute Resolution' (2007) 31.1 FordhamIntlLJ 138, 156.

119 Salacuse *(n 118)*, 157; Gene Hamilton, 'Alternative Dispute Resolution (ADR) – Definitions, Types and Feasibility' in UNCTAD, *Investor-State Disputes: Prevention and Alternatives to Arbitration II* (United Nations 2011), 6.

120 Salacuse *(n 118)*, 154-155.

121 See eg Hamilton *(n 119)*, 6-7; UNCITRAL WG III, Dispute prevention and mitigation, WP 190 (2020) *(n 96)*, para 29.

122 See eg Catherine Kessedjian et al, 'Mediation in Future Investor-State Dispute Settlement', Academic Forum on ISDS Concept Paper 2020/16, 5 March 2020, 3; Titi *(n 100)*, 21; Jack J Jr Coe, 'Toward a Complementary Use of Conciliation in Investor-State, Disputes - A Preliminary Sketch' (2005) 12.1 UC Davis J Int' L & Pol'y 7, 14.

123 See eg Salacuse *(n 118)*, 172; Wolf von Kumberg, Jeremy Lack, and Michael Leathes, 'Enabling Early Settlement in Investor-State Arbitration: The Time to Introduce Mediation Has Come' (2014) 29.1 ICSID Review 133, 134-136; Monde Marshall, 'Investor-State Dispute Settlement Reconceptionalized: Regulation of Disputes, Standards and Mediation' (2017) 17.2 Pepp Disp Resol LJ 233, 249-251; Edna Sussman, 'The Advantages of Mediation and the Special Challenges to its Utilization in Investor State Disputes' (2011) 7.27 Rev Bras Arb 54, 56. See also Nancy A Welsh and Andrea K Schneider, 'The Thoughtful Integration of Mediation into Bilateral Investment Treaty Arbitration' (2013) 18 Harv Negot L Rev 71, 109-114; Susan D Franck, 'Using Investor-State Mediation Rules to Promote Conflict Management: An Introductory Guide' (2014) 29.1 ICSID Review 66, 72-75 distinguishing between 'evaluative mediation', where the legal position of the parties becomes relevant, and 'facilitative mediation', which refers to a purely interest-based mediation.

Proponents of ADR refer to the lower procedural costs and shorter duration compared to arbitration.[124] In particular, they stress that mediation and conciliation are more flexible and lead to amicable solutions that take into account the interests of the parties, which regularly allows the investment relationship between the investor and the State to be maintained or restructured.[125] All these advantages are also being put forward by a number of countries within Working Group III.[126] For States, controlling the outcome of the proceedings also means that a possibly undesirable line of jurisprudence can be avoided.[127] Against this background, a greater use of mediation or conciliation as an alternative is being promoted, however, without fully replacing arbitration.[128] Obstacles to its use are seen, for example, in the fact that the relationship between the parties may already be too dysfunctional. There are also particular difficulties States face in conducting mediation such as the fear of non-acceptance of settlements by the public.[129]

Mediation and conciliation already have a firm place in the settlement of disputes between private parties but have not yet played a major role in investor-State disputes, despite the existing legal framework.[130] Examples

---

124 See eg Salacuse *(n 118)*, 176; Welsh, Schneider *(n 123)*, 77, 82-83; Franck *(n 123)*, 77-78; Shahla F Ali and Odysseas G Repousis, 'Investor-state mediation and the rise of transparency in international investment law: Opportunity or threat' (2017) 45.2 Denv J Int'l L & Pol'y 225, 234-235; Titi *(n 100)*, 21-25.

125 ibid; see also Coe *(n 122)*, 15; von Kumberg, Lack, and Leathes *(n 123)*, 141; Marshall *(n 123)*, 253-254; Daniel Weinstein and Mushegh Manukyan, 'Making Mediation More Attractive For Investor-State Disputes' (Kluwer Arbitration Blog, 26 March 2019) <http://arbitrationblog.kluwerarbitration.com/2019 /03/26/making-mediation-more-attractive-for-investor-state-disputes/?doing_wp_cron=1593761940. 8679230213165283203125> accessed 13 January 2022; Sussman *(n 123)*, 61.

126 UNCITRAL WG III, Dispute prevention and mitigation, WP 190 (2020) *(n 96)*, para 30; see also UNCITRAL Working Group III, 'Possible reform of investor-State dispute settlement (ISDS) Mediation and other forms of alternative dispute resolution (ADR), Note by the Secretariat' (2021), para 1 et seqq.

127 Franck *(n 123)*, 78-80.

128 This is expressly emphasized by eg Coe *(n 122)*, 32 and Salacuse *(n 118)*, 176.

129 Titi *(n 100)*, 35-38. See for an overview about different obstacles to investor-State mediation Seraphina Chew, Lucy Reed, and J Christopher Thomas, 'Report: Survey on Obstacles to Settlement of Investor-State Disputes' (2018) NUS Centre for International Law Working Paper 18/01.

130 UNCITRAL WG III, Dispute prevention and mitigation, WP 190 (2020) *(n 96)*, paras 37-44.

are the ICSID Conciliation Rules[131], the UNCITRAL Model Law[132] or the IBA Investor–State Mediation Rules[133]. In addition, there are complementary soft law approaches such as the 'Code of Professional Conduct' of the International Mediation Institute.[134] With regard to the enforcement of settlements, the new UNCITRAL Singapore Convention may become especially important in practice.[135] It has entered into force in September 2020 and aims at ensuring that settlements can be enforced as effectively as arbitral awards under the New York Convention.[136]

Furthermore, a number of investment treaties already contain provisions that provide for settlement proceedings at a preliminary stage to arbitration.[137] Yet, they are not considered as a real alternative to arbitration.[138] At the same time, however, around one third of all ICSID cases are settled or otherwise discontinued, without the exact procedural circumstances or

---

131 ICSID Conciliation Rules 2006 <http://icsidfiles.worldbank.org/icsid/icsid/staticfiles/basicdoc/partE. htm> accessed 13 January 2022.

132 UNCITRAL Model Law on International Commercial Mediation and International Settlement Agreements Resulting from Mediation (2018), Annex II, <https://uncitral.un.org/en/texts/mediation/ modellaw/commercial_conciliation> accessed 13 January 2022.

133 IBA Investor-State Mediation Rules (2012) <https://www.ibanet.org/MediaHandler?id=C74CE2C9-7E9E-4BCA-8988-2A4DF573192C> accessed 13 January 2022. See on this Anna Joubin-Bret and Barton Legum, 'A Set of Rules Dedicated to Investor-State Mediation: The IBA Investor-State Mediation Rules' (2014) 29.1 ICSID Review 17, 17-24.

134 International Mediation Institute, Code of Professional Conduct <https://www.imimediation.org/ practitioners/code-professional-conduct/> accessed 13 January 2022.

135 Convention on International Settlement Agreements Resulting from Mediation (Singapore Convention) (adopted by UN Res 73/198 2018).

136 Convention on the Recognition and Enforcement of Foreign Arbitral Awards (New York Convention) (1959) 330 UNTS 3; Iris Ng, 'The Singapore Mediation Convention: What Does it Mean for Arbitration and the Future of Dispute Resolution?' (Kluwer Arbitration Blog, 31 August 2019) <http://arbitrationblog. kluwerarbitration.com/2019/08/31/the-singapore-mediation-convention-what-does-it-mean-for-arbitration-and-the-future-of-dispute-resolution/?doing_wp_cron=1593443930.04997706413269042 96875> accessed 13 January 2022.

137 See eg Article 23 US-Uruguay BIT requiring consultation or negotiation before the initiating a claim of arbitration; Article 9 (1) Thailand-Peru BIT stipulating that investor-State disputes 'shall, if possible be settled through consultation or negotiation'; Article 11 (1) requiring amicable settlement of disputes before submitting them to arbitration.

138 Kessedjian et al *(n 122)*, 4-12.

the motives being sufficiently clear.[139] Proponents of ADR see this statistic as a potential driver for a greater use of ADR in the future.[140] Comprehensive rules on mediation can also be found within the new free trade and investment treaties concluded between the EU and Canada (CETA),[141] Singapore[142] and Vietnam[143] respectively.[144]

Thus, the decisive question is not *whether* mediation or conciliation can be considered as alternative dispute resolution methods, but *how* they can be used more widely. In this regard, a fundamental question is whether the use of mediation or conciliation should be mandatory in any form, for example in the form of an obligatory participation in a kind of preliminary meeting to inform the parties about the possibilities and advantages of an amicable settlement[145] or as mandatory mediation for certain types of disputes only.[146] However, there is no treaty so far that contains a provision of compulsory ADR.[147] Moreover, it may be difficult to add elements of coercion without a legitimate policy basis.[148] It could also be seen as a logical contradiction to the idea of ADR as a voluntary procedure.[149] Instead, primary emphasis should be placed on careful design of the specific ADR regime and education of the parties.[150] Overall, it is most important that both parties are committed to the process in order for it to be successful.[151]

One option would be to use existing IIA clauses that provide for a 'cooling-off period', during which the parties can settle an investment dispute

---

139 Titi *(n 100)*, 33-34.

140 von Kumberg, Lack, and Leathes *(n 123)*, 135; Ali, Repousis *(n 124)*, 232; Marshall *(n 123)*, 251; Weinstein, Manukyan *(n 125)*.

141 Article 8.20 (1) Comprehensive Trade and Economic Agreement between Canada and the European Union (CETA) (2016).

142 Article 3.4, Annexes 6 and 10 Investment Protection Agreement between the European Union and its Member States, of the one part, and the Republic of Singapore, of the other part (2019).

143 Article 3.4, Annexes 9 and 10 Investment Protection Agreement between the European Union and its Member States, of the one part, and the Socialist Republic of Viet Nam, of the other part (2019).

144 See also on this Titi *(n 100)*, 21-25.

145 Welsh, Schneider *(n 123)*, 132.

146 Weinstein, Manukyan *(n 125)*.

147 Kessedjian et al *(n 122)*, 4.

148 Coe *(n 122)*, 35-36.

149 ibid, 34-36.

150 ibid, 36.

151 Franck *(n 123)*, 76.

amicably.[152] These clauses could be combined with an explicit reference to procedures such as mediation or conciliation, making them an option for a preliminary stage in the form of a precondition to an arbitral procedure.[153] This may filter out a number of cases that would be settled instead of coming before an arbitration tribunal. For example, Article 26 (1) and (2) of the Energy Charter Treaty (ECT)[154] refers to amicable settlement and is complemented by mediation guidelines developed by the ECT Secretariat.[155]

A second possibility would be to provide for a first round of mediation or conciliation during the cooling-off period and for a second attempt at a later stage[156] since the parties may assess their own position at different stages of the proceedings differently when their understanding of the dispute evolves.[157] This automatically affects the possibility of reaching an agreement.[158] This attempt should 'reflect a balance between information completeness and cost considerations' and could take place before the hearing.[159]

A third option would be to enable the parties to initiate mediation or conciliation proceedings at any time in parallel to arbitration.[160] This approach can be found, for example, in new free trade or investment agreements such as CETA.[161] *Coe* suggests authorising a conciliator or mediator to 'shadow' the arbitral process and to apply mediation techniques at

152 See UNCITRAL WG III, Dispute prevention and mitigation, WP 190 (2020) *(n 96)*, paras 34-35; UNCITRAL WG III, Mediation and other forms of ADR (2021) (*n 126*), para 30-31. See also the statistical overview by Kessedjian et al *(n 122)*, 4-8.

153 Salacuse *(n 118)*, 184-185; von Kumberg, Lack, and Leathes *(n 123)*, 137; UNCITRAL WG III, Dispute prevention and mitigation, WP 190 (2020) *(n 96)*, para 36.

154 Energy Charter Treaty (ECT) (signed 17 December 1994, entered into force 16 April 1998).

155 Marshall *(n 123)*, 258-259.

156 Coe *(n 122)*, 41-42.

157 ibid, 41. This is also mentioned by Kessedjian et al *(n 122)*, 13.

158 ibid.

159 Coe *(n 122)*, 41.

160 Nancy A Welsh and Andrea K Schneider, 'Becoming Investor-State Mediation' (2012) 1.1 Penn St JL & Int'l Aff 86, 94-95; Welsh and Schneider *(n 123)*, 108-115; Marshall *(n 123)*, 255; see also UNCITRAL WG III, Mediation and other forms of ADR (2021) (*n 126*), para 32-33.

161 Article 8.20 (1) CETA states: 'The disputing parties may at any time agree to have recourse to mediation.'

various instances throughout that procedure.[162]. However, the closer mediation or conciliation and arbitration are intertwined, the more questions arise regarding the relationship of both procedural mechanisms.

In addition to the question of the legal integration of ADR into the existing ISDS system, a number of reform proposals deal with ways to make the use of ADR more attractive overall. For example, the implementation of ADR should be promoted more strongly, thereby explaining the procedure as well as the advantages.[163] Moreover, there is a large number of suggestions to make mediation or conciliation easier to handle, including the development of independent procedural rules, guidelines, checklists, templates and other tools, as well as assistance in identifying suitable mediators.[164]

Salacuse proposes the establishment of an International Investment Mediation Service (IIMS) that provides for qualified mediators on short-notice.[165] The International Mediation Institute already offers a database where parties can find mediators.[166] In principle, a number of supporters see a stronger role for institutions already qualified in the field of ADR, such as UNCITRAL or ICSID, which should offer coaching and comprehensive procedural support.[167]

With regard to the internal administrative system of the State, some proposals suggest the establishment of a central competent authority that leads and coordinates settlement procedures, as well as developing a comprehensive communication strategy that builds an understanding of the benefits of ADR.[168] To deal with fears of State representatives of being criticised by the public for the outcome of mediation, *Weinstein* and *Manukyan* propose further that mediators should issue a letter confirming that '(i) the negotiated deal is fair, (ii) the terms agreed upon by the parties are commercially reasonable, and (iii) negotiations were conducted in good faith'.[169] However, it is unclear whether mediators would be willing to take on this responsibility.

---

162 Coe *(n 122)*, 42. As this ongoing role would add to the costs of the proceeding, he argues for a combination of one mediator or conciliator together with a sole arbitrator, ibid 42-43.

163 von Kumberg, Lack, and Leathes *(n 123)*, 137; Salacuse *(n 118)*, 180-181.

164 von Kumberg, Lack, and Leathes *(n 123)*, 137-139; Salacuse *(n 118)*, 180-82; Kessedjian et al *(n 122)*, 131-134.

165 Salacuse *(n 118)*, 182.

166 See <https://www.imimediation.org/find-a-mediator/> accessed 13 January 2022.

167 von Kumberg, Lack, and Leathes *(n 123)*, 137; Salacuse *(n 118)*, 181.

168 von Kumberg, Lack, and Leathes *(n 123)*, 141; Salacuse *(n 118)*, 183-184.

169 Weinstein, Manukyan *(n 125)*.

III. DPA and ADR in the Context of the MIC

DPA and ADR are fundamentally different mechanisms than the MIC. While the former aim at finding a mutually acceptable solution, the latter represents a contradictory procedure and is, in that way, comparable to the fundamental characteristics of investor-State arbitration. ADR could be established as a multilateral institution like the MIC whereas DPA is, in principle, better suited for a unilateral or bilateral approach adopted by individual States unless it is coordinated through a multilateral focal point.

Accordingly, the study by *Bungenberg/Reinisch* does not contain any comments or concrete proposals on DPA. In addition, Article 1 (2) MIC Draft Statute states that the MIC 'shall exercise jurisdiction over all disputes related to the protection of investments (...)'. Hence, the focus of the MIC is linked to the subsequent resolution of a dispute that has already been substantiated. This is also logical, since the MIC is concerned with a multilateral mechanism for dispute resolution, whereas DPA is basically organised by each individual State independently or in a bilateral relationship. The concrete form of dispute prevention must be geared to the needs, but also the possibilities of individual States.

However, the MIC as an international organisation can serve as a focal point for coordinating national or bilateral DPA policies or mechanisms without having to make specific arrangements. Existing DPA models can be presented and promoted among the members within the framework of the MIC without the need for a specific provision. The States can exchange their experiences and thus possibly optimise their own system. For an institutional structuring of this dialogue, MIC Member States can make use of Article 8 (6) MIC Draft Statute that allows the formation of committees in this context. Hence, it would be possible for States to establish their own committee for a joint exchange on DPA methods.

In addition, *Bungenberg/Reinisch* propose the establishment of an Advisory Centre that 'could support small and medium-sized enterprises and developing countries by preventing and settling disputes and offering legal advice during arbitration'.[170] On the one hand, Article 10 (2) MIC Draft Statute states that the Advisory Centre may 'provide legal assistance for disputes in the MIC', thereby indicating that DPA might be excluded. On the other hand, Article 10 (4) MIC Draft Statute allows the Plenary Body to draft rules that specify the role of the Advisory Centre. The possible mandate of the Advisory Centre does not seem to be limited by the MIC

170 Bungenberg, Reinisch *(n 2)*, para 17.

Draft Statute in such a way that it only allows for a legal service to be provided after a dispute has been brought before the MIC.

With regard to ADR, *Bungenberg/Reinisch* state that it is an alternative also to the investment court proceedings of the MIC.[171] Against this background, the authors see either the possibility to keep ADR proceedings and the MIC separated, or to create a mediation centre as a sub-unit within the framework of the MIC that would then only have subsidiary jurisdiction in cases where no provisions on this topic exist in the bilateral IIAs.[172] Thereby, the jurisdiction of the MIC would be extended.[173]

The MIC Draft Statute remains silent on ADR indicating that both types of proceeding should remain separated. Article 23 MIC Draft Statute, on the one hand, underlines the exclusivity of the jurisdiction of the MIC for 'disputes arising out of an investment agreement between two States that are both Members of the MIC'. This leads to the question if members of the MIC will be allowed to continue making use of ADR based on their IIAs after having consented to the jurisdiction of the MIC. On the other hand, Article 27 MIC Draft Statute recognizes additional jurisdictional requirements resulting from the underlying IIA. This may include for example a cooling-off period and thereby leaves the door open for ADR. However, it does not cover parallel ADR. In this respect, there may be the possibility to consider ADR after initiation of an MIC procedure as a reason to stay the MIC proceedings pursuant to Article 36 MIC Draft Statute. In addition, the parties may have recourse to ADR and agree to withdraw the claim (Article 39 MIC Draft Statute). Finally, MIC Member States could draft procedural rules that regulate the implementation of ADR mechanisms and their relationship with the court proceeding (Article 8 (2) MIC Draft Statute).

E. Multilateral Institution for Dispute Settlement on Investment

This chapter has already shown that a plethora of different reform options based on various diverging political conceptions exist. For that reason, *Schill* and *Vidigal* consider it unlikely that a global consensus can be

171 ibid, para 264.
172 ibid, paras 264 and 599.
173 ibid, para 196.

found.[174] In order to avoid further fragmentation of investor-State dispute resolution, they propose establishing a Multilateral Institution for Dispute Settlement on Investment (MIDSI) which they describe as 'an umbrella for dispute settlement options that participating members could chose [sic] from 'à la carte'.[175] The authors argue that the MIDSI would be equipped to address the problems that the current ISDS is facing while at the same time providing a solution that all States could agree on.[176]

The MIDSI would include several 'pillars' of dispute settlement which the parties could select from, including a permanent investment court[177], SSDS, and investor-State arbitration – possibly in a revised form.[178] The concept is based on a comparative institutional analysis[179] of a number of international organisations and dispute settlement mechanisms such as the United Nations Convention on the Law of the Sea (UNCLOS)[180] and the International Tribunal for the Law of the Sea (ITLOS), ICSID, the International Court of Justice (ICJ), and the Court of Justice of the European Union (CJEU).[181]

---

174 Stephan W Schill and Geraldo Vidigal, 'Designing Investment Dispute Settlement à la Carte: Insights from Comparative Institutional Analysis' (2019) 18.3 Law & Prac Int'l Cts & Tribunals 314, 321.

175 ibid, 321. This idea has also been taken up by UNCITRAL's Working Group III, see UNCITRAL, Working Group III, 'Possible reform of investor-State dispute settlement (ISDS) – Multilateral instrument on ISDS Reform' (16 January 2020), A/CN.9/WG.III/WP.194.

176 ibid, 342-343.

177 In their paper, the authors speak of a permanent investment court Multilateral Investment Court (or MIC) in the form suggested by the EU, see ibid, 319. The permanent court as one of the pillars can but does not have to be the MIC as envisaged by Bungenberg, Reinisch (see above Section B.). Therefore, in this context, the authors will use the term 'investment court'.

178 ibid, 322; see already Stephan W Schill and Geraldo Vidigal, 'Cutting the Gordian Knot: Investment Dispute Settlement à la Carte' Amsterdam Law School Legal Studies Research Paper No 2019-20 21.

179 Comparative institutional analysis is related to comparative constitutional analysis as is reflected in Sergio Puig and Gregory Shaffer, 'Imperfect Alternatives: Institutional Choice and the Reform of Investment Law' (2018) 112.3 AJIL 361. For more details see Schill, Vidigal *(n 171)*, n 7.

180 United Nations Convention on the Law of the Sea (UNCLOS) (1994) 1836 UNTS 42.

181 Schill, Vidigal *(n 171)*, 316-318.

I. Principles

Schill/Vidigal primarily argue that the MIDSI would provide parties with enormous flexibility in a number of aspects. First, the membership in the MIDSI would be separated from jurisdiction, so that the MIDSI member States would not be required to accept compulsory jurisdiction under the MIDSI over investor-State disputes.[182]

Furthermore, parties would be granted maximum flexibility in deciding which dispute settlement mechanism(s) they wish to submit to. For example, they could consent only to one specific mechanism, select a default mechanism while permitting alternative mechanisms, or even leave it completely open.[183] Moreover, MIDSI members would be free to accept only ISDS, only SSDS or consent to both.[184]

Similarly, States could require investors to pursue or even exhaust local remedies before bringing an international claim.[185] Finally, States could through agreements or declarations choose to omit monetary awards and thereby limit awards to the identification of IIA breaches and an obligation to stop the violations.[186] However, a number of open questions remain, including MIDSI's funding, location, and costs as well as its legitimacy and its reception by the investment law community.[187]

II. Roles of the Investment Court

A great degree of flexibility comes at the cost of fragmentation. According to *Schill/Vidigal*, this fragmentation can be reduced by giving the investment court more functions.[188] First of all, the investment court could be tasked with reviewing decisions of MIDSI tribunals – similar to *Bungenberg/Reinisch's* MIAM. The authors favour an appeals mechanism, pointing to the coherence in the interpretation of WTO law created by the Appel-

182 ibid, 324-326 referring to the UN Charter and the ICJ, the ICSID Convention, and the OAS.
183 ibid, 326-327, referring to the UCLOS and the WTO DSU.
184 ibid, 329.
185 ibid, 329-330.
186 ibid, 330.
187 ibid, 343-344.
188 ibid, 331; see already Schill, Vidigal *(n 175)*.

late Body.[189] Alternatively, they propose a review mechanism in the form of an annulment comparable to the ICSID Annulment Committees.[190]

Comparable to EU domestic courts, which can request a preliminary ruling from the CJEU on EU law, tribunals could also request such rulings from the investment court.[191] Requests would have to relate to norms shared by all MIDSI dispute settlement mechanisms, questions regarding transparency, evidence or principles of international investment law. Tribunals could request preliminary rulings when the arbitrators disagree on an interpretation or if they want to deviate from the interpretation of another tribunal. The preliminary ruling could either be binding for the requesting tribunal or for all future tribunals or be non-binding but authoritative. Outside a specific case, the investment court could issue binding or non-binding interpretative opinions.[192] In order to avoid abuse of this instrument, the agreement could either provide that a certain proportion of the parties must submit to the application (eg two-thirds) or stipulate that the different MIDSI pillars must have adopted divergent interpretations.[193]

Finally, the investment court could assume auxiliary tasks to ensure a proper function of the MIDSI's arbitral pillar. On the one hand, this could include prescribing, modifying, or revoking provisional measures during the period of time where the arbitral tribunal is constituted.[194] On the other hand, the investment court could constitute an independent body charged with the challenges of arbitrators based on a lack of qualification, independence or impartiality.[195]

III. *Institutional Features Beyond Dispute Settlement*

Finally, *Schill/Vidigal* propose a number of institutional features for the MIDSI to deal with other 'concerns' with the current ISDS system. For example, ADR mechanisms could be organised under the roof of the

189 Schill, Vidigal *(n 171)*, 332-333.
190 ibid, 333-334.
191 ibid.
192 ibid, 335-336.
193 ibid.
194 ibid, 335, referring to Article 290 para 5 UNCLOS empowering ITLOS with this task.
195 ibid, 337.

MIDSI[196] as well as DPMs such as legal advice, capacity-building or impact assessment but also legal aid in a specific proceeding.[197] Finally, if States wish to develop more coherent and uniform IIAs, the MIDSI could provide an inter-governmental platform to discuss and develop multilateral rules.[198]

IV. *Interim Conclusion*

Both MIC and MIDSI are quite comprehensive reform proposals. They entail the creation of international organisations and, appropriately, both submissions consist of a rather detailed institutional structure. Furthermore, it is noteworthy that both MIC and MIDSI are based on existing mechanisms in the international legal order: the WTO Dispute Settlement Body in the case of the former and various international and supranational dispute settlement mechanisms in the case of the latter. This can be considered an advantage of both proposals since the model institutions have already been tested in practice and their strengths and weaknesses can be used as a lesson for ISDS.

As this section has shown, the MIDSI is the most flexible approach to ISDS reform. This means that it includes an MIC which is comparable to *Bungenberg/Reinisch's* proposal above, even though it would only serve as one of several pillars. The voluntary nature of submitting disputes to MISDI can be regarded as one of the most important differences between the two proposals.

At the same time, this is an enormous practical advantage of the MIDSI as it could unite all different perspectives on the desirability of ISDS reform and on the design of these reforms. Each State could choose from the menu of reform options that best fits its needs. On the other hand, this also reveals MIDSI's biggest weakness. Offering States anything and everything will most probably only contribute to the already existing fragmentation of international investment law. *Schill* and *Vidigal* have proposed some additional duties for the MIC in order to minimise further fragmentation. However, it is doubtful whether tasks like reviewing decisions or a preliminary ruling are efficient remedies against fragmentation.

196 ibid, 338-339 drawing on the experience under ICSID, ICSID AF and Article 33 UN Charter.

197 ibid, 339-341 referring to the Council of Europe and the Advisory Centre for WTO Law.

198 ibid, 341-342 based on the WTO experience.

Different from the above-mentioned institutional approaches, the MIDSI would not fit into the MIC's institutional framework. To the contrary, it would be the MIC which would have to be incorporated into the MIDSI's structure. For this purpose, detailed suggestions or even a MIDSI Statute will have to be awaited.

F. Conclusion

As has been shown, the MIC represents a detailed institutional reform proposal which creates a comprehensive dispute settlement mechanism. Due to its institutional structure and openness it can unite several other proposals such as ADR, JACs and SSDS and further serve as a focal point for different DPA mechanisms. It is, however, a clear turn away from ISDS in the form of arbitration towards a permanent court system. In this regard it is clearly a different approach than the proposed MIDSI under which ad hoc arbitration would still remain possible.

This may be one of the MIDSI's biggest advantages since it makes finding a political agreement much more likely. On the other hand, it would also make a comprehensive reform addressing the whole variety of criticism towards the current system more difficult as it would prevent a unified approach. Against this background, the MIC which combines a unified approach with an open institutional structure could be more advantageous in the end.

Chapter 3: An Advisory Centre for International Investment Law

by Johanna Braun and Philipp Reinhold[*]

Selected Bibliography: Nicolas Angelet et al, 'Note on the costs and financing of an Advisory Centre on International Investment Law' (18 July 2020) International Law Institute <https://uncitral.un.org/sites/uncitral.un.org/files/aciil_note_on_costs_financing_24_august_2020_final_updated.pdf> accessed 13 January 2022; Petina Gappah, 'An Evaluation of the Role of Legal Aid in International Dispute Resolution with Emphasis on the Advisory Centre on WTO Law' in Harald Hohmann (ed), *Agreeing and Implementing the Doha Round of the WTO* (CUP 2008), 309; Lise Johnson and Brooke Guven, 'Securing Adequate Legal Defense in Proceedings Under International Investment Agreements – A Scoping Study' (Prepared for the Ministry of Foreign Affairs of the Netherlands by the Columbia Center on Sustainable Investment, 2019) <https://uncitral.un.org/sites/uncitral.un.org/files/media-documents/ uncitral/en/securingadequatedefense.pdf> accessed 13 January 2022; Anna Joubin-Bret, 'Establishing an International Advisory Centre on Investment Disputes?' (2015) E15 Task Force on Investment Policy Think Piece <https://e15initiative.org/wp-content/uploads/2015/09/E15-Investment-Joubin-Bret-Final.pdf> accessed 13 January 2022; Niall Meagher and Leah Buencamino, 'Advisory Centre on WTO Law (ACWL)' in Anne Peters (ed), *Max Plack Encyclopedia of Public International Law* (online edn, last updated April 2018) <https://opil.ouplaw.com/view/10.1093/law-mpeipro/e1195.013.1195/law-mpeipro-e1195?prd=OPIL> accessed 13 January 2022; Karl P Sauvant, 'An Advisory Centre on International Investment Law: Key Features' (2019) Academic Forum on ISDS Concept Paper 2019/14 <https://www.jus.uio.no/pluricourts/english/projects/leginvest/academic-forum/papers/papers/sauvant-advisory-center-isds-af-14-2019.pdf> accessed 13 January 2022; Alisher Umirdinov, 'The case for an advisory center on international investment law' (2016) Columbia FDI Perspectives No 175 <https://academiccommons.columbia.edu/doi/10.7916/D8445MNH> accessed 13 January 2022.

[*] Johanna Braun is a PhD candidate at the University of Cologne. Philipp Reinhold is a research associate at Saarland University.

A. Introduction

The discussions on ISDS reform do not only concern the procedure for the settlement of future investor-State disputes. They also involve the establishment of a level playing field in a dispute settlement mechanism which involves developed and developing countries as well as multinational and small and medium-sized enterprises (SMEs). In this context, the creation of an Advisory Centre is currently being discussed within UNCITRAL Working Group III.[1]

Probably the best-known Advisory Centre in the field of international economic law to date is the Advisory Centre on World Trade Law (ACWL). This chapter will therefore begin by outlining the development and basic structure of the ACWL, which could function as a model for the Advisory Centre for investment law (B.). Subsequently, an overview of the reform process within UNCITRAL Working Group III will be given (C.) as well as an evaluation of reform proposals submitted so far (D.). The chapter will then discuss whether and how these proposals would be compatible with a Multilateral Investment Court (MIC) (E.) and will, on this basis, draw a conclusion (F.).

B. The Advisory Centre on World Trade Law (ACWL)

The emergence of the ACWL as an intergovernmental organisation located in Geneva is closely linked to the development of the WTO since its founding in 1995.[2] Different from the preceding quasi-diplomatic GATT system, the WTO has been given greater autonomy and it is generally characterised

---

1 On the topics currently discussed in UNCITRAL's Working Group III see <https://uncitral.un.org/en/working_groups/3/investor-state> accessed 13 January 2022.

2 On the development of the ACWL see Petina Gappah, 'An Evaluation of the Role of Legal Aid in International Dispute Resolution with Emphasis on the Advisory Centre on WTO Law' in Harald Hohmann (ed), *Agreeing and Implementing the Doha Round of the WTO* (CUP 2008), 309-332; Niall Meagher, 'Representing Developing Countries before the WTO: The Role of the Advisory Centre on WTO Law (ACWL)' (2015) RSCAS Policy Papers 2015/02 <https://cadmus.eui.eu/bitstream/handle/1814/35747/RSCAS_PP_2015_02.pdf> accessed 13 January 2022; Niall Meagher and Leah Buencamino, 'Advisory Centre on WTO Law (ACWL)' in Anne Peters (ed), MPEPIL (online edn, last updated April 2018) <https://opil.ouplaw.com/view/10.1093/law-mpeipro/e1195.013.1195/law-mpeipro-e1195?prd=OPIL> accessed 13 January 2022.

by a stronger legal focus.[3] One of its key innovations is the creation of a two-stage dispute settlement mechanism, whose final decisions can only be rejected by consensus.[4]

The dispute settlement mechanism has become a decisive factor in the acceptance and further development of WTO law and is not without reason called the 'jewel in the crown of the WTO'.[5] At the same time, however, the strong development of subsequent jurisdiction based on a large number of agreements that became binding for all members following the establishment of the WTO has posed immense challenges for developing countries.[6]

Due to their limited economic and human resources, they could not – like the industrial countries – rely on 'in-house' legal service to participate in the dispute settlement system but had to resort to external law firms, which is not only costly but also prevented their own learning process.[7] This lack of good knowledge of WTO law is also problematic as the work of the WTO takes place in a large number of committees that deal with institutional issues, the negotiation of further legal texts or the analysis of individual members' trade policies.[8]

Overall, it became clear shortly after the creation of the WTO that the new system prevents developing countries from equal participation.[9] For participation in the dispute settlement system, this was recognised from the outset by Article 27.2 DSU, which refers to the need for special sup-

3 John H Jackson, *The World Trade Organization, Constitution and Jurisprudence* (Royal Institute of International Affairs 1998), 41-47 and 60-63.

4 ibid, 59-60 and 72. See also Articles 16.4 and 17.14 Understanding on Rules and Procedures Governing the Settlement of Disputes (DSU).

5 See eg WTO, 'WTO disputes reach 400 mark' (6 November 2009) <https://www.wto.org/english/news_e/pres09_e/pr578_e.htm> accessed 13 January 2022.

6 Gappah *(n 2)*, 311-313; Meagher *(n 2)*, 2-3; Meagher, Buencamino *(n 2)*, paras 10-14. See also Constantine Michalopoulos, 'The Developing Countries in the WTO' (1999) 22.1 The World Economy, 117; Van der Borght, 'The advisory center on the WTO law: advancing fairness and equality' (1999) 2.4 Journal of International Economic Law 723, 723; Jan Bohanes and Fernanda Garza, 'Developing countries as plaintiffs and defendants in GATT/WTO trade disputes' (2012) 4.1 Trade, Law and Development 45, 69-72.

7 Michalopoulos *(n 6)*, 136-137; Van der Borght *(n 6)*, 723; Bohanes, Garza *(n 6)*, 71; Meagher, Buencamino *(n 2)*, para 10.

8 Michalopoulos *(n 6)*, 135-136; Meagher *(n 2)*, 2; Meagher, Buencamino *(n 2)*, paras 11 and 14.

9 Meagher *(n 2)*, 3; Meagher, Buencamino *(n 2)*, para 10.

port for developing countries.[10] On this basis, the WTO Secretariat offers training courses and information and, on request, also makes available qualified legal experts from the WTO technical cooperation services to developing countries.[11] At the same time, however, the independence of the WTO Secretariat must be preserved, as it also supports the panels in their work. Overall, this excludes dispute settlement support in any form.[12]

Against this background, some WTO delegates came up with the idea of creating a support mechanism, originally as an internal office of the WTO.[13] However, since it was expected that some members would not financially support a body that would potentially assist other members in proceedings against them, and due to the limitations imposed by Article 27.2 DSU, it was decided to create the ACWL as an independent organisation outside the WTO framework.[14] At the Seattle Ministerial Conference in 1999, a number of WTO members finally decided that the ACWL should be established as an intergovernmental organisation separate from the WTO, with its own treaty and seat agreement with the Swiss government, but following wherever possible WTO rules and regulations on matters such as salaries and staff rules.[15]

On this basis, the ACWL was established in 2001 pursuant to the Agreement Establishing the Advisory Centre on WTO Law (ACWLA)[16] to provide legal advice, dispute settlement support and training activities to developing and least-developed countries.[17] Accession to the ACWL is open to all countries that are either already WTO members or have started

10 Gappah *(n 2)*, 315-316 and 317-318; Meagher *(n 2)*, 3; Meagher, Buencamino *(n 2)*, para 17.

11 Gappah *(n 2)*, 315-316; Meagher *(n 2)*, 3; Meagher, Buencamino *(n 2)*, para 17.

12 Gappah *(n 2)*, 317-318; Meagher *(n 2)*, 3; Meagher, Buencamino *(n 2)*, para 17. Article 27.2 DSU states: 'While the Secretariat assists Members in respect of dispute settlement at their request, there may also be a need to provide additional legal advice and assistance in respect of dispute settlement to developing country Members. To this end, the Secretariat shall make available a qualified legal expert from the WTO technical cooperation services to any developing country Member which so requests. This expert shall assist the developing country Member in a manner ensuring the continued impartiality of the Secretariat.'.

13 Meagher, Buencamino *(n 2)*, paras 15-16.

14 Meagher *(n 2)*, 3; Meagher, Buencamino *(n 2)*, paras 16-17.

15 Gappah *(n 2)*, 318 Meagher *(n 2)*, 3; Meagher, Buencamino *(n 2)*, paras 18-19.

16 The Agreement establishing the Advisory Centre on WTO Law (adopted 13 November 1999) 2299 UNTS 249.

17 See the Preamble, as well as Article 2 ACWLA. For the following see Gappah *(n 2)*, 318-324; Meagher *(n 2)*, 4-9; Meagher, Buencamino *(n 2)*, paras 24-67.

accession negotiations, irrespective of their level of development.[18] Least-developed countries receive automatic access to assistance by the ACWL if they are WTO members or have started an accession process.[19]

The multi-level structure of the ACWL includes a General Assembly, a Management Board and an Executive Director.[20] The General Assembly as the highest decision-making body consists of the representatives of the members of the Centre and the representatives of the least-developed countries that are entitled to the services under the ACWLA.[21] The General Assembly meets regularly to evaluate performance, to elect the Management Board, to adopt the annual budget and to adopt regulations proposed by the Management Board.[22] The Management Board takes decisions necessary to ensure the efficient and effective operation of the ACWL.[23] It consists of four members, a representative of the least-developed countries and the Executive Director; all being selected on the basis of their professional qualifications in the field of WTO law or international trade relations and development.[24] The Executive Director *inter alia* manages the Centre's day-to-day operations, is responsible for the staff of the Centre and represents the ACWL externally.[25] The actual service provided by the ACWL is currently performed by 11 lawyers.[26]

The institutional structure serves the independence and impartiality of the ACWL, as does the limitation of its activities to legal advice, ie no political or strategic advice.[27] The developed countries bear the main financial burden of the ACWL through contributions to the Endowment Fund[28], so care must be taken to ensure that the Centre serves exclusively

18 Article 16 ACWLA. The ACWL has currently 93 members (12 developed countries, 37 developing countries, 44 least-developed countries). For a list of all ACWL members, see <https://www.acwl.ch/ members-introduction/> accessed 13 January 2022.

19 See Article 7 and Annex III ACWLA.

20 Article 3 (1) ACWLA. See also <https://www.acwl.ch/organisational-structure/> accessed 13 January 2022.

21 Article 3 (1) and Annex III ACWLA.

22 Article 3 (2) ACWLA.

23 Article 3 (3) and (5) ACWLA.

24 Article 3 (3) and (4) ACWLA.

25 Article 3 (6) ACWLA.

26 ACWL, 'Report on Operations 2019' <https://www.acwl.ch/download/dd/reports_ops/Report-on-Operations-2019-website.pdf> accessed 13 January 2022.

27 Gappah *(n 2)*, 319; Meagher *(n 2)*, 4-6; Meagher, Buencamino *(n 2)*, paras 27-33.

28 Articles 5 (1), 6 (2) and Annex I ACWLA.

to improve developing countries' access to the WTO legal system.[29] At the same time, the developed countries must not be allowed to directly influence the ACWL through their financial contribution.[30] The developing countries pay a membership fee based on income and their share in world trade and a service fee for support in WTO dispute settlement proceedings.[31] The least-developed countries only pay a service fee for dispute settlement support.[32]

The ACWL offers legal advice on every aspect of WTO law, including institutional questions, and assists States in every step of a dispute settlement procedure.[33] However, such services are only provided upon request (no 'ambulance chasing').[34] In addition, the ACWL offers weekly training, ad-hoc seminars and secondment programmes whereby lawyers from member countries' governments spend nine months working at the ACWL and then return to their respective governments.

If two countries entitled to support in WTO dispute settlement proceedings are involved in the same proceeding, the ACWL operates on a first-come-first-served basis whereby priority is however given to least-developed countries.[35] In this case, the ACWL offers a roster of external legal experts to the other party that agreed to provide support on terms equivalent to those normally used by the ACWL.

The ACWL is generally regarded as crucial for improving developing countries' access to the WTO legal system.[36] Nevertheless, there are calls

---

29 Gappah *(n 2)*, 323, Meagher *(n 2)*, 4 and 6; Meagher, Buencamino *(n 2)*, paras 27-28 and 46.

30 ibid.

31 See Articles 5 (1), 6 (2) and Annex II ACWLA (membership fee); Article 5 (2) and Annex IV ACWLA (service fee). Developing countries that are not Members of the Centre have access to its legal support subject to an hourly rate between USD 250 and 350 (see Annex IV).

32 Articles 5 (2), 7 and Annex IV ACWLA.

33 See on the services offered by the ACWL Gappah *(n 2)*, 322-332; Meagher *(n 2)*, 6-9; Meagher, Buencamino *(n 2)*, paras 47-67.

34 Meagher *(n 2)*, 6; Meagher, Buencamino *(n 2)*, para 31.

35 Article 8 ACWLA. See Gappah *(n 2)*, 322-323; Meagher *(n 2)*, 8; Meagher, Buencamino *(n 2)*, para 62.

36 Gappah *(n 2)*, 326-331; Meagher *(n 2)*, 9-10; Meagher, Buencamino *(n 2)*, paras 68-71. See also Kenneth R Schunken, 'The Advisory Centre on WTO Law: A Success Story, But for Whom?' (2008) 7 The Law and Practice of International Courts and Tribunals, 59-79, 67-74; Bohanes, Garza *(n 6)*, 72-6; Gregory Shaffer, 'Assessing the Advisory Centre on WTO Law from a Broader Governance Perspective' (2011) University of Minnesota Law School Legal Studies Research Paper No 11-46 1-4.

for an even stronger role of the ACWL, for example through additional support possibilities or the creation of regional ACWLs.[37]

C. *UNCITRAL Working Group III and States' Submissions*

From the beginning of the discussions on the reform of ISDS, UNCITRAL Working Group III has referred to the possible introduction of an Advisory Centre.[38] Initially, both the UNCITRAL Secretariat and States' submissions focused on the potential of an Advisory Centre to improve cost-effectiveness of ISDS for beneficiaries.[39] However, according to later Secretariat Notes, the Advisory Centre may also address other concerns such as the correctness and consistency of decisions, and access to justice or transparency.[40]

While there is wide support for the establishment of an Advisory Centre of some sort, almost all details still have to be sorted out. This includes such fundamental questions like whether there should be one central institution or different regional Advisory Centres.[41]

Moreover, there seems to be some level of disagreement on who should benefit from the Centre's services. The Secretariat proposes that both developing countries and SMEs receive assistance,[42] which finds support

---

37 See eg Schunken *(n 36)*, 74-76; Bohanes, Garza (*n 6*), 76-9; Meagher *(n 2)*, 9.

38 See already UNCITRAL, 'Possible future work in the field of dispute settlement: Reforms of investor State dispute settlement (ISDS)' (20 April 2017), A/CN.9/917, para 56.

39 UNCITRAL, 'Report of Working Group III (Investor-State Dispute Settlement Reform) on the work of its thirty-fourth session (Vienna, 27 November-1 December 2017), Part I' (19 December 2017), A/CN.9/930/Rev. 1, paras 71-72; UNCITRAL, 'Report of Working Group III on the work of its thirty-sixth session (Vienna, 29 October–2 November 2018)', (6 November 2018), A/CN.9/964, para 119; Working Group III, 'Submission from the Government of Thailand' (8 March 2019), A/CN.9/WG.III/WP.162, para 26; 'Submission from the Government of Costa Rica' (22 March 2019), A/CN.9/WG.III/WP.164, Annex I.

40 UNCITRAL, 'Report of Working Group III (Investor-State Dispute Settlement Reform) on the work of its thirty-eighth session (Vienna, 14–18 October 2019)' (23 October 2019), A/CN.9/1004*, para 28.

41 UNCITRAL, Report WG III, Session 38, A/CN.9/1004* (2019) *(n 40)*, para 36. Korea suggested a network of regional Advisory Centres that would be more effective than a central institution, 'Submission from the Republic of Korea', (31 July 2019), A/CN.9/WG.III/WP.179, 5.

42 UNCITRAL, Working Group III, 'Possible reform of investor-State dispute settlement (ISDS)' (5 September 2018), A/CN.9/WG.III/WP.149, para 62; UNCITRAL,

among some States,[43] while other States[44] prefer limiting the services only to developing countries.

The Secretariat has suggested a wide array of services that the Advisory Centre could potentially offer, including capacity-building[45] and legal assistance before and during ISDS proceedings[46]. This takes into account the requests of various States whose submissions have exclusively focused on legal assistance and capacity-building.[47] However, the Secretariat also names various other possible services such as the provision of financial aid[48] or of a platform to share best practices,[49] offering guidance in treaty interpretation[50] or services in the area of alternative dispute resolution.[51] Moreover, it could monitor compliance with a code of conduct for ISDS decision makers and could provide a database on challenges and sanctioned arbitrators.[52]

Naturally, both the choice of services and the scope of the beneficiaries will impact the costs of establishing and running an Advisory Cen-

---

Working Group III, 'Cost and Duration - Note by the Secretariat' (31 August 2018), A/CN.9/WG.III/WP.153, para 101.

43 UNCITRAL, Working Group III, 'Submission from the Government of Turkey' (11 July 2019), A/CN.9/WG.III/WP.174, 3; 'Submission from the Government of the Russian Federation' (30 December 2019), A/CN.9/WG.III/WP.188, 4 speaking of 'interested parties, including developing countries'.

44 UNCITRAL WG III, Submission Thailand, WP 162 (2019) *(n 39)*, para 26; UNCITRAL WG III, Submission Korea, WP 179 (2019) *(n 41)*, 5.

45 UNCITRAL, Working Group III, 'Possible reform of investor-State dispute settlement (ISDS) Advisory Centre' (25 July 2019), A/CN.9/WG.III/WP.168, paras 23-24; 'Possible reform of investor-State dispute settlement (ISDS), Dispute prevention and mitigation - Means of alternative dispute resolution, Note by the Secretariat' (15 January 2020), A/CN.9/WG.III/WP.190, paras 27-28 and 47.

46 UNCITRAL WG III, Advisory Centre, WP 168 (2019) *(n 45)*, paras 8-18.

47 UNCITRAL WG III, Submission Thailand, WP 162 (2019) *(n 39)*, para 26; Submission Turkey, WP 174 (2019) *(n 43)*, 3; Submission Korea, WP 179 (2019) *(n 41)*, 5; Submission Russian Federation, WP 188 (2019) *(n 43)*, 4.

48 UNCITRAL, Working Group III, 'Possible reform of investor-State dispute settlement (ISDS) Third-party funding – Possible solutions' (2 August 2019), A/CN.9/WG.III/WP.172, paras 17-18.

49 UNCITRAL, Report WG III, Session 38, A/CN.9/1004* (2019) *(n 40)*, para 35.

50 UNCITRAL, Working Group III, 'Possible Reform of Investor-State Dispute Settlement (ISDS) – Interpretation of Investment Treaties by Treaty Parties' (17 January 2020), A/CN.9/WG.III/WP.191, paras 49-52.

51 UNCITRAL WG III, Dispute prevention and mitigation, WP 190 (2020) *(n 45)*, paras 27-28 and 47; UNCITRAL WG III, Advisory Centre, WP 168 (2019) *(n 45)*, paras 21-22.

52 UNCITRAL, Report WG III, Session 38, A/CN.9/1004* (2019) *(n 40)*, para 64.

tre.[53] The Secretariat therefore stressed that the scope of services needs to be narrowed and duplication of services already provided by other institutions should be avoided.[54] If regional centres were established, the existing UNCITRAL Regional Centre for Asia and the Pacific could possibly assume an Asian and Pacific Advisory Centre's responsibilities.[55] The Secretariat pointed out that the Centre could either be financed through member States' contributions or through fees that would be paid by the Centre's users or by users of a bigger structure like an MIC.[56] However, no preference for one mechanism over another was voiced.

Based on the State submissions and its own previous notes, the Secretariat recently prepared a draft note for further discussions which includes provisions governing the Advisory Centre and its operations, services that would be available to key beneficiary States and financing options.[57] According to the draft note, the Advisory Centre would consist of two pillars: an 'Assistance Mechanism' and a 'Forum'.[58] Whereas the Assistant Mechanism would provide the services foreseen in the statute, the Forum would allow for beneficiaries to discuss, share information, engage in training and potentially develop guidelines of best-practices. Overall, the draft note contains provisions on the general scope of the Advisory Centre[59], the services offered[60], the beneficiaries[61], the membership[62] and the location of the Centre[63].

In line with its comprehensive approach, the Secretariat prepared draft provisions covering all stages of conflict resolution.[64] In addition, the pro-

53 UNCITRAL WG III, Advisory Centre, WP 168 (2019) *(n 45)*, paras 7, 26, 63, 65.

54 UNCITRAL, Report WG III, Session 38, A/CN.9/1004* (2019) *(n 40)*, paras 32, 34.

55 UNCITRAL WG III, Submission Korea, WP 179 (2019) *(n 41)*, 5.

56 UNCITRAL, Report WG III, Session 38, A/CN.9/1004* (2019) *(n 40)*, para 38.

57 UNCITRAL, Working Group III, 'Possible reform of investor-State dispute settlement (ISDS) Advisory Centre', Initial draft on the establishment of an advisory centre by the Secretariat <https://uncitral.un.org/sites/uncitral.un.org/files/media-documents/uncitral/en/draft_wp_advisory_centre_for_comment.docx> accessed 13 January 2022.

58 ibid, paras 7-8.

59 UNCITRAL, Working Group III *(n 57)*, Draft provision 1.

60 UNCITRAL, Working Group III *(n 57)*, Draft provision 2 and 3.

61 UNCITRAL, Working Group III *(n 57)*, Draft provision 4.

62 UNCITRAL, Working Group III *(n 57)*, Draft provision 5.

63 UNCITRAL, Working Group III *(n 57)*, Draft provision 6.

64 UNCITRAL, Working Group III *(n 57)*, Draft provision 2 (a), 2 (b) and 2 (c). They are described as 'pre-dispute and dispute avoidance', 'mediation and other alternative dispute resolution (ADR) services' and 'representation and assistance

vision of legal and policy advisory services is foreseen, as well as different services related to capacity building and sharing of best practices.[65] Furthermore, the Secretariat prepared a general clause which would allow the Centre to perform any service assigned to it.[66] At the same time, however, the draft note points to existing support mechanisms.[67] With regard to the beneficiaries, the draft note reflects the discussions about access for SMEs and includes possible options for a limitation to specific services.[68] The draft note is open for comments until 15 June 2021.

Overall, it becomes clear that even though there is wide support for the establishment of an Advisory Centre on International Investment Law, a plethora of questions regarding its exact structure, beneficiaries, services, and financing remains open. Even though the Secretariat has created draft provisions, substantial decisions on the shape of an Advisory Centre are lacking so far.

D. *Evaluation of Current Reform Proposals*

The approval of an Advisory Centre extends not only to Working Group III and States but also to international investment law scholars, some of whom have already made suggestions as to its concrete form. The purpose of this section is to consolidate and evaluate the proposals for such a Centre regarding its possible structure (I.), beneficiaries (II.), services (III.), and financing (IV.).

I. *Structure*

The first significant decision the Working Group III has to make is on the structure of a prospective Advisory Centre. A great number of contributions take the ACWL as a model in this regard.[69] This would lead to

services in ISDS'. See on the different stages of conflict resolution Braun/Reinhold, Chapter 2.

65 UNCITRAL, Working Group III *(n 57)*, Draft provision 2 (d) and 2 (e).

66 UNCITRAL, Working Group III *(n 57)*, Draft provision 3.

67 ibid, paras 43-47.

68 ibid, paras 48-59 and Annex 2.

69 Stephan W Schill and Geraldo Vidigal, 'Designing Investment Dispute Settlement à la Carte: Insights from Comparative Institutional Design Analysis' (2019) 18.3 The Law and Practice of International Courts and Tribunals 314, 340; Karl P

the establishment of a new institution, that could either be independent[70] or affiliated with an existing[71] or a new organisation (a Multilateral Investment Court[72] or an Appellate Body or a Multilateral Institution for Dispute Settlement on Investment[73]). On the other hand, there are already a number of support mechanisms. This becomes particularly clear in the comprehensive study conducted by *Johnson/Guven* in which a wide range of existing services is presented.[74] In addition, the authors describe past attempts to establish an Advisory Centre that have failed, in part due to institutional reasons such as the nationality of staff or the location of the centre.[75] This may speak against the establishment of a central body.

However, international investment law lacks a multilateral forum comparable to the WTO.[76] The existing system is very decentralised and therefore difficult to access especially for less developed countries and SMEs without any or substantive experience in ISDS. This is even more relevant for countries that face only a few cases and therefore the high opportunity

---

Sauvant, 'An Advisory Centre on International Investment Law: Key Features' (2019) Academic Forum on ISDS Concept Paper 2019/14, 5 <https://papers.ssrn.com/sol3/papers.cfm?abstract_id=3450919> accessed 13 January 2022; Jeremy Sharpe, 'An International Investment Advisory Center: Beyond the WTO Model' (EJIL: Talk!, 26 July 2019) <https://www.ejiltalk.org/an-international-investment-advisory-center-beyond-the-wto-model/> accessed 13 January 2022; Rob Howse, 'Designing a Multilateral Investment Court: Issues and Options' (2017) 36 Yearbook of European Law 209, 232; Hamed El-Kady and Mustaqeem De Gama, 'The Reform of the International Investment Regime: An African Perspective' (2019) 34.2 ICSID Review Special Focus Issue 1, 11; Marc Bungenberg and August Reinisch, *From Bilateral Arbitral Tribunals and Investment Courts to a Multilateral Investment Court* (2nd edn, Springer Open 2019).

70 Sharpe *(n 69)*; Sauvant *(n 69)*; Anna Joubin-Bret, 'Establishing an International Advisory Centre on Investment Disputes?' (2015) E15 Task Force on Investment Policy Think Piece 11, 12. This piece was published prior to Joubin-Bret's 2017 appointment as UNCITRAL Secretary.

71 Alisher Umirdinov, 'The case for an advisory center on international investment law' (June 2016) Columbia FDI Perspectives No 175, 2 <http://ccsi.columbia.edu/files/2013/10/No-175-Alisher-FINAL.pdf> accessed 13 January 2022.

72 Bungenberg, Reinisch *(n 69)*, para 188; Howse *(n 69)*, 232.

73 Schill, Vidigal *(n 69)*, 314, 339-340.

74 Lise Johnson and Brooke Guven, 'Securing Adequate Legal Defense in Proceedings Under International Investment Agreements – A Scoping Study' (Prepared for the Ministry of Foreign Affairs of the Netherlands by the Columbia Center on Sustainable Investment, 2019), <https://uncitral.un.org/ sites/uncitral.un.org/files/media-documents/uncitral/en/securingadequatedefense.pdf> accessed 13 January 2022, Sections 2 and 4.

75 ibid, Section 3.

76 Sharpe *(n 69)*; Umirdinov *(n 71)*, 1.

costs for capacity-building is not seen as being justified. Relying on regional centres would only add to the decentralisation and may incur logistical problems as well as additional costs.[77]

Against this background, it is crucial to establish a central body all beneficiaries can access for all relevant services. This is without prejudice to the exact range of services provided by the centre. Even if no specific ISDS related service was offered by the Advisory Centre itself, a central body could refer incoming requests to regional centres or specialised organisations or to a private consultant. It would function as a contact point, which answers the questions of what services are available to whom and where they could be handled. This may include, for example, setting up a platform to bring together the need for support and service offerings.[78]

For the functioning of a central contact point, the establishment of an independent body would be useful but not mandatory. Should the Centre be established as an independent institution, however, the question of its location will arise. If the tasks of the Centre are limited to the coordination of support within a network of different assistant mechanisms (including regional centres), a specific geographical location is not decisive. It would then not be necessary to locate the Centre in an 'ISDS hub' like Washington or Paris. This could be different if a wide range of services like legal representation is offered. However, it should be pointed out in principle that a large part of the necessary communication is nowadays possible via e-mail, telephone and video conferencing.

The governance structure could be drawn from ACWL which would include a general assembly, a management board, and an executive director. However, the structure also depends on the number of services provided. A special feature could be a forum of representatives of all assistant mechanisms that form part of the network. Such a forum could be useful to coordinate support, share experiences and identify areas in which more support is needed. This has to be contrasted with the approach taken by the Secretariat which provides for a 'Forum' for beneficiaries.[79]

Finally, it should be pointed out that the creation of a central body that does not provide all services itself but is integrated into a network of many different assistant mechanisms could mitigate conflicts over the nationality

77 Robert W Schwieder, 'Legal Aid and Investment Treaty Disputes: Lessons Learned from the Advisory Centre on WTO Law and Investment Experiences' (2018) 19.4 Journal of World Investment & Trade 628, 660-661.

78 See also below Section D.III.

79 See UNCITRAL, Working Group III *(n 57)*, paras 7-8.

of the staff and the location. It could thus also prove to be consensual from a political point of view.

II. Beneficiaries

With regard to the question of beneficiaries, there seems to be one controversial question, which relates to the provision of access to a support mechanism for SMEs. Despite a number of experts who argue for opening the assistant mechanisms for SMEs as well[80], there seem to be widespread concerns raised by public parties and scholars.[81] One explanation might be the fact that until now it remains unclear what services will be provided by a future Advisory Centre and how the centre will be financed.

In comparison to multinational corporations that are frequent users of ISDS, SMEs generally face a lack of resources putting them at a disadvantage. Thus, by taking the basic idea of a level playing field in ISDS as the basis for the provision of assistance, the exclusion of SMEs does not seem warranted.[82] However, two general questions need to be addressed beforehand:

First of all, there needs to be a common understanding of what should be considered as an SME in the context of the Advisory Centre.[83] One option could eg be a turnover threshold affecting access or the amount of fees. A different option would be to limit access to SMEs 'headquartered in the developing world'.[84]

A second question would be how to set up an Advisory Centre in a way that guarantees its impartiality and independence while offering services to States and SMEs. This could be achieved eg by limited access only to specific services for SMEs or by dividing the workforce in such a way that

80 See eg Bungenberg, Reinisch *(n 69)*, para 190; Howse *(n 69)*, 232; Schwieder *(n 77)*, 656-657.

81 See eg Eric Gottwald, 'Leveling the Playing Field: Is it Time for a Legal Assistance Center for Developing Nations in Investment Treaty Arbitration?' (2007) 22.2 American University International Law Review 237, 270; Joubin-Bret *(n 70)*; Johnson, Guven *(n 74)*, 105-106.

82 Bungenberg, Reinisch *(n 69)*, para 190.

83 On the definition of an SME in the context of the establishment of an Advisory Centre see Johnson, Guven *(n 74)*, Section 6.1.

84 Schwieder *(n 77)*, 656-657.

States and SMEs are served by separate staff.[85] In principle, the allocation of staff seems advisable against the background of the hypothetical case that a State and an SME may both use the Advisory Centre in the same case.

Apart from this, the question whether SMEs should be included in the provision of support is a principal one which needs to be separated from the question of the specific services provided. There can be no question as to the fact that not every service possibly offered would equally be accessible for SMEs, such as the prevention of investment disputes. At the very least, an institution acting as central contact point could provide SMEs with information on support offered by other assistant mechanisms and consultants. This approach somewhat reflects the approach taken by the Secretariat in its draft notes.[86]

The question of general access to an Advisory Centre should further be separated from the question of financing the support. Countries may have an interest in supporting national SMEs as they do by providing export credits for trade. SMEs themselves could also have an interest in participating in a network and pay a membership or a service fee. Equal treatment with regard to the amount of contributions to be paid is not required. By this, SMEs could help to finance the overall system.

As a result, access for developing countries and SMEs to an Advisory Centre can be considered useful. Although developing countries are in particular need of support, it is not clear why the imbalance on the investor side between multinational corporations and SMEs should be maintained. Especially SMEs from developing countries could benefit from the creation of a level playing field for investors. After all, industrialised countries already have possibilities to support their companies abroad. Nevertheless, the concerns expressed by individual countries about the access of SMEs to an Advisory Centre should be taken seriously. A compromise could be found by not granting access on equal terms and by providing for necessary separations.

85 On the possibility to limit access on certain services see Johnson, Guven *(n 74)*, Section 6.3.2. On the internal separation of services see Bungenberg, Reinisch *(n 69)*, para 190.

86 See UNCITRAL, Working Group III *(n 57)*, paras 48-59 and Annex 2.

III. Services

A number of bodies already provide all kinds of assistance in international investment law and policy.[87] Since it cannot be in the interest of an Advisory Centre to duplicate the work of other institutions or to compete with existing excellent offers, it should, first of all, identify the services that are already provided by others.[88] If the Centre offers services like building capacities and gathering resources such as arbitral awards, treaties, and commentary it should be limited to areas which are not already covered by other institutions or States. As regards services that are already on the market, it should focus on compiling information on the existing programs and, if necessary, bringing together suppliers of such services and their beneficiaries.[89]

Nevertheless, there is still a strong demand for services like training in international investment law and policy,[90] assistance in drafting investment agreements and contracts,[91] and secondments or internships with arbitral institutions[92]. Here, the Advisory Centre could fill the gaps that are left by the existing services.[93] Training on international investment instruments, law, and policies may be especially efficient since it could help States to avoid ISDS proceedings in the future. It is also one of the more cost-efficient services because once the training programs are set up, they can be used again.[94] However, States must keep in mind that advising developing States on their investment policy may be a (perceived or actual) challenge to the body's independence.[95]

In addition, the Advisory Centre could serve as a forum for States to exchange information and experiences on investment law and arbitra-

---

87 See eg Johnson, Guven *(n 74)*, Section 2.2; Sharpe *(n 69)*; UNCITRAL, Report WG III, Session 38, A/CN.9/1004* (2019) *(n 40)*, para 34.

88 UNCITRAL, Report WG III, Session 38, A/CN.9/1004* (2019) *(n 40)*, para 42.

89 Cf Johnson, Guven *(n 74)*, 83; Gottwald *(n 81)*, 270; UNCITRAL WG III, Submission Korea, WP 179 (2019) *(n 41)*, 5; see also above Section D.I.

90 Schill, Vidigal *(n 69)*, 339; Bungenberg, Reinisch *(n 69)*, para 191; Gottwald *(n 81)*, 270; Joubin-Bret *(n 70)*, 11; El-Kady, De Gama *(n 69)*, 11; Sharpe *(n 69)*; UNCITRAL WG III, Submission Korea, WP 179 (2019) *(n 41)*, 5.

91 Joubin-Bret *(n 70)*, 11.

92 UNCITRAL, Report WG III, Session 38, A/CN.9/1004* (2019) *(n 40)*, para 33; Gottwald *(n 81)*, 271.

93 UNCITRAL, Report WG III, Session 38, A/CN.9/1004* (2019) *(n 40)*, para 34.

94 See also Johnson, Guven *(n 74)*, 88.

95 Schwieder *(n 77)*, 658-659.

tion.[96] Due to the decentralised nature of the international investment law regime, there is no multilateral forum dealing with international investment law and policies in an as comprehensive manner as the WTO does with regard to international trade law.[97] States would, therefore, benefit greatly from a setting for discussions, exchanges, and networking.[98]

However, these programs benefit above all (developing) States. While it cannot be ruled out that there may be some training programs that would be interesting for SMEs, it is rare that a company, and especially an SME, is party to more than one investor-State dispute. Thus, SMEs generally do not need training on investment law. Similarly, they would probably not be interested in exchanging experiences in a global forum. The Centre should, therefore, be mindful that offering these kinds of services could create an impression of favouring developing countries at the expense of SMEs.

With regard to legal support in the conduct of a case, an Advisory Centre could represent the beneficiaries in the arbitration. This would include tasks like managing the appointment of arbitrators, drafting and filing memorials, producing of documents, the representation in hearings, and dealing with experts.[99] Qualitative legal representation is very effective in creating a level playing field both between claimant and respondent. On the other hand, it is very costly and time-consuming.[100] Considering the limited resources of an Advisory Centre, this could mean that only a few companies or States might benefit from the Centre's services. In addition, it could also prevent developing States from acquiring their own expertise or creating an internal organisation to deal with investment-related issues.[101]

In order to prevent a too limited access, the Advisory Centre should charge a fee for its services. This fee could be adapted to the economic capacities of the parties and, in the case of LDCs, be lifted entirely.[102] In addition, the fee could be lifted for small enterprises whose turnovers fall

96 UNCITRAL, Report WG III, Session 38, A/CN.9/1004* (2019) *(n 40)*, para 35; Sharpe *(n 69)*; Gottwald *(n 81)*, 270; Joubin-Bret *(n 70)*, 11; Sauvant *(n 69)*, 10.

97 See above Section D.I.

98 This mirrors the approach taken by the Secretariat in its draft notes, see UNCITRAL, Report WG III, Session 38, A/CN.9/1004* *(n 40)*.

99 Gottwald *(n 81)*, 272; Sharpe *(n 69)*; Sauvant *(n 69)*, 9.

100 The defence of an average ISDS case costs USD 5 million, see Johnson, Guven *(n 74)*, 88.

101 See Schwieder *(n 77)*, 645-650 for this criticism of the ACWL.

102 UNCITRAL, Report WG III, Session 38, A/CN.9/1004* (2019) *(n 40)*, paras 32-33.

below a certain threshold. Second, it may be advisable not to offer full legal representation but rather focus on a significant number of individual measures. In addition to the representation tasks described above,[103] these measures could include advice on compiling a team of inhouse and/or external personnel,[104] drafting opinions on specific legal questions,[105] or assessing risks of adopting a certain measure[106] or of entering into a specific dispute[107]. If legal advice is given to both claimants and respondents, the Centre should create mechanisms to ensure confidentiality and impartiality.[108]

Legal support could also be extended to assisting claimants and respondents in alternative dispute resolution like settlements, mediation, or conciliation.[109] In addition, the Centre might keep a list of qualified mediators and conciliators for interested parties.[110] This can help to settle conflicts amicably without the need to recourse to expensive ISDS proceedings.

Finally, some authors suggest providing legal aid, for example in the form of a trust fund[111] or as relief from bearing the litigation costs of the winning party[112]. Other possible financial aid mechanisms are third-party funding and contingent fee representation.[113] While financial help for parties may be an efficient way to create a level playing field and to avoid the problems associated with private third-party funding,[114] it should not be provided under the umbrella of an Advisory Centre which offers capacity building and legal support. Combing these services may lead to conflicts

---

103 Managing the appointment of arbitrators, drafting and filing memorials, producing of documents, representation in hearings, and dealing with experts.

104 Joubin-Bret *(n 70)*, 9.

105 Gottwald *(n 81)*, 272.

106 Schill, Vidigal *(n 69)*, 339-340.

107 Gottwald *(n 81)*, 272; Joubin-Bret *(n 70)*, 9; Sauvant *(n 69)*, 9.

108 Bungenberg, Reinisch *(n 69)*, para 190; see also above Section D.II.

109 Joubin-Bret *(n 70)*, 9; see also Bungenberg, Reinisch *(n 69)*, para 189; UNCITRAL WG III, Dispute prevention and mitigation, WP 190 (2020) *(n 45)*, paras 27-28; UNCITRAL, Working Group III, 'Submission from the Government of Morocco' (4 March 2019), A/CN.9/WG.III/WP.161, 3.

110 Joubin-Bret *(n 70)*, 12.

111 El-Kady, De Gama *(n 69)*, 11; Sharpe *(n 69)*; see also Schill, Vidigal *(n 69)*, 340-341.

112 Howse *(n 69)*, 232.

113 See Johnson, Guven *(n 74)*, Sections 4.3.2 and 4.3.3.

114 UNCITRAL WG III, Third-party funding – Possible solutions, WP 172 (2019) *(n 48)*, para 17.

of interests which should not be underestimated. A legal aid mechanism should therefore rather be set up as a stand-alone body.[115]

IV. Financing

An Advisory Centre must ensure reliable and sustainable funding.[116] In general, it is expected that due to the complexity of ISDS cases, an Advisory Centre for international investment law needs more funding than other assistance mechanisms.[117] Naturally, the exact amount of financing needed depends on a number of preliminary questions, including the Centre's structure, beneficiaries, and range of services.[118] A body affiliated with an international organisation could be financed, at least partially, through its budget[119] while an independent organisation would need not only funding to be set up initially but also in the long run. Regional offices would increase the costs.[120] Finally, the number of personnel and their qualification influence the Centre's financial needs.[121]

As regards the scope of services, full representation is more costly than the provision of individual support measures. As opposed to the provision of training and resources, legal representation will most probably not generate economies of scale.[122] The Centre could start by offering a limited number of services while closely monitoring their success and utility. If the services are well received, the Centre could either gradually expand their scope or fill possible gaps.

---

115 This alternative is also included in UNCITRAL WG III, Third-party funding – Possible solutions, WP 172 (2019) *(n 48)*, para 18.

116 See specifically on estimated costs of establishing and operating an Advisory Centre, as well as possible sources of finance for the Centre's operation Nicolas Angelet et al, 'Note on the costs and financing of an Advisory Centre on International Investment Law' (International Law Institute, 18 July 2020) <https://uncitral.un.org/sites/uncitral.un.org/files/aciil_note_on_costs_financing_24_august_2020 _final_updated.pdf> accessed 13 January 2022.

117 Johnson, Guven *(n 74)*, 89-90. For example, the authors note that compared with WTO proceedings, ISDS cases could require 40-50 times more hours worked.

118 UNCITRAL WG III, Advisory Centre, WP 168 (2019) *(n 45)*, paras 7, 26, 63, 65; Angelet et al *(n 116)*, paras 4-45.

119 Bungenberg, Reinisch *(n 69)*, para 192.

120 Schwieder *(n 77)*, 660-661.

121 Johnson, Guven *(n 74)*, 99.

122 Johnson, Guven *(n 74)*, 88.

The more parties contribute, the more secure the funding is. If the Centre was to be established as an independent international organisation, it should not only be its beneficiaries who contribute but all member States. If necessary, third-party donors could provide additional financial support.[123] On the other hand, the more parties are involved, the more tensions may possibly arise, both between and among beneficiaries and other contributors (whether member States or third-party donors).[124] It is important to keep an equilibrium so that the Centre is not dependent on individual donors or contributors.[125] Member States should therefore not reject donations altogether but should provide clear regulations for potential donors.

In the initial phase, the Centre would have to rely on member States' contributions and third-party donations.[126] Once it is working, however, the Centre should charge fees for its services[127] which may either be capped or adjusted to the respective beneficiary's means[128] and subsidised by member States' contributions.[129] This ensures that it can offer quality services to all beneficiaries. Relying entirely on member States' contributions may jeopardise reliable funding while relying on donations from developed States or private donors can create dependencies and conflicts of interests. Adding fees can finally prevent beneficiaries from frivolously using the Centre's services.[130]

E. Compatibility of an Advisory Centre with a Multilateral Investment Court

The following section aims to clarify whether and how these options would be compatible with an MIC. In principle, the creation of an MIC does not conflict with any of the above-mentioned options for an Advisory Centre, which can be created either as an integral part of the MIC or as an independent intergovernmental organisation.

---

123 Umirdinov *(n 71)*, 2; Sauvant *(n 69)*, 10; Angelet et al *(n 116)*, para 87.
124 Johnson, Guven *(n 74)*, Sections 5.2.3.
125 Schwieder *(n 77)*, 659-660; Angelet et al *(n 116)*, paras 12 and 61.
126 Gottwald *(n 81)*, 274; Joubin-Bret *(n 70)*, 13.
127 Joubin-Bret *(n 70)*, 13; Sauvant *(n 69)*, 11. See also Angelet et al *(n 116)*, paras 63-77 and 83-84.
128 UNCITRAL, Report WG III, Session 38, A/CN.9/1004* (2019) *(n 40)*, para 47.
129 Gottwald *(n 81)*, 274.
130 Johnson, Guven *(n 74)*, 94; Angelet et al *(n 116)*, para 84.

If the Centre forms part of the institutional structure of the MIC, questions arise about the interaction with other bodies of the MIC such as the Plenary Body or the Secretariat. This concerns, for example, the staffing of the Centre, which can be decided either by the member States, the MIC Secretariat or by a sub-committee. The member States could elect the staff of the Centre, whereby the procedure and composition would have to be clarified or delegate the selection process. An open application procedure managed by the Secretariat could thereby depoliticise the selection of personnel.

In terms of financing, costs could be covered by the MIC budget, but also by independent contributions or mixed financing. This could depend on the type of support provided by the Centre. In principle, the Centre does not have to be exclusively focused on the legal system of the MIC. It could offer comprehensive support instead, including for example dispute avoidance. However, it is unlikely that members will be willing to provide financial support if there is no alignment with the procedures of the MIC. The same may apply to support for SMEs. Should the Advisory Centre therefore offer a wide range of services and/or address both developing countries and SMEs, independent or additional funding might be necessary. A further limitation could result from the fact that the establishment of the MIC already represents a financial burden.[131]

As with the creation of the ACWL, the unwillingness of individual members of the MIC to support developing countries and/or SMEs could be a strong argument for the creation of the Centre as an independent organisation. The ACWL is a good example of how the Centre's services can still be directed towards the MIC. If the Centre were to focus solely on MIC proceedings, however, funding from the developed members of the MIC would be required. The ACWL depends heavily on financial contributions by the developing countries.[132] Even if the new Centre receives additional contributions from SMEs, it is not clear whether or at what level these could replace the contribution from developed countries. In any case, however, the independence of the Advisory Centre must be safeguarded. This means that the financial support must not be accompanied by any possibility of influence. Similar to the ACWL, the financial support of developed countries can also mean that the range of services must be limited to purely legal advice.

131 See Braun/Reinhold, Chapter 2.

132 Meagher *(n 2)*, 5-6; Meagher, Buencamino *(n 2)*, paras 43-46.

Irrespective of whether an Advisory Centre is created as an integral part of the MIC or independently of it, it must in any event be assumed that its creation can be justified by the establishment of the MIC, which would create a certain 'momentum'. The ACWL as a 'spin off' of the WTO[133] represents a good example. The creation of a new institution on investment law leading to a new form of dispute settlement is similar to the creation of the WTO dispute settlement mechanism. Active participation in the MIC, as well as equal access to its judicial procedures, justifies additional support for developing countries. While it can be argued that developing countries are already at a disadvantage by the current ISDS system due to lack of economic and human resources, a multilateral framework creates a common interest in its functioning among all members. This does not apply to ad hoc arbitration and is not apparent with regard to ICSID in a way comparable to the WTO.

Overall, it can therefore be concluded that while the creation of an MIC does not impose any fundamental restrictions on the establishment of an Advisory Centre, it does have a particular impact on its concrete structure. Furthermore, the creation of an MIC as a multilateral framework for investment dispute settlement implies a particular need for the simultaneous creation of an Advisory Centre.

F. Conclusion

There seems to be a general agreement among the participants in UNCITRAL Working Group III on the need for a support mechanism in international investment law. Apart from this, however, a large number of individual questions appear to be open so far. An overly ambitious approach carries the risk of failure, be it in reaching an agreement on structure, access or in financing. At the same time, the creation of an Advisory Centre offers a historic opportunity to create equal access to investment protection.

The ACWL already provides an established model for assistance in international economic law, but it is unclear whether and to what extent it is transferable. Moreover, it may be doubted whether the momentum of current reform efforts in international investment law is comparable to the creation of world trade law and the emergence of the WTO. The latter

---

133 See Meagher *(n 2)*, 4; Meagher, Buencamino *(n 2)*, para 24.

could be assessed differently, depending on whether an MIC is created, and investor-State dispute settlement is profoundly reformed as a result.

In any case, the creation of an Advisory Centre must take into account the specificities of international investment law. It should build on existing structures and, at best, actively involve them. The exact need for support and the associated costs are difficult to estimate. Therefore, a flexible adaptation of the structures as well as the services offered might be desirable.

In the end, it is crucial that the States can agree on a concept at all. Whether this actually succeeds remains to be seen.

Chapter 4: Appeal Mechanism and the Issue of Consistency in International Investment Arbitration

by Niclas Landmann[*]

Selected Bibliography: Charris Benedetti and Pablo Juan, 'The proposed Investment Court System: does it really solve the problems?' (2019) 42 Revista Derecho del Estado 83; Marc Bungenberg and Stefan Reinisch, *From Bilateral Arbitral Tribunals and Investment Courts to a Multilateral Investment Court – Options Regarding the Institutionalization of Investor-State Dispute Settlement* (2nd edn, Springer 2019); Nicolette Butler, 'In Search of a Model for the Reform of International Investment Dispute Resolution: An Analysis of Existing International and Regional Dispute Settlement Mechanisms' in Jean E Kalicki and Anna Joubin-Bret (eds), *Reshaping the Investor-State Dispute Settlement System: Journeys for the 21st Century* (Brill/Nijhoff 2015); Anna De Luca et al, 'Responding to Incorrect Decision-Making in Investor-State Dispute Settlement: Policy Options' (2020) 21 Journal of World Investment & Trade 374, Robert Howse, 'Designing a Multilateral Investment Court: Issues and Options' (2017) 36.1 Yearbook of European Law 209; Gabrielle Kaufmann-Kohler and Michele Potestà, 'Can the Mauritius Convention serve as a model for the reform of a permanent investment tribunal or an appeal mechanism? Analysis and roadmap' CIDS 2016; Malcolm Langford, Daniel Behn, and Maria Chiara Malaguti, 'The Quadrilemma: Appointing Adjudicators in Future Investor-State Dispute Settlement' Academic Forum on ISDS' (13 October 2019) Concept Paper 2019/12; Jaemin Lee, 'Introduction of an Appellate Review Mechanism for International Investment Disputes: Expected Benefits and Remaining Tasks' in Jean E Kalicki and Anna Joubin-Bret (eds), *Reshaping the Investor-State Dispute Settlement System: Journeys for the 21st Century* (Brill/Nijhoff 2015); Stephan Schill, 'Sources of International Investment Law: Multilateralization, Arbitral Precedent, Comparativism, Soft Law' in

---

* Niclas Landman is a doctoral candidate at Cologne University. He studied German law at Frankfurt University, Germany and Investment Treaty Arbitration at Uppsala University, Sweden. Currently, he works as a legal clerk at the Regional Court of Hanau and as a research assistant in the dispute resolution team of a corporate law firm in Frankfurt.

Jean d'Aspremont and Samantha Bessoneds (eds), *The Oxford Handbook on the Sources of International Law* (OUP 2017), 1104.

A. Introduction

The debate about the legitimacy of ISDS is partly rooted in inconsistent arbitral decision-making which has created legal uncertainty for States and investors alike.[1] Within the current system of ad hoc arbitration, every tribunal is established for the settlement of one specific dispute without being bound by previous case law or precedent.[2] Thus, ad hoc tribunals make their decision based on all particularities of the given case and dissolved upon rendering the award.[3] Even though tribunals tend to contribute to the development of international investment law by building on each other's decisions, inconsistencies in jurisprudence under these circumstances are almost impossible to avoid.[4] Considering arbitral tribunals' short-lived nature, this outcome may not be a surprise.

Hence, the discussions on ISDS reform have emphasised that a multilateral appeal mechanism would be an important step towards achieving the objective of consistent case law and legal certainty for States and investors. In 2013, the United Nations Conference on Trade and Development (UNCTAD) identified the creation of a standing international Multilateral Investment Court (MIC) as well as the introduction of a self-contained and standalone appeals facility (Appellate Body) as two of five broad paths for

1 Charris Benedetti and Pablo Juan, 'The proposed Investment Court System: does it really solve the problems?' (2019) 42 Revista Derecho del Estado 83, 90, 91.

2 Stephan Schill, 'Sources of International Investment Law: Multilateralization, Arbitral Precedent, Comparativism, Soft Law' in Jean d'Aspremont and Samantha Besson (eds), *The Oxford Handbook on the Sources of International Law* (OUP 2017), 1104; Anna De Luca et al, 'Responding to Incorrect Decision-Making in Investor-State Dispute Settlement: Policy Options' (2020) 21 Journal of World Investment & Trade 374, 377.

3 Jaemin Lee, 'Introduction of an Appellate Review Mechanism for International Investment Disputes: Expected Benefits and Remaining Tasks' in Jean E Kalicki and Anna Joubin-Bret (eds), *Reshaping the Investor-State Dispute Settlement System: Journeys for the 21st Century* (Brill/Nijhoff 2015), 481.

4 See UNCTAD, 'Reform of Investor-State Dispute Settlement: In Search of a Roadmap' IIA Issues Note 2 (2013), 3 <https://unctad.org/en/PublicationsLibrary/webdiaepcb2013d4_en.pdf> accessed 13 January 2022. See also Benedetti, Juan, *(n 1)*, 91; UNCITRAL Working Group III, 'Possible reform of investor-State dispute settlement (ISDS): Consistency and related matters' (28 August 2018), A/CN.9/WG.III/WP.150, para 37.

reform of the current ISDS system.[5] Against this background, a number of scholars have addressed possible options for the establishment of a uniform dispute settlement mechanism in ISDS either through an MIC or a free-standing Appellate Body that supervises all ad hoc arbitration proceedings. In particular, ground-laying works of *Kaufmann-Kohler/Potestà*[6] and *Bungenberg/Reinisch*[7], as well as the Draft Statute of the Multilateral Investment Court (MIC Draft Statute) by *Bungenberg/Reinisch*[8] and the Draft Provisions on the Appellate Procedure (UNCITRAL Draft Provisions)[9] by the UNCITRAL Secretariat will be considered in the following analysis.

This chapter, therefore, aims to explore the advantages and disadvantages of the introduction of an appeal mechanism to ISDS. First, the main decisions will be outlined that States must consider when implementing some type of appeal mechanism in order to enhance consistency in ISDS (B.). General institutional and procedural choices will be portrayed and their respective influence on the design of any possible review structure will be examined. Second, the question will be assessed which design options exist for a court structure like an MIC or a standalone Body of Appeal (C.). This also includes procedural aspects, such as the sope of appeal, the issue of remand, as well as the introduction of any type of time limitations. Last, a conclusion will be drawn which of the appeal options can be considered most suitable to achieve the proclaimed goals of the ISDS reform effectively (D.).

---

5 UNCTAD *(n 4)*, 4. See also De Luca et al, *(n 2)*, 397-407.

6 Gabrielle Kaufmann-Kohler and Michele Potestà, 'Can the Mauritius Convention serve as a model for the reform of a permanent investment tribunal or an appeal mechanism? Analysis and roadmap' CIDS 2016.

7 Marc Bungenberg and August Reinisch, *From Bilateral Arbitral Tribunals and Investment Courts to a Multilateral Investment Court – Options Regarding the Institutionalization of Investor-State Dispute Settlement* (2nd edn, Springer 2019).

8 Marc Bungenberg and August Reinisch, *Draft Statute of the Multilateral Investment Court* (Nomos 2021) (MIC Draft Statute).

9 Draft Provisions on the Appellate Procedure of the UNCITRAL Secretariat, in UNCITRAL Secretariat, 'Possible Reform of Investor State Dispute Settlement (ISDS) Appellate Mechanism And Enforcement Issues', para 59 <https://icsid.worldbank.org/sites/default/files/Possible%20Improvements%20of%20 the%20Framework%20of%20ICSID%20Arbitration.pdf> accessed 13 January 2022.

B. *The Issue of Consistency - Institutional and Procedural Choices*

The implementation of an appeal mechanism in search of consistency has two dimensions. On one side lies the question of what institutional structure should be the basis for appeal (I.). On the other side, the question must be assessed which procedure should be adopted (II.). Both questions are independent of whether the review mechanism will be designed as an MIC or a standalone Appellate Body. Therefore, a general assessment can be made irrespective of a specific mechanism.

I. *Institutional Choices in Search for Consistency*

Before examining the reform options, a number of fundamental issues need to be assessed which are relevant regardless of the design of the new ISDS system. First of all, the implications of the choice between a court system and a permanent arbitral tribunal will be briefly portrayed (1.). Second, it needs to be considered whether the newly formed ISDS system should adopt a system of stare decisis or remain more flexible in its decision-making (2.). Third, less demanding alternatives to an appeal mechanism will be considered (3.). Lastly, reform efforts made by States and the international community will be examined (4.).

1. *Ad hoc or Permanent Dispute Settlement Mechanism*

Regularly, the starting point to develop a concrete design for a multilateral dispute settlement mechanism in international investment law is the WTO dispute settlement process. It is seen as a role-model for a multi-tiered dispute settlement body which has encountered great acceptance in international law.[10] The Investment Court System (ICS) envisaged by the Comprehensive Economic and Trade Agreement (CETA)[11] and other EU Free Trade Agreements (FTAs) and Investment Protection Agreements

---

10 Nicolette Butler, 'In Search of a Model for the Reform of International Investment Dispute Resolution: An Analysis of Existing International and Regional Dispute Settlement Mechanisms' in Kalicki and Joubin-Bret (eds), *Reshaping the Investor-State Dispute Settlement System: Journeys for the 21st Century* (Brill/Nijhoff 2015), 356.

11 Comprehensive Economic and Trade Agreement between Canada and the European Union (CETA) (2016).

(IPAs) was also considered a template for a review instance in ISDS.[12] The WTO experience allows for the presumption that a review instance with a standing body of adjudicators will have the most significant influence on predictability as well as certainty and establish constant jurisprudence.[13] However, such a system would come at the expense of the core advantage of the current ISDS system, ie strong party control in the dispute settlement proceedings with high flexibility.[14] On the upside, the diminished influence of the parties on the proceedings would legitimise the permanent court due to its higher degree of autonomy and independence from the parties.[15] This independence argument may of course only be validly raised if the appointment procedure limits the influence of the Contracting States on the appointment of respondent-friendly adjudicators.[16]

In addition, despite all the criticism of ad hoc ISDS, it must not be forgotten that the current investment law regime consists of more than 3,000 legal texts with most of them having individual language or different context.[17] This may lead to varying interpretations of the underlying treaty language and hence – on the first glance – inconsistent outcomes.[18] Given this fractured nature of investment law, any type of uniform review mechanism may have difficulty achieving the consistency and coherence that proponents of a reform expect.[19] Any comparison to the WTO dispute

12 Kaufmann-Kohler, Potestà *(n 6)*, paras 47-55; Bungenberg, Reinisch *(n 7)*, paras 70, 71; Sardinha, 'The New EU-Led Approach to Investor-State Arbitration' (2017) 32.3 ICSID Review 625.

13 Rob Howse, 'Designing a Multilateral Investment Court: Issues and Options' (2017) 36.1 Yearbook of European Law 209, 215.

14 Lee *(n 3)*, para 493.

15 Howse *(n 13)*, 226.

16 See Malcolm Langford, Daniel Behn, and Maria Chiara Malaguti, 'The Quadrilemma: Appointing Adjudicators in Future Investor-State Dispute Settlement' (13 October 2019), Academic Forum on ISDS Concept Paper 2019/12, 33, 34. See Kittelmann/Dünkelsbühler, Chapter 6.

17 De Luca et al *(n 2)*, 377; Stephan Schill and Geraldo Vidigal, 'Designing Investment Dispute Settlement à la Carte: Insights from Comparative Institutional Design Analysis' (2019) The Law & Practice of International Courts and Tribunals 314, 318.

18 UNCTAD *(n 4)*, 8.

19 Barton Legum, 'Appellate Mechanisms for Investment Arbitration: Worth a Second Look for the Trans-Pacific Partnership and the Proposed EU-US FTA?' in Kalicki and Joubin-Bret (eds), *Reshaping the Investor-State Dispute Settlement System: Journeys for the 21st Century* (Brill/Nijhoff 2015), 438; Łukasz Kułaga, 'A Brave, New, International Investment Court in Context' (2019) 38 Polish Yearbook of International Law 115, 139; UNCITRAL WG III, Consistency, WP 150 (2018) *(n 4)*, para 30.

settlement mechanism may thus be flawed because the WTO framework is based on a network of multilateral agreements and not thousands of bilateral treaties as in investment law.[20] Therefore, it is argued that any review mechanism in ISDS would be unable to reach the envisioned goal of consistency and predictability unless and until BITs, IPAs, and FTAs between the Contracting States are coordinated.[21] Substantive language divergences may also be the cause of inconsistency. Nonetheless, ISDS practice shows that cases of general importance are regularly relied upon by disputing parties irrespective of the underlying BIT provision invoked in the arbitration.[22] Therefore, it can be assumed that adjudicators under international law decide in the light of basic principles that are not necessarily linked to the specific wording of the respective treaty.[23]

The argument can be made that both ad hoc tribunals, as well as permanent court or court-like structures, can produce decisions, which follow these basic principles in international law. The only requirement is that these decisions are regarded by subsequent panels of adjudicators.[24] However, it would be comprehensible if States perceived a permanent body of adjudicators as more authoritative than ad hoc panels, regardless of whether such a view would actually hold true.

2. *Permanent Tribunal or International Court*

If States consider a permanent body as the preferable form of ISDS, the next question must be whether the reformed ISDS system should be designed as an international court system or as a standing, permanent tribunal. In a court system, the adjudicators would be appointed by States in advance, independent of a specific dispute, and for a longer period of time.[25] A permanent tribunal, however, also bears court-like features.

20 Butler *(n 10)*, 378.

21 Kaufmann-Kohler, Potestà *(n 6)*, para 73; Giovanni Zarra, 'The New Investor-State Dispute Settlement Mechanisms Proposed by the EU and the Geneva Centre for International Dispute Settlement. A Step Forward or a Hasty Reform?' (2018) XIII Studi sull'integrazione europea 389, 400; De Luca et al *(n 2)*, 405.

22 See also Gabriel Bottini, 'Reform of the Investor-State Arbitration Regime: The Appeal Proposal' in Kalicki and Joubin-Bret (eds), *Reshaping the Investor-State Dispute Settlement System: Journeys for the 21st Century* (Brill/Nijhoff 2015), 468.

23 Schill *(n 2)*, 1100-1103; Bottini *(n 22)*, 468.

24 Lee *(n 3)*, para 492.

25 Bungenberg, Reinisch, *(n 7)*, para 55; UNCITRAL WG III, Consistency, WP 150 (2018) *(n 4)*, para 47.

In contrast to ad hoc tribunals, permanent tribunals lack party influence on the appointment process, their adjudicators are appointed for a specific term rather than only for a single dispute, and panels are assigned disputes randomly.[26] In general, there is no binding definition of where an international court starts and a permanent tribunal ends.[27] However, permanent tribunals are characterised by a stronger detachment from State-structures and a greater say of the parties regarding procedural aspects.[28] Notwithstanding this, the largest field of party influence in arbitration, the appointment of arbitrators, is foreclosed in a permanent tribunal system. This makes the distinction between a permanent tribunal and a court system from a procedural perspective seem marginal in any case.

There is a strong movement amongst scholars and States that lean towards a two-tiered MIC instead of a permanent tribunal.[29] This approach mirrors domestic judicial review in traditional public law as it envisions two independent permanent judicial bodies that derive their competence from the Contracing States' sovereign authority to resolve disputes stemming from an individual's claim based on unlawful State conduct.[30] In light of the policy goal of achieving profound consistency, it can be argued that appointed judges would be likely to develop a more cohesive decision-making practice.[31]They may also demonstrate stronger independence and neutrality than party-appointed arbitrators.[32] However, critics to a court system argue that there is no conclusive evidence of government-appointed adjudicators rendering decisions in a more competent, objective and impartial manner.[33] Moreover, resorting to a court system could also strip the dispute settlement mechanism from the advantages arbitral awards have with regard to enforcement.[34] The advantages include inter alia

26 Kaufmann-Kohler, Potestà *(n 6)*, para 85.
27 ibid, para 86.
28 ibid, para 86.
29 See above Section A.1.
30 UNCTAD (*n 4*), 9.
31 Bungenberg, Reinisch *(n 7)*, paras 55, 607; Nicolette Butler, 'Possible Improvements to The Framework of International Investment Arbitration' (2013) 14.4 The Journal of World Investment & Trade, 637.
32 Bungenberg, Reinisch *(n 7)*, paras 55, 607; Butler *(n 32)*, 637.
33 Benedetti, Juan (*n 1*), 108; Koeth, 'Can the Investment Court System (ICS) save TTIP and CETA?' (2016) EIPA Working Papers, 12 <https://www.eipa.eu/wp-content/uploads/2017/11/20161019072755 _Workingpaper2016_W_01.pdf> accessed 13 January 2022.
34 See Bungenberg, Reinisch (*n 7*), paras 534-536; Zarra (*n 21*), 405. See also, Müller, Chapter 9, Section B.I.1.

the recognition of decisions of any new MIC/Appellate Body under the New York Convention on the Recognition and Enforcement of Foreign Arbitral Awards (New York Convention)[35] or the Convention on The Settlement of Investment Disputes Between States and Nationals of other States (ICSID Convention)[36]. The lack of these enforcement options poses a major disadvantage of a court system. It would call for the development of a new multilateral enforcement system by the Contracting States or a modification of the existing conventions.[37] This would require consent by all State parties involved and whether such broad consent can be found between the different States is at least questionable.

However, the final decision whether the reformed dispute settlement mechanism should be designed as a court system or a permanent tribunal is up to the Contracting States. Thus, for further analysis, the premise is that all reform options considered could be designed as an international court or a permanent arbitral tribunal. Hence the compatibility of both systems with a two-tiered MIC or a standalone Appellate Body is assumed. Accordingly, from this point going forward, the judges and permanent arbitrators will be commonly referred to as 'adjudicators'.

3. *System of 'Stare Decisis' or 'de facto' Precedent*

One reaction to the criticism of inconsistent jurisprudence may be the implementation of a system of *stare decisis*, ie subsequent tribunals following rules or principles laid down by previous tribunals in their decisions unless they contravene the ordinary principles of justice. Therefore, it might seem surprising at first glance that scholars are generally reluctant when confronted with the idea of introducing a system of *stare decisis* and binding precedent in ISDS. A major point of concern is, inter alia, flexibility in the decision-making process.[38] In principle, adjudicators require leeway to adequately adapt to the specific facts and circumstances in each

35 Convention on the Recognition and Enforcement of Foreign Arbitral Awards (New York Convention) (1959) 330 UNTS 3.

36 Convention on The Settlement of Investment Disputes Between States and Nationals of other States (ICSID) (1965) 575 UNTS 159.

37 Kułaga (*n 19*), 136. See also, Müller, Chapter 9.

38 Kaufmann-Kohler, Potestà (*n 6*), paras 188, 189; Bungenberg, Reinisch (*n 7*), para 362; Alexander M Heideman, 'Investment Law for Investors: A Case against Multilateral Investment Courts' (2018) 19 UC Davis Bus LJ 1, 14; Zarra (*n 21*), 401.

case, which could be overly restricted by binding precedent.[39] It must be understood that the lack of a system of *stare decisis* does not imply that prior decisions should not be regarded by adjudicators as guidance for future disputes. A system of soft-precedent has already been established in arbitral jurisprudence.[40] Therefore, it can be expected that decisions by a future review body will be regarded as 'authoritative' beyond the scope of the dispute at hand and will lead to a system of *de facto* precedent.[41]

Consistency can also be reached without stipulating binding precedent. This would require, however, that the chambers of the MIC or the panels of the permanent tribunal are permanently staffed and are obligated to consult a grand chamber or the plenary of adjudicators in cases of fundamental disagreement.[42] In order to avoid extraordinary delay, this consultation procedure should be limited to exceptional cases on a party's request based on important reasons, such as a divergence in the decisions of the review body.[43]

Given the fractured nature of investment law, considerable doubts can be raised as to whether truly consistent and coherent decisions can be reached without its interpretation by a common instance of review.[44] The role of this common review mechanism will be to further form and define principles of international investment law that can be used as guidance by other adjudicative bodies, thereby leading to a system of *de facto* precedent.[45] Thus – regardless of its final form – the body of review, must

39 This does not imply that systems of stare decisis are generally inflexible. However, adjudicators may be more compelled to follow prior jurisprudence without making the decision based on the individual factors in the case at hand. Stare decisis are particularly difficult in the context of ISDS, as the fractured nature of international investment law to find truly comparable case-law. Comparing cases based on different BIT provisions may violate the rules of interpretation set out by the Vienna Convention on the Law of Treaties of 23 May 1969, which requires each international treaty to be interpreted in light of its individual context and wording, see Heideman (*n 38*), 14.

40 Heideman (*n 38*), 14; Kułaga (*n 19*), 136; UNCITRAL WG III, Possible reform of investor-State dispute settlement (ISDS), WP 150 (2018) (*n 4*), para 40.

41 Kaufmann-Kohler, Potestà (*n 6*), paras 188, 189; Bungenberg, Reinisch (*n 7*), para 362. Critical hereto Sardinha (*n 12*), 671.

42 Bungenberg, Reinisch (*n 7*), para 362.

43 ibid, para 360.

44 Legum (*n 19*), 438; UNCITRAL WG III, Consistency, WP 150 (2018) (*n 4*), para 20.

45 Bungenberg, Reinisch (*n 7*), para 640.

be able to pronounce clear jurisprudence on some of the key issues of investment law.[46]

4. *Reform Efforts in State Practice*

The introduction of a uniform review instance to ISDS is controversial and faces a number of practical obstacles.[47] However, current State practice and solutions presented by practitioners and scholars all point to one conclusion: a permanent and uniform review instance will have a beneficial effect on the functioning of ISDS.[48] Such a conclusion is also justified in light of the recent reform efforts made by the European Union (EU) and the conclusions reached in the 39th session of the UNCITRAL Working Group III in October 2020.[49]

Especially the EU paved the way towards the introduction of some type of review mechanism within the ICS in its recently concluded bilateral and multilateral investment protection treaties. These treaties explicitly reference a permanent 'Appeal Tribunal' whose function is to hear appeals against the awards rendered by a first instance tribunal.[50] However, none of the bilateral treaties provides for a detailed description of how such a permanent Appeal Tribunal should be constituted. Similarly, the UNCITRAL Working Group III considered the reform options of a standalone review or appellate mechanism and a standing MIC.[51] Additionally, State practice concerning recently concluded non-EU investment treaties

46 Lee (*n 3*), para 492.

47 See below Section C.

48 Bungenberg, Reinisch (*n 7*), paras 50-51; Kaufmann-Kohler, Potestà (*n 6*), paras 28-30; Bottini (*n 22*), 472.

49 See UNCITRAL, 'Report of Working Group III (Investor-State Dispute Settlement Reform) on the work of its thirty-ninth session (Vienna, 5-9 October 2020)' (10 November 2020), A/CN.9/1044. This is a continuation of previous reform efforts, see Andreea Nica, 'UNCITRAL Working Group III: One Step Closer to a Multilateral Investment Court?' Kluwer Arbitration Blog (24 March 2020) <http://arbitrationblog.kluwerarbitration.com/2020/03/24/uncitral-working-group-iii-one-step-closer-to-a-multilateral-investment-court/> accessed 13 January 2022.

50 Article 8.28 CETA; Article 3.10 EU-Singapore Investment Protection Agreement (IPA) (2018); Article 3.39 EU-Vietnam IPA (2019).

51 UNCITRAL, Working Group III, 'Possible reform of investor-State dispute settlement (ISDS) – Multilateral instrument on ISDS Reform' (16 January 2020), A/CN.9/WG.III/WP.194. See also Nica (*n 49*).

clearly demonstrates a trend towards a bilateral or multilateral appellate mechanism in ISDS.[52]

This strong support among States indicates that both the introduction of an MIC or a permanent Appelate Body are more than just academic discussions and that the 'if' of a reform of ISDS is less of a question than the 'how' of an appeal mechanism's implementation.

Notwithstanding the general support by the international community, any reform faces serious practical hurdles as it would require a complete overhaul of the current regime and the participation of a large number of States.[53] Practical and political difficulties when appointing adjudicators were showcased only recently by the example of the WTO Appellate Body.[54] A similar risk of politicisation has also been addressed with regard to the constitution of an MIC.[55] However, such a risk can only be evaluated if the procedural rules and the caseload of the hypothetical MIC are known.

Therefore, it could be argued that it is unnecessary to undergo the struggle of creating a new framework since the ICSID Convention already offers a self-contained mechanism for the settlement of disputes which alleviates any legitimacy concerns. Even the former Commissioner for Trade of the European Commission conceded that '[t]he objective would be to multilateralise the court either as a self-standing international body or by embedding it into an existing multilateral organization'.[56] The Annulment Committee under the ICSID Convention could thus be the starting point for the development of a uniform standalone Appellate Body in international investment law. An *inter se* modification of the ICSID Convention

---

52 For example Articles 28 (10) and 34, Annex D United States Model Bilateral Investment Treaty (2012); Article 9.23 (11) Comprehensive and Progressive Trans Pacific Partnership (2018); Article 10.20 (10), Annex 10 F Central America Free Trade Agreement (CAFTA-DR) between Costa Rica, Dominican Republic, Guatemala, Honduras, Nicaragua, El Salvador, and USA (2009); Article 15 Dutch Model Investment Agreement (2018). See for an extensive overview of investment treaties concluded in the last two decades providing for an appeal mechanism: UNCITRAL Secretariat (*n 9*), para 64.

53 UNCTAD (*n 4*), 9. The adherence of the MIC adjudicators with the rule of law and the principle of uniform and consistent interpretation of the law could be guaranteed by including the decisions in the Court's Statute, see for example Article 28 (1) MIC Draft Statute.

54 See Lee (*n 3*), para 480.

55 Benedetti, Juan (*n 1*), 107; Butler (*n 32*), 635; Zarra (*n 21*), 404.

56 Cecilia Malmström, 'Investment in TTIP and beyond – the path for reform' (2015), 11 <http://trade.ec.europa.eu/doclib/docs/2015/may/tradoc_153408.PDF> accessed 13 January 2022.

is a viable approach to the reform.[57] Nonetheless, ICSID in its current state faces the same criticism with regard to want of legitimacy as well as inconsistency as general ISDS and does not offer the option of appealing on the merits.[58] Particularly the denunciation of the ICSID Convention by some Member States demonstrates diminished support in the international community.[59] Moreover, if the reform attempts for the ICSID Convention fail, the current dispute settlement mechanism may lose more of its good reputation, authority, and legitimacy.[60] A newly developed system would, hence not face the same resentments as current ISDS mechanisms and would allow for the implementation of ideas regarding new and innovative structures. It might, however, be difficult to find sufficient support among States to create a completely new and costly dispute settlement system.

In sum, the international community is pushing towards reform of ISDS and the introduction of some form of review mechanism. However, both the MIC as well as the standalone Appellate Body face significant practical challenges.[61] Any type of standing adjudicative body, may it be the two-tiered MIC or the self-contained Appellate Body, must have broad international consensus among States.[62] Otherwise, any type of reform is bound to fail.

---

57 See also ICSID Secretariat, 'Possible Improvements of the Framework for ICSID Arbitration', paras 20-23 <https://icsid.worldbank.org/sites/default/files/Possible%20Improvements%20of%20the%20Framework%20of%20ICSID%20Arbitration.pdf> accessed 13 January 2022; Bungenberg, Reinisch (*n 7*), paras 497-498; Kaufmann-Kohler, Potestà (*n 6*), paras 244, 245; August Reinisch, 'Will the EU's Proposal Concerning an Investment Court System for CETA and TTIP Lead to Enforceable Awards?' (2016) 19.4 J Int Economic Law 761, 780.

58 Butler (*n 10*), 361.

59 Bolivia in 2007, Ecuador in 2009, Venezuela in 2012 denounced the ICSID Convention. However, it must also be considered that in the meantime a larger number of States signed the ICSID Convention, of which most notable are Iraq (2015) and Mexico (2018). See also Sergio Puig and Gregory Shaffer, 'Imperfect Alternatives: Institutional Choice and the Reform of Investment Law' (2018) 112.3 The American Journal of International Law, 365.

60 Kristina Anđelić, 'Why ICSID Doesn't Need an Appellate Procedure, and What to Do Instead' in Jean E Kalicki and Anna Joubin-Bret (eds), *Reshaping the Investor-State Dispute Settlement System: Journeys for the 21st Century* (Brill/Nijhoff 2015), 498.

61 UNCTAD (*n 4*), 9.

62 Lee (*n 3*), para 482. Summarising the pluralistic approaches regarding the reform, see Anthea Roberts, 'Incremental, Systemic, and Paradigmatic Reform of Investor-State Arbitration' (2018) 112.3 American Journal of International Law, 431, 432.

II. Procedural Choices in Search for Consistency

Procedural choices can be manyfold, depending on the final structure chosen for the review mechanism by the States. However, there can be identified a number of procedural questions, which should be discussed in advance. In the beginning of this section, the criticism to any type of review mechanism must be addressed (1.). In reaction to the criticism, less burdensome consultation procedures will be assessed, which may constitute considerable alternatives to the introduction of an MIC or standalone Appellate Body (2.). Last, the difference between appeal and annulment will be explained and examined whether the difference has to be taken into account in the structural design of an MIC or the standalone body.

1. Criticism of the Introduction of a Review Mechanism in ISDS

Some authors raise doubts whether a two-tiered system is necessary. First, a review mechanism may not necessarily increase the consistency of decisions.[63] The argument is made that any type of review would simply shift the risk of misapplication of investment treaty obligations from ad hoc tribunals to permanently placed adjudicators.[64] It does, however, not necessarily follow that these adjudicators render 'enhanced' decisions, just because they are elected for a fixed term.[65] Second, the efficiency of ISDS could be adversely affected. Since the introduction of a review mechanism prolongs the arbitration procedure, it could be called into question whether an ISDS reform actually needs a second instance.[66]

A review mechanism would undermine the finality of the award and hence the timely conclusion of the proceedings and efficient enforcement of arbitral decisions.[67] Moreover, the introduction of a review mechanism is a mostly procedural system change, which may not be sufficient to address all consistency concerns.

---

63 De Luca et al (*n 2*), 407; Benedetti, Juan (*n 1*), 108.

64 De Luca et al (*n 2*), 407.
ibid, 407.

65 De Luca et al (*n 2*), 407; Benedetti, Juan (*n 1*), 108.

66 Kaufmann-Kohler, Potestà (*n 6*), paras 122-123; Heideman (*n 38*), 15.

67 Eun Young Park, 'Appellate Review in Investor-State Arbitration' in Jean E Kalicki and Anna Joubin-Bret (eds), *Reshaping the Investor-State Dispute Settlement System: Journeys for the 21st Century* (Brill/Nijhoff 2015), 444; Heideman (*n 38*), 15.

Instead of overhauling the procedural aspects of ISDS, the role of adjudicators may have to be redefined.[68] Adjudicative panels deciding on investment law cases do not only resolve a private dispute between two parties. They decide on matters of public interest in the field of public international law, which requires them not to act as a panel established only for resolving one dispute but as part of a global ISDS system. Hence, adjudicators would need to accept more responsibility and a greater role in the regulation of international investment relations.[69] Such a change in the role of first instance adjudicators is perceived by some as preferable, as their authority would only be diminished if there was a second review instance.[70] This, however, would not have any benefit in light of consistency and legitimacy but only prolong the procedure.

The annulment procedure under the ICSID Convention gives credence to the risk of prolongation by only allowing recourse to the Annulment Committee in exceptional cases, in which fundamental principles of law were violated.[71] It is evident that leaving such decisions to become final and binding for the sake of procedural swiftness would be a grave violation of basic principles of justice, especially because arbitral practice regularly does not actually work with such swiftness but rather proves to be a lengthy process with proceedings stretching over several years.[72] The concern with regard to delays caused by an additional review instance in the models as described above is further refuted by the fact that a standing body of adjudicators does not require a lengthy arbitrator-appointment procedure.[73] It is additionally noteworthy that experience with the WTO Appellate Body shows that a review instance does not necessarily invite undue delays.[74] Finally, a limitation of the scope of review could significantly decrease the number of cases for which review would be admissible in the first place.

The claim can also be made that there is a general lack of data on ISDS decisions. Therefore, there are no empirical grounds to effectively determine coherence or incoherence in arbitral jurisprudence. On this basis, it could be called into question whether the decision making is inconsistent or whether the divergence in the holdings simply results from differing

---

68 Anđelić (*n 60*), 503-505.

69 Anđelić (*n 60*), ibid.

70 Benedetti, Juan (*n 1*), 108; Anđelić (*n 60*), 499.

71 Park (*n 67*), 444.

72 Kułaga (*n 19*), 133-134.

73 Bottini (*n 22*), 471 Butler (*n 32*), 635.

74 Benedetti, Juan (*n 1*), 94, 108; Butler (*n 32*), 635.

facts, arguments, and evidence.[75] At least indications for the existence of inconsistencies are, however, decisions in the early 2000s. There can be found a number of arbitral decisions, which show clear signs of contradictory findings without substantial factual differences.[76] Considering this, the rule of law and the public interest at stake in investment disputes must mean that the correctness of awards should not be subordinated to finality.[77]

Therefore, despite the criticism, it is advisable to introduce at least some kind of control mechanism in international investment law to review arbitral awards.[78] Such a control mechanism, however, must not necessarily be a full-fledged appellate mechanism. Thus, less burdensome alternative consultation procedures will be explored next.

2. *Alternative Consultation Procedures*

As less burdensome alternatives, consistency of decisions could also be enhanced by *ex ante* procedures, such as preliminary ruling reference to the body of review or a plenary (en-banc) decision. These alternatives to a built-in review have generally the potential to be less burdensome for ISDS users.[79] In comparison to the traditional ISDS system, the establishment of a review mechanism would represent a fundamental system change.[80] Accordingly, the associated uncertainties should only be risked if this really seems necessary.[81] Against this background, possible alternatives will be discussed first.

75 Legum (*n 19*), 439.

76 Park (*n 67*), 444-450, with reference to cases against Argentina in the aftermath of its economic crisis. See also Benedetti, Juan (*n 1*), 91, with reference to *CME v Czech Republic*, Final Award, 14 March 2003 and *Lauder v Czech Republic*, Final Award, 3 September 2001, and UNCITRAL WG III, Consistency, WP 150 (2018) (*n 4*), para 11, 12, 16-18.

77 Benedetti, Juan (*n 1*), 108.

78 Kaufmann-Kohler, Potestà (*n 6*), para 105.

79 Kaufmann-Kohler, Potestà (*n 6*), para 105.

80 Katia Yannaca-Smal, 'Improving the System of Investor-State Dispute Settlement: The OECD Governments' Perspective' in Karl P Sauvant and Michael Chiswick-Patterson (eds), *Appeals Mechanism in International Investment Disputes* (OUP 2008), 223; Kaufmann-Kohler, Potestà (*n 6*), para 42.

81 See the criticism portrayed below in Section C.I.

a) Preliminary Rulings

According to critics, arbitral decisions are inherently prone to inconsistency.[82] Since scrutiny of legal holdings after the award was rendered affects not only the duration of the proceedings but also the finality and binding effect of the award, it would be a valid option to introduce a facility or body for arbitral tribunals to turn to when encountering a crucial issue of the law. Therefore, as a less intrusive reform of the ISDS system, it is suggested to establish a consultation facility, which bindingly pre-determines crucial issues of the case in order to achieve greater consistency in the arbitral decision making.[83]

The proposals for a preliminary ruling procedure are often modelled after a similar procedure at the Court of Justice of the European Union (CJEU), which allows a national court to refer a question concerning European law for final determination before rendering a decision.[84] Applied to ISDS, this would require a system in which ad hoc tribunals can submit questions to a permanent body of adjudicators. Such a procedure would allow for decentralised dispute resolution using ad hoc tribunals, while ensuring a uniform interpretation of international investment law.[85] To prevent abuse of the procedure it has been suggested that certain requirements could be imposed as to by whom and under which circumstances it can be requested.[86] For example, the right to request a preliminary ruling could be limited to situations where there is a serious concern for the investment treaty system as a whole, a new legal question, inconsistent case-law, or the intention to depart from an established line of cases.[87] Such preliminary ruling procedure could either be supplementary or alternative to an instance of review.[88]

b) En-Banc Decisions

As another alternative to a review system, the option of an en-banc determination and consulting is considered. En-banc decisions refer to a proce-

---

82 UNCTAD *(n 4)*, 4.
83 Kaufmann-Kohler, Potestà (*n 6*), para 129; Schill, Vidigal (*n 17*), 334-336.
84 Article 267 Treaty on the Functioning of the European Union (TFEU).
85 Kaufmann-Kohler, Potestà (*n 6*), paras 129, 130.
86 Schill, Vidigal (*n 17*), 335.
87 Kaufmann-Kohler, Potestà (*n 6*), para 130.
88 See Kaufmann-Kohler, Potestà (*n 6*), para 208.

dure in which determinations of great importance are made not by an individual panel but by the plenary tribunal or a chamber consisting of a larger choice of adjudicators.[89] In a such reformed ISDS system, a question of law could thusly be referred for final determination where there is a risk of inconsistent decisions or awards.[90] The difference to the preliminary ruling procedure is that decisions are not rendered by a pre-determined chamber of adjudicators but the plenary.[91] It can be argued that either preliminary rulings or en-banc decisions would be much less burdensome to implement and sustain than a full-fledged review mechanism.[92] Since they aid in streamlining decision-making rather than correcting already rendered decisions, they can be expected to ensure coherent jurisprudence as well as foster judicial continuity within the dispute settlement body.[93]

While the models for en-banc decisions vary in some minor details, they mostly share the same flaw: A plenary can only be formed where a number of standing panels exist. Hence, en-banc decisions must be regarded as a mere supplementary measure for ensuring consistency between the different chambers of the Appellate Body.[94] Such a supplementary approach is demonstrated by the Iran-US Claims Tribunal whose procedural rules allow for the determination of important questions to be referred to the plenary by one of its chambers.[95] This flaw could be circumvented by envisioning a separate procedure before a permanent tribunal only established for determining otherwise inconsistently decided issues.[96] However, it is not evident why such a design should be preferable to the preliminary ruling procedure. Thus, en-banc decisions seem (only) a reasonable supplementary tool, which can foster coherence in ISDS decision-making practice.

---

89 ibid, para 132.
90 ibid, paras 132-136.
91 ibid, para 133.
92 ibid, para 137.
93 ibid, para 137.
94 Bungenberg, Reinisch (*n 7*), para 255, acknowledge the option of a preliminary ruling procedure in an MIC context without further comment. See also Article 18 (4) and Article 47 (2) MIC Draft Statute, which suggest that larger chambers or a plenary of Appellate Court judges may be called upon to decide on specific disputes which are deemed to be of high importance.
95 Iran-US Claims Tribunal, Presidential Order No 1, 19 October 1981, para 6, cited in Kaufmann-Kohler, Potestà (*n 6*), para 132.
96 Kaufmann-Kohler, Potestà (*n 6*), paras 125-137, 207-210.

3. *Difference between Appeal and Annulment*

The main choice to be made is whether the review system should be structured as an appeal or an annulment instance.[97] The first refers to a system where the second instance can amend a decision of the first instance, while the latter only allows the second instance to annul such decisions. In general, an appeal is the reconsideration of decisions as one of the regular phases of the proceedings, whereas an annulment is concerned only with the legitimacy of the process of decision-making.[98] Hence, a system based on annulment would correspond to considerably less scrutiny than a system allowing for a full appeal.

Grounds for annulment could – closely related to the grounds of annulment listed in Article 52 of the ICSID Convention – include lack of jurisdiction, irregular constitution of the tribunal as well as lack of impartiality and independence of its members or breach of due process closely related to. Additionally, it is suggested that these grounds could be complemented by the grounds for challenge in Article 34 of the UN Commission on International Trade Law (UNCITRAL) Model Law.[99] Such a limited number of grounds would save the parties to the proceedings time and lower the costs of trying the case before a second instance.[100] However, a simple annulment procedure with a limited scope of review does not reflect the purpose sought by reforming ISDS. UNCTAD noted with reference to the annulment decision in CMS v Argentina that under the ICSID annulment rules, a simple annulment body may find itself unable to annul or correct an award, even after having identified 'manifest errors of law'.[101] This would be an unbearable situation in any legal system that follows the rule of law.[102] No court or tribunal has jurisdiction to decide based on a manifestly erroneous understanding of the law.[103] So far, ICSID Annulment Committees have attempted to circumvent these shortcomings by finding that manifest misapplication of the law amounts to non-application of the proper law or qualifying the reasoning as 'frivolous' or 'contradictory'

97 Kaufmann-Kohler, Potestà (*n 6*), para 107.
98 Anđelić (*n 62*), 502, 503.
99 Kaufmann-Kohler, Potestà (*n 6*), para 112.
100 Zarra (*n 21*), 410.
101 UNCTAD (*n 4*), 3, citing *CMS Gas Transmission Company v The Republic of Argentina* ICSID Case No. ARB/01/8, Decision of the ad hoc Committee on the application for annulment, 25 September 2007, paras 97, 127, 136, 150, 157-159.
102 Bottini (*n 22*), 461.
103 Bottini (*n 22*), ibid.

and hence no proper Statement of reason at all.[104] Such 'workarounds', however, foster procedural legal insecurity in practice and do not help diminish legitimacy concerns. Thus, simple annulment grounds do not seem suitable to achieve the aim of legal certainty and uniform judicial decisions sought by the reform.

Were there an appeal instance instead, the grounds for appeal could be based on the grounds for annulment listed in Article 52 of the ICSID Convention as well. However, in order to review the content of the award, it has been demanded that the body of appeal should also have the authority to scrutinise the awards' substance with regard to errors in the application or interpretation of the applicable law as well as manifest errors of fact.[105] The EU's recently concluded IPAs demonstrate a similar approach.[106] Alternatively, 'autonomous' formulations could be introduced, without attempting to combine new grounds with the grounds set out in Article 52 of the ICSID Convention.[107] This could avert any unintentional mutual influence on the interpretation between the rules of competence developed under the new regime and the grounds of annulment in the ICSID Convention.[108]

Some concerns may arise regarding the swiftness of the review process of decisions if the losing party can challenge the decision on such a broad variety of grounds.[109] However, the comparison between annulment and appeal makes it clear that, in the light of consistency and the rule of law, an appeal mechanism offers the better option for an effective review instance. Thus, States should procedurally route for appeal rather than annulment.

III. Interim Conclusion

When considering a central and permanent appeal mechanism for ISDS, States have a wide variety of general choices to make. First, the decision must be made whether a permanent body of adjudicators is actually more effective to reach the goals of more legitimacy and consistency than ad

104 De Luca et al (*n 2*), 385, 386.

105 Bungenberg, Reinisch (*n 7*), paras 356-358.

106 Article 8.28 (2) CETA; Article 3.54 EU-Vietnam IPA; Article 3.19 EU-Singapore IPA. See also Kułaga (*n 19*), 134; Sardinha (*n 12*), 641.

107 Kaufmann-Kohler, Potestà (*n 6*), para 118.

108 ibid.

109 Reinisch (*n 59*), 780.

hoc tribunals. Second, the States are faced with the choice between a permanent tribunal or an international court system. Third, it must be considered whether this newly formed body of adjudicators should render its decision under a system of *stare decisis* or may simply rely on a system of *de facto* precedent.

In addition to the procedural reforms, there may be the need to reform the investment law framework by harmonising the substantive protection standards contained in the current network of international investment agreements (IIAs). In order for ISDS to function as effectively as other bodies of international law, a multilateral and more centralised structure of the fractured investment law framework would be required.

In case a full-fledged appeal mechanism is considered too burdensome by the States, a preliminary ruling or an en-banc consultation procedure could be an effective measure to avoid conflicting decisions even before they were rendered. With regard to the scope of the legal grounds for review, the better arguments speak for a broader appeal than a simple annulment procedure. It has been demonstrated that annulment is too narrow and would not allow for correction of manifest errors of fact or misinterpretation of the law. However, leaving such manifest errors uncorrected would not comply with the rule of law.

C. Creating an Appeal Mechanism – Institutional and Procedural Design

The amendment of existing structures in international investment law will require a great effort by as many States as possible. Even more so would the creation of an entirely new system of ISDS. Therefore, the most prominent options, the introduction of a two-tiered MIC or a standalone Appellate Body will be reviewed and evaluated in light of the participation required by the States and the possible benefit they may bring to ISDS. Subsequently, specific procedural decisions, that must be taken depending on whether a two-tiered or a standalone appellate mechanism is chosen, will be examined.

I. Institutional Design of an Appeal Mechanism

There are two basic designs for an appellate mechanism in investment law. The MIC[110] would completely replace the current ad hoc tribunals by a first instance consisting of permanent adjudicators. Their decisions would be reviewed by an appellate body consisting of permanently placed adjudicators as well. In the event of the establishment of a standalone Appellate Body, the system of ad hoc tribunals would remain unaltered. However, their decisions would be reviewed by a standing and standalone body of adjudicators.

1. Two-Tiered 'Multilateral Investment Court'

Structure-wise, the adjudicating body in the first instance would take the role currently assigned to investment tribunals. This includes conducting fact-finding and applying the relevant law to the facts under its own rules of procedure.[111] The second instance would then hear appeals against the decisions of the first instance in accordance with its competence.[112]

The WTO Dispute Settlement Mechanism with a first and review instance is often used as a template for MIC designs.[113] It has been suggested to elect the adjudicators of the appellate instance from the adjudicators serving in the first instance of the MIC.[114] Nonetheless, the review instance would be a separate organ of the MIC and its adjudicators would not serve in the first instance at the same time.[115] In general, the proficiency of appellate-level adjudicators is a key factor in the discussion whether a second-level should be introduced at all.[116] This is mainly due to the fact that the review instance has to deal with the most complex and controver-

---

110 Any two-tiered dispute settlement structure, may it be a court system or permanent tribunals, will be referred to as an MIC.

111 UNCITRAL, Working Group III, 'Possible reform of investor-State dispute settlement (ISDS) - Appellate and multilateral court mechanisms, Note by the Secretariat' (29 November 2019), A/CN.9/WG.III/WP.185, para 52; Benedetti, Juan (*n 1*), 103.

112 UNCITRAL WG III, Appellate and multilateral court mechanisms, WP 185 (2019) (*n 111*), para 52. See below Section C.I.

113 Bungenberg, Reinisch (*n 7*), para 176; Butler (*n 10*), 377, 378; Benedetti, Juan (*n 1*), 102; De Luca et al (*n 2*), 404, 405.

114 Article 18 (1) MIC Draft Statute.

115 ibid.

116 De Luca et al (*n 2*), 409.

sial cases, whereas less complex cases can also be handled well in the first instance by less experienced adjudicators. The prolongation of the ISDS procedure can only be justified if the second-level review significantly enhances the quality of the decisions rendered.[117] Additionally, a standing body with predetermined adjudicators in the first and second instance would generally enhance transparency and address the criticism regarding party-appointed adjudicators and double-hatting.[118] Likewise, members of the *Academic Forum on ISDS* suggest bolstering the proposed dispute settlement body's authority by demanding 'extraordinary' qualifications from its adjudicators.[119] Extraordinary qualifications could be secured by requiring a fixed number of adjudicators to be selected from a diverse list of candidates for both instances.[120] Transparency could further be fostered by permitting third parties, for example representatives of affected communities, to participate in the proceedings in one or both instances.[121]

Independent of the exact design of the MIC, the general structure as a two-tiered standing court would make it easier to streamline processes making ISDS proceedings more efficient. It may also prevent opportunistic forum-shopping tactics by investors.[122] Moreover – as seen at the WTO Appellate Body – decisions of the appellate instance will offer guidance to the first instance.[123] Then, once a *jurisprudence constante* has developed with regard to key legal standards, the decisions of the MIC adjudicators will become more predictable.[124]

2. *Standalone Appellate Body*

The two-tiered MIC model is not uniformly regarded as the most favourable reform option for ISDS. As an alternative to the two-tiered system, authors also considered a self-contained multilateral Appellate Body, which would serve as a review instance for all ad hoc arbitration proceed-

117 ibid.

118 Bottini (*n 22*), 462, 465.

119 Bjorklund et al, 'Selection and Appointment of International Adjudicators: Structural Options for ISDS Reform' Academic Forum on ISDS Concept Paper 2019/11, 19.

120 Bjorklund et al (*n 119*), 19; Malmström (*n 56*), 11.

121 UNCITRAL WG III, Appellate and multilateral court mechanisms, WP 185 (2019) (*n 111*), para 54.

122 Howse (*n 13*), 216.

123 Schill, Vidigal (*n 17*), 333.

124 ibid.

ings.[125] Such an Appellate Body would give the parties more leeway to determine the rules of the arbitration while pressuring parties and arbitrators to abide by general principles of investment law as well as the rule of law.[126] For example, parties might be more inclined to select adjudicators that have demonstrated the ability to change their stance towards a certain topic of law or fact depending on the circumstances and details of each individual case.[127] Regarding current practice in investment arbitration, parties have shown a tendency to appoint such arbitrators that have a certain pre-determined opinion in a crucial topic of the case.[128] Such practice may change if all participants are aware of the possibility of meaningful scrutiny by a standing Appellate Body. As UNCTAD pointed out, concerns of inconsistency and illegitimacy regarding ad hoc arbitrations could be reduced by a uniform second-level supervision and thus 'would add direction and order to the existing decentralised, non-hierarchical and ad hoc regime'.[129]

Some authors suggest that such an Appellate Body could be created by simply reforming the annulment proceedings under the ICSID Convention.[130] Such an approach would have the significant advantage that the reformed system could use the already established structures and the reputation of the ICSID system. The ICSID signatory States could then modify the ICSID Convention to allow for the establishment of a standing tribunal or court.[131] This approach would additionally have the benefit that the new Appellate Body would have a clearly defined jurisdiction from the outset.[132] In accordance with the Vienna Convention on the Law of Treaties (VCLT)[133], this modification could be implemented without the unanimous consent of the signatory States.[134]

---

125 Bungenberg, Reinisch (*n 7*), para 607; Kaufmann-Kohler, Potestà (*n 6*), para 105; Bottini (*n 22*), 467; Lee (*n 3*), para 495.

126 Lee (*n 3*), para 477; Puig, Shaffer (*n 59*), 393.

127 Bottini (*n 22*), 469.

128 ibid.

129 UNCTAD (*n 4*), 8.

130 Considered inter alia by the ICSID Secretariat (*n 57*), paras 20-23; Bungenberg, Reinisch (*n 7*), paras 497-498; Kaufmann-Kohler, Potestà (*n 6*), paras 237-245.

131 ICSID Secretariat (*n 57*), paras 20-23; Bottini (*n 22*), 459.

132 Lee (*n 3*), para 495.

133 Vienna Convention on the Law of Treaties (VCLT) (1969) 1155 UNTS 331.

134 Article 41 VCLT provides that two or more of the parties to a multilateral treaty, such as the ICSID Convention, may conclude an agreement to modify the treaty as between themselves alone as long as the agreement does not have an adverse

However, it is questionable whether such modification to the ICSID Convention is permissible depending on how drastic the chosen reform option would be.[135] The modification would inter alia require that the method of constituting the tribunal would be changed from an ad hoc appointment of Annulment Committee members for one dispute to an appointment of adjudicators for the Appellate Body for a fixed period of time.[136] However, if such changes were implemented, it could be argued that the decisions made under the reformed system are no longer to be regarded as awards rendered pursuant to the ICSID Convention.[137] This could undermine the obligation of other Contracting States to recognise and enforce such awards.[138] Therefore, the Appellate Body could also be developed as an autonomous structure. This autonomous structure can be either based on the Annulment Committee under the ICSID Convention or a completely newly developed system.[139] The latter would allow a great level of flexibility to tailor the dispute resolution mechanism to the needs of the Contracting States.[140]

As far as the competence with regard to appeal or annulment is concerned, it is argued that the Appellate Body should have the authority to scrutinise the awards for errors in the application or interpretation of the applicable law and manifest errors of fact.[141] These grounds would be supplementary to the grounds for annulment laid out in Article 52 of the ICSID Convention.[142]

Additionally, plenary decisions should be possible in order to prevent substantively divergent decisions of different chambers.[143]

---

effect on the other parties. Concerns regarding the admissibility of an inter se modification of the ICSID Convention can be found in Zarra (*n 21*), 407.

135 Potestà, 'Investment Arbitration, Challenges And Prospects For The Establishment of a Multilateral Investment Court' (2018) Austrian Yearbook on International Arbitration, 169; Reinisch, 'Will the EU's Proposal Concerning an Investment Court System for CETA and TTIP Lead to Enforceable Awards?' (2016) 19.4 J Int Economic Law 761, 779.

136 Potestà (*n 135*), 169; Reinisch (*n 57*), 781, 782. See also Müller, Chapter 9.

137 ibid.

138 ibid.

139 Schill, Vidigal (*n 17*), 342-344; Roberts (*n 62*), 432; Puig, Shaffer (*n 59*), 408, 409. Raising concerns of a fragmentation of the ICSID dispute settlement mechanism: ICSID Secretariat (*n 57*), paras 20-23.

140 Roberts (*n 62*), 432; Puig, Shaffer (*n 59*), 408, 409.

141 Bungenberg, Reinisch (*n 7*), para 633. See also Section C.I.

142 ibid.

143 ibid, para 636.

II. Procedural Design of an Appeal Mechanism

Regardless of whether the appellate mechanism will take the form of a two-tiered MIC or as a self-standing Appellate Body for ad hoc awards, it needs to be determined how the appeals procedure should be designed. The standard of review of the appeal is an important decision in this context. Thus, it must be determined whether the scope of review should only cover errors of law or also errors of fact (1.). Then, as a subsequent issue, it must be assessed whether the review instance should only remand the dispute back to the first instance or correct the decision itself (2.). Finally, the introduction of time limits for the lodging of the appeal and the duration of the review procedure must be determined in order to maintain ISDS' swiftness (3.).

1. Scope of the Appeal

As identified by the UNCITRAL Secretariat, the choice must be made whether the instance of review should have the competence to scrutinise the first instance's decisions based on errors of fact.[144] This choice has also an immediate influence on the duration of the proceeding and thus raises concerns that an excessively wide scope of review would significantly increase costs and lead to delays.[145] In general, a second factual analysis would add to the thoroughness of the review. However, it could also negatively influence the duration of the proceedings because factual evidence might have to be taken at the appellate stage.[146] The assessment of legal errors is generally quicker than the assessment of factual errors, which becomes apparent when assessing the duration of the proceedings before the WTO's Appellate Body.[147] Therefore, a system in which the instance of review re-examines factual circumstances or remands the case back to the first instance would significantly prolong the proceedings compared to a purely legal review.

However, while the separation of errors of law and fact may seem sensible, practical concerns are raised with regard thereto as legal and fac-

---

144 UNCITRAL WG III, Appellate and multilateral court mechanisms, WP 185 (2019) (*n 111*), para 11.

145 Howse (*n 13*), 234; Zarra (*n 21*), 402.

146 Reinisch (*n 57*), 780.

147 UNCITRAL WG III, Appellate and multilateral court mechanisms, WP 185 (2019) (*n 111*), para 12. See also Lee (*n 3*), para 486.

tual issues are usually closely intertwined.[148] When examining this issue, the UNCITRAL Secretariat took into consideration the scope of appellate scrutiny under international criminal law and observed that the review of factual errors is frequently limited to those that 'occasioned a miscarriage of justice'.[149] Similarly, the review of legal issues is limited to those errors which would 'invalidat[e] the decision'.[150] This aligns with the practice in civil law as well as common law legal systems, in which final scrutiny is limited to questions of law and manifest errors in giving reasons.[151] In this context, the 'manifest error of fact' approach would grant the body of appeal the authority to assess whether the adjudicators in the first instance made an 'objectively reasonable assessment of the facts'.[152]

Restricting the factual and legal review to such extreme cases seems necessary to make sure that the review instance can resolve appeals within a tight timeframe and at a reasonable cost.[153] Therefore, it is suggested that formulations limiting the appeal to 'clear', 'serious' or 'manifest' errors of law or assessment of the facts would aid to define the balance of power between the first instance and the Appellate Body.[154] Nonetheless, there is consensus among scholars that the scope of review of the body of appeal should extend to issues of law and fact in order to guarantee a level of scrutiny that strengthens trust in a reformed ISDS system.[155]

Accordingly, *Bungenberg/Reinisch* suggest in Article 46 of their proposition for an MIC Statute that the grounds for appeal should include lack of jurisdiction of the MIC, excess of power, corruption of a judge, a serious departure from a fundamental rule of procedure, and failure to provide reasoning.[156] Moreover, the body of appeal within the MIC shall also have the power to review the decision of the first instance for errors in the application or interpretation of applicable law or manifest errors in the appreciation of the facts. Notably, the MIC Draft Statute only requires a manifest error in the appreciation of fact but not in the interpretation of

---

148 ibid.

149 ibid, paras 20, 21.

150 ibid.

151 ibid, para 18.

152 Sardinha (*n 12*), 642.

153 Howse (*n 13*), 234. Malmström *(n 56)*, 8.

154 UNCITRAL WG III, Appellate and multilateral court mechanisms, WP 185 (2019) *(n 111)*, para 19; Kaufmann-Kohler, Potestà (*n 6*), para 118.

155 Bungenberg, Reinisch, (*n 7*), para 357; Howse (*n 13*), 234; Sardinha (*n 12*), 643; UNCITRAL WG III, Appellate and multilateral court mechanisms, WP 185 (2019) (*n 111*), para 53.

156 Article 46 lit a-e MIC Draft Statute.

law.[157] This indicates that errors of law weigh heavier in light of the principle of the rule of law and do not have to be manifest. The UNCITRAL Secretariat leaves this differentiation in its Draft Provisions explicitly open. It suggests that the procedural rules for the body of appeal can allow review on the grounds of the violation of procedural or substantive protective standards.[158] With regard to the ICS system, CETA stipulates that grounds for appeal can be 'errors in the application or interpretation of applicable law' and 'manifest errors in the appreciation of the facts, including the appreciation of relevant domestic law'.[159]

However, the restrictions on the scope of review should be depending on whether a two-tiered MIC or the self-contained Appellate Body is chosen. If the adjudicators in the first instance are experienced in investment disputes and follow a uniform procedure, the need for thorough scrutiny of the first instance's decisions may be lower than that for ad hoc tribunals, which are constituted only for the purpose of resolving a single dispute, regardless of the adjudicators' individual high qualification.[160]

Additionally, likewise depending on the structure of the appellate mechanism, it must be addressed whether both issues of merits and procedure can be appealed.[161] The UNCITRAL Working Group III considered that not all procedural matters should be subject to appeal, as such a broad scope would overburden the appellate mechanism.[162] This especially excludes issues such as challenges to ISDS tribunal members and decisions on interim measures.[163]

157 Article 46 lit f-g MIC Draft Statute.

158 No 1 UNCITRAL Draft Provisions. Procedural protective standards are, inter alia, material and prejudicial errors of law, errors in the application or interpretation of the applicable law. Substantive protective standards are, inter alia, expropriation, fair and equitable treatment, and non-discrimination.

159 Article 2.28 (2) CETA.

160 Howse (*n 13*), 234.

161 UNCITRAL, 'Report of Working Group III (Investor-State Dispute Settlement Reform) on the work of its resumed thirty-eighth session' (28 January 2020), A/CN.9/1004/Add.1, para 31.

162 UNCITRAL, Report WG III, Resumed Session 38, A/CN.9/1004/Add.1 (2020) (*n 161*), para 31.

163 ibid, para 32.

2. The Issue of Remand

As part of the competence of the review instance, within either of the proposed structures, it must also be determined to what extent it can correct any mistakes found. The review instance could either have the authority to examine these issues *de novo* and modify the award accordingly or remand the case back to the first instance in cases of uncertainties regarding decisive facts of the case.[164] *De novo* review means that the review instance considers submissions of facts and law as if they were made for the first time, whereas a remand requires the tribunal in the first instance to take action again.[165] The answer to the question of which system is preferable depends on the impact on the overall duration of the procedure and the nature of the first instance.[166]

Such a separation between the first instance and the review instance may reduce both time and cost of further proceedings.[167] Such cost and time savings could be realised because each instance would have a distinct set of duties to focus on, such as fact-finding or legal review.

In general, however, scholars have demonstrated reluctance towards giving the review instance the power to refer cases back to the first instance in order to avoid delays to proceedings.[168] Particularly in the case of a standalone Appellate Body for ad hoc arbitral tribunals, it seems impractical to force an already dissolved tribunal to re-establish in order to render an improved decision based on the prerequisites named by the review instance.[169] But even in the case of a standing MIC, it is suggested that the appellate instance should only uphold, modify or reverse the decision of first instance.[170]

If there is no possibility to refer cases back to the first instance, it is evident that the principles of investigation, celerity, oral hearing, and transparency must also apply in the appellate stage. Facts and evidence

164 See options assessed in UNCITRAL, Report WG III, Resumed Session 38, A/CN.9/1004/Add.1 (2020) (*n 161*), paras 29, 30 and UNCITRAL WG III, Appellate and multilateral court mechanisms, WP 185 (2019) (*n 111*), para 19.

165 UNCITRAL Secretariat (*n 9*), para 19.

166 UNCITRAL WG III, Appellate and multilateral court mechanisms, WP 185 (2019) (*n 111*), para 24.

167 Legum (*n 19*), 442.

168 Bungenberg, Reinisch (*n 7*), para 350; Bottini (*n 22*), 469, 471; Lee (*n 3*), para 490.

169 UNCITRAL, Report WG III, Resumed Session 38, A/CN.9/1004/Add.1 (2020) (*n 161*), para 42.

170 See Article 47 (3) MIC Draft Statute; No 7 UNCITRAL Draft Provisions.

already submitted in the first instance should be taken into account.[171] Therefore, it seems most practical to equip the review instance with the authority to assess errors of fact on its own, thereby enabling it to render 'improved' decisions, instead of remanding them to the first instance.[172]

3. *Introduction of a Time Limit*

Each instance added in a dispute settlement system prolongs the proceedings significantly.[173] To limit this negative impact of an appeal on the parties to the dispute in terms of cost and time, the design of the procedure before the instance of review must consider the introduction of time limits. This includes the reduction of time-consuming aspects that do not add significant value to the overall outcome.

On the one hand, a deadline for the filing of the appeal should be set. It is suggested that the time period for lodging appeals should be limited to 30 to 90 days.[174] Such provisions can be found in a number of the EU's recent IPAs.[175]

On the other hand, it must be determined whether the procedural rules should set a time limit for the duration of the appeal procedure. The Draft Provisions of the UNCITRAL Secretariat recommend the introduction of a time limit, but do not specify its extent.[176] In a number of recently concluded investment treaties, the Parties agreed on a timeline of 180 days for the review instance to render its decision, starting from the commencement of the proceedings.[177] Drawing once again from the WTO Dispute Settlement Procedure, an even shorter duration of the review procedure is

---

171 Bungenberg, Reinisch (*n 7*), para 352.

172 Bottini (*n 22*), 469, 471.

173 Langford, Behn, and Malaguti (*n 16*), 21, suggest a standing tribunal with no appellate mechanism. The wider the Appellate Body's scope of review, the longer the proceedings will be. On the other hand, the authors consider that no time would be lost if an annulment tribunal comparable to the ICSID system was established.

174 Bungenberg, Reinisch (*n 7*), para 347 and Article 47 (1) MIC Draft Statute.

175 See Article 8.28 (9) (a) CETA; Article 3.54 (1) EU-Vietnam IPA; Article 3.19 (1) EU-Singapore IPA. See also Sardinha (*n 12*), 646.

176 No 11 UNCITRAL Draft Provisions.

177 Article 3.54 (5) EU-Vietnam IPA; Article 3.19 (5) EU-Singapore IPA. See also Kułaga (*n 19*), 132.

possible. It could be limited to a maximum of 60 days for regular and 90 days for extraordinary cases.[178]

The duration of the review process can further be influenced significantly by the design of the parties' procedural rights, the scope of review and whether there is a standing panel or the appointment of adjudicators is still required.[179] The duration of the review process can also be influenced by the timeframe in which such procedural rights can be exercised. As an example, if the scope of review includes challenges to the jurisdiction of the adjudicative body, the appellants should be able to lodge their appeals immediately after the decision on jurisdiction was rendered. Having to wait until a decision on the merits is rendered, would unnecessarily increase costs and duration of the proceedings.[180]

It must further be determined which party or participant in the proceedings should have the right to appeal. Some authors consider a limitation of the right to appeal to the respondent States in order to reduce frivolous arbitration proceedings by foreign investors. This raises immediate concerns regarding the rule of law.[181] With respect to the intervention of third parties in the proceedings, authors tend to be in favour of allowing *amicus curiae* briefs by third parties with a substantial interest in the outcome, such as the European Commission or NGOs.[182] Whether such third parties should also be granted the right to appeal a decision of the first instance is generally left unanswered.[183] However, it must be asked if there is any substantial benefit to the correctness of the award from such third-party-appeals or whether it might just add to the duration of the proceedings against the parties' will. Additionally, any participation of third parties would jeopardise the short standard duration for dispute settlement procedures envisioned by the EU's recently concluded treaties.[184]

---

178 Section 17.5 Annex 2 WTO Agreement (Understanding on rules and procedures governing the settlement of disputes - DSU).

179 See Sections C.I and C.II.

180 UNCITRAL Secretariat (*n 9*), para 21.

181 Lee (*n 3*), 485.

182 Bungenberg, Reinisch (*n 7*), para 345.

183 See Bungenberg, Reinisch (*n 7*), para 345.

184 See for a comment on the duration of arbitral proceedings Sardinha (*n 12*), 635.

III. "Takeaways" for the Creation of an Appeal Mechanism

In case States route for the introduction of a centralised appeal mechanism, they have to decide between the MIC or the standalone Appellate Body. The MIC gives ISDS a firmer institutional and procedural structure and diminishes legitimacy concerns, such as double-hatting. However, there is no empirical proof that MIC adjudicators would render more consistent decisions than adjudicators in a standalone Appellate Body. Notwithstanding this, the Appellate Body seems to face fewer practical hurdles with regard to State support, both financially and from a cooperation standpoint in the implementation process. Regarding the procedural design, the newly reformed appellate mechanism must balance between maintaining the swiftness of ISDS and adjudicators producing a 'correct' decision. The analysis has demonstrated that it seems most preferable to allow the appellate instance to review both issues of law and fact in cases of manifest error. Adjudicators of the appellate instance may, however, not refer cases back to the first instance but may only uphold, modify, or reverse rendered decisions. To minimise the effect on the duration of ISDS procedures, tight but realistic time limitations should be implemented procedural-wise.

D. Conclusion

From a procedural point of view, bilateral treaties must have clear rules as to whether the reformed appellate mechanism applies and what the specific requirements for appeals are.[185] The EU already announced that the MIC would replace the bilateral ICS included in EU trade and investment agreements so far.[186] Such a step must also be taken with regard to other ISDS provisions in BITs or national law. States must set out clear rules of conflict to regulate possible collision between the proceedings before the uniform appellate mechanism and other review proceedings, like the ICSID annulment procedure or the challenges before domestic courts.[187] These rules must be set out in the treaty establishing the appellate mech-

---

185 Lee (*n 3*), paras 491, 495.

186 European Commission, 'The Multilateral Investment Court Project' <http://trade.ec.europa.eu/doclib/ press/index.cfm?id=1608> accessed 13 January 2022. See for example Article 8.29 CETA.

187 UNCITRAL Secretariat (*n 9*), para 9.

anism and may have to be incorporated into domestic law by States, in order to avoid loopholes and legal uncertainty.[188]

With regard to reform options, one must bear in mind that they are not exclusive but can be implemented jointly. As an example, the dual function of the International Court of Justice (ICJ) is taken into consideration when assessing the scope of the appellate mechanism's competence.[189] On one hand, the ICJ settles disputes within its jurisdiction.[190] On the other hand, however, the ICJ may also be called upon by UN organs or authorised entities for an advisory opinion.[191] ICJ decisions have also become a reference point for other judicial bodies operating in international law. Given that a newly formed dispute settlement body of either presented format would constitute authority in investment law, its decisions may not only contribute to legal certainty in cases falling under its jurisdiction but also act as guidance for other bodies interpreting international investment law.[192]

Therefore, both a preliminary ruling procedure and a plenary (en-banc) determination as an alternative to a built-in appeal are considered. These two procedures could be combined with an annulment mechanism restricted to serious procedural violations, excess of jurisdiction and issues of impartiality of the tribunal. Taken together, annulment in conjunction with preliminary rulings and/or en banc determinations could serve as an alternative to an appeal mechanism.[193] However, for such a solution to work, it would have to be ensured that ad hoc arbitral tribunals are entitled to make submissions and will comply with decisions.[194] Correspondingly, States would have to create in their reform efforts the legal framework for ad hoc tribunals to have the right to submit preliminary

188 Gabrielle Kaufmann-Kohler and Michele Potestà, *Investor State Dispute Settlement and National Courts. Current Framework and Reform Options* (Springer 2020), paras 185, 186.

189 Butler (*n 10*), 364.

190 Pursuant to Article 36 International Court of Justice Statute (ICJ Statute) (1945) 33 UNTS 993 '[t]he jurisdiction of the Court comprises all cases which the parties refer to it and all matters specially provided for in the Charter of the United Nations or in treaties and conventions in force'.

191 Pursuant to Article 64 ICJ Statute '[t]he Court may give an advisory opinion on any legal question at the request of whatever body may be authorized by or in accordance with the Charter of the United Nations to make such a request'.

192 Bottini (*n 22*), 468.

193 Kaufmann-Kohler, Potestà (*n 6*), para 125. See Section B.II.2.

194 See Section B.II.2.a).

questions. Non-compliance with these decisions would then have to constitute some ground of challenge of the arbitral award.

In the discussions about creating legal certainty through increased consistency in decision-making, the main advantages of the current ISDS system must be kept in mind. Today's ISDS system offers flexibility, a high degree of party autonomy, finality of awards and an advanced enforcement system.[195] It follows that at least three questions need to be addressed. The first question is whether and to which extent a multilateral review process would weaken the finality of arbitral awards. If such a process is considered necessary or useful, different options such as appeal, annulment or preliminary ruling are possible. Once the type of review process is clear, the scope and standard of review have to be considered. Finally, it needs to be decided whether such multilateral review process should be implemented as a built-in or standalone mechanism. The answer to all these questions should reflect a sound compromise between consistency and correctness of decisions on the one hand and efficiency and flexibility of the proceedings on the other.

With regard to legitimacy and transparency concerns, it can be argued that creating an MIC would be most advantageous, as investment disputes would be decided by State-appointed adjudicators in accordance with strict and pre-determined procedural rules. However, it is also the most demanding reform option because it completely overhauls the current ISDS system. The MIC also faces serious practical and political issues as it requires a high degree of consensus among States and is at the same time prone to potential sabotage by Contracting States, as seen recently with the WTO dispute settlement mechanism.[196] Moreover, a standing court or tribunal will have to be funded by Contracting States. If they do not offer sufficient funding, the MIC might be staffed with too few adjudicators to handle the caseload in an appropriate period of time.[197] In comparison, the standalone Appellate Body would be less intrusive as the parties are free to agree on their ad hoc proceedings as they wish. Additionally, the Appellate

---

195 Benedetti, Juan (*n 1*), 89, 90.

196 In 2019, the USA threatened to delay the appointment of judges, which would have effectively shut down the WTO Appellate System, see Tom Miles, 'U.S. blocks WTO judge reappointment as dispute settlement crisis looms' (Reuters, 27 August 2018) <https://www.reuters.com/article/us-usa-trade-wto-idUSKCN1LC19O> accessed 13 January 2022. See also De Luca et al (*n 2*), 406.

197 UNCITRAL, Report WG III, Resumed Session 38, A/CN.9/1004/Add.1 (2020) (*n 161*), 14, 15; Langford, Behn, and Malaguti (*n 16*), 19; Heideman (*n 38*), 19.

Body is more cost-efficient as it lacks a standing first instance.[198] Another practical aspect is that the Appellate Body could (arguably) be established by amending the Annulment Committee under the ICSID Convention.[199] This, however, would still require a change of the appointment procedure from ad hoc appointments to permanent adjudicators.[200] The Appellate Body also offers the option to combine the judicial ex-post review with the ex-ante alternatives of preliminary rulings and/or en-banc decisions. Nonetheless, it can be argued that an ex-post review is not needed if ad hoc tribunals are given the opportunity to request a preliminary ruling from a standing body of experienced adjudicators with high reputation. This option of a preliminary ruling would also be the least intrusive since the current ISDS system would only have to be supplemented by a free-standing body that pre-determines questions of law with binding effect.

Hence, the most practical and feasible reform option would be an Appellate Body in the form of a permanent tribunal to which ad hoc tribunals may submit questions for preliminary determination but that may also – in cases of extraordinary errors of law and fact – review and, if necessary, amend the ad hoc awards rendered under its jurisdiction[201].

---

198 See Bottini (*n 22*), 471, 472.

199 ICSID Secretariat (*n 57*), paras 20-23; Bungenberg, Reinisch (*n 7*), paras 497-498; Kaufmann-Kohler, Potestà (*n 6*), paras 244, 245; Reinisch (*n 57*), 780.

200 Pursuant to Article 52 (3) ICSID Convention, three arbitrators from a pre-determined Panel of Arbitrators are appointed to the ad hoc Annulment Committee. In contrast, the MIC or Appellate Body would require an appointment for a fixed term regardless of the individual case, see Bungenberg, Reinisch (*n 7*), para 55; Kaufmann-Kohler, Potestà (*n 6*), para 85.

201 Advocating for an Appellate Body without considering preliminary rulings: Bottini (*n 22*), 467, 473; Lee (*n 3*), para 495.

Chapter 5: Mass Investment Claims in the ISDS Reform Process: Promoting Procedural Efficiency and the Rights of Individuals and Small and Medium-Sized Enterprises

*by Petyo Nikolov**

Selected Bibliography: Manish Aggarwal and Simon Maynard, 'Investment Treaty Arbitration Post-*Abaclat*: Towards a Taxonomy of 'Mass' Claims' (2014) 3.3 Cambridge Journal of International and Comparative Law (CJICL), 825; Sandrine Giroud and Sam Moss, 'Mass Claims Processes under Public International Law' in Eva Lein et al (eds), *Collective Redress in Europe: Why and How?* (British Institute for International & Comparative Law 2015), 481; Marine Koenig, 'Mass Proceedings in the Investor-State Arbitration Setting' (2019) 1.1 ITA in Review, 33; Friedrich Rosenfeld, 'Mass Claims in International Law' (2013) 4.1 Journal of International Dispute Settlement, 159; Stacy I Strong, *Class, Mass, and Collective Arbitration in National and International Law* (OUP 2013).

A. Introduction

The plurality of claimants in a single international investment claim is not uncommon anymore. According to a survey conducted in 2017, 46% of the pending cases were initiated by more than one claimant.[1] No jurisdictional or other objections had typically been expressed based on the plural-

* Petyo Nikolov is Research Fellow at the International Investment Law Centre Cologne (IILCC). This Chapter is based on the author's LLM thesis. The author is grateful to Professor Christian Borris (thesis supervisor) for helpful comments on the drafts.

1 Jeffery Commission and Rahim Moloo, *Procedural Issues in International Investment Arbitration* (OUP 2018), 9.69. Despite the limited empirical evidence, similar tendency is observed in international commercial arbitration too, see Gary Born, *International Commercial Arbitration* (Kluwer Law International 2014), 2566.

ity of claimants of the same nationality.[2] Cases where the claims arise out of the same investment, such as multiple shareholders claims, also usually did not pose any problems on this matter.[3] This has drastically changed since the jurisdiction of the tribunals in *Abaclat v Argentina*, *Alemanni v Argentina*, and *Ambiente v Argentina* cases[4] – also called the 'Argentinean Trilogy'[5] – regarding their capability of adjudicating disputes with respectively 60,000 (initially 180,000), 74 (initially 183) and 90 (initially 119) claimants in a single claim was challenged.[6] Before that, no mass claims in international investment arbitration were publicly known.[7] Up to that point, the cases filed with the ICSID had involved more than one claimant and were therefore handled as 'traditional' multi-party arbitrations.[8]

During, but also in the aftermath of the aforementioned disputes, serious concern was expressed about the possibility of dealing with claims brought by such a high number of claimants, since both the applicable bilateral investment treaties (BITs) and the ICSID Convention are silent on the capability of administering claims with multiple claimants.[9] Even if all three tribunals in these cases decided consistently in favour of the

---

2 Marine Koenig, 'Mass Proceedings in the Investor-State Arbitration Setting' (2019) 1.1 ITA in Review 33, 38.

3 Campbell McLachlan, Laurence Shore, and Matthew Weininger, *International Investment Arbitration* (OUP 2017), 4.206.

4 *Abaclat and others v Argentine Republic* ICSID Case No. ARB/07/5; *Giovanni Alemanni and others v Argentine Republic* ICSID Case No. ARB/07/8; *Ambiente Ufficio S.p.A. and others v Argentine Republic* ICSID Case No. ARB/08/9.

5 Koenig *(n 2)*, 33, 34.

6 Eloïse Obadia, 'Mass Arbitrations in International Investment Cases: Introductory Remarks' in Bernard Hanotiau and Eric Schwartz (eds), *Class and Group Actions in Arbitration* (Kluwer Law International 2016), 105, 108.

7 Summary of the factual background of *Abaclat v Argentina* is provided in Manish Aggarwal and Simon Maynard, 'Investment Treaty Arbitration Post-*Abaclat*: Towards a Taxonomy of 'Mass' Claims' (2014) 3.3 Cambridge Journal of International and Comparative Law (CJICL) 825, 828 et seq. See also Siegfried Wiessner, 'Democratizing International Arbitration? Mass Claims Proceedings in Abaclat v. Argentina' (2014) 1.1 Journal of International and Comparative Law 55, 57-60.

8 Commission, Moloo *(n 1)*, 9.67.

9 Koenig *(n 2)*, 33, 52 et seq; Katarzyna Barbara Sczcudlik, 'Mass Claims under ICSID' (2014) 4.2 Wroclaw Review of Law, Administration & Economics 70, 85 et seq; Jennifer Permesly and Meredith Craven, 'Where Are We Now? Investment Treaty Arbitration, Sovereign Debt, and Mass Claims in the Post-Abaclat Era' (2018) 15.1 Transnational Dispute Management 1, 6; Relja Radović, 'Problematizing *Abaclat's* Mass Claims Investment Arbitration Using Domestic Class Actions' (2017-2018) 4 McGill Journal of Dispute Resolution 1, 12 et seq; Veijo Aulis Heiskanen, 'Mass Claims in ICSID Arbitration' in Meg Kinnear et al (eds), *Building*

claimants on this matter, it seems that serious doubts remain about the suitability of these legal instruments to govern such claims. When reforming existing or drafting new regimes for the settlement of investment disputes, lessons should be drawn from the 'Argentinean Trilogy' in regard to claims brought by such a high number of claimants.

Against this background, the following chapter shall examine whether multi-party and mass claim procedures should be included when establishing a permanent Multilateral Investment Court (MIC)[10]. It is argued that, on the one hand, they will contribute to the enhancement of the procedural efficiency of investor-State dispute settlement (ISDS) proceedings. On the other hand, they will also strengthen the rights of individuals and small and medium-sized enterprises (SMEs) in the international investment law regime. Before delving into the complex issues raised by the procedural devices of multi-party and mass claims in ISDS (C.), some terminological difficulties must be clarified (B.). After the approach to multi-party and mass claims in the practice of investment tribunals is discussed, it shall be ascertained whether there is necessity for regulation (D.), and whether the inclusion of such claims in an MIC Statute would be beneficial for the MIC system and its stakeholders (E.). The analysis then turns to the issue of finding the most appropriate method to implement multi-party arbitration and mass claims in the MIC system (F.). In conclusion, the findings of this chapter shall be summarised briefly (G.).

International Investment Law: The First 50 Years of ICSID (Kluwer Law International 2015), 613, 619; Aggarwal, Maynard *(n 7)*, 825, 839 et seq.

10 For a profound analysis of how such an MIC could be designed, see Marc Bungenberg and August Reinisch, *From Bilateral Arbitral Tribunals and Investment Courts to a Multilateral Investment Court – Options Regarding the Institutionalization of Investor-State Dispute Settlement* (Springer 2019). UNCITRAL, Working Group III, 'Possible reform of investor-State dispute settlement (ISDS) – Multilateral instrument on ISDS Reform' (16 January 2020), A/CN.9/WG.III/WP.194, para 38: '[…] the Working Group may wish to note that it is feasible to develop a multilateral instrument that would apply the reforms in a coherent and flexible manner'. For other approaches by Gabrielle Kaufmann-Kohler and Michele Potestà: 'Can the Mauritius Convention serve as a model for the reform of a permanent investment tribunal or an appeal mechanism?' CIDS 2016; 'The Composition of a Multilateral Investment Court and of an Appeal Mechanism for Investment Awards' CIDS Supplemental Report 2017.

B. Terminological Conundrum

This chapter focuses on the situation in which multiple claimants bring their claims before one single tribunal as a coordinated group. [11] In this regard, the differentiation between multi-party and mass claims proves especially unclear.[12] A multi-party arbitration is deemed to be given when at least three parties are involved. The term *mass claim* has been used to describe a much higher number of claimants which are resolved jointly because of the similarity of the issues.[13] However, this definition leaves many questions in the blur, in particular, as to about the precise number of claimants which should be involved in an investment arbitration to confer mass character on a multi-party arbitration – several dozen, hundreds, thousands, hundreds of thousands etc?[14] As the tribunals in the Argentinean cases implied by cautiously rejecting pre-existing terminology, however, the characterisation of the proceedings as multi-party or mass does not assist in assessing whether investment arbitration is the suitable place for disputes with a large number of claimants bringing a single claim.[15] Even though it is generally considered that the number of claimants in *Alemanni* and *Ambiente* was insufficient to constitute mass claims,[16] the

11 It should be noted that the present chapter does not deal with consolidation. Typically, in the situation of multi-party and mass claims, the parties agree on collectively filing a single claim against the respective respondent or multiple respondents, whereas 'consolidation is defined as the joinder of two or more proceedings that already are pending before different courts or arbitral tribunals.' Gabrielle Kaufmann-Kohler et al, 'Consolidation of Proceedings in Investment Arbitration: How Can Multiple Proceedings Arising from the Same or Related Situations Be Handled Efficiently?' (2006) 21.1 ICSID Review 59, 64. Basically, the simplest criterion to make precise distinction between the concepts of multi-party claims and consolidation is the relevant time of action. See eg McLachlan, Shore, and Weininger *(n 3)*, 4.201.

12 Stacy I Strong, *Class, Mass, and Collective Arbitration in National and International Law* (OUP 2013), 3.10 et seq. See also Carolyn B Lamm, Eckhard R Hellbeck, and Onur Saka, 'Mass Claims in Investment Arbitration: Jurisdiction and Admissibility' in Bernard Hanotiau and Eric Schwartz (eds), *Class and Group Actions in Arbitration* (Kluwer Law International 2016), 114, 116.

13 Lamm, Hellbeck, and Saka *(n 12)*, 114, 115.

14 Commission, Moloo *(n 1)*, 9.68. See also Sandrine Giroud and Sam Moss, 'Mass Claims Processes under Public International Law' in Eva Lein et al (eds), *Collective Redress in Europe: Why and How?* (British Institute for International & Comparative Law 2015) 481, 493.

15 Koenig *(n 2)*, 33, 37. See also McLachlan, Shore, and Weininger *(n 3)*, 4.208; Obadia *(n 6)*, 105, 106-107.

16 Giroud, Moss *(n 14)*, 481, 498.

nature of the claims and the underlying issues in the proceedings of all three cases were similar to a very high degree.[17] Some argue further, that the proceedings in *Abaclat* are in fact not purely mass, as the cases were not decided individually.[18] Thus, the Argentinean Trilogy 'appear[s] to be a new form of multiparty proceeding, which raises questions about the alleged novelty of the debate about mass proceedings.'[19] Therefore, the mass proceedings procedure developed in the Argentinean Trilogy is rightly regarded as 'the heir of multiparty arbitrations'[20]. Accordingly, from that point on, multi-party and mass claims in investment arbitration shall be discussed only together as one singular procedural device (*uniting approach*)[21]. For the sake of convenience, the term *mass investment claims* will be used in this chapter.

At this point, it should also be noted that there is a widespread consensus that the *multi* or *mass* element is of rather descriptive than normative nature.[22] Accordingly, the plurality of claims could pose difficulties on almost every stage of the tribunal's decision-making: its jurisdiction, admissibility of the claims, and the decision on the merits. Consequently, the tribunals in the Argentinean Trilogy structured their decisions differently because of the matter of mass investment claims. For instance, the approach developed by the *Abaclat* tribunal of drawing a clear line between jurisdiction and admissibility was not adopted by the tribunals in the other two Argentinean cases.[23]

17 Heiskanen *(n 9)*, 613, 620. See also Koenig *(n 2)*, 33, 39.

18 Hans van Houtte and Bridie McAsey, 'Case Comment Abaclat and others v Argentine Republic, ICSID, the BIT and Mass Claims' (2012) 27.2 ICSID Review 231, 231-233. It should be noted that a 'traditional mass claims process (TMCP) is characterized by a numerosity of claims which have some commonality of legal and factual issues but which are decided individually.'

19 Koenig *(n 2)*, 33, 38.

20 ibid, 33, 59.

21 Such approach is used by the jurisdictions of Ontario (Canada) and Australia. They make class actions and multi-party suits indistinguishable by determining a very low number of claimants involved to be sufficient to form a class (respectively 2 and 7). Cf Strong *(n 12)*, 3.17.

22 Koenig *(n 2)*, 33, 38-39; Heiskanen *(n 9)*, 613, 621. See also *Theodoros Adamakopoulos and others v Republic of Cyprus* ICSID Case No. ARB/15/49 Decision on Jurisdiction, 7 February 2020, para 191.

23 Lamm, Hellbeck, and Saka *(n 12)*, 114, 114-115.

C. Status quo in International Investment Law

In the absence of relevant provisions regarding mass investment claims in the investment arbitration legal framework, the respective case law must be analysed. As the Argentinean cases have already been discussed widely elsewhere, [24] they will not be repeated here, rather only the main issues will be outlined. This approach is also applied here to the recent decision on jurisdiction in *Adamakopoulos v Cyprus*[25] concerning 950 claimants because this chapter is not the appropriate place to discuss it in detail.

I. Paucity of Provisions in International Investment Agreements

Because of the silence of both investment treaties concluded between States (International Investment Agreements - IIAs)[26] and the ICSID Convention[27], serious concern was expressed about the capability of administering claims with multiple claimants in the dissenting opinions[28] in all

---

24 Koenig *(n 2)*, 33-60; Giroud, Moss *(n 14)*, 481, 498-503; van Houtte, McAsey *(n 18)*, 231-236; Sczcudlik *(n 9)*, 70, 84-93; Wiessner *(n 7)*, 55-83; Permesly, Craven *(n 9)*, 1, 6 and 10; Radović *(n 9)*, 1-21; Heiskanen *(n 9)*, 613-626; Aggarwal, Maynard *(n 7)*, 825-852; Lamm, Hellbeck, and Saka *(n 12)*, 114-124.

25 *Adamakopoulos v Cyprus*, Decision on Jurisdiction *(n 22)*.

26 Within the international investment law regime, there are basically three different legal mechanisms which confer substantive protection to foreign investors and usually contain an arbitration clause: IIAs, Investor-State contracts and national investment laws. In the present context, the major focus is put on IIAs as they form the centrepiece of the regime. Theoretically, under certain circumstances claims based on different legal mechanisms for investment protection can be combined in a single multi-party or mass arbitration. However, such scenarios are much less likely than joining many claims resulting from one or more IIAs.

27 Other arbitration rules being used for the settlement of investment disputes such as the UNCITRAL Arbitration Rules and the ICC Arbitration Rules are also silent on the matter of mass investment claims. Still, Article 8 (1) ICC Arbitration Rules (2021), for instance, expressly admits 'arbitration with multiple parties'. However, it is not absolutely clear if Article 8 (1) is applicable to mass investment claims at least for two reasons. First, the provision is primarily designed for commercial arbitration ('claims may be made by any party against any other party'). Second, the term 'multiple' does not necessarily mean *mass*; a restrictive interpretation of the term may exclude mass claims from the scope of Article 8 (1).

28 *Abaclat and others v Argentine Republic* ICSID Case No. ARB/07/5 Dissenting Opinion of Georges Abi-Saab, 28 October 2011; *Giovanni Alemanni and others v Argentine Republic* ICSID Case No. ARB/07/8 Concurring Opinion of J Christopher Thomas QC, 17 November 2014; *Ambiente Ufficio S.p.A. and others v Argen-*

four cases as well as by many commentators[29]. It was reported that the ICSID Secretariat intended to develop rules and procedures for multi-party disputes, but such plans have not been implemented in practice so far.[30] Conversely, though the negotiations of the Transatlantic Trade and Investment Partnership (TTIP) came to a dead end, the European Union's proposal for Investment Protection and Resolution of Investment Disputes was one of the rare cases where an agreement contained a provision accounting for mass, class or collective claims, namely by putting a ban on class actions.[31] Until a sound legal framework regarding mass investment claims is established, they may become one of the new major jurisdictional battlegrounds in investment treaty arbitration, since they are considered as 'one of the most noteworthy developments of investment law over the past decade'[32].

II. Consent

In ICSID arbitration, the consent of the parties to the arbitration is 'an indispensable requirement for a tribunal's jurisdiction'[33]. Pursuant to Article 25 (1) ICSID Convention, each party to a dispute must consent in writing in order for the dispute to be submitted to ICSID arbitration. Within the framework of investment treaty arbitration, consent is perfected when the investor accepts the offer of consent contained in an IIA concluded between the host and home State ('Arbitration without Privity'[34]). Therefore, each of the claimants desiring to participate in a mass investment arbitration must individually consent to arbitration. The dissenting arbitrators in

tine Republic ICSID Case No. ARB/08/9 Dissenting Opinion of Santiago Torres Bernárdez, 2 May 2013; *Theodoros Adamakopoulos and others v Republic of Cyprus* ICSID Case No. ARB/15/49, Statement of Dissent of Marcelo G Kohen, 3 February 2020.

29 See *(n 9)*.

30 *Alemanni v Argentina*, Concurring Opinion *(n 28)*, para 4.

31 Cf Article 6.5. of the Proposal, available at <https://trade.ec.europa.eu/doclib/docs/2015/november/ tradoc_153955.pdf> accessed 13 January 2022.

32 Koenig *(n 2)*, 33, 33.

33 Rudolf Dolzer and Christoph Schreuer, *Principles of International Investment Law* (OUP 2012), 254.

34 Jan Paulsson, 'Arbitration Without Privity' (1995) 10.2 ICSID Review 232-257.

Abaclat[35] and *Ambiente*[36] as well as some commentators[37] argued, however, that such an approach is insufficient due to the fundamental difference between regular bilateral arbitration and mass investment arbitration. Because the ICSID Convention is silent on this issue, they additionally require explicit consent not only to arbitration of the dispute but also to the procedure to be used in it (secondary consent)[38] in order to conduct mass investment proceedings.[39]

In principle, there is no need for secondary consent solely based on the plurality of claimants. After all, the State's standing offer is not limited to a particular number of claimants. Unlike an arbitration clause in a standard commercial contract, offers to arbitrate in investment treaties are inherently directed not only to particular individual investors, but to all investors that are nationals of one of the other contracting States.[40] Accordingly, an indefinite number of investors should be able to accept this offer.[41] If one shareholder holding 100,000 shares is entitled to consent to investment arbitration, it should be equally possible for 100,000 shareholders each holding one share to do the same.[42] Hence, mass investment claims are a sheer consequence of the general and abstract nature of consent in investment treaty arbitration.[43] In this context, the *Abaclat* majority noted that, since it confirmed its jurisdiction over individual claimants, it was difficult to see how it could lose 'such jurisdiction where the number of Claimants outgrows a certain threshold'[44]. In addition, the use of singular terms such as *investor* and *dispute* in IIAs and the ICSID Convention also does not provide a sound basis for the necessity of a secondary consent, since the

---

35 *Abaclat v Argentina*, Dissenting Opinion *(n 28)*, paras 173-175.

36 *Ambiente v Argentina*, Dissenting Opinion *(n 28)*, para 103.

37 Szczudlik *(n 8)*, 70, 94-96.

38 This term is discussed in detail in Strong *(n 12)*, 3.118 et seq.

39 See eg *Abaclat v Argentina*, Dissenting Opinion *(n 28)*, paras 173-175.

40 Andrew Newcombe, 'Mass claims and the distinction between jurisdiction and admissibility' (2011) Kluwer Arbitration Blog <http://arbitrationblog.kluwerarbitration.com/2011/12/16/mass-claims-and-the-distinction-between-jurisdiction-and-admissibility-part-ii/> accessed 13 January 2022. See also Heiskanen *(n 9)*, 613, 619.

41 Newcombe *(n 40)*. See also Aggarwal, Maynard *(n 7)*, 825, 835; Lukas Vanhonnaeker, *Shareholders' Claims for Reflective Loss in International Investment Law* (CUP 2020), 328.

42 Newcombe *(n 40)*. In a similar way argues Friedrich Rosenfeld, 'Mass Claims in International Law' (2013) 4.1 Journal of International Dispute Settlement 159, 174.

43 Heiskanen *(n 9)*, 613, 619.

44 *Abaclat and others v Argentine Republic* ICSID Case No. ARB/07/5 Decision on Jurisdiction and Admissibility, 4 August 2011, para 490.

use of these terms in singular often implies the plural and *vice versa*.[45] Nevertheless, in order to avoid any misinterpretations, treaty drafters should use the plural form when explicitly liberalising mass claims in future legal instruments regarding investment disputes.

III. Interpretation of Silence

Interpreting the silence of IIAs and the ICSID regime on the matter of mass investment claims is closely related to the issue of consent and raises major difficulties. In this regard, the two suggested approaches reflect the general question in international investment law of how much investment protection through IIAs is both needed and desirable.[46] On the one hand, the 'sovereigntist approach' ensures the States' right to regulate[47] and sets limits to their exposure to investment claims.[48] As a consequence, leaving out mass investment claims of the ICSID framework should be interpreted as qualified silence.[49] On the other hand, the 'liberal internationalist approach' supports the proposition that international investment law primarily aims at enhancing the freedom of capital movements by providing a secure and predictable investment climate.[50] Following this, the ICSID Convention's silence on the possibility of adjudicating mass investment claims should be interpreted not as a restriction on such claims, but merely as indicating a gap, which the tribunal is free to fill within the limits of the ICSID Convention.[51] The latter approach should prevail in this situation. As indicated by the *Abaclat* tribunal, it was fully aware that such course of action could diminish the rights of the parties to the dispute to some extent.[52] However, the alternative of each claimant bringing an indi-

45 See eg *Ambiente Ufficio S.p.A. and others v Argentine Republic* ICSID Case No. ARB/08/9 Decision on Jurisdiction and Admissibility, 8 February 2013, para 99.

46 Koenig *(n 2)*, 33, 60.

47 Cf Aikaterini Titi, *The Right to Regulate in International Investment Law* (Nomos 2014).

48 Koenig *(n 2)*, 33, 60. In the context of treaty interpretation, this approach is also known as the *in dubio mitius* principle. See Markus Petsche, 'Restrictive Interpretation of Investment Treaties: A Critical Analysis of Arbitral Case Law' (2020) 37.1 Journal of International Arbitration 1-26.

49 Heiskanen *(n 9)*, 613, 619.

50 Koenig *(n 2)*, 33, 60.

51 Permesly, Craven *(n 9)*, 1, 6.

52 *Adamakopoulos v Cyprus*, Decision on Jurisdiction *(n 22)*, para 228.

vidual claim would lead to denial of justice.[53] Accordingly, the exclusion of mass investment claims 'would be shocking given that the investment at stake is protected under the BIT, which expressly provides for ICSID jurisdiction and arbitration'[54].

IV. Link between Claims

In order to proceed mass investment claims in a single arbitration, the tribunals in the aforementioned cases presupposed that a genuine link (*homogeneity*) between the claims exists. The requirement of homogeneity is satisfied where the interests represented on each side of the dispute are 'in all essential respects identical'[55]. By establishing identity of interest, it enables both the aggregation of claims, and ensures that the respondent State is not exposed to claims which substantially differ from the interest supposed to be vindicated.[56] In the *Argentinean Trilogy* of cases, the homogeneity requirement did not seem to pose considerable difficulties for the tribunals since in each case, the source of consent (Italy-Argentina BIT), the measures affecting the investors (measures taken by Argentina in the aftermath of the 2001 financial crisis), and the type of investment (government bonds) were the same. The sole difference of the *Adamakopoulos* case – namely the investors' reliance on two different BITs[57] – did not prevent the tribunal from affirming the homogeneity of the claims since the two BITs were also 'essentially the same'[58].[59] However, the tribunals failed to establish a more precise general standard or threshold which has to be

53 *Abaclat v Argentina*, Decision on Jurisdiction *(n 44)*, para 537.

54 ibid, para 537. In a similar way argue Lamm, Hellbeck, and Saka *(n 12)*, 114, 121.

55 *Giovanni Alemanni and others v Argentine Republic* ICSID Case No. ARB/07/8 Decision on Jurisdiction and Admissibility, 17 November 2014, para 292.

56 McLachlan, Shore, and Weininger *(n 3)*, 4.214.

57 The issue of applicable law in such situations is discussed in Vanhonnaeker *(n 41)*, 334 et seq.

58 *Adamakopoulos v Cyprus*, Decision on Jurisdiction *(n 22)*, para 213.

59 Other cases where the tribunal dismissed the Respondents' objection that they did not consent to a single arbitration in which claimants invoked breaches of different IIAs but arising from the same investment dispute: *Flughafen Zürich A.G. and Gestión e Ingenería IDC S.A. v Bolivarian Republic of Venezuela* ICSID Case No. ARB/10/19 Award, 18 November 2014; *Noble Energy, Inc. and Machalapower Cia. Ltda. v The Republic of Ecuador and Consejo Nacional de Electricidad* ICSID Case No. ARB/05/12 Decision on Jurisdiction, 5 March 2008.

fulfilled by future groups of multiple investors.[60] It is, therefore, to expect that tribunals will continue to apply the homogeneity test by weighting the similarities and differences between the claims.[61] The refusal of several tribunals[62] to collectively adjudicate claims brought by multiple unrelated claimants highlights the importance of an in-depth examination of homogeneity as a prerequisite to mass investment claims.[63] In order to obtain consistency to some extent, a homogeneity test should be stipulated in the provisions liberalising mass investment claims in future legal instruments regarding investment disputes.

V. *Procedures, Techniques, and Hybridity of Proceedings*

Admittedly, the regulatory framework of investment treaty arbitration has not been designed to deal with mass investment claims.[64] In particular, the ICSID regime does not contain any specific provisions stipulating the procedural steps and techniques needed by tribunals in order to conduct arbitrations involving a large number of claimants.[65] Nevertheless, the tribunal in *Adamakopoulos*, for instance, found that a mass investment arbitration could be managed within the existing ICSID framework without any adaptions.[66] Whereas that might be true for proceedings with around 1,000 claimants, the manageability of proceedings with, for example, 60,000 claimants takes on a whole different dimension. The decision on jurisdiction in *Abaclat* is therefore considered ground-breaking in a number of ways, but mostly for the tribunal's procedural adaptations to make mass investment arbitrations work in the ICSID regime.[67] Accordingly, the tribunal invoked Article 44 ICSID Convention and Rule 19 ICSID Arbitration Rules which provided the legal basis to fill the gaps and

60 Aggarwal, Maynard *(n 7)*, 825, 846.

61 Permesly, Craven *(n 9)*, 1, 9.

62 See eg *Erhas and Others v Turkmenistan* PCA Case No. 2013-27 Award (not public). Analysis of the case is provided by IA Reporter <https://www.iareporter.com/articles/an-uncitral-tribunal-declines-jurisdiction-over-a-joint-treaty-claim-brought-against-turkmenistan-by-a-series-of-unrelated-claimants/> accessed 13 January 2022. See also Obadia *(n 6)*, 105, 109-111.

63 Permesly, Craven *(n 9)*, 1, 12-14.

64 Giroud, Moss *(n 14)*, 481, 499.

65 Commission, Moloo *(n 1)*, 9.77.

66 *Adamakopoulos v Cyprus* Decision on Jurisdiction *(n 22)*, para 247.

67 Commission, Moloo *(n 1)*, 9.77.

to make the procedural adaptations necessary to hear the claims.[68] In particular, due to the homogeneous nature of the claims, the tribunal amended 'the method of examination from individual to group treatment'[69], which is commonly applied in mass claims processing.[70] Another procedural mechanism adopted by the tribunal and commonly employed in mass claims processes is the delegation of claims review to a secretariat or an expert. Such an expert was assigned in *Abaclat* to verify whether all claimants met the specific jurisdictional requirements.[71] In addition, there is a variety of procedures and techniques – such as the development of flexible standards of proof – concerning the establishment and normative assessment of facts which could be adopted to overcome difficulties generated by mass investment claims.[72] It is rightly argued that the selection and adaptation of such techniques should be guided by the principles of economic analysis of law, by which i.a. the allocation of scarce resources and the impact of techniques upon the substantive outcome of a particular case are evaluated.[73]

In the context of procedure, it should also be mentioned that the tribunal in *Abaclat* combined the two most common forms of collective actions: aggregate and representative proceedings.[74] In aggregate proceedings a group of individually known claimants jointly files a claim and participates in the proceedings, whereas in representative proceedings a named representative acts on behalf of a group of unnamed claimants and they participate in the proceedings only passively.[75] The proceedings in *Abaclat* started as aggregate because they were initiated by a number of individually identified claimants, but continued in a representative manner as the claimants' interests were represented by *Task Force Argentina*

---

68 Whether these provisions can serve as a basis for adapting the procedure or not, is not relevant for the main question of this chapter and would not be further discussed. Critical analysis is provided in Radović *(n 9)*, 1, 16 et seq.

69 *Abaclat v Argentina*, Decision on Jurisdiction *(n 44)*, para 539.

70 Howard M Holtzmann, 'Mass Claims' (July 2008) Max Planck Encyclopedias of International Law (MPIL) 1, 5 <https://opil.ouplaw.com/view/10.1093/law:epil/9780199231690/law-9780199231690-e189 1> accessed 13 January 2022.

71 *Abaclat and others v Argentine Republic* ICSID Case No. ARB/07/5 Procedural Order No. 17, 8 February 2013. See also Giroud, Moss *(n 14)*, 481, 501.

72 Rosenfeld *(n 42)*, 159, 162 et seq.

73 ibid 159, 168-170.

74 *Abaclat v Argentina*, Decision on Jurisdiction *(n 44)*, para 488.

75 ibid, para 483. See also Strong *(n 12)*, 6.61 et seq.

(TFA).[76] Hence, the tribunal classified the proceedings as 'hybrid'[77]. This is considered 'a compromise that allows the *Abaclat* tribunal to depart from the traditional US class arbitration scheme while creating a new category in the well-established nomenclature'[78]. When regulating mass investment claims in future legal instruments regarding investment disputes, the issue of choosing the best appropriate procedures and techniques for their conduct in a way which guarantees the compliance with the principles of the rule of law would be the most crucial and challenging at the same time.

VI. *Investment Mass Claims – Quo vadis?*

The rulings in the aforementioned cases regarding the adjudication of mass investment claims are widely considered a positive development in international investment arbitration, although not all arguments of the respective tribunals are entirely convincing. Some commentators go one step further and argue that mass investment claims 'do not raise legal issues, but acknowledging their possibility is rather a matter of a psychological threshold that needs to be overcome.'[79] Others still express worries which inter alia address the potential for abuse by third-party funders or law firms, restrictions on cross-examination, or limited assessment of individual claims.[80] However, the decision to adjudicate mass investment claims did not provoke more criticism than the decision to extend investment protection to claims regarding sovereign bonds.[81] Not less controversial is the question whether government bonds should qualify as protected

76 'TFA is organized under Italian law as an *associazione non riconosciuta*, funded by its members' contributions and headed by Dr. Nicola Stock as its president. The aim of TFA is to represent the interests of the Italian bondholders in pursuing a negotiated settlement with Argentina.' *Abaclat v Argentina* Decision on Jurisdiction *(n 44)*, paras 65 et seq. According to the TFA Mandate Package, the Claimants were passive participants of the arbitration and all relevant decision were made by TFA and White & Case (as appointed counsel in the arbitration proceedings by the TFA) on behalf of them. See also Radović *(n 9)*, 1, 2; Strong *(n 12)*, 2.123 et seq.

77 *Abaclat v Argentina*, Decision on Jurisdiction *(n 44)*, para 488.

78 Koenig *(n 2)*, 33, 40.

79 Vanhonnaeker *(n 41)*, 332.

80 Permesly, Craven *(n 9)*, 1, 6 and 10.

81 Permesly, Craven *(n 9)*, 1, 14. See also Michael Waibel, 'Opening Pandora's Box: Sovereign Bonds in International Arbitration' (2007) 101.4 American Journal of International Law 711-759.

investments in the sense of an IIA or Article 25 ICSID Convention. These issues directly concern the future importance of mass claims in investment arbitration, since in all of the four aforementioned cases the claimants were sovereign bondholders.[82] Whether mass investment claims will also play a considerable role outside the financial sector, remains to be seen. As it will be argued in the next section, the increased globalisation of investment flows would undoubtedly trigger the need of other sectors for investment tribunals to effectively adjudicate investment claims brought by a large number of investors.

D. Necessity for Regulation

The conflicting views among both the arbitrators in the aforementioned cases and many commentators leave some doubts about the attitude of future tribunals towards mass claims in international investment arbitration. Although all tribunals decided in the affirmative and might have created a guiding framework, i.e. a persuasive line of consistent cases in investment arbitration, there is no binding precedent within the ICSID framework and future tribunals could deviate from the previous decisions.[83] In view of legal certainty, the regulation of these procedural devices in IIAs and the legal instruments governing the proceedings would be an important step forward towards their proper functioning.[84]

At the same time, the necessity for regulation could result from the line of consistent decisions rendered in favour of the possibility of dealing with mass investment claims in investment proceedings. It has been studied that investment arbitration tribunals nearly always take earlier cases into account.[85] This way 'a progressive emergence of rules through lines of consistent cases on certain issues'[86] comes into being. Their development by the tribunals unambiguously sends a clear message about the necessity for regulation to international policy makers and treaty drafters.

On the contrary, one could argue that the discussed investment arbitrations have so far remained isolated cases because of their identical subject

82 In the Argentinean cases the bonds are issued by the State, whereas in the Cyprian case by a bank.

83 Koenig *(n 2)*, 33, 34-35.

84 In a similar vein Vanhonnaeker *(n 41)*, 332.

85 Gabrielle Kaufmann-Kohler, 'Arbitral Precedent: Dream, Necessity or Excuse?' (2006) 23.3 Arbitration International 357, 368-373.

86 ibid 357, 373.

matter. Such argument does not convince for at least two reasons. First, there is a considerable number of instances where a mass of individuals or SMEs could be affected by State measures. Basically, each State's regulation with abstract and general nature affects a wide range of persons. One should just take into account the series of claims triggered by Spain's extensive amendments in its energy law regulations. Second, the reluctance of individuals and SMEs to collectively bring investment claims is at least partly related to the lack of suitable dispute resolution mechanisms. That and other obstacles such as the high amount of arbitration costs make it nearly impossible for individuals and SMEs to pursue and obtain redress before independent international tribunals.

However, 'for the time being the prospect that the ICSID Convention will be amended any time soon to accommodate mass claims processing seems highly unlikely'[87]. The regulation of mass investment proceedings represents therefore an excellent opportunity for the eventual MIC regime to additionally increase its attractiveness for stakeholders. But even if the drafters of the MIC Statute would consider mass investment claims as counterproductive development, they should at least include a provision expressing this decision in order to enhance legal certainty.[88] The MIC Draft Statute does not, unfortunately, mention mass, class or collective claims at all.[89]

E. *Desirability of Mass Investment Claims in the MIC Statute*

Given the intricacies of the system described thus far, there are ostensibly three options available for regulators, legislators, and treaty drafters to deal with mass investment claims. First, the conservative approach would consist in a complete ban of such proceedings and claims. Second, the sovereigntist approach which is in favour of creating procedures and techniques for the conduct of mass investment claims, but only provided there is a provision requiring the express secondary consent of the respondent State. Third, the liberalist approach: It focuses on the development of procedures and techniques by sticking to the general and abstract nature of the consent to arbitrate given by States in investment treaties. This is,

87 Heiskanen *(n 9)*, 613, 624.

88 In this context Radović *(n 9)*, 1, 20-21.

89 Marc Bungenberg and August Reinisch, *Draft Statute of the Multilateral Investment Court* (Nomos 2021).

however, a question of legal policy implicating fundamental beliefs about the role of investment law in international affairs, to which a clear and fully correct answer is not possible to give. In more general terms, it touches upon delicate topics such as the future of a global society, the structure of the international legal order, and the roles of individuals and SMEs therein.

I. Ongoing Debate

The case law has stirred a fierce debate about the suitability and desirability of the investment treaty framework for conducting mass investment claims.[90] Unfortunately, this debate has thus far received only marginal attention in the ongoing suggestions for the establishment of an MIC and in the ISDS reform process in general.[91] Admittedly, the MIC proposal has emerged from criticism of other aspects of the current ISDS mechanism. However, instead of limiting the reform process to 'old problems', the negotiating parties should also take into consideration 'things that the existing system cannot do, or at least cannot do well'[92], such as giving 'access of the common man or woman to the hallowed venues of international [investment adjudication]'[93]. At the same time, it is argued that the new and improved system for resolving international investment disputes must preserve the German and continental European legal traditions, and mass, class or collective claims should therefore be explicitly ruled out.[94] As it will be argued in the following, such unjustified protectionism can particularly intensify the alleged legitimation crisis in international investment

90 Giroud, Moss *(n 14)*, 481, 503.

91 To my knowledge, only two publications briefly deal with the topic: Bungenberg, Reinisch *(n 9)*, para 336; Jeremy K Sharpe, 'The Future of International Claims Commissions: Conceptualizing the EU's Proposed Multilateral Investment Court as an International Claims Tribunal' (2017) 111 American Society of International Law Proceedings 102-106.

92 Sharpe *(n 91)*, 102, 103.

93 Wiessner *(n 7)*, 55, 82.

94 Steffen Hindelang, 'Grundzüge eines modernen Investitionsschutzes – Ziele und Handlungsempfehlungen' (2015) Harnack-Haus Reflections, 2, 20, <https://www.dihk.de/resource/blob/ 4116/792177c2901dd2b7cf15930e921026dd/harnack-haus-reflections-data.pdf> accessed 13 January 2022. See also Bungenberg, Reinisch *(n 9)*, para 336.

law. Instead, it would be more helpful to consider to what extent the benefits of these procedural devices 'inure to society as a whole'[95].

II. Preconceptions about Mass Investment Claims

Principally, the terms *mass*, *class* and *collective* claims appear to have only marginal differences in their meaning. Each of them is used in different systems in order to depart from the legal cultures shaping and surrounding the other terms.[96] Therefore, the terms *class* action and arbitration are basically used in the US, *collective* action or arbitration in Europe and *mass* claims in public international law in order to describe claims processes before international claims commissions and other international tribunals.[97] For practical reasons, they are often used synonymously. However, when discussing the desirability of mass investment claims on the international level, it is misleading to refer to concerns generally expressed about class actions from the perspective of the European legal tradition since the 'hybrid proceedings'[98] in the Argentinean Trilogy significantly differ from the traditional US-American class action.

Class action is a procedural device of private law enforcement that aims at stimulating individual private initiatives in order to legally reinforce supra-individual interests.[99] It enables representative action brought by an injured class member on behalf of the other members – often not known by name in major proceedings. Furthermore, the legal effects of a judgment are extended not only to persons who did not actively participate in the trial, but also to persons who were not even aware of the conduct of such proceedings.[100] However, class members not present during the proceedings may avert the binding effects of a decision or a settlement terminating the proceedings if they opt out from the class in due time.[101] The opt-out mechanism is considered problematic for a couple of reasons such

95 Strong *(n 12)*, 3.79.

96 In this sense ibid, 1.31.

97 See eg ibid, 1.12-1.36. See also Lamm, Hellbeck, and Saka *(n 12)*, 114, 115.

98 *Abaclat v Argentina*, Decision on Jurisdiction *(n 44)*, para 488. See above Section C.V.

99 Bernard Hanotiau, *Complex Arbitrations: Multiparty, Multicontract, Multi-Issue and Class Actions* (Kluwer Law International 2006), para 560.

100 Marc Orgel, *Class Arbitration, Von der Gruppenklage zum Gruppenschiedsverfahren und zurück? Eine Untersuchung zum U.S.-amerikanischen Schiedsverfahrensrecht* (Mohr Siebeck 2013), 12.

101 Hanotiau *(n 99)*, para 562.

as curtailing the right to be heard and interpreting inactivity as a consent to the class action.[102] In the mass investment claims procedures, however, only claimants who expressly consented to the ISDS were involved.[103]

The supra-individual character of class actions has also further consequences which engender scepticism among lawyers educated in continental Europe. Inherent in traditional class arbitration is that not the individual but the collective interest forms the centrepiece of the proceedings, which leads to an abstraction of individual enforcement.[104] It is argued, therefore, that the outcome of class action disputes results in a kind of veiled legislation in mass proceedings and thus create interference in the classical field of functions of the parliamentary legislator.[105] In the context of investment arbitration, the possibility of such an extension of the tribunal's authority may be seen by the antagonists of ISDS as a serious encroachment on State sovereignty, whereas the assumption of this function by a permanent international court such as the projected MIC might be more easily to abide by. In any case, the risk for an interference with certain legislative powers does not seem to be such an issue on the international level since there is no centralised legislation in international law.

Further factors, which make class actions to seem unappealing for European lawyers, are the complex discovery procedure, the generous jurisdiction rules inviting to tactical forum shopping, jury trial in liability cases, the fear of exorbitant compensation on the basis of punitive damages, negative publicity effect for the defendant company etc.[106] These are, however, not specific to class action litigation, but rather to the US legal order in general.

102 Harald Koch and Joachim Zekoll, 'Europäisierung der Sammelklage mit Hindernissen' (2010) 18.1 Zeitschrift für Europäisches Privatrecht 107, 128.

103 See eg *Abaclat v Argentina* Decision, on Jurisdiction *(n 44)*, paras 458 et seq.

104 Alexander Bruns, 'Instrumentalisierung des Zivilprozesses im Kollektivinteresse durch Gruppenklagen?' (2018) 69.38 Neue Juristische Wochenschrift (NJW) 2753, 2754.

105 ibid, 2753, 2754 et seq.

106 Koch, Zekoll *(n 102)*, 107, 125-126.

III. Promoting Procedural Efficiency

One of the essential benefits arising out of mass investment proceedings is the enhancement of procedural efficiency.[107] In a similar vein, the Working Group III referred to procedural efficiency[108] as one of the guiding principles when considering whether a reform is desirable.[109] In this context, efficiency is assimilated with benefits such as costs and time saving[110], conduct of expeditious and economical procedures[111], and avoidance of incoherence and inconsistency[112]. For example, unnecessary oral hearings and overlapping oral witness testimonies are avoided when applying the principle of an economical procedure.[113] The procedural efficiency inures to the benefit of both, investors and respondent States.[114]

In the context of mass investment claims, however, it should be recognised that tension emerges between procedural efficiency and due process – in particular procedural fairness – which shall be addressed by the MIC treaty drafters. As the aforementioned cases showed, procedural efficiency is achieved at the expense of equal treatment and procedural fairness.[115] For example, the respondent State's right to defend itself against each

---

107 Strong *(n 12)*, 4.19-4.22.

108 At this point, it should be noted that procedural efficiency is also sought in the situations of *multiple proceedings*. Under the topic *multiple proceedings* are discussed shareholder claims and reflective loss within the ISDS reform process. These situations have different features from the situations of multi-party proceedings and mass claims. They pose different difficulties which cannot be solved by the mechanisms discussed here. Cf UNCITRAL, Working Group III, 'Possible reform of investor-State dispute settlement (ISDS), Shareholders claims and reflective loss' (9 August 2019), A/CN.9/WG.III/WP.170.

109 UNCITRAL, 'Report of Working Group III on the work of its thirty-fifth session' (14 May 2018), A/CN.9/935, para 44; UNCITRAL, Working Group III, 'Possible reform of investor-State dispute settlement (ISDS), Multiple proceedings and counterclaims' (22 January 2020), A/CN.9/WG.III/WP.193, para 17.

110 UNCITRAL, Working Group III, 'Possible reform of investor-State dispute settlement (ISDS)' (5 September 2018), A/CN.9/WG.III/WP.149, paras 57-58.

111 ibid, para 61.

112 UNCITRAL, Report WG III, Session 35, A/CN.9/935 (2018) *(n 109)*, para 24.

113 Fabricio Fortese and Lotta Hemmi, 'Procedural Fairness and Efficiency in International Arbitration' (2015) 3.1 Groningen Journal of International Law 110, 121.

114 Heiskanen *(n 9)*, 613, 624.

115 Fortese, Hemmi *(n 113)*, 110, 123. See also Giroud, Moss *(n 14)*, 481, 495-496; Irene M Ten Cate, 'Multi-Party and Multi-Contract Arbitrations: Procedural Mechanisms and Interpretation of Arbitration Agreements Under U.S. Law' (2004) 15.1 The American Review of International Arbitration 133, 157.

claim may be limited in cases where the number of claimants is particularly high. However, sticking to extremely stringent application of the doctrine of due process would make the application of procedural devices bringing together multiple claims impossible. Therefore, in order to protect the principle of due process as much as possible, it is crucial to adopt an opt-in mechanism, pursuant to which the decisions only bind those who have expressly consented to the proceedings.[116] Furthermore, as modern electronic and communications technologies have become easily available[117] and legal tech solutions more common, the inclusion of a large number of participants in the proceedings would not be an insurmountable obstacle and thus, the potential risk of a due process violation would considerably decrease. In any case, the MIC drafters should, however, strike a reasonable balance between procedural efficiency and due process.

IV. Strengthening the Rights of Individuals and Small and Medium-Sized Enterprises

The enhanced access to justice for individuals and SMEs is the second key benefit which stands out of mass investment proceedings.[118] When this goal is achieved, it also creates a serious disincentive for States to embark on risky or socially harmful behaviour.[119]

The international investment law is proving to be one of the few specialised international regimes granting a high level of autonomy to individuals and private enterprises on an international level.[120] This has been achieved through conferring them the right to bring action against internationally responsible States directly before independent arbitral tribunals, which historically was partly a result of the expressed mistrust by foreign investors towards the impartiality of national courts and the ineffectiveness of diplomatic protection.[121] One of the main points of criticism on inter-

116 Similar Obadia *(n 6)*, 105, 106.

117 Wiessner *(n 7)*, 55, 56.

118 Strong *(n 12)*, 3.80.

119 ibid, 3.81.

120 Pierre-Marie Dupuy and Jorge E Viñuales, 'Human Rights and Investment Disciplines: Integration in Progress' in Marc Bungenberg et al (eds), *International Investment Law, A Handbook* (Beck/Hart/Nomos 2015) 1739, 1742-1745.

121 Dolzer, Schreuer *(n 33)*, 232-237. ISDS prevents investors from becoming a pinball of diplomatic imbroglios between home and host States, and has a stabilising effect on the international relations between States at the same time, thus preventing the escalation of (armed) conflicts.

national investment law, however, picks up on the small number of investors being able to effectively rely on the ISDS mechanism. Principally, if the costs of claiming a breach against substantive IIA provisions exceed the expected compensation, there is a high probability that the claim will not be pursued before an international arbitration tribunal, as the individual legal claim is not worth the effort of initiating an ISDS procedure. Such scenarios appear to be unavoidable for smaller investments since the total costs of a single party in investment arbitration proceedings on average exceed the amount of USD 8 million.[122] Accordingly, the ISDS mechanism has been critically viewed as a privilege for financially strong multinational corporations, abovementioned financial obstacles namely hinder a high number of foreign individuals and SMEs from enjoying the benefits of the international investment law regime.[123] Even if the individual amount of damage is basically small, the overall damage to the general public might be of considerable significance because of the high number of individual damages.[124]

So, taking into account the current involvement of individuals and SMEs in international investment arbitration, a necessity for improvement becomes apparent. The latter are generally considered as 'the backbone of almost all economies'[125]. However, the investment arbitration regime lacks mechanisms enabling financially less strong individuals and SMEs to use it and thus, the substantive provisions of IIAs become meaningless for them.[126] Without such mechanisms, investment arbitration perpetuates the societal discontent with unresolved wrongs resulting from 'various crises and incidents, such as armed conflicts, environmental disasters or large-scale economic crises'[127]. In the example of Argentina's economic crisis, individual Italian bondholders would end up with minimal or no

---

122 UNCITRAL, 'Report of Working Group III (Investor-State Dispute Settlement Reform) on the work of its thirty-fourth session (Vienna, 27 November-1 December 2017), Part I' (19 December 2017), A/CN.9/930/Rev. 1, para 36.

123 ibid, para 41.

124 Orgel *(n 100)*, 4.

125 Joachim Karl, 'The Treatment of Small and Medium-Sized Enterprises in International Investment Law' in Thilo Rensmann (ed), *Small and Medium-Sized Enterprises in International Economic Law* (OUP 2017) 241, 241.

126 Rosenfeld *(n 42)*, 159. See also Alexander Gebert, 'Legal Protection for Small and Medium-Sized Enterprises through Investor-State Dispute Settlement, Status Quo, Impediments, and Potential Solutions' in Thilo Rensmann (ed), *Small and Medium-Sized Enterprises in International Economic Law* (OUP 2017) 291, 301-303.

127 Giroud, Moss *(n 14)*, 481, 502. See also p 493.

compensation, whereas leading global companies such as *Siemens*[128] and *Daimler*[129] would have much better chances to minimise their losses.

Admittedly, there are several initiatives for the creation of hybrid spaces of regulation on the international level such as the International Swaps and Derivatives Association (ISDA) or the International Accounting Standards Board (IASB), which enable individuals, private corporations, and organisations to play a more significant role in decision-making processes.[130] However, it is a long way to go until they would be able to create highly effective regulations on their own. Until then, States mainly remain responsible for the establishment of a sound framework protecting the rights of individuals and SMEs. Accordingly, the European Union (EU) pioneered for the creation of a 'standing mechanism for the settlement of international investment disputes'[131] as a part of the ISDS reform process. In order to fulfil the internal requirements of EU law, the EU needs to induce the adoption of regulations strengthening the rights of individuals and SMEs. This assignment was specified by the Court of Justice of the European Union (CJEU) in its ruling regarding the compatibility of the Comprehensive Economic and Trade Agreement (CETA) between Canada and the European Union with EU law:

> It is accordingly apparent that, in the absence of rules designed to ensure that the CETA Tribunal and Appellate Tribunal are financially accessible to natural persons and small and medium-sized enterprises, the ISDS mechanism may, in practice, be accessible only to investors who have available to them significant financial resources. Such a situation would give rise to an inconsistency with the scope *ratione personae* […], which extends to all the enterprises and natural persons of one of the Parties that invest in the territory of the other Party, as well as with the objective of free and fair trade, laid down in Article 3 (5) TEU […]. The approval of the CETA by the Union is thus dependent on the abovementioned commitment by the Union to guarantee effective access to the envisaged tribunals for all EU investors subject to the CETA.[132]

---

128 *Siemens A.G. v Argentine Republic* ICSID Case No. ARB/02/8.

129 *Daimler Financial Services AG v Argentine Republic* ICSID Case No. ARB/05/1.

130 Peer Zumbansen, 'Transnational Legal Pluralism' (2010) 1.2 Transnational Legal Theory 141-189.

131 UNCITRAL, Working Group III, 'Possible reform of investor-State dispute settlement (ISDS) Submission from the European Union and its Member States' (24 January 2019), A/CN.9/WG.III/WP.159/Add.1 para 1.

132 Opinion 1/17 CETA (2019) CJEU ECLI:EU:C:2019:341, paras 213, 221.

In order to participate in the establishment of an MIC, the EU would have to comply with the CJEU's ruling in the *CETA* Opinion.[133] Therefore, it should be taken stock of the interests of individuals and SMEs in the MIC proposal.[134] For this purpose, mass investment proceedings constitute appropriate procedural mechanisms.[135]

V. Commentary

By implementing a suitable framework for the conduct of mass investment claims on the basis of an MIC, policy makers would succeed in achieving two things in a single action: promotion of procedural efficiency of investment arbitration proceedings and strengthening the rights of individuals and SMEs. For sure, there are much more benefits of these procedural devices such as 'stability, rationality and predictability in the resolution of collective disputes'[136] which make their inclusion in the MIC Statute even more desirable. It can also be argued that mass actions and ISDS share common concerns: they require transparency, efficiency, and a reinforced sense of equality between the parties. In addition, while international arbitration undoubtedly will remain 'the forum of choice for sophisticated dispute resolution of complex disputes'[137] arising out of large foreign direct investments, the implementation of procedural devices vested with social function in a court-like MIC becomes indispensable. As already shown, the expressed concerns about class actions are not entirely specific

---

133 For an extensive analysis of the correlation between CETA and ISDS reform process see Steffen Hindelang, 'The Price for a Seat at the ISDS Reform Table' (2020) – forthcoming, available at <https:// www.steffenhindelang.de/wp-content/uploads/2020/03/20200303_Hindelang_The_Price_for_a_Seat_at_the_ISDS_Reform_Table_FINAL.pdf> accessed 13 January 2022. On the EU Law requirements for the establishment of the MIC see Borgdorf, Chapter 10.

134 Cf also Gloria Alvarez et al, 'Submission by the European Federation for Investment Law and Arbitration (EFILA) to the UNCITRAL Working Group III on ISDS Reforms – Ensuring Equitable Access to all Stakeholders: Critical Suggestions for the MIC' (2019) <https://efila.org/wp-content/uploads/2019/07/EFILA-WG-III-submission-15-July-2019.pdf> accessed 13 January 2022.

135 Cf also Gebert *(n 126)*, 291, 301-303.

136 Elie Kleiman, 'The Future of Class, Collective and Mass Arbitrations in Europe: A European Approach to Collective Redress' in Bernard Hanotiau and Eric Schwartz (eds), *Class and Group Actions in Arbitration* (Kluwer Law International 2016), 183, 197.

137 ibid, 183, 191.

to it but result from other concepts inherent to the US legal system. The predicted 'flood of claims'[138] after the Argentinean Trilogy has not become a reality in international investment arbitration yet. Finally, developing a legal framework for mass investment claims in new regimes such as the MIC would extend their legitimising function.[139]

F. Implementation of Mass Investment Claims into the MIC Statute

Once a policy decision on the desirability of mass investment claims has been made, the issue of their implementation into the MIC Statute will become relevant.

First, the definition of essential terms such as *investment*, *investor* and *dispute* must be drafted in a way which explicitly allows for the settlement of mass investment claims. The simplest way would be to use their plural form. Furthermore, when drafting the provisions regarding third-party funding (TPF)[140] – another essential tool for facilitating access to justice – the possibility of bringing multiple claims together in a single claim should also be taken into account. In the context of TPF, but also beyond it, tribunals began more frequently to order a security for costs from claimants.[141] In regard to mass investment claims, this could pose some major difficulties for investors, since it is expected that each individual claimant is not particularly financially strong. Thus, there could emerge a disagreement between claimants on whether to provide the security for cost or on how to allocate expenditure for it between them. Another interesting question may become whether counterclaims should be available against a large number of claimants. In order to, again, enhance procedu-

138 Sczcudlik *(n 9)*, 70, 101.

139 Rosenfeld *(n 42)*, 159, 174. See also Heiskanen *(n 9)*, 613, 624; Kleiman *(n 136)*, 183, 195-196; Wiessner *(n 7)*, 55, 83.

140 About TPF in the ISDS reform process Stavros Brekoulakis and Catherine Rogers, 'Third-Party Financing in ISDS: A Framework for Understanding Practice and Policy' (2019) Academic Forum on ISDS Concept Paper 2019/11, 1-32.

141 Lately in *Theodoros Adamakopoulos and others v Republic of Cyprus* ICSID Case No. ARB/15/49 Procedural Order No. 8, 8 June 2020. See <https://www.iareporter.com/articles/cyprus-reveals-that-it-was-granted-a-5-million-usd-security-for-costs-in-bondholder-mass-arbitration/> accessed 13 January 2022.

ral efficiency and maintain the balance between investors and State, such a provision may also be included in the MIC Statute.[142]

In addition, MIC drafters should avoid the pitfall of ignoring the *Dutco*[143] rule. It aims to prevent the disadvantage on the respondent side that may occur in regard to the appointment of arbitrators if there is more than one respondent. Whereas claimants autonomously decide whether they prefer to start arbitral proceedings alone or in conjunction with other parties, no such choice exists for the respondent parties.[144] Depriving a single respondent of its right to appoint its own arbitrator could lead to a breach of the *Dutco* rule. From today's perspective, it may be difficult to imagine claims against more than one State. However, large-scale or transnational investments such as inter-State pipelines could become more common.[145] In the case of the EU or similar supranational organisations, there is usually an internal regulation which stipulates whether the Union as a whole or the respective Member State should be responsible for wrongful actions.[146]

As important as these related topics indeed are, most essential for treaty drafters would be to establish an accurate procedure and techniques for the conduct of such proceedings and to make the awards enforceable. If the enforcement provisions are not adapted to mass investment claims and *vice versa*, awards would become more vulnerable to challenges and anti-enforcement actions.[147] In regard to procedure and techniques, the right recipe seems to be the attainment of a reasonable balance between procedural efficiency and due process which would be able to meet the rule of law threshold especially set by CJEU in the *Opinion 1/17*, since the EU will play a central role in the creation of the MIC. Either the

---

142 Unlike mass investment claims, counterclaims have already been discussed in the ISDS reform process, see UNCITRAL WG III, Multiple proceedings and counterclaims, WP 193 (2020) *(n 109)*, paras 32 et seq.

143 *Siemens AG/BKMI Industrianlagen GmbH v Dutco Construction Company* (1993) XVIII YBCA 140 Cour de Cassation, 7 January 1992, JDI 119, 707.

144 Julian D M Lew, Loukas A Mistelis, and Stefan M Kröll, *Comparative International Commercial Arbitration* (Kluwer Law International 2003), 16-22.

145 Aggarwal, Maynard *(n 7)*, 825, 849.

146 See eg Regulation (EU) No 912/2014 of the European Parliament and of the Council of 23 July 2014 establishing a framework for managing financial responsibility linked to investor-to-state dispute settlement tribunals established by international agreements to which the European Union is party, <https://eur-lex.europa.eu/legal-content/EN/TXT/?uri=uriserv:OJ.L_.2014.257.01.0121.01.ENG> accessed 13 January 2022.

147 For issues regarding enforcement of mass investment claims, see Strong *(n 12)*, 7.5 et seq. On the recognition and enforcement of MIC decisions see Müller, Chapter 9.

hybrid procedure in the *Abaclat* case might be the most proper source of inspiration for developing mass investment claims procedure in the MIC Statute, or the one stipulated in the provisions of the recently adopted EU Directive 2018/0089(COD) on representative actions for the protection of the collective interests of consumers[148], or any domestic collective redress mechanisms in particular States[149], would require further in-depth research. If the parties to the MIC cannot consent on this matter, the approach developed in Article 19 (1) of the recently published Hague Rules[150] seems vastly preferable. According to it, it is left to the tribunal to adopt special procedures for class, mass, collective or multi-party claims.

Finally, the MIC drafters may also consider a twofold approach of implementation. On the one hand, they could create regulations which govern *ad hoc* mass investment claims similar to the Argentinean Trilogy and *Adamakopoulos v Cyprus*. On the other hand, a regulatory framework for the formation and functioning of specialised mass claims commissions could be established within the MIC system. Such commissions could be convened on an ad hoc basis when needed.

G. Conclusion

Despite the commencing liberalisation of collective claims in Europe, there are still some fundamental discrepancies between the different legal traditions in regard to their desirability and way of conducting both judicial and arbitral proceedings. Nonetheless, an increasing convergence of positions can be traced in the international sphere. Especially when the perceived shortcomings of class actions are overcome in the eyes of European legal culture, it can be assumed that mass claims will be generally

148 The text of the proposal can be seen here: <https://eur-lex.europa.eu/legal-content/EN/ TXT/?uri=CELEX%3A52018PC0184> accessed 13 January 2022.

149 To mention only one of many examples, the German Institution of Arbitration's (*DIS*) Supplementary Rules, which are limited in scope to corporate law disputes, have characteristic features of collective arbitration. Cf Christian Borris, 'Collective Arbitration: The European Experience - Germany and the DIS Supplementary Rules for Corporate Law Disputes (DIS-SRCoLD)' in Bernard Hanotiau and Eric Schwartz (eds), *Class and Group Actions in Arbitration* (Kluwer Law International 2016), 80, 85. See also Kleiman *(n 136)*, 183, 194-195.

150 The Hague Rules on Business and Human Rights Arbitration, December 2019 <https://www.cilc.nl/cms/wp-content/uploads/2019/12/The-Hague-Rules-on-Business-and-Human-Rights-Arbitration_CILC-digital-version.pdf> accessed 13 January 2022.

accepted in international law. In spite of that, they have been used only occasionally thus far, probably because of the absence of a legal framework and – aside from few exceptions such as international human rights law – the lack of sufficient mechanisms to involve individuals and SMEs within the realm of international public law.

At the same time, due to increased globalisation, high level of international networking and cooperation, and thus shrinking costs for capital export, foreign investments flows rise constantly.[151] This accordingly leads to situations where a group or mass of foreign individuals or SMEs with similar investments would need an effective remedy against wrongful host States acts. Since no such efficient remedies are currently available under regional or universal human rights regimes, which allow them to claim compensation for wrongful States' actions, the international investment law regime is being put in the spotlight. Even if it does not contain a proper regulative framework for dealing with mass investment claims yet, the respective tribunals managed somehow to adapt the current regulations in order to effectively conduct the proceedings. By doing so, they launched 'the intrusion of the common man or woman — pensioners and other retail investors — into the marbled halls of international investment arbitration.'[152] However, some major uncertainties about the meaning of silence in the ICSID system, the principle of consent, and the correct procedure in such cases throw a shadow over these new developments in international investment arbitration.

Meanwhile, within the ISDS reform process administered by the Working Group III, the proposal for the establishment of an MIC takes on concrete shape. In this context, mass investment claims have received only marginal attention until now. Against the background of their benefits, i.e. to promote procedural efficiency of investment arbitration proceedings and to strengthen the rights of individuals and SMEs, such approach seems quite surprising. The participants in the reform process have rather focused on other instruments which are supposed to overcome the concerns which have been identified in the current ISDS. However, they might try to be more innovative by establishing new procedural devices and mechanisms in order to provide additional incentives for all stakeholders to choose the MIC instead of the other ISDS regimes. Therefore, international policy makers may thoughtfully take into account the benefits of mass investment claims. Such approach should then result in the implementation of

151 Lamm, Hellbeck, and Saka *(n 12)*, 114, 115.
152 Wiessner *(n 7)*, 55, 57.

the legacy of *Abaclat*, *Ambiente*, *Alemanni* and *Adamakopoulos* cases into the MIC Statute.

Even if Working Group III reached the final third phase of the ISDS reform process where concrete proposals are developed and then recommended to the Commission, it seems not too late for new aspects to be included into the debates. As much as phase one and two are concerned, this chapter has illustrated that, first, the regulation of these procedural devices is necessary and, second, their inclusion in the MIC Statute is desirable.

Chapter 6: Selection and Appointment of Adjudicators

by Caroline Kittelmann and Alexander Dünkelsbühler[*]

Selected Bibliography: Marc Bungenberg and August Reinisch, *Draft Statute of the Multilateral Investment Court* (Nomos 2021); Marc Bungenberg and August Reinisch, *From Bilateral Arbitral Tribunals and Investment Courts to a Multilateral Investment Court – Options Regarding the Institutionalization of Investor-State Dispute Settlement* (Springer 2018/19); Gabrielle Kaufmann-Kohler and Michele Potestà, 'The Composition of a Multilateral Investment Court and of an Appeal Mechanism for Investment Awards' CIDS Supplemental Report, 15 November 2017; Andrea Bjorklund, Marc Bungenberg, Manjiao Chi and Catharine Titi, 'Selection and Appointment of International Adjudicators: Structural Options for ISDS Reform' (17 September 2019) Academic Forum on ISDS Concept Paper 2019/11; Ruth Mackenzie, Kate Malleson, Penny Martin, and Philippe Sands, *Selecting International Judges: Principle, Process, and Politics* (OUP 2010); Anna De Luca, Mark Feldman, Martins Paparinskis, and Catharine Titi, 'Responding to Incorrect ISDS Decision-Making: Policy Options' (21 January 2020) Academic Forum on ISDS Concept Paper 2020/1, 23; George Abi-Saab, 'Ensuring the Best Bench: Ways of Selecting Judges' in Connie Peck and Roy S K Lee (eds), *Increasing the Effectiveness of the International Court of Justice: proceedings of the ICJ/UNITAR Colloquium to Celebrate the 50th Anniversary of the Court* (Martinus Nijhoff 1997); Aida Torres Pérez, 'Can Judicial Selection Secure Judicial Independence? Constraining State Governments in Selecting International Judges' in Michal Bobek (ed), *Selecting Europe's Judges: A Critical Review of the Appointment Procedures to the European Court* (OUP 2015), 196.

* Caroline Kittelmann is a Senior Foreign Lawyer in the International Arbitration team of Clifford Chance, Frankfurt. Comments expressed in this piece are made strictly in a personal capacity. Alexander Dünkelsbühler is a doctoral candidate at the University of Cologne's International Investment Law Centre.

A. Introduction

In the current system of investor-state dispute settlement (ISDS), the identification and selection of arbitrators is characterised by its lack of formality or regulation. The disputing parties are permitted to conduct their own search for potential candidates, screen their experience and qualifications, assess the potential for conflicts of interest, and ascertain their availability to be nominated. This system has generally resulted in high quality decisions rendered by individuals who, crucially, understand both the applicable framework of public international law as well as the specialist facts of the particular dispute. One consequence of the current system of free party choice of arbitrators is that the pool of candidates from which parties generally choose has remained small (and necessarily highly specialised), with candidates who are overwhelmingly (i) male, and (ii) from western Europe and the United States.[1]

In the discussions surrounding the potential reform of ISDS away from *ad hoc* tribunals and towards a permanent institution, the issues of free party choice and the lack of diversity in current practice have been addressed in the context of the effort to establish a Multilateral Investment Court (MIC).[2] Various proposals have been made to (i) use a permanent bench or closed lists/rosters of adjudicators in order to minimise party influence over the selection of arbitrators (with States likely retaining at least some influence over the nomination process), and (ii) increase diversity among appointees.

The aim of this chapter is to provide an overview of the mechanisms for the selection and appointment of adjudicators that an MIC could make use of, as well as setting out the rationales and conflicting interests underlying these. First, this chapter will discuss how the selection and subsequent appointment to the MIC bench of adjudicator candidates could be organised (B.). In this context it will map out the issue of transitioning from an *ad hoc* system to permanent adjudicators (B.I.); discuss the issue of the extent of the representation of Member States on the MIC bench (B.II.); the question of who has the power to nominate, and who is eligible for

1 See generally Susan D Franck, 'Empirically Evaluating Claims about Investment Treaty Arbitration' (2007) 86 NCL Rev 1, 75-83; ICCA, 'Report of the Cross-Institutional Task Force on Gender Diversity in Arbitral Appointments and Proceedings' (2020) The ICCA Reports No 8, 3 et seq.

2 See ia UNCITRAL, Working Group III, 'Possible reform of investor-State dispute settlement (ISDS), Note by the Secretariat, Selection and appointment of ISDS tribunal members' (31 July 2019), A/CN.9/WG.III/WP.169.

nomination (B.III.); elaborate on the mechanisms for adjudicator selection currently proposed (B.IV.), and discuss the merits of a mechanism to screen the candidates' competence (B.V.). Then, it will address the issue of arbitrator diversity (C.). In particular, it will discuss the diversity deficit in investment arbitration (C.I.), elaborate on specific diversity gaps (C.II.), analyse the treatment of diversity in the published MIC models (C.III.), and address the lessons to be learned from the CETA adjudicator nominations (C.IV.), before finishing with a conclusion (D.).

B. Selection Procedure

The nomination and selection of candidates is one of the fundamental matters an MIC would need to resolve. Several questions would need to be answered: How 'representative' should the MIC bench be (1)? Who should nominate the individuals as candidates – the Member States, the individuals themselves, or an independent entity (2)? Which examples should the MIC selection and appointment procedures draw inspiration from, and to what extent are these reflected in the existing proposals for its structure and selection procedure (3)? And finally, to what extent should there be preliminary stages, such as a screening or consultation stage (4)?[3]

I. From ad hoc panels to permanent adjudicators

Ad hoc ISDS tribunals as currently used are created after a dispute arises and disband after reaching their verdict. By contrast, permanent or 'standing' international dispute resolution mechanisms are composed of adjudicators forming part of a 'bench' that would already exist prior to the dispute arising. Unlike current *ad hoc* appointed arbitrators, these adjudicators are assigned to cases once they are filed and serve fixed terms of office.[4] Such mechanisms can be found in the World Trade Organization (WTO) Appellate Body and the European Court of Human Rights (ECtHR). There is also the possibility of a middle ground, whereby rosters

3 See UNCITRAL, 'Report of Working Group III (Investor-State Dispute Settlement Reform) on the work of its resumed thirty-eighth session' (28 January 2020), A/CN.9/1004/Add.1, paras 114-122.

4 Gabrielle Kaufmann-Kohler and Michele Potestà, 'The Composition of a Multilateral Investment Court and of an Appeal Mechanism for Investment Awards, CIDS Supplemental Report' (15 November 2017) CIDS Report 2017, 11.

or closed list models are used. In that context there are elements of both permanent and *ad hoc* mechanisms, as roster membership could be determined by the participating States according to formalised criteria, but the parties could be permitted to exercise their autonomous choice within the constraints of the roster or list.[5]

The permanence of a standing international dispute resolution mechanism would inherently constrain the parties' freedom to participate in the selection of adjudicators: in a permanent system, the fact that a permanent body pre-exists the dispute logically reduces the parties' influence in the selection and appointment of adjudicators.[6] While States as treaty parties exercise influence over the composition of the bench in international dispute resolution mechanisms such as the ECtHR[7] or the WTO Appellate Body,[8] as disputing parties, they have no influence over the identity of the adjudicators ultimately assigned to their particular case. The ICJ Statute falls somewhere in between, as it allows for compromise: disputing parties may appoint *ad hoc* judges in limited circumstances where one of the judges is a national of a disputing State, or through the constitution of particular chambers.[9]

Whether or not the form of an MIC is taken, any permanent body competent to settle investment disputes will need to establish a procedure to populate any bench or roster. This procedure is likely to encompass distinct stages. First, Member States will have to *nominate* individuals as potential adjudicators (i.e. propose or formally enter as a candidate to serve on the court). Then, from this pool of eligible candidates, a *selection* must be made according to certain pre-determined criteria. Finally, the MIC will

5 Kaufmann-Kohler, Potestà *(n 4)*, 10.

6 See UNCITRAL WG III, Selection and appointment of ISDS tribunal members, WP 169 (2019) *(n 2)*, para 41; UNCITRAL, Working Group III, 'Possible reform of investor-State dispute settlement (ISDS) Standing multilateral mechanism: Selection and appointment of ISDS tribunal members and related matters, Note by the Secretariat' (8 December 2021), A/CN.9/WG.III/WP.213 (advance copy), para 5.

7 Articles 20-23 European Convention for the Protection of Human Rights and Fundamental Freedoms (ECHR) (1950).

8 Articles 17 (1) and 17 (2) WTO Dispute Settlement Understanding, Annex 2 to the Marrakesh Agreement establishing the World Trade Organization (WTO Agreement) (1995) 1867 UNTS 3.

9 Article 31 (2) and Article 26 (2) International Court of Justice Statute (ICJ Statute) (1945) 33 UNTS 993. See Serena Forlati, *The International Court of Justice: An Arbitral Tribunal or a Judicial Body?* (Springer 2014), 31-49; Kaufmann-Kohler, Potestà *(n 4)*, 13.

require a procedure by which the candidates who have successfully been selected can be formally *appointed* to the MIC's bench.

How this nomination, selection and appointment procedure is reflected in a final MIC statute will be of particular relevance in judging how much of a change of course an institutionalised mechanism will present for the conduct of ISDS proceedings. Under the current ISDS appointment system, owing to a lack of formal regulation of the selection and appointment process of arbitrators, the individual freedom of the parties is virtually unencumbered.[10] Therefore, with any systemic reform towards a more centralised and permanent court system likely to encroach on this near total freedom to choose an arbitrator, such a change in degree of party autonomy may ultimately be a decisive factor in determining to what extent such a Court would be accepted and used by the relevant stakeholders, in particular investors.

This is particularly relevant with regard to an MIC, but is also a broader issue – examples can also be seen in the permanent Investment Court System (ICS) established by the new Trade and Investment Agreements between the European Union and (i) Canada, (ii) Vietnam, and (iii) Singapore.[11] Additionally, as investment arbitration would undergo a metamorphosis into a more judicial procedure under an MIC, the experience of international tribunals such as the International Court of Justice (ICJ), the International Criminal Court (ICC), the International Tribunal for the Law of the Sea (ITLOS) or the ECtHR in selecting and appointing their bench members may serve as another useful point of comparison.

There is a clear need to define principles governing the selection and subsequent appointment of candidates. Such principles carry the burden of ensuring that a balance between competence, diversity, representative-

10 Ksenia Polonskaya, 'Diversity in the Investor-State Arbitration: Intersectionality Must Be a Part of the Conversation' (2018) 19.1 Melbourne Journal of International Law, 15; Kaufmann-Kohler, Potestà *(n 4)*, para 16; Van Vechten Veeder, 'The Historical Keystone to International Arbitration: The Party-Appointed Arbitrator - From Miami to Geneva' in David D Caron, Stephan W Schill, Abby Cohen Smutny, and Epaminontas E Triantafilou (eds), *Practising Virtue: Inside International Arbitration* (OUP 2015), 128-149.

11 Chapter 8 Comprehensive Economic and Trade Agreement between Canada and the European Union (CETA) (2016); Chapter 3 of the EU-Vietnam Investment Protection Agreement (EU-Vietnam IPA) (2019); Chapter 3 of the EU-Singapore Investment Protection Agreement (EU-Singapore IPA) (2018); see also Section C of the Chapter on Investment of the EU-Mexico Agreement in Principle.

ness, impartiality and the interests of the different parties is ultimately achieved.[12] This is, however, no simple task.

II. Full vs selective representation

In terms of the selection of adjudicators, Member States of an MIC will first have to address the question of its constitution. Most importantly, States will have to decide whether they wish to have one of their representatives on the bench at all times (so-called *full representation*), or whether the number of adjudicators should be smaller than the number of participating States (*selective representation*).[13] Full representation would not necessarily mean restricting States to choosing representatives from their own nationals alone, just as States may currently select foreign nationals for the ICSID panels of arbitrators and conciliators.[14]

Full representation is the option preferred by bodies such as the ECtHR[15] and the Court of Justice of the European Union (CJEU),[16] while Courts such as the International Court of Justice (ICJ),[17] the International Tribunal for the Law of the Sea (ITLOS),[18] the African Court of Human

12 Cf UNCITRAL WG III, Selection and appointment of ISDS tribunal members, WP 169 (2019) (*n 2*).

13 See Kaufmann-Kohler, Potestà *(n 4)*; Marc Bungenberg and August Reinisch, *From Bilateral Arbitral Tribunals and Investment Courts to a Multilateral Investment Court – Options Regarding the Institutionalization of Investor-State Dispute Settlement* (Springer 2018 and 2019) (in the following, references will be made to the 2019 edn), para 87; UNCITRAL WG III, Selection and appointment of ISDS tribunal members, WP 169 (2019) *(n 2)*, para 48; UNCITRAL WG III, Selection and appointment of ISDS tribunal members and related matters, WP 213 (2021) (*n 6*), Draft Provision 4, para 3 et seqq.

14 As long as they fulfil the requirements of Article 14 Convention on the Settlement of Investment Disputes between States and Nationals of Other States (ICSID Convention) (1965) 575 UNTS 159, no additional nationality requirements apply.

15 Article 20 ECHR.

16 Article 48 Rules of Procedure of the European Court of Justice (2012) OJ L265/1; Article 254 Treaty on European Union.

17 Article 3 ICJ Statute.

18 Article 2 Statute of the International Tribunal for the Law of the Sea (ITLOS) (1994) 1833 UNTS 3.

and Peoples' Rights,[19] the Inter-American Court of Human Rights,[20] and the Caribbean Court of Justice[21] have opted for selective representation. The perhaps closest existing multilateral equivalent to a proposed MIC – the WTO's Dispute Settlement Body, and, in particular, its Appellate Body – also provides for the selective representation of (in theory) 7 members for 164 Member States.[22]

The first option would be to have the MIC Plenary Body confirm government-chosen candidates without choosing from a larger pool. The second option would see Member States nominate individuals to a larger pool of candidates, from which an international committee or body would ultimately be able to make selections. These individuals would then go on to be appointed as adjudicators to the MIC bench.[23]

Even though both procedures may be considered to be inherently political,[24] using a larger pool of potential adjudicators will be less politicised than opting for a mere confirmation of government-chosen candidates. There are practical considerations that could make full representation less effective, such as a potential need for the number of adjudicators to be able to remain flexible in order to handle a changing caseload.[25] Also, selective representation is likely to be the more transparent option, as it encourages nominating Member States to put forward candidates that have the potential to also convince other participants in the MIC.[26]

Opting for a selective representation mechanism would also likely lead to an increase in collective decision-making by States at the election stage.[27] As in other international bodies that practice selective representation, a system of rotation – whether formal or informal – could ensure that

19 Article 11 Protocol to the African Charter on Human and Peoples' Rights on the Establishment of an African Court of Human and Peoples' Rights (1998).

20 Article 4 Statute of the Inter-American Court of Human Rights, Organisation of American States Resolution No 448 (October 1979).

21 Article IV Agreement Establishing the Caribbean Court of Justice (2001).

22 Article 17 of the Understanding on Rules and Procedures Governing the Settlement of Disputes, Uruguay Round Agreement (1994).

23 Kaufmann-Kohler, Potestà *(n 4)*, para. 88.

24 ibid.

25 UNCITRAL, Report WG III, Resumed Session 38, A/CN.9/1004/Add.1 (2020) *(n 3)*, para 115; see also UNCITRAL WG III, Selection and appointment of ISDS tribunal members and related matters, WP 213 (2021) (*n 6*), Draft Provision 4, para 17 et seqq.

26 Bungenberg, Reinisch *(n 13)*, para 89.

27 UNCITRAL WG III, Selection and appointment of ISDS tribunal members, WP 169 (2019) *(n 2)*, para 52.

all Member States have the chance of seeing their own candidate eventually appointed to the bench. However, the possibility of the international politicisation of the nomination process would increase with selective representation; a negative example may be found in the selection procedure for appointments to the ICJ.[28] Furthermore, the current crisis surrounding the WTO Appellate Body may also serve as cautionary tale – having a reduced number of adjudicators and the necessity of a form of collective decision-making for their appointment carries a risk of paralysis if the appointment procedure can be held hostage by the foreign policy concerns of individual Member States.[29]

The number of adjudicators would further likely be subject to change over time. In an MIC with a full representation of Member States on the bench, the number of adjudicators would evolve every time a new Member State accedes to the MIC, or if a participating Member State leaves. In both selection alternatives, the final statute of an MIC could provide for the adjustment of the number of adjudicators in the event of an increasing caseload. In the case of full selection, reactivity to caseload developments can be included by multiplying the number of adjudicators consistently for all Member States. Examples of international tribunals incorporating such flexibility into their statutes can be found in the International Criminal Court,[30] the CETA Tribunal,[31] the EU-Vietnam Tribunal;[32] and the Iran – United States Claims Tribunal.[33]

Finally, the question arises as to whether nationals of MIC Member States may be involved in the adjudication of their cases (a scenario that is not possible within the ICSID framework). The statutes of several international tribunals that have elected for full representation provide for the possibility for Member States to appoint one of their representatives as an

---

28 See George Abi-Saab, 'Ensuring the Best Bench: Ways of Selecting Judges' in Connie Peck and Roy S K Lee (eds), *Increasing the Effectiveness of the International Court of Justice: proceedings of the ICJ/UNITAR Colloquium to Celebrate the 50th Anniversary of the Court* (Martinus Nijhoff 1997), 184; Ruth Mackenzie, Kate Malleson, Penny Martin, Philippe Sands, *Selecting International Judges: Principle, Process, and Politics* (Oxford University Press 2010), 10, 25.

29 See UNCITRAL, Report WG III, Resumed Session 38, A/CN.9/1004/Add.1 (2020) *(n 3)*, para 119.

30 Article 36 (2) Rome Statute of the International Criminal Court (ICC) (2002) 2187 UNTS 3.

31 Article 8.27.3 CETA.

32 Article 12 (3) EU-Vietnam FTA.

33 First sentence Article III (1) Iran-United States Claims Tribunal, Claims Settlement Declaration.

ad hoc adjudicator when they are party to a proceeding. In some instances, this occurs with the aim of alleviating concerns of States with regards to the adjudicators' possible lack of familiarity with their domestic legal system. This is the case in the context of *inter alia* the ECtHR[34] and the Central American Court of Justice (CACJ).[35] While these examples all come from courts favouring full representation, a version of this could possibly be extended to an MIC with selective representation, perhaps combined with an adjudicator roster to complement the permanent bench, similar to the system of *ad hoc* Judges at the ECtHR. This list could, in turn, be drawn up on the basis of the same criteria used for the selection and appointment of the permanent adjudicators.[36] However, there are trade-offs to such a solution, as the concerns expressed as to the impartiality and independence of *ad hoc* arbitrators are one of the reasons a standing ISDS mechanism such as the MIC started to be contemplated in the first place.[37]

In order to secure the highest possible quality of decision-making, the qualification requirements for adjudicators should be equivalent to those of the highest national judges.[38] Alternatively, individuals of recognised competence, for example academics, should also be permissible. If arbitration experts with qualifications other than that of a judge or a scholar were to be included in the list of acceptable 'backgrounds' for MIC adjudicators, the qualification requirements would need to be tailored accordingly. However, this would pose a question of policy – does building an MIC aim at a *tabula rasa* of adjudicators, or should the experienced arbitrators of the existing system be allowed to carry on in a new, modernised form, just without the opportunity to act as counsel in parallel?[39] This question

34 Rule 29 ECtHR Rules of Court (2 June 2021).

35 Article VI Convention for the Establishment of a Central American Court of Justice (adopted 10 December 1992).

36 See UNCITRAL WG III, Selection and appointment of ISDS tribunal members, WP 169 (2019) *(n 2)*, para 48.

37 See Gus Van Harten, 'Perceived Bias in Investment Treaty Arbitration?' in Michael Waibel et al (eds), *The Backlash Against Investment Arbitration. Perceptions and Reality* (Kluwer Law International 2010), 436.

38 Noting that all elements of selection and appointment to a standing court and a standing appellate system should ideally be contained in the respective statute: Andrea Bjorklund, Marc Bungenberg, Manjiao Chi, and Catharine Titi, 'Selection and Appointment of International Adjudicators: Structural Options for ISDS Reform' (17 September 2019), Academic Forum on ISDS Concept Paper 2019/11, 18.

39 idem, 8; Philippe Sands, 'Developments in Geopolitics: The End(s) of Judicialization?' 12 September 2015, ESIL Conference Closing Speech, reprinted in EJIL Talk!

remains to be answered, in particular in the context of the uptake of any new framework by the relevant stakeholders. Investors used to highly specialised decision makers may not, for example, welcome the former option.

III. Nomination and selection – whom, how?

Were an MIC to opt for a separate nomination phase prior to the steps of selecting and appointing the adjudicators, three models appear practicable: first, direct nominations by the Member States of an MIC; second, establishing an independent entity in charge of nominations within the permanent body, and third, giving individuals the opportunity to declare their candidacy individually.[40]

With regard to the selection procedure, there are arguments in favour of a 'consultation' phase. Such a consultation phase could be designed as a preliminary sub-phase within the nomination process at the national level. Otherwise, it could take place at the appointment phase and at the supra-national level, with the body entrusted with the appointment having to incorporate the outcome of the process into its decision.[41] The advantage of such a consultation mechanism would be to take into account the currently perceived asymmetry of ISDS.[42] Accordingly, NGOs, other arbitral institutions, and associations of international law professionals would gain the opportunity to participate in order to ensure representation and expertise.[43] Some commentators go further and propose that all stakeholders – especially representatives of investors – be included in the appointment and selection procedure,[44] especially to compensate for the fact that under an MIC system, investors would lose their ability to autonomously choose their arbitrator.[45] This is all the more important as

40 See UNCITRAL, Report WG III, Resumed Session 38, A/CN.9/1004/Add.1 (2020) *(n 3)*, para 116.

41 Kaufmann-Kohler, Potestà *(n 4)*, para 126.

42 idem, para 133.

43 See UNCITRAL, Report WG III, Resumed Session 38, A/CN.9/1004/Add.1 (2020) *(n 3)*, paras 114-122.

44 Submission by the European Federation for Investment Law and Arbitration (EFILA) to the UNCITRAL Working Group No III on ISDS Reforms, 'Ensuring Equitable Access to all Stakeholders: Critical Suggestions for the MIC' (15 July 2019) <https://efila.org/wp-content/uploads/2019/07/EFILA-WG-III-submission-15-July-2019.pdf>, accessed 13 January 2022, para 12.

45 idem, para 15.

some commentators fear that investors would be treated less fairly in an MIC where States would entirely control the nomination of adjudicators. Arguably, as treaty parties selecting permanent adjudicators *ex ante* rather than as dispute parties selecting *ex post*, States have an interest to balance their interests as importers and exporters of capital. As both home States and possible respondents, it may be in their own best interests to choose balanced adjudicators, rather than overtly pro-State individuals.[46]

Whether a selective or full representation model is followed, MIC electors are likely to be representatives of State parties – be it governments or a supra-national parliamentary body, as with the Parliamentary Assembly of the Council of Europe for the ECtHR.[47] Therefore, political considerations are likely to be unavoidable.[48] The presence of multiple procedural checks and balances with only a final 'political' determination would however increase the likelihood of the most qualified candidates being elected.[49]

IV. Selection procedures in MIC model proposals

The issue of selection and appointment procedures in the MIC has so far been addressed by a number of commentators. We first briefly set out the various MIC proposals on the arbitrator selection method (sections 1. to 3.), and then reflect on the possible ways forward (section 4.).

Accordingly, in the following, we explore certain of the MIC proposals (which we address as the proposals as made by the European Union and its Member States from 12 December 2017 and 18 January 2019[50] (the

46 See Sergio Puig and Gregory Shaffer, 'Imperfect Alternatives: Institutional Choice and the Reform of Investment Law' (July 2018) 112 AJIL 3, 361-409; Stephen Schwebel, 'The Proposals of the European Commission for Investment Protection and an Investment Court System' ISDS blog (17 May 2016), <http://isdsblog.com/wp-content/uploads/sites/2/2016/05/THEPROPOSALSOFTHEEUROPEANCOMMISSION.pdf> accessed 13 January 2022.

47 Kaufmann-Kohler, Potestà *(n 4)*, para 157.

48 idem, para 160.

49 ibid.

50 UNCITRAL, Working Group III, 'Possible reform of investor-State dispute settlement (ISDS): Submission from the European Union and its Member States' (12 December 2017), A/CN.9/WG.III/WP.145 and UNCITRAL, Working Group III, 'Possible reform of investor-State dispute settlement (ISDS) Submission from the European Union and its Member States' (24 January 2019), A/CN.9/WG.III/WP.159/Add.1 (together 'EU Proposals').

'EU Proposals'), the proposals of *Bungenberg and Reinisch*,[51] including their 'MIC Draft Statute' of November 2020[52] (the '*Bungenberg/Reinisch* Proposals') and also the proposals of *Kaufmann-Kohler and Potestà*[53] (the '*Kaufmann-Kohler/Potestà* Proposals')) and how these interact with the selection and appointment of arbitrators (or 'adjudicators').

1. The EU Proposals

In the 2017 submission, the EU Proposals refer to 'permanent bodies with full-time and tenured adjudicators' that can 'deliver predictability and consistency'.[54] In matters of appointment, the focus is on 'a long-term approach', with the permanency of the body 'free[ing] the adjudicators from the need to be remunerated from other sources and typically provid[ing] some form of tenure' which 'prevents the adjudicators from coming under pressure to take short-term considerations into account and ensures that there are no concerns as to their impartiality'.[55] In the 2017 submission, the EU Proposals also note that members of standing bodies on both the domestic and international level 'are composed of full time adjudicators who are appointed by states, associated with a high degree of independence and impartiality.'[56] The 2017 submission also notes that:

> The ad hoc nature of the investor-state arbitration wherein the arbitrators, by definition, have other activities creates significant perception problems. These perception problems derive from the fact that the professional and/or personal interests of the persons involved in the system might be perceived to have an effect on the outcomes of the disputes. Whilst the detailed reality and the complex interactions

---

51 Bungenberg, Reinisch *(n 13)* (*Bungenberg/Reinisch Proposals*).

52 Bungenberg and August Reinisch, *Draft Statute of the Multilateral Investment Court* (Nomos 2021).

53 Gabrielle Kaufmann-Kohler and Michele Potestà, 'Can the Mauritius Convention serve as a model for the reform of investor-State arbitration in connection with the introduction of a permanent investment tribunal or an appeal mechanism?: Analysis and Roadmap' (3 June 2016) and 'The Composition of a Multilateral Investment Court and of an Appeal Mechanism for Investment Awards' (15 November 2017) CIDS Supplemental Report (together 'Kaufmann-Kohler/Potestà Proposals').

54 UNCITRAL WG III, Submission European Union and its Member States, WP 145 (2017) *(n 50)*, para. 7.

55 ibid.

56 idem, para 8.

> between arbitrators themselves and the actors which appoint them undoubtedly paints a more complex picture, the combination of the unidirectional nature of the system and the importance of perception, of justice being seen to be done, raises concerns.[57]

In the 2017 submission, the EU Proposals contrast the process of (i) appointing standing adjudicators before a dispute has arisen, whereby States 'have an incentive to balance their interests, ensuring the selection of fair and balanced adjudicators that they would be happy to live with whether a future case is brought by their investors or against them as respondents', with (ii) appointing an arbitrator only once a dispute has arisen, 'which means that investors and state respondents make decisions about arbitrators with a view to best serving their interests in that particular case.'[58] This, according to the EU Proposals, means that there is a 'focus on arbitrators who are already known in the system and who are considered as having a predisposition towards one or other side (being perceived as investor or state-friendly).'[59] The EU Proposals lament this, as 'parties are looking at appointment to the dispute primarily in their capacity as disputing party and not in their capacity as sovereigns, where their long term interests lies in providing for adjudicative bodies that faithfully interpret and apply the underlying substantive provisions.'[60] This, the EU Proposals note, 'is heightened by [inter alia] the repeat nature of potential disputes.'[61] The 2017 finally notes that:

> In addition to encouraging the appointment of predisposed (i.e. perceived as investor or state friendly) arbitrators and a small number of repeat players, one of the problems with this approach is that it leads to a continued high concentration of persons who have gained their experience as arbitrators primarily in the field of commercial arbitration involving disputes of 'private law' rather than public international law disputes. Such persons often are professionally less familiar with public international law (investment treaties are of course a field of public international law) and public law (which is important because the cases concern the actions of states in their sovereign capacity).[62]

---

57 idem, para 27.
58 idem, para 31.
59 ibid.
60 ibid.
61 ibid.
62 idem, para 32.

In the 2019 submission, the EU Proposals begin by noting that the adjudicators should be employed on a full-time basis, without any 'outside activities'.[63] Adjudicators should be subject to 'strict ethical requirements', ensured not only by their full-time employment and the prohibition on outside activities (noted as 'other remunerated or political activities'), but also by eliminating conflicts of interest, and should in this regard 'disclose past interests, relationships or matters that could affect their independence or impartiality and, after the end of their term, they should remain subject to obligations to ensure that their independence and impartiality in office are not called into question.'[64] Making adjudicators' terms of office (i) long (referring to nine-year terms), and (ii) non-renewable, should in combination with 'a robust and transparent appointment process' ensure independence from governments.[65] The EU Proposals make suggestions as to the qualifications of adjudicators by reference to the practice of international courts more generally, i.e. 'the qualifications required in their respective countries for appointment to the highest judicial offices or are jurisconsults of recognised competence in international law (see for example, Article 2 of the Statute of the International Court of Justice)' with specific requirements as to 'expertise in certain areas of law, and it would be desirable to have persons with judicial experience and case-management skills'.[66]

On the appointment process itself, the EU Proposals highlight the importance of neutrality of the adjudicators and reiterate that '[a] robust and transparent appointment process would be necessary to ensure the independence and impartiality of the adjudicators.'[67] In this regard, the EU Proposals refer to the screening mechanisms (with independent staff, who could be appointed ex officio) used by international or regional courts.[68] The EU Proposals also state that candidates could be proposed by the contracting States, or apply directly (with consideration of the possibility for non-nationals of contracting States to be appointed, subject to a majority vote of the contracting States).[69] The EU Proposals expect the contracting States to 'appoint objective adjudicators, rather than ones

63 UNCITRAL WG III, Submission European Union and its Member States, WP 159 (2019) *(n 50)*, para 16.

64 idem, para 18.

65 idem, para 19.

66 idem, para 20.

67 idem, para 22.

68 ibid.

69 ibid.

that are perceived to lean too heavily in favour of investors or states, because they are expected to internalise not only their defensive interests, as potential respondents in investment disputes, but also their offensive interests, i.e. the necessity to ensure an adequate level of protection to their investors.'[70] On this basis, the EU hopes that they 'will therefore take a longer term perspective.'[71] Finally, the EU Proposals suggest that adjudicators be 'appointed to divisions of the standing mechanism on a randomised basis to ensure that the disputing parties would not be in a position to know in advance who will hear their case'.[72]

The EU Proposals specifically address 'double-hatting', suggesting that adjudicators having long, non-renewable terms will mean that 'the concerns on independence and impartiality [according to the heading, such concerns related to ethics, double hatting and incentives flowing from the current system] can be definitively addressed', as double-hatting would no longer be possible.[73] The EU Proposals also focus on how this would 'remove incentives flowing from the phenomenon of repeat appointments' as it would 'remove the link between arbitrators (or candidates to be arbitrators) and counsel for investors and states who are the gate-keepers to appointment.'[74] This, suggest the EU Proposals, 'plays a large role in raising concerns around the legitimacy of the regime'.[75] The EU Proposals also point to the recent decision of the International Court of Justice not to allow its sitting Members to act as arbitrators in either investor-state dispute settlement or in commercial arbitration.[76] With regard to the expertise of candidates, the EU Proposals suggest requiring proficiency in public international law as well as expertise in judging and 'detailed fact-finding'.[77]

Finally, the EU Proposals suggest that there would be three key benefits to their suggested appointment methods:

- Eliminating the arbitrator selection process (which, the EU Proposals note, has been estimated by ICSID to take on average 6–8 months) would significantly reduce counsel costs.[78]

---

70 idem, para 23.
71 ibid.
72 idem, para 24.
73 idem, para 47.
74 ibid.
75 ibid.
76 idem, para 48.
77 idem, para 49.
78 idem, para 52.

- There would only be challenges to arbitrators in very limited circumstances, saving both time and money.[79]
- Fixed remuneration means that any perceived incentive in prolonging the duration of a particular proceeding would be removed and is 'likely to lead to better case management'.[80]

Although the EU has advocated for the application of the IBA Guidelines in other settings,[81] this is not included in its MIC proposals.

2. *The Bungenberg/Reinisch Proposals and the MIC Draft Statute*

The *Bungenberg/Reinisch* Proposals favour a selection process whereby the MIC Member States propose a pool of suitable candidates, from which the MIC Plenary Body (composed of representatives of all member States, independent administrative entities and international organisations[82]) chooses appointees.[83] The Plenary Body would generate guidelines for the selection of candidates by the MIC Member States, which could be based on the Council of Europe's approach for judges of the European Court of Human Rights, whereby the selections 'must reflect the principles of democratic procedure, transparency and non-discrimination'.[84] The authors reject the idea of direct applications made by candidates to the organisation itself,[85] because although the influence of the home States of the candidates would be limited, *Bungenberg and Reinisch* see here an issue as to acceptance if Member States have no possibility to influence the selection process.[86]

---

79 idem, para 53.
80 idem, para 54.
81 ICSID, UNCITRAL, 'Draft Code of Conduct, Comments by State/Commenter' (14 January 2021), 36 'With regard to the ICSID reform process, the European Union and its Member States suggested that pending the availability of a code of conduct, the acceptance of appointment should include a specific commitment to comply with existing relevant ethic rules, such as the IBA Guidelines on Conflicts of Interest in International Arbitration.'; see also Article 8.30(1) CETA ('The Members of the Tribunal shall […] comply with the International Bar Association Guidelines on Conflicts of Interest in International Arbitration or any supplemental rules adopted […].')'.
82 Bungenberg, Reinisch *(n 13)*, para 81.
83 idem, para 89.
84 idem, para 90.
85 idem, para 91.
86 idem, para 92.

After nomination, a Screening Committee that could take the form of a sub-committee of the Plenary Body could vet the candidates 'for their personal suitability, i.e. professional qualifications, ethical standards as well as independence and neutrality', which would function as an 'additional instance to mitigate the possibility of politically motivated and non-transparent national nominations of candidates, to prevent the candidacy of unsuitable persons'.[87]

Bungenberg and Reinisch suggest that MIC judges should not act as representatives of States, but rather act to perform an 'international task'.[88] Moreover, the 'suitability and behaviour' of MIC judges should be governed by the MIC's statute.[89] The IBA Guidelines should also be 'taken into consideration'[90]; moreover there should be disclosure requirements that could be modelled on the IBA Guidelines (with an 'exemplary' rather than 'exclusive' list of hypothetical cases), with a disclosure breach constituting prima facie grounds for disqualification.[91]

The *Bungenberg/Reinisch* Proposals also directly address parallel engagements, proposing that although engagement at the MIC should be the 'predominant activity' of a judge, 'parallel engagements should still be considered permissible'.[92] However, parallel professional engagements should be subject to an approval,[93] and there should be temporal limitations as well as consideration of the issue of independence.[94] The authors propose that teaching at public institutions should be permissible, but that representation of parties in other investment law proceedings should not be allowed due to 'the danger of bias or that a person may wear a 'double hat'.'[95]

The *Bungenberg/Reinisch* Proposals reject direct appointment by States, concluding that this should be the task of the Plenary Body.[96] They also discuss the appropriate length of term for judges, weighing a longer term without the option of reappointment as advantageous from the perspective

87 idem, para 94.
88 idem, para 131.
89 idem, para 133.
90 idem, para 136.
91 idem, para 139.
92 idem, para 151.
93 idem, para 152.
94 idem, para 153.
95 idem, para 154.
96 idem, para 155.

of independence,[97] against shorter terms that would be less likely to deter new MIC Member States.[98]

The authors also address the framework for decisions on challenges for bias, suggesting that the second instance of the proposed MIC should have jurisdiction to rule on challenges brought against first instance judges. In addition, the plenary of the second instance should decide on bias of judges of the second instance. Alternatively, a third instance such as the ICJ could decide on any alleged bias of the second instance.[99]

Based on the above, the MIC Draft Statute (November 2020) contains a concrete provision addressing the appointment process, as follows:

> *Article 12*
> *Nomination, Screening, and Election of Judges*
> *1. Each Member of the MIC has the right to nominate candidates to a list for consideration to be elected as a judge of the MIC, through an internal selection procedure conducted by the Member.*
> *2. The persons nominated to the list shall be evaluated by a sub-committee of the Plenary Body called the 'Screening Committee' for their suitability to be appointed as judges of the MIC on the parameters of professional qualifications, ethical standards, independence, and impartiality. The Screening Committee shall comprise seven persons chosen by the Plenary Body from among former judges of the MIC, members of national supreme and international courts, and lawyers of recognised competence. The Screening Committee may use additional criteria for the screening process as it deems fit and would seek to ensure that the persons who are finally selected represent the principal legal systems of the world.*
> *3. The Screening Committee shall publish the names of the candidates who are eligible for election as judges of the MIC by classifying them in one of the following regional groups based on the nationality of the country which nominated them for the election: Asia, Africa, Latin America and the Caribbean, Western Europe and others, and Eastern Europe. The names will be published in an alphabetical order and each name will indicate the regional group which has the right to vote for the candidate.*
> *4. The Members of a particular regional group in the Plenary Body will vote on the candidates eligible for election from their regional group with the aim to select an initial number of 15 judges, of which the following number of judges shall be chosen from each regional group:*

97 idem, para 156.
98 idem, para 157.
99 idem, para 159.

Asia: ### judges
Africa: ### judges
Latin America and the Caribbean: ### judges
Western Europe and others: ### judges
Eastern Europe: ### judge
5. In addition to the judges elected under paragraph 4 above, each regional group will be allotted a quota of judges out of the remaining nine MIC judges who shall be elected as provided under Article 12(1 - 4) of this Statute and subject to any amendment under Article 9(4). The number of judges which can be elected by a regional group will be commensurate with the number of MIC Members present in the regional group as a share of the total number of MIC Members.
6. Each Member of the MIC has one vote, which may be exercised in the election process for the judges of the MIC. Legal entities that are Members of the MIC can exercise their right to vote having a number of votes equal to the number of votes of their members which are Members of the MIC. Based on the number of votes received and the quota allotted to the regional group, the persons who receive the highest number of votes in a particular regional group will be selected as judges of the MIC.
7. The appointed judges will take an Oath of Office before the Plenary Body before the commencement of their tenure.[100]

3. *The Kaufmann-Kohler/Potestà Proposals*

Regarding decision-makers in the current ISDS framework, the *Kaufmann-Kohler/Potestà* Proposals note that current criticisms include an 'alleged lack of sufficient guarantees of independence and impartiality' due to their remuneration creating a 'vested interest in perpetuating the regime'.[101] The authors take the view that, because investment treaty disputes are generally commenced by investors rather than states, arbitrators would be dependent on future appointments and so 'inclined to cater to the investors' interests'.[102] They also mention current criticisms as including (i) party appointments negatively impacting impartiality, (ii) practitioners acting in different proceedings as counsel and arbitrator giving rise to conflicts of interest and issue conflicts, (iii) insufficient relationships be-

100 Bungenberg, Reinisch *(n 52)*.
101 Kaufmann-Kohler, Potestà *(n 53)*, para 20.
102 ibid.

tween arbitrators and the States whose regulatory frameworks they are examining, and (iv) a lack of acceptability of private individuals ruling on decisions of democratically elected officials.[103]

The Proposals discuss the benefits and drawbacks of a standing body, and regarding the adjudicators, they take the view that 'tenured judges would offer better guarantees of impartiality and independence than arbitrators appointed on an *ad hoc* basis'[104] but also that bringing an end to the system of party appointment could 'entail undesirable consequences', as it may not be possible to find individuals with the same level of experience, reputation and competence who are willing to devote all of their time to a long-term position; nor might the level of remuneration attract the best candidates.[105] Kaufmann-Kohler and Potestà also mention that the creation of a permanent body might 'mean reintroducing politics into investor-State dispute settlement and would be contrary to the fundamental purpose of the regime, which may affect its legitimacy.'[106]

The *Kaufmann-Kohler/Potestà* Proposals examine two different models, an 'International Tribunal for Investments' ('ITI') and an appeal mechanism ('AM'). The AM is considered both as a possible addition to the ITI and also as an alternative. In relation to the appointment of arbitrators to the ITI and/or AM, the authors note that party appointments would no longer be possible in a system with tenured members who have been nominated by States.[107] However, they state that consulting business organisations (representative of investor interests) with regard to the election process would mitigate the risk of shifting to an 'interstate paradigm', which would neglect the asymmetric nature of investor-State dispute settlement.[108]

The *Kaufmann-Kohler/Potestà* Proposals discuss how to determine an appropriate length of term of service, noting that while 'a shorter term of office accompanied by the possibility of re-election would enable States (possibly in consultation with business organisations) to confirm sitting members with a good performance record, while excluding those with which they are dissatisfied', at the same time, 'a longer non-renewable mandate would shield members from the possible (conscious or unconscious) pressure deriving from the desire to be re-elected and would thus

103 idem, para 21.
104 idem, para 29.
105 idem, para 33.
106 idem, para 34 (footnotes omitted).
107 idem, para 92.
108 idem, para 168.

strengthen their actual and perceived independence'.[109] The authors also examine how disputes would be assigned at the ITI, and set out two models: (i) a roster from which the parties could select the arbitrators,[110] and (ii) a standing tribunal without any party choice (although the right to challenge should be retained), whereby for example the President of the ITI could appoint arbitrators.[111]

The Proposals encompass a separate and detailed paper on the composition of an ITI. Some of the main relevant issues emphasised in the paper are:

a) Structural independence

It is suggested that as an entity, ITI would need to be independent of States, independent of the organs of any international organisation the ITI might be under the aegis of, and also independent of non-State actors such as business organisations, NGOs and civil society groups.[112] Such structural independence could be established through inter alia a depoliticised selection method, security of tenure, longer and non-renewable terms of office, financial security, and rules on incompatibilities with other activities.[113]

b) Individual independence (and impartiality)

The authors first note that issues of individual independence 'are less likely to arise' in an ITI setting but that the independence and impartiality of individual adjudicators should be protected by way of a standard for disqualification of 'justifiable doubts' and possibly also a code of conduct.[114]

109 idem, para 170.
110 idem, para 171.
111 idem, para 172 (noting that both CETA and the EU-Vietnam FTA take this approach). The Kaufmann-Kohler/Potestà Proposals *(n 53)* also address the issue of nationality, see paras 173-174, the ideal number of members to hear a dispute, see para 175 and the role of an institutional structure, see para 176.
112 idem, para 82.
113 idem, paras 85-93.
114 idem, para 94.

c) 'Internal' repeat appointments:

In addition, the *Kaufmann-Kohler/Potestà* Proposals point out that certain current criticisms will 'lose relevance or take on a different shape', and specifically note in this regard that if the ITI takes the form of a permanent institution, the removal of party choice of adjudicators will 'largely alleviate' current concerns as to repeat appointments of particular individuals.[115] However, if the ITI were to instead be semi-permanent, with parties able to select adjudicators from a roster, 'concerns over repeat appointments are bound to continue, if not even become more acute due to the limited pool of adjudicators from which disputing parties will be able to choose'.[116]

d) 'External' repeat appointments

Kaufmann-Kohler and Potestà note that concerns about external repeat appointments would still remain in the event that adjudicators were to be permitted to continue to sit in commercial and investment treaty arbitration cases alongside their tenure at the ITI, and note that in a permanent ITI, stricter rules on incompatibilities between ITI tenure and other activities would be 'desirable', whereas with a semi-permanent ITI, 'room would have to be made for the adjudicators' external activities, as a member of the roster would have no assurance of ever being appointed to a panel.'[117]

e) 'Issue conflicts':

The *Kaufmann-Kohler/Potestà* Proposals address three kinds of issue conflicts:

(1) **'Double-hatting'** (prior or current service as counsel/expert): The authors note that 'different constellations may arise depending on whether the ITI is permanent or semi-permanent and whether the potentially conflicting service is performed within or outside the ITI.'[118]

115 idem, para 96.
116 idem, para 96.
117 idem, para 97.
118 idem, para 99.

They conclude that '[w]ith proper incompatibility rules in place, concerns about double hatting are likely to diminish, if not disappear'.[119]

(2) **Decision on same (or similar) legal issue:** It is suggested that in a permanent setting, concerns about conflicts based on the adjudicator having rendered a prior decision on the same or similar legal issues 'to the extent that they are justified at all, should vanish'.[120] Concerns about issue conflicts may however still arise where an adjudicator sits in a proceeding in a forum other than the ITI.[121]

(3) **Scholarly writings:** The authors note that although 'scholarly opinions unrelated to the case at issue are generally not considered to affect an arbitrator's impartiality',[122] in the ITI setting where the parties will have little or no choice in the selection of adjudicator, concerns about predispositions as to particular issues are in any case simply less likely to arise.[123]

f) Other relationships of ITI adjudicators

Furthermore, they note that 'other types of relationships between an ITI member and a disputing party, counsel, or the dispute would not be substantively impacted by a possible reform',[124] and in these cases 'the same facts and circumstances will continue to raise doubts and potentially disqualify an adjudicator as presently'.[125] The authors list these circumstances as where an ITI member:

(i) is 'judge in his or her own cause';
(ii) has a financial or personal interest in the dispute or in one of the disputing parties;
(iii) had a prior involvement in the dispute;
(iv) had (nontrivial) business dealings with a disputing party;
(v) has a personal or family relationship with a disputing party or its counsel; and

119 ibid.
120 idem, para 100.
121 ibid.
122 idem, para 101.
123 ibid.
124 idem, para 103.
125 ibid.

(vi) has shown bias vis-à-vis a disputing party or the dispute prior to or during the proceedings in such a manner that he or she cannot be expected to keep an open mind and render an impartial judgment.[126]

Finally, the *Kaufmann-Kohler/Potestà* Proposals conclude that 'the main bulwark to safeguard individual independence and impartiality is the provision for the disputing party's power to request a disqualification of an adjudicator',[127] noting that there would need to be a decision as to who should decide on a challenge. Whilst the decision could be left to the ITI, the authors see advantages in conferring such power on an external authority instead (such as the PCA Secretary General, ICSID, or the ICJ) in order to avoid unchallenged ITI members being entrusted with the power to disqualify one of their colleagues, noting that this approach at ICSID has often been criticised.[128]

Kaufmann-Kohler and Potestà also address the selection process itself: They suggest that the selection process would need to be multi-layered (with a number of procedural phases constraining State discretion),[129] open (such that views from multiple stakeholders, not only States, are taken into account),[130] and lastly transparent, by subjecting the procedure to public scrutiny.[131] On the national level, the *Kaufmann-Kohler/Potestà* Proposals set out various options for the nomination of candidates.[132]

They also favour a 'consultation' phase to take into account the asymmetry of ISDS.[133] Accordingly, NGOs, other arbitral institutions, and associations of international law professionals would gain the opportunity to participate to ensure representation and expertise.[134] The authors also view a screening procedure (as a check and balance) as an advantage.[135]

Kaufmann-Kohler and Potestà point out that the 'electors' (i.e. persons tasked with the appointment of candidates) are likely to be representatives of State parties.[136] Therefore, political considerations are likely to be un-

126 ibid.
127 idem, para 104.
128 ibid.
129 idem, para 112.
130 idem, para 113.
131 idem, para 115.
132 idem, paras 120-125.
133 idem, para 133.
134 idem, para 134.
135 idem, para 135.
136 idem, para 157.

avoidable.[137] In the authors' view, the presence of multiple procedural checks and balances and a final 'political' determination would increase the likelihood of the most qualified candidates being elected.[138]

4. *Preliminary Conclusion: Criteria for a Selection Procedure*

With any switch from *ad hoc* arbitration to a permanent institution, there will need to be effective safeguards against over-politicisation of the selection procedure. Not addressing the danger of a politicisation of appointments would risk undermining the independence, credibility and legitimacy of the adjudicators and of the MIC.[139] With all of the present models offering both advantages and drawbacks, it is perhaps most helpful to think about them in terms of the criteria they need to fulfil in order to secure a representative and competent roster.

First, the process of selection and appointment should provide for checks and balances, with a number of procedural phases potentially constraining the wide discretion of States.[140] Second, and following the argumentation of *Kaufmann-Kohler/Potestà*, it needs to be *inclusive*, taking into consideration views from multiple stakeholders, not only States.[141] And third, the procedure must be *transparent*, by subjecting the procedure to public scrutiny.[142]

In this context, *checks and balances* imply a selection procedure with the highest possible level of procedural safeguards against misuse. Multiple procedural phases could help balance the broad autonomy that MIC Member States have with regard to the selection of adjudicators and limit possibilities for abuse.[143] One of the possibilities to ensure a multi-layered selection process lies in the incorporation of a screening or consultative phase. This is an element of the architecture of numerous courts and tribunals, whereby an advisory panel or body vets the qualifications of candidates put forward by the States parties to the relevant underlying treaty.[144]

---

137 idem, para 160.
138 ibid.
139 idem, paras 107-108.
140 idem, para 112.
141 idem, para 113.
142 idem, para 115.
143 idem, para 112.
144 See below Section B.V.

In order to be *inclusive*, the selection procedure should try to involve all stakeholders to the highest possible extent. Inclusion could mean giving a voice to parties with no direct power in the MIC selection procedure. Thus, the involvement of civil society representatives, NGOs, representatives of investors and associations of international law professionals could make sure that the interests of all stakeholders are, if not represented, then at least taken into account at the selection stage. It should not be forgotten, however, that the impact of this for investors is the replacement of their free choice with at best having their interests merely taken into account.

Finally, in order to transcend some of the common criticisms of *ad hoc* ISDS procedures, *transparency* could be one of the defining criteria when drafting the selection procedure for MIC adjudicators at the international level. Other international dispute resolution institutions have been criticised for the level of discretion they exercise over appointments in the absence of full transparency, such as ICSID regarding its annulment procedures, and the WTO regarding panel appointments.[145] In the case of ICSID, the institution itself forms the annulment committees. While ICSID is bound by certain constraints, such as a negative nationality criterion and the obligation to select only from the panel of State-selected arbitrators, it enjoys otherwise broad discretion.[146] In particular, there is little in the rules governing the formation of annulment committees that would increase the chance of the committee being more qualified, or more representative, than the tribunal that rendered the award.[147] Although both the manner by which the Chairman of the Administrative Council of ICSID composes committees as well as the national procedures by which States select individuals to be appointed to the panel has been criticised as opaque,[148] the issue of committee selection by the Chairman would be unlikely to present itself in the same way in a permanent MIC.

Therefore, the selection procedure within the MIC should subject itself to public scrutiny. In the end, this may also contribute to the overall quality of candidates, as treaty parties would find it harder to allow improper motives to factor into their choice of candidates for the bench.[149] This

145 Bjorklund et al *(n 38)*, 8.
146 Article 52 (3) ICSID Convention.
147 Bjorklund et al *(n 38)*, 8.
148 ICSID Administrative and Financial Regulation 21: ibid.
149 See Aida Torres Pérez, 'Can Judicial Selection Secure Judicial Independence? Constraining State Governments in Selecting International Judges' in Michal Bobek (ed), *Selecting Europe's Judges: A Critical Review of the Appointment Procedures to the European Court* (OUP 2015), 196; Mackenzie et al *(n 28)*, 138.

could involve steps that are already mandatory in similar frameworks, such as the publication of the candidates' resumés;[150] public hearings of candidates; and the public advertisement of openings.[151]

V. Competence and Screening

In parallel to a consultation phase, it may be advantageous to have a separate 'screening' stage in the selection and nomination procedure, whereby an independent body of the MIC scrutinises the proposed candidates for the MIC bench. Such an additional layer of scrutiny with a special emphasis on qualifications in the selection process is something that has been discussed in several of the models developed for an MIC.[152]

Although a screening stage may generally be seen as beneficial to the quality of MIC decision-making, by ensuring only individuals with the requisite knowledge of international law are ultimately nominated to the bench, it does not come without drawbacks. Weighing professional qualifications too heavily could run counter to other necessary skills, as well as to aims of an MIC with regard to the composition of the adjudicator pool, by effectively reducing the pool of eligible individuals.[153] Indeed, relying only on experience as a metric may mean the favouring of older and more experienced individuals. If greater diversity on the bench is to be a goal of an MIC, this aspect has to be given proper consideration, as will be discussed below (C.).[154]

A potential MIC screening mechanism would not be without precedent. In particular, a screening committee similar to the ones existing within the ICC, CJEU and ECtHR has been proposed to vet the qualifications of the candidates, including expertise and general suitability

150 This is notably the case at the International Criminal Court and at the European Court of Human Rights.

151 See eg, UK Department for International Trade, Guidance: Appointments to ICSID panels: call for expressions of interest (19 March 2020) <https://www.gov.uk/government/publications/appointments-to-icsid-panels-call-for-expressions-of-interest/appointments-to-icsid-panels-call-for-expressions-of-interest> accessed 13 January 2022.

152 See Bungenberg, Reinisch (n 13), paras 94-95; Kaufmann-Kohler, Potestà (n 4), paras 74-86.

153 See UNCITRAL, Report WG III, Resumed Session 38, A/CN.9/1004/Add.1 (2020) *(n 3)*, para 120.

154 See more generally John R Crook, 'Dual Hats and Arbitrator Diversity: Goals in Tension' (2019) 113 AJIL Unbound 284.

(independence, integrity and neutrality) prior to election by the Plenary Body.[155] Such a screening process could contribute to transparency and objectivity and lead Member States to set high standards in their internal nomination procedures.[156]

With regard to the composition of a possible MIC screening mechanism charged with assessing candidates' eligibility, similar questions arise to those concerning the selection of adjudicators to be screened. Again, one may look to the CJEU's appointment of former judges of the Court on the advisory panel as an example.[157]

Furthermore, if such a screening phase were to be implemented, the screening mechanism's findings should be binding, if the screening exercise is to have any added value. At the very least, the procedure should be final and removed from challenge by candidates.[158]

However, there would at the same time need to be trust in the screening procedure. In the interests of transparency, the criteria for evaluation should be contained in the constitutive instrument and cover the fulfilment of the eligibility criteria. This would be more precise than simply asking for the candidates' 'suitability', which may leave too much room for interpretation in the hands of the MIC screening mechanism.[159]

In terms of transparency, there exists a possibility to diversify the confidentiality levels of the screening procedure, depending on the recipients.[160] An MIC screening mechanism thus structured would be likely to improve the chances of choosing qualified and independent MIC adjudicators. Different confidentiality levels might also temper potential politicisation and avoid unsuitable candidates being put forward in the first place.

In the end, the following recommendations for a screening mechanism could be issued in order to reflect the aforementioned concerns: First, States as constituting parties could draw up the applicable criteria for office. Second, the screening panel's role could be limited to applying pre-determined criteria and weeding out unsuitable candidates. And third,

155 Bungenberg, Reinisch *(n 13)*, para 94. Emphasizing that arbitrators' expertise and experience should, in addition to international law, also include commercial law: Malcolm Langford, Daniel Behn, and Maria Chiara Malaguti, 'The Quadrilemma: Appointing Adjudicators in Future Investor-State Dispute Settlement' (13 October 2019), Academic Forum on ISDS Concept Paper 2019/12, 27.

156 Bungenberg, Reinisch *(n 13)*, para 95; Bjorklund et al *(n 38)*,19.

157 Bungenberg, Reinisch *(n 13)*, para 137; Article 255 TFEU.

158 Bungenberg, Reinisch *(n 13)*, paras 149, 152.

159 idem, paras 145-146.

160 idem, para 154.

with the benefit of the panel's advice, the ultimate responsibility for the appointment of MIC adjudicators, including the determination of the MIC's composition to reflect the diversity requirements, could lie with the electors.[161]

With regard to professional qualifications, it may be argued that selecting and screening adjudicators with a specific emphasis on substantive competence in public international law in particular could provide a means of countering diverging decisions stemming from treaty interpretation issues.[162] This is emphasised, for instance, in the CETA with regard to tribunal members.[163] However, again, it must be remembered that a decisive emphasis on professional qualifications may come at a cost in bench diversity.

Finally, the example of the International Criminal Court's Advisory Committee on Nomination of Judges ('the Advisory Committee'), one of the obvious models, shows that the mere existence of a screening phase does not resolve all issues surrounding qualifications. For instance, the Advisory Committee's September 2020 report on the evaluation of the 20 candidates nominated by State parties for the 2020 elections for six ICC judicial seats scored candidates as 'highly qualified', 'qualified', 'only formally qualified', or 'not qualified'. Commentators have pointed out that while the Advisory Committee made liberal use of the 'only formally qualified' label, no candidate was scored 'not qualified' (i.e. not meeting the formal requirements set out in the Rome Statute). The 'only formally qualified' label received criticism for its lack of clarity; it was deemed to signify that the candidate met the requirements set out in the Rome Statute for election as a judge, but the Advisory Committee was uncertain whether the candidate could make a noteworthy contribution to the work of the Court. Furthermore, the scoring of individual candidates has received criticism for placing extraordinary importance on familiarity with the Rome Statute and the jurisprudence of the ICC, even when candidates were highly experienced former judges from previous international criminal tribunals.[164]

---

161 idem, para 155.

162 Anna De Luca, Mark Feldman, Martins Paparinskis, and Catharine Titi, 'Responding to Incorrect ISDS Decision-Making: Policy Options, Academic Forum on ISDS Concept Paper 2020/1' (21 January 2020), 22-23.

163 Article 8.27.4 CETA: '[...] They shall have demonstrated expertise in public international law.'

164 Owiso Owiso and Sharon Nakandha, 'Grading' the Nominees for the International Criminal Court Judges Election 2021-2030: The Report of the Advisory

This makes the importance of clear, balanced, and unambiguous criteria for an MIC screening mechanism all the more evident. It also shows that expectations vis-à-vis such a screening phase need to be realistic. Screening alone will not protect the selection phase from political considerations and will not insulate individual candidates from criticism.

C. *Diversity*

I. *The Diversity Deficit in International Investment Arbitration*

UNCITRAL Working Group III considers the issue of diversity as central to any potential remodelling of the ISDS landscape. Indeed, it has said that 'the view was generally shared that the current lack of diversity in decision makers in the field of ISDS contributed to undermine the legitimacy of the ISDS regime.'[165] Therefore, any effort to successfully address issues of representation in a planned MIC would have to address adjudicator diversity. This issue plays into a larger structural debate about diversity in arbitration – both commercial and investor-State[166] – and has been addressed both through the work of Working Group III and also by various scholars.[167] Whatever the final structure of an MIC, an improvement in diversity and inclusiveness will require commitment by States. While the creation of a standing tribunal is an opportunity to ensure the diversity of the bench,

---

Committee on Nomination of Judges – Part I, Opinio Juris' (9 October 2020), <http://opiniojuris.org/2020/10/09/grading-the-nominees-for-the-international-criminal-court-judges-election-2021-2030-the-report-of-the-advisory-committee-on-nomination-of-judges-part-i/>, accessed 13 January 2022; Mark Kersten, The Politics of Electing ICC Judges: Some Unpopular Thoughts, Justice In Conflict, 22 October 2020, <https://justiceinconflict.org/ 2020/10/22/the-politics-of-electing-icc-judges-some-unpopular-thoughts/> accessed 13 January 2022.

165 UNCITRAL, Working Group III, 'Report of Working Group III on the work of its thirty-sixth session (Vienna, 29 October–2 November 2018)' (6 November 2018), A/CN.9/964, para 92; This is also emphasised in UNCITRAL WG III, Selection and appointment of ISDS tribunal members and related matters, WP 213 (2021), para 23.

166 *See inter alia* the Equal Representation in Arbitration (ERA) Pledge (18 May 2016) <http://www.arbitr ationpledge.com/about-the-pledge>, accessed 13 January 2022.

167 *See inter alia* Andrea K Bjorklund, Daniel Behn, Susan Franck, Chiara Giorgetti, Won Kidane, Arnaud de Nanteuil, and Emilia Onyema, 'The Diversity Deficit in International Investment Arbitration' (21 January 2020), Academic Forum on ISDS Concept Paper 2020/1.

States will need to devote time and attention to this, and, importantly, agree on what aspects of diversity to emphasise.[168]

II. Diversity Gaps

1. Elements of Representation

How to conceptualise diversity is itself a complex issue and encompasses a multitude of factors. The ones more consistently mentioned by existing provisions in the statutes of international dispute settlement bodies are (i) regional representation, and (ii) gender.[169] Regional representation, however, can itself cover more complex forms of diversity: diversity of language, ethnicity; legal system, religion, level of development, etc. But other factors fall outside this scope: social and economic class, level of education, age, and work experience are all elements of diversity that have received less attention in ISDS. Such factors, moreover, may overlap and intersect to varying degrees.[170]

2. Geographical Diversity

Since the shift to a permanent system would imply a more structured appointment process, diversity would no longer depend on the goodwill and self-regulation of the actors in the arbitral process.[171] An argument can be made in favour of the system aiming at considering geographical diversity *lato sensu*, ensuring that representativeness extends beyond a nominal assignation of a number of adjudicators to specific continents. This would incorporate related elements mentioned above, such as language, level of development, and legal tradition.[172] In order to further this diversity, the inclusion of a negative nationality requirement in order not to have more than one judge per State seems advisable.[173] Here, MIC Member States

---

168 ibid, 20.

169 Kaufmann-Kohler, Potestà (*n 4*), para 53.

170 *See* Susan D. Franck, 'The Diversity Challenge: Exploring the "Invisible College" of International Arbitration' (2015), 53 Colum J Transnat'l L 429, 440.

171 Kaufmann-Kohler, Potestà (*n 4*), para 52.

172 idem, para 54.

173 idem, para 57; UNCITRAL WG III, Selection and appointment of ISDS tribunal members and related matters, WP 213 (2021), para 19.

might draw on the example of the WTO Appellate Body, where no two members may be drawn from one Member State.[174] At least with regard to the example of the ITLOS, a possible role for regional groupings of States in the selection of a common candidate and of possible rotation schemes within the group is worthy of discussion.[175] The alternative – an absence of such regional groups – would mean a freer choice, but coupled with the possibility that stronger States may ultimately prevail.[176]

3. Gender Diversity

Opportunities to increase gender diversity present themselves at different phases of the selection process: Guidance could be provided to States to avoid male-only candidate lists,[177] as well as later during the selection and appointment phases.[178] As a point of comparison, the Rome Statute requires 'a fair representation of female and male judges'. [179] This is a relatively recent development, and one that would be among the most urgent aspects of improving diversity among adjudicators. However, a forward-thinking MIC Statute could embrace greater gender diversity without necessarily anchoring binary gender norms into its founding document. The inclusion of 'invisible minorities' such as sexual minorities or people with disabilities is however a perhaps more complex challenge.[180]

4. Age Diversity

In order to ensure age diversity – realistically understood as securing the representation of younger adjudicators in arbitral panels hitherto dominated by older individuals – treaty parties to a future MIC could consider incorporating an age range.[181] Instances of age limits include 70 at the

174 Bungenberg, Reinisch (*n 13*), para 96; see also Bjorklund et al (*n 38*),18.
175 Bungenberg, Reinisch (*n 13*), para 97. *See* Bungenberg, Reinisch (*n 11*), Article 12 (3) MIC Draft Statute.
176 Bungenberg, Reinisch (*n 13*), paras 100-101.
177 Kaufmann-Kohler, Potestà (*n 4*), para 64.
178 idem, para 66.
179 Article 36 para. 8 lit a) sublit iii Rome Statute of the International Criminal Court.
180 Kaufmann-Kohler, Potestà (*n 4*), para 53.
181 Kaufmann-Kohler, Potestà (*n 4*), para 164.

ECtHR[182] and 72 at the Caribbean Court.[183] How age is reflected in the bench's make-up will in part depend on the design of the adjudicators' terms of office, in particular their length and renewability.[184]

5. 'Background Diversity'

The concept of 'background diversity' combines the issues of diversity and professional competence of adjudicators. In this context, emphasising the diversity of professional backgrounds among adjudicators would lead to a departure from what has been labelled a 'rigid dual judge-scholar track'[185]. Indeed, if States are truly dedicated to diversity in the MIC, it only seems reasonable to include individuals with a background as lawyers, officials, and representatives of international organisations or NGOs active in international dispute settlement among those considered for adjudicator positions. An argument can be made that it is competence in international law, investment law, and international dispute settlement that should be taken into consideration when screening for knowledge of the MIC's subject matter, as opposed to specific prior professional activity.[186]

III. Diversity in MIC Model Proposals

The lack of diversity in arbitrator appointments has been taken up by all of the MIC proposals (sections 1 to 3), on which we then provide our comments in the following section.

1. The EU Proposals

In their 2017 submission, the EU Proposals note that 'the ad hoc appointment system also impacts on the regional and gender diversity of the

---

182 , Article 23(2) ECHR.
183 Article IX(3) Statute of the Caribbean Court.
184 Kaufmann-Kohler, Potestà (*n 4*), paras 161-164.
185 idem, para 35.
186 idem, para 39.

individuals chosen to sit as arbitrators, with the system leading to relatively limited diversity on both fronts'.[187]

In their 2019 submission, the EU Proposals accordingly state that mechanisms to ensure 'both geographical and gender diversity' should be used.[188] However, the EU Proposals do not flesh this out beyond a reference to Article 36(8) of the Rome Statute of the International Criminal Court for an example of the types of rules which can be set for adjudicators in a permanent body (i.e. 'representation of the principal legal systems of the world, equitable geographical representation and a fair representation of female and male judges').[189] The EU Proposals do provide some underlying reasoning, stating that '[a] permanent two-tier system provides more opportunities for the appointment of adjudicators from underrepresented regions and to seek gender balance' since 'selection criteria could be built-in which would ensure geographical and gender diversity'.[190] However, the EU Proposals note, such opportunities are impossible 'without moving away from the system of party-appointment because in such a system the disputing parties will naturally default to arbitrators with a known profile.'[191]

187 UNCITRAL WG III, Submission European Union and its Member States, WP 145 (2017) *(n 50)*, para 32.

188 UNCITRAL WG III, Submission European Union and its Member States, WP 159 (2019) *(n 50)*, para 21.

189 idem, para 21, Fn 15: 'The Assembly of States Parties, that elects the International Criminal Court (ICC) judges, is required to 'take into account the need for the representation of the principal legal systems of the world, equitable geographical representation and a fair representation of female and male judges.' (Art. 36(4)(8)(a)). For the election of ICC judges, regional and gender voting requirements have been established. According to those requirements, at least six judges should be female and at least six male. There are currently 6 female judges out of 18 at the ICC. Additionally, each regional group of the United Nations has at least two judges. If a regional group has more than sixteen states parties this leads to a minimum voting requirement of three judges from this regional group, see Resolution of the Assembly of the State Parties, Procedure for the nomination and election of judges, the Prosecutor and the Deputy Prosecutors of the International Criminal Court (ICC-ASP/3/Res.6), paras 20(b) and (c), <https://asp.icc-cpi.int/iccdocs/asp_docs/Publications/Compendium/Resolution-ElectionJudges-ENG.pdf> accessed 13 January 2022.

190 idem, para 50.

191 ibid.

2. *The Bungenberg/Reinisch Proposals and the MIC Draft Statute*

The *Bungenberg/Reinisch* Proposals also address diversity. Regarding geographical diversity, they suggest that the adjudicators 'should reflect the legal systems and regions of the Members and seek gender balance – and at the same time have the highest professional qualifications.'[192] They draw on the example of the WTO Appellate Body, and conclude that 'there should not be two judges of the same nationality'.[193] By reference to ITLOS, the authors discuss the possibility of appointing adjudicators by regional group.[194] The alternative – 'a free choice [...] made exclusively on the basis of the qualifications of candidates without an allocation of seats on the bench to regional groups' would, in their view, risk that politically stronger States would ultimately prevail.[195] Regarding gender diversity, Bungenberg and Reinisch note that 'the aim for a balanced appointment of judges from a gender perspective' is a 'relatively recent development',[196] only proposing in the context of assignment of adjudicators that gender balance should be taken into account, 'if possible'.[197]

The MIC Draft Statute envisages geographical diversity in the appointment of judges in its Article 12 (together with a power for the screening committee to consider in that context 'additional criteria'[198]) and includes broader diversity considerations in the context of the assignment of judges in its Article 16(5):

The President will consider criteria such as gender and regional diversity as well as diversity of expertise of legal systems and subject area in addition to the guidelines provided under the Rules of Procedure adopted by the Plenary Body while assigning the judges to the chambers of the MIC and the Appellate Court.

---

192 Bungenberg, Reinisch (*n 13*), para 96.
193 ibid.
194 idem, para 97.
195 idem, paras 100-101.
196 idem, para 105.
197 idem, paras 167.
198 Article 12(2) MIC Draft Statute ('...The Screening Committee may use additional criteria for the screening process as it deems fit and would seek to ensure that the persons who are finally selected represent the principal legal systems of the world').

3. *The Kaufmann-Kohler/Potestà Proposals*

The *Kaufmann-Kohler/Potestà* Proposals state that a permanent system with a criteria-based (rather than party preference-based) appointment process would mean that diversity would no longer 'depend exclusively on the goodwill and self-regulation of the actors involved in the arbitral process' and accordingly 'the potential to achieve diversity goals appears more promising in the new system than in the current one'.[199] The authors mention 'nationality, ethnicity, race, geographical provenance, gender, sexual orientation, presence of disabilities, and age' as examples of 'varied backgrounds'[200] but focus in detail on (i) geographical diversity, and (ii) gender diversity.

Regarding geographical diversity, which in the *Kaufmann-Kohler/Potestà* Proposals is stated to extend to related elements such as 'ethnicity, legal system, culture, religion, tradition, and – especially relevant in an investment context – a State's level of development',[201] it is suggested that an ITI could adopt 'the general criteria on geographical diversity present in the statutes of international courts and tribunals'.[202] It is highlighted that States will generally wish to see 'negative' nationality requirements, in order to limit the number of adjudicators from a single State.[203] The question is also posed as to whether the main legal traditions should be represented,[204] and whether there should be a balance between emerging and developed economies.[205]

Regarding gender diversity, Kaufmann-Kohler and Potestà suggest that considerations could be 'built in' to various phases, for example the nomination phase (if there is one)[206] and then also the election phase (using either aspirational or mandatory wording).[207]

199 Kaufmann-Kohler, Potestà (*n 4*), para 52.
200 idem, para 40.
201 idem, para 54.
202 idem, para 56.
203 idem, para 57.
204 idem, para 58.
205 idem, para 59.
206 idem, para 64.
207 idem, para 66.

IV. The CETA Lesson – Diversity is up to the Parties

While all of these models have value, it should not be forgotten that the appointment of adjudicators to the bench of an MIC as the sole remit of States will not in and of itself guarantee greater diversity. Achieving greater diversity would depend entirely on the decisions taken by States when choosing candidates.[208] The example of the bilateral tribunals established by the EU through the CETA and its Investment Protection Agreements with Vietnam and Singapore show that while such instruments might give consideration to diversity at least with regard to nationality through quotas for judges from each side and from third countries,[209] they fall short in bringing about any other forms of diversity. Indeed, the proposed roster of arbitrators for potential State-to-State disputes arising under the EU-Japan free trade agreement consists of more than 75% male candidates.[210] For State-to-State disputes under CETA, a similar picture emerges – of the 16 arbitrators initially proposed by the EU and Canada, only four were women. [211]

However, the discourse surrounding the ISDS reform process has incorporated influences from the diversity requirements of various international courts. The International Criminal Court and the Appellate Body of the WTO, in particular, are examples of panels requiring some form of gender parity and representation of adjudicators from both the 'global north' and the 'global south'.[212]

---

208 ibid.

209 *See* Article 8.27(2) CETA, Article 15.23 EU-Vietnam Investment Protection Agreement; Article 3.9(2) EU-Singapore IPA.

210 *See* Council Decision (EU) 2019/1317 of 18 July 2019 on the position to be adopted on behalf of the European Union within the Joint Committee established under the Agreement between the European Union and Japan for an Economic Partnership, as regards the establishment of the list of arbitrators (5 August 2019), OJ L 205, <http://data.europa.eu/eli/dec/2019/1317/oj>, accessed 13 January 2022.

211 *See* Council Decision (EU) 2019/2246 of 19 December 2019 on the position to be taken on behalf of the European Union in the CETA Joint Committee as regards the adoption of the List of Arbitrators pursuant to Article 29.8 of the Agreement, OJ L 336 <http://data.europa.eu/eli/dec/2019/2246/oj>, accessed 13 January 2022.

212 Article 36(8)(i)-(iii) Rome Statute of the International Criminal Court; Article 17(3) WTO Dispute Settlement Understanding; see De Luca et al *(n 162)*, 23; Olof Larsson, Theresa Squatrito, Øyvind Stiansen, and Taylor St John, 'Selection and Appointment in International Adjudication: Insights from Political Science', Academic Forum on ISDS Concept Paper 2019/10 (17 September 2019), 11 *et seq*.

Achieving such a balance on the MIC bench would, however, require careful and centralised coordination by the participating States.[213] If the CETA Tribunal and its bench of 21 adjudicators (15 in the first instance, 6 in the second) is taken as an example, these 21 arbitrators evenly reflect a balance of the different metrics of diversity – whether gender, age, nationality, experience, race, legal system of origin, and experience – could realistically only be achieved by the centralised creation of a roster according to these metrics. Otherwise, the fact that each Member State has the power to nominate candidates without coordination could just as likely lead to each adjudicator possessing similar characteristics.[214]

The outcome of such a dispersed responsibility for selection, paired with a strong preference for experience over other criteria and the small size of the candidate pool, can be seen in the roster of the EU-Japan free trade agreement mentioned above. The example of the EU and its conception of investment courts demonstrate that the creation of a standing adjudication mechanism, as opposed to the *ad hoc status quo*, by no means guarantees an increase in adjudicator diversity.[215] Such diversity ultimately stands and falls with the decisions of the nominating parties, not with the architecture of the adjudication mechanism *per se*. However, the architecture may impose some constraints on the choices of the nominating parties.

D. Conclusion

Transitioning from an *ad hoc* dispute resolution system to a standing body decreases the role of the disputing parties, but in turn necessarily increases the role – and responsibility – of the treaty parties, i.e. the future MIC Member States, in the selection and appointment of adjudicators. In setting up the MIC, the treaty parties will have to design a mechanism for the selection and appointment of adjudicators that answers a great number of political and technical questions. In order for an MIC to successfully address the concerns surrounding the current ISDS system, the selection and appointment procedure would need to address several issues in greater emphasis: the diversity of adjudicators, to free ISDS from its perception as

213 De Luca et al *(n 162)*, 23.

214 idem, p. 24.

215 José M. Zárate, 'Legitimacy Concerns of the Proposed Multilateral Investment Court: Is Democracy Possible?' (2018), 59 BCL Rev 2765), 2769.

'pale, male, and stale'; transparency with regard to the selection of its pool of adjudicators, in order to bring ISDS 'out of the backroom and into the light'; and the perception of greater independence and impartiality of the adjudicators.

Furthermore, the future MIC Member States need to design a procedure for the selection and appointment of adjudicators not only from the perspective of respondents (that is, themselves in future disputes), but would also be well-advised to integrate the perspectives of their own investors abroad. MIC Member States might perceive the possibility of greater influence over the composition of the adjudicator bench as an immediate advantage; but at least capital-exporting States should not forget their national investor's needs, if ISDS is still to retain its key advantages for (and attractiveness to) foreign investors – namely, access to neutral, international adjudicators not potentially beholden to the relevant respondent State.[216]

The inherent politicisation of the selection procedure in a treaty-party-controlled mechanism is an issue that should not be understated. The WTO Appellate Body's nomination crisis should serve as a warning that a greater 'judicialisation' of ISDS and the centralisation of adjudicator selection would not come without risks. The experiences of the International Criminal Court's Advisory Committee on Nomination of Judges also shows that a screening procedure for candidates is no silver bullet, as it does not operate in a politics-free environment, either. Either way, as long as the treaty parties' political choice of selection and nomination can draw from a pool of highly qualified candidates, politicisation should be treated as unavoidable and instead addressed as manageable through procedural means,[217] to the extent possible.

Finally, States pursuing the creation of an MIC should consider the costs and benefits of abandoning the current *ad hoc* ISDS system in favour of a centralised architecture. Reforming individual ISDS instruments and changing ingrained behaviours in the selection of *ad hoc* adjudicators may make it possible to achieve the reform aims concerning the way individuals adjudicating investment disputes are selected and appointed. However, greater formalisation and centralisation will not automatically solve all concerns, and will likely also raise multiple new ones.

216 See Schwebel *(n 46)*.
217 Abi-Saab *(n 28)*, 184.

Chapter 7: Code of Conduct of Adjudicators

by Alexander Dünkelsbühler[*]

Selected Bibliography: Marc Bungenberg and August Reinisch, *Draft Statute of the Multilateral Investment Court* (Nomos 2021); Marc Bungenberg and August Reinisch, *From Bilateral Arbitral Tribunals and Investment Courts to a Multilateral Investment Court – Options Regarding the Institutionalization of Investor-State Dispute Settlement* (Springer 2018/19); Jeffrey L Dunoff and Chiara Giorgetti, 'Introduction to the Symposium: A Focus on Ethics in International Courts and Tribunals' (2019) 113 AJIL Unbound, 279; Hélène Ruiz Fabri, 'Conflicts of Interests: Navigating in the Fog' (2019) 113 AJIL Unbound, 307; Chiara Giorgetti, Steven Ratner, Jeffrey Dunoff, Shotaro Hamamoto, Luke Nottage, Stephan Schill, and Michael Waibel, 'Independence and Impartiality in Investment Dispute Settlement: Assessing Challenges and Reform Options' (21 January 2020) Academic Forum on ISDS Concept Paper 2020/1; Gabrielle Kaufmann-Kohler and Michele Potestà, 'The Composition of a Multilateral Investment Court and of an Appeal Mechanism for Investment Awards' (15 November 2017) CIDS Supplemental Report; Phillipe Sands, 'Conflict and Conflicts in Investment Treaty Arbitration: Ethical Standards for Counsel' in Arthur Rovine (ed), *Contemporary Issues In International Arbitration And Mediation: The Fordham Papers 28-49* (Brill 2012); Elsa Sardinha, 'The New EU-Led Approach to Investor-State Arbitration: The Investment Tribunal System in the Comprehensive Economic Trade. Agreement (CETA) and the EU-Vietnam Free Trade Agreement' (2017) 32 ICSID Review 3, 625; Gus Van Harten, 'Perceived Bias in Investment Treaty Arbitration' in Michael Waibel et al (eds), *The Backlash against Investment Arbitration* (Kluwer Law International 2010), 433.

---

* Alexander Dünkelsbühler is a doctoral candidate at the University of Cologne's International Investment Law Centre.

A. Introduction

The question of ethics in international law is not unique to investor-state dispute settlement (ISDS). In fact, cases such as *Chagos*,[1] as well as the *Arbitration between Croatia and Slovenia* case,[2] serve as a reminder that questions surrounding the ethics of adjudicators can impact state-to-state disputes as well. However, much of the public opprobrium that has long dogged investment arbitration has been particularly tied to ethical questions surrounding the perceived lack of independence and impartiality of arbitrators in investor-state dispute settlement cases. Arbitrators, often perceived to be unfairly beholden to private interests, face accusations of favouring investors in order to create further opportunities for appointments.[3] The duties of disclosure currently applying to arbitrators have not adequately remediated this perception, which undermines public trust in ISDS.[4]

To be successful, a Multilateral Investment Court (MIC) will have to address this issue head-on. Even if all participants in ISDS under an MIC were to respect the procedural rules of an MIC Statute, even hints of improper conduct by the adjudicators would suffice to taint the proceedings and tarnish the sheen of transparency and independence that the MIC

1 Arbitral Tribunal Constituted Under Annex VII of the 1982 United Nations Convention on the Law of the Sea, *Mauritius v UK* Reasoned Decision on Challenge, 30 November 2011.

2 *Arbitration Between the Republic of Croatia and the Republic of Slovenia* PCA Case No. 2012-04 Final Award, 29 June 2017; see Arman Sarvarian and Rudy Baker, 'Arbitration Between Croatia and Slovenia: Leaks, Wiretaps, Scandal' (28 July 2015) EJIL:TALK! <https://www.ejiltalk.org/arbitration-between-croatia-and-slovenia-leaks-wiretaps-scandal/> accessed 13 January 2022.

3 Gus Van Harten, 'Perceived Bias in Investment Treaty Arbitration' in Michael Waibel et al (eds), *The Backlash against Investment Arbitration* (Kluwer Law International 2010), 436, 441; Kate Miles, *The Origins of International Investment Law: Empire, Environment and the Safeguarding of Capital* (CUP 2013) 377; Daniel Behn, 'Legitimacy, Evolution and Growth in Investment Arbitration: Empirically Evaluating the State-of-the-Art' 1 Georgetown Journal of International Law 2015, 363, 380; Nicolette Butler and Surya Subedi, 'The Future of International Investment Regulation: Towards a World Investment Organisation?' (2017) 1 Netherlands International Law Review 1, 43, 47; see also the issue of concerns regarding independence and impartiality of arbitrators raised within UNCITRAL, Working Group III, 'Possible Reform of Investor-State Dispute Settlement (ISDS)' (5 September 2018), A/CN.9/WG.III/WP.149, paras 11 et seqq.

4 Freya Baetens, 'The European Union's Proposed Investment Court System: Addressing Criticisms of Investor-State Arbitration While Raising New Challenges' (2016) 43 Legal Issues of Economic Integration 4, 367, 382 et seqq.

would seek to provide for ISDS. Therefore, once suitable candidates have been selected and appointed as adjudicators to the permanent body, the rules according to which they exercise their mandate, and how these rules and circumstances influence their independence and impartiality, become highly relevant.[5]

Finding its source in the idea of the rule of law, the independence and impartiality of adjudicators are necessary preconditions of judicial legitimacy, both domestically and internationally, and accepted as general principles of law under Article 38(1)(c) of the ICJ Statute.[6] Therefore, the influence of external factors in arbitral decision-making and its impact on the legitimacy of investment arbitration have been important concerns in the ISDS reform debate. Thus, the terms of appointment of MIC adjudicators should reflect commonly identified elements of concern such as multiple appointments, double-hatting, issue conflict, alleged pro-investor bias, and connections between parties and arbitrators. The UNCITRAL Working Group III in particular has re-affirmed that 'in order to be considered effective, the ISDS framework should not only ensure actual impartiality and independence of decision makers, but also the appearance thereof.'[7]

How this would be addressed on a structural level remains to be seen. Options include incorporating such provisions in an MIC Statute; by referencing existing Codes of Conduct such as the current ICSID and UNCITRAL-led Code of Conduct for Adjudicators in Investor-State Dispute Settlement effort;[8] or by the creation of an MIC-specific code of conduct. This MIC Code of Conduct could perhaps be inspired by the European Union's efforts in creating Codes of Conduct for its ICS un-

5 See Michael Waibel and Yanhui Wu, 'Are Arbitrators Political? Evidence from International Investment Arbitration' (January 2017) <http://www.yanhuiwu.com/documents/arbitrator.pdf> accessed 13 January 2022; Elsa Sardinha, 'The Impetus for the Creation of an Appellate Mechanism' (2017) 32 ICSID Review 3-FILJ, 503.

6 See United Nations Economic and Social Council Commission on Human Rights, Report of the Special Rapporteur Param Cumaraswamy, 'Independence and Impartiality of the Judiciary, Jurors and Assessors and the Independence of Lawyers' (6 February 1995), UN Doc E/CN.4/1995/39, para 34.

7 UNCITRAL, 'Report of Working Group III on the work of its thirty-sixth session (Vienna, 29 October–2 November 2018)' (6 November 2018), A/CN.9/964, paras 66-83.

8 ICSID, UNCITRAL, 'Draft Code of Conduct for Adjudicators in International Investment Disputes, Version Two' (19 April 2021) <https://icsid.worldbank.org/sites/default/files/Draft_Code_Conduct_Adjudicators_ISDS.pdf> accessed 13 January 2022 (a third Draft Code of Conduct has been published in September 2021 by the UNCITRAL Secretariat).

der the CETA[9] and the EU-Vietnam Free Trade Agreement (EU-Vietnam FTA).[10]

This chapter will address the issue of how an MIC could safeguard the independence and impartiality of its adjudicators through a code of conduct. First, it will look at the effects the shift from an *ad hoc* system to a permanent bench on the incentives of the adjudicators (B.). It will secondly assess whether these adjudicators should rather be attached to the MIC full- or part-time (C.). It will then deal with the individual elements of relevance for a potential MIC Code of Conduct (D.). First, it will provide an overview of existing Codes of Conducts for international adjudicators (D.I.); then, it will discuss the core duties of independence and impartiality (D.II.). It will go on to examine individual issues such as double hatting (D.III.), issue conflicts (D.IV.), the duty of disclosure (D.V.), the obligations of former adjudicators (D.VI.), as well as remedies for perceived bias (D.VII.), before coming to a final conclusion (F.).

B. Changing Incentives: From Ad Hoc Appointments to a Permanent Bench

A switch away from *ad hoc* arbitration to a permanent ISDS institution would in itself remedy several concerns regarding the independence and impartiality of arbitrators. Most obviously, replacing the current system of party appointments with a roster of tenured adjudicators would ease concerns about a lack of independence of party-appointed arbitrators. Tenured adjudicators could be perceived as less beholden to the appointing parties for future appointments and would therefore benefit from an increased public perception of impartiality.[11] While critics argue that putting the appointment mechanism entirely in the hands of participating States could lead to a roster of overly State-friendly adjudicators, States could as well adopt a long-term perspective in the selection process, recognising that

9 See Art. 8.44 (2) Canada-EU Comprehensive Economic and Trade Agreement (CETA), (2016); investment chapter not yet in force (final text published 29 February 2016) <https://trade.ec.europa.eu/doclib/docs/2014/september/tradoc_152806.pdf> accessed 13 January 2022.

10 Free Trade Agreement between the European Union and the Socialist Republic of Vietnam (EU-Vietnam FTA) (draft text published 1 February 2016) <http://trade.ec.europa.eu/doclib/press/index.cfm?id=1437> accessed 13 January 2022.

11 Chiara Giorgetti, Steven Ratner, Jeffrey Dunoff, Shotaro Hamamoto, Luke Nottage, Stephan Schill, and Michael Waibel, 'Independence and Impartiality in Investment Dispute Settlement: Assessing Challenges and Reform Options' (21 January 2020) Academic Forum on ISDS Concept Paper 2020/1, 31.

they and their citizens might find themselves on both sides of potential disputes.[12] In any way, an argument can be made that the *perception* of independence and impartiality would increase with a permanent court staffed by full-time judges.[13]

A State-led appointment process would also limit the damaging perception of close contacts between arbitrators and private interests;[14] and longer, non-renewable terms for the adjudicators would ease concerns regarding multiple appointments and issue conflicts.[15] Most importantly, the alleged implicit pro-investor bias of arbitrators would hardly persist in a permanent court with State-appointed adjudicators. This is likely to help alleviate the allegation that arbitrators in the current system possess an incentive to decide in favour of investors in the hope of repeat appointments in future disputes.[16]

C. Full-Time vs. Part-Time Adjudicators

In this regard, one of the most important points concerning the individual independence of the adjudicators is the question of the temporal nature of their appointment and whether states chose to opt for full-time or part-time judges.

Employing full-time adjudicators would effectively prevent "double-hatting" – the ability to combine activities as both arbitrator and counsel in arbitration proceedings. Furthermore, it is also likely to contribute both to a more effective case management and to a higher degree of independence and quality in the work done by the MIC. This could, in turn, ultimately lead to an increase in caseload, with the added benefit of reducing any incentives for prolonging the settlement of a case.[17] In the beginning, a system of part-time judges, who would receive a stand-by fee plus a fee for the actual work, would probably be less expensive.[18] This reflects

---

12 ibid.
13 ibid.
14 ibid.
15 ibid.
16 idem, 32.
17 Marc Bungenberg and August Reinisch, *From Bilateral Arbitral Tribunals and Investment Courts to a Multilateral Investment Court – Options Regarding the Institutionalization of Investor-State Dispute Settlement* (Springer 2018/19), paras 120 et seqq.
18 Bungenberg, Reinisch *(n 17)*, paras 120 et seqq.

current proposals; consistent with the practice in other international tribunals, [19]the judges would be barred from engaging in other remunerated activities (with the possible exception of teaching appointments).[20]

In a permanent system, availability could, for example, be ensured by an obligation to reside at the seat of the court. Consequently, stand-by fees would have to be paid by the Member States of the MIC; these could allow for variation between adjudicators in the first and second instance.[21] In such a constellation, to which extent parallel engagements could be permissible would depend on the classification of individual adjudicators as part-time or full-time. With part-time adjudicators, parallel engagements would logically remain necessary but could also be made subject to approval and include temporal obligations to ensure availability. With full-time adjudicators, parallel engagements should be minimized but permissible if the judicial activity is not affected. Independence must be guaranteed by excluding engagements as government representatives except where they are not obliged to follow instructions (for example as an academic or judge).[22] Here, the MIC would arguably benefit from the Member States drawing up precise guidelines to prevent adverse effects on the perception of the judicial activity. Most realistically, such guidelines would be drafted in the form of a code of conduct.

Be they full- or part-time adjudicators, a switch away from an ad hoc arbitrator-based system could have an impact on the overall costs of arbitration, as panel members of the MIC would in all likelihood receive a fixed salary, as opposed to the hourly rates charged by arbitrators. This would have the potential to reduce arbitration-related expenses, assuming that the MIC has a reasonably busy caseload.[23]

---

19 See for instance Articles 16 (1), 17 (1), 23 (3) International Court of Justice Statute (ICJ Statute) (1945) 33 UNTS 993 ; Article 20 (2) International Court of Justice Rules of Court (ICJ Rules of Court) (adopted 14 April 1978, entered into force 1 July 1978); Article 35 (3) Rome Statute of the International Criminal Court (ICC) (2002) 2187 UNTS 3; Article 10 (1) ICC Code of Judicial Ethics (2021) Article 21 (3) ECHR; Article VII ECtHR Resolution on Judicial Ethics (23 June 2008); Rule 42 ECtHR Rules of Court (2 June 2021); Article 7 Statute of the International Tribunal for the Law of the Sea (ITLOS) (1994) 1833 UNTS 3.

20 Giorgetti et al (*n 11*), 32.

21 Gabrielle Kaufmann-Kohler and Michele Potestà, 'The Composition of a Multilateral Investment Court and of an Appeal Mechanism for Investment Awards' (15 November 2017) CIDS Supplemental Report, para 146.

22 idem, paras 130 et seqq.

23 Gabriel Bottini, Julien Chaisse, Marko Jovanovic, Facundo Pérez Aznar, and Catherine Titi, 'Excessive Costs and Recoverability of Cost Awards in Investment

With full-time adjudicators, security of tenure rules should ensure impartiality against the appointing entities, especially limiting the reasons to be removed from office.[24] Furthermore, in the interest of securing the future independence of the MIC, adequate financial resources for the adjudicators and for the MIC as a whole should be provided.[25]

D. Designing a Code of Conduct for the MIC

I. The Existing Landscape of Code of Conducts for International Adjudicators

The impartiality and independence of adjudicators is an issue included in all arbitration rules relevant for the settlement of both commercial and investment disputes.[26] Such provisions can be complemented by specific ethics codes. Examples include the American Bar Association and the American Arbitration Association, whose Code of Ethics includes 10 canons on matters such as neutrality, confidentiality and trust obligations, integrity and fairness in the arbitration process, duties of disclosure, standards of integrity and fairness concerning expenses, rules governing the communication with parties, provisions on advertising, and the obligations of arbitrators to reach their decisions 'in a just, independent and deliberate manner.'[27] The Singapore International Arbitration Center (SIAC) has also enacted a Code of Ethics for Arbitrators, which governs appointment, disclosure, bias, communications, fees, conduct, and confidentiality.[28] Arbitral institutions such as the Milan Chamber of Arbitration[29] and

---

Arbitration' (17 September 2019) Academic Forum on ISDS Concept Paper 2019/9, 12.

24 idem, para 86. For more details on the removal of judges see Olof Larsson, Theresa Squatrito, Øyvind Stiansen, and Taylor St John, 'Selection and Appointment in International Adjudication: Insights from Political Science' (17 September 2019) Academic Forum on ISDS Concept Paper 2019/10, 25.

25 Bottini et al (*n 23)*, paras 88-89.

26 See ia Articles 11, 12 UNCITRAL Arbitration Rules; Articles 5, 10 LCIA Arbitration Rules; Article 11 International Chamber of Commerce (ICC) Rules of Arbitration; Article 18 SCC Arbitration Rules; Article 14 Convention on the Settlement of Investment Disputes between States and Nationals of Other States (ICSID Convention) (1965) 575 UNTS 159 ; Article 9 DIS Arbitration Rules.

27 See generally American Arbitration Association, 'Code of Ethics for Arbitrators in Commercial Disputes' (2004).

28 Articles 1-7 SIAC Code of Ethics for An Arbitrator.

29 Milan Chamber of Arbitration Code of Ethics for Arbitrators.

the Hong Kong International Arbitration Centre (HKIAC)[30] have enacted Codes of Ethical Conduct as well.

Professional and learnt societies have developed soft-law instruments giving practitioners guidance in ethical matters as well, which incorporate similar elements.[31] Here, the most renowned examples include the IBA Guidelines on Conflicts of Interest in International Arbitration (IBA Guidelines) and the IBA International Principles on Conduct for the Legal Profession,[32] as well as the Burgh House Principles on the Independence of the International Judiciary adopted by the International Law Association, which in turn are aimed at all members of the international judiciary rather than at arbitrators in commercial arbitrations.[33]

Such codes of ethics have also been adopted by international courts and tribunals. Examples include the ECtHR Resolution on Judicial Ethics of 2008, which encompasses ten general ethical principles applicable to the members of the ECtHR in their work, such as the duties of independence, impartiality, integrity, diligence, competence, and discretion.[34] Courts specialising in international criminal law have adopted codes of conducts as well. Here, the International Criminal Court (ICC) has followed the International Tribunal for the Former Yugoslavia (ICTY) and the International Criminal Tribunal for Rwanda (ICTR) in adopting codes of conducts for judges, counsel, and members of the Office of the Prosecutor.[35]

However, this is not the case for all international courts; for instance, at the International Court of Justice (ICJ), neither the judges nor the other

---

30 HKIAC Code of Ethical Conduct.

31 Chiara Giorgetti and Mohammed Wahab, 'A Code of Conduct for Arbitrators and Judges' (13 October 2019) Academic Forum on ISDS Concept Paper 2019/12, para 5.

32 See International Bar Association, 'International Principles on conduct for the legal profession' (2011), paras 5-7.

33 See Study Group of the International Law Association on Practice and Procedure of International Courts and Tribunals, and the Project on International Courts and Tribunals, 'The Burgh House Principles on the Independence of the International Judiciary' (2004) <https://docs.pca-cpa.org/2020/04/ef1f0fb6-burgh-house-principles.pdf> accessed 13 January 2022 (Burgh House Principles).

34 European Court of Human Rights, Resolution on Judicial Ethics (2008); See generally Arman Sarvarian, 'Common Ethical Standards for Counsel Before the European Court of Justice and European Court of Human Rights' (2012) 23 EJIL 991.

35 Core ICC texts, International Criminal Court (Code of Judicial Ethics, Code of Professional Conduct for Counsel, Regulations of the Office of the Prosecutor, and Regulations of the Registry) and Regulations and Policies; UN International Residual Mechanism for Criminal Tribunals (codes and directives).

participants in proceedings are bound by a specific code of conduct.[36] Instead, provisions touching on professional ethics are – although sporadically – directly incorporated in the ICJ Statute and in the Rules of Court, in particular into the judges' oath of office.[37] Most other international tribunals, such as the ITLOS, also lack codes of conduct that apply generally in their respective proceedings.[38]

In recent years, investment arbitration has witnessed an increase in efforts to incorporate binding codes of conducts for arbitrators into ISDS proceedings.[39] In April 2021, the Secretariats of ICSID and UNCITRAL published a second Draft Code of Conduct for Adjudicators in International Investment Disputes, which is currently still debated by Member States.[40]

Furthermore, the European Union has incorporated such provisions in its Investment Court Systems under CETA and the EU-Vietnam FTA.[41] In the case of the EU-Vietnam FTA, a detailed code of conduct for Members of the Tribunal and the Appellate Tribunal is included in an annex.[42]

In this regard, an innovative feature of CETA is that the European Union and Canada chose not to include a code of conduct in the Treaty itself. Instead, the Treaty imposes a 'best efforts' obligation on the Parties 'to ensure that the code of conduct is adopted no later than the first day of the provisional application or entry into force of this Agreement', and in any event no later than two years after such date.[43] This mandate set out by the Treaty was fulfilled in January 2021, when the CETA Committee on Services and Investment finally adopted a code of conduct for Members of the Tribunal, Members of the Appellate Tribunal, and mediators, which encompasses aspects such as disclosure obligations, independence and im-

---

36 Jeffrey L Dunoff and Chiara Giorgetti, 'Introduction to the Symposium: A Focus on Ethics in International Courts and Tribunals' (2019) 113 AJIL Unbound, 279, 280.

37 Art 4 ICJ Rules of Court.

38 Dunoff, Giorgetti (*n 36*), 279, 281.

39 See International Council for Commercial Arbitration (ICCA), 'Report Of The ASIL-ICCA Joint Task Force On Issue Conflicts In Investor-State Arbitration' (17 March 2016) The ICCA Reports No 3.

40 ICSID, UNCITRAL *(n 8)*.

41 See Elsa Sardinha, 'The New EU-Led Approach to Investor-State Arbitration: The Investment Tribunal System in the Comprehensive Economic Trade Agreement (CETA) and the EU-Vietnam Free Trade Agreement' (2017) 32 ICSID Review 3, 625, 632.

42 EU-Vietnam FTA *(n 10)*, Annex II.

43 Article 8.44 (2) CETA.

partiality, confidentiality, expenses, and obligations of former Members of the Tribunal or Appellate Tribunal. [44] However, it should be noted that CETA itself already contains a code of conduct for arbitrators and mediators for *State-to-State* dispute resolution.[45] In addition, CETA includes detailed language on ethics, and makes the IBA Guidelines binding on its Tribunal and Appeal Tribunal.[46]

This shows the possibility of temporally decoupling the code of conduct from the future MIC Statute. A code of conduct for adjudicators could also be adopted by a potential MIC Plenary Body instead of an MIC Committee.[47]

II. The Core Duties of Impartiality and Independence

In the end, these various codes of ethics or codes of conduct, be they from international tribunals, arbitral bodies, or professional societies, share broadly similar concerns: a focus on independence and impartiality, diligence and integrity, and competence.[48]

As outlined above, the duties of independence and impartiality form a central part of the canon of ethics codes in international arbitration (and legal proceedings *senso latu*).[49] In this context, 'independence' means that the adjudicators must not depend – be it financially or otherwise – on one of the parties.[50] Impartiality, on the other hand, is understood as both

---

44 See CETA, 'Decision No 001/2021 of the Committee on Services and Investment of January 29, 2021 adopting a code of conduct for Members of the Tribunal, Members of the Appellate Tribunal and mediators'.

45 Annex 29-B CETA.

46 Article 8.30 CETA.

47 See Marc Bungenberg and August Reinisch, *Draft Statute of the Multilateral Investment Court* (Nomos 2021), 51: 'Article 8(4): The Plenary Body shall adopt: a code of ethics and a code of conduct for the judges of the MIC, rules of conduct and ethics for all staff members, and regulations on procedure to be followed for the registration, allocation and conduct of proceedings before the Court of First Instance and the Appellate Court, transparency, costs and Court fees. These regulations will be drafted in accordance with the principles of the rule of law and will implement the UNCITRAL Rules of Transparency in Treaty-based Investor-State Arbitration.'

48 Giorgetti, Wahab (*n 31*), para 5.

49 The Burgh House Principles, para 1.1.

50 Giorgetti, Wahab (*n 31*), para 17.

not favouring one of the parties and the absence of inappropriate predispositions towards the issues in dispute or the applicable legal principles.[51]

But how to best preserve the independence and partiality of the MIC adjudicators? To this end, parties to an MIC would need to identify the factors influencing the autonomy of adjudicators. This necessitates a focus on both structural and individual independence as well as impartiality.[52] *Structural* independence aims at protecting the adjudicatory body from external interferences, threats, or pressure from States, international organisations, and non-State actors such as businesses or NGOs. States as respondents might be especially tempted to control the selection and appointment process in a dangerous way, considering the asymmetric settlement mechanism in investment disputes. Whether or not adjudicators could serve multiple terms, and would therefore have to factor in their possible re-appointment into their decision-making, is another issue tied to their structural independence.[53] *Individual* independence, on the other hand, centres on the non-existence of personal relationship with a disputing party.[54] As is argued in *Suez v. Argentina*, 'the concepts of independence and impartiality, though related, are often seen as distinct, although the precise nature of the distinction is not always easy to grasp'.[55]

Realistically, Article 3 of the ICSID-UNCITRAL Draft Code of Conduct for Adjudicators in Investor-State Dispute Settlement is likely to either

---

51 IBA Minimum Standards of Judicial Independence of the International Judiciary, para 1.1.

52 Bungenberg, Reinisch (*n 47*), 25; Kaufmann-Kohler, Potesta (*n 21*), para 71. In addition, Larsson et al (*n 24*), focus on managerial and interpretative autonomy. While the former concerns the question whether the court can administer its own operations, eg select its staff, the latter asks whether it can render judgments without concern about the States' reactions 26, 28-30.

53 Kaufmann-Kohler, Potesta (*n 21*), para 79. Malcolm Langford, Daniel Behn, and Runar Hilleren Lie, 'The Revolving Door in International Investment Arbitration' (June 2017) 20 Journal of International Economic Law 2, 301-332, recommend less party control over appointment which would enhance the independence and impartiality of adjudicators.

54 Kaufmann-Kohler, Potesta (*n 21*), paras 73 et seq, 94 et seqq. The proposal especially refers to the aforementioned IBA guidelines for examples of questionable individual independence.

55 *Suez, Sociedad General de Aguas de Barcelona, S.A. and Vivendi Universal, S.A. v Argentine Republic* ICSID Case No. ARB/03/19 Decision on the Proposal for the Disqualification of a Member of the Arbitral Tribunal, 22 October 2007, para 29 (formerly *Aguas Argentinas, S.A., Suez, Sociedad General de Aguas de Barcelona, S.A.and Vivendi Universal, S.A. v Argentine Republic*).

serve as an inspiration for an MIC or be adopted wholesale.[56] In a similar way, Article 4 of the proposed Code of Conduct for the CETA Investment Court System (ICS), as well as Articles 10-14 of the EU-Vietnam FTA's Code of Conduct[57], are likely to serve as building blocks.

These different codes emphasise similar substantive issues with regards to the adjudicators' duty of impartiality and independence. However, depending on whether or not the MIC would opt for full-time adjudicators, a number of ethical questions and quandaries differ from their counterparts in the *ad hoc* arbitration framework. While this may sound obvious, it is tied to several more complicated issues concerning the work of adjudicators, namely double hatting, issue conflicts, duties of disclosure, the obligations of former adjudicators once they retire from the MIC bench, and remedies for bias.

III. Double Hatting

The phenomenon of 'double hatting' – the ability to combine activities as both arbitrator and counsel in arbitration proceedings – has become of focal point of criticism of investment arbitration. How this issue would be framed in an MIC Code of Conduct will largely depend on what architecture the Member States would choose for the MIC itself; namely, whether or not to include full-time adjudicator positions. Employing full-time adjudicators would most effectively prevent the so-called 'double-hatting' as it is commonly understood.[58] However, the MIC could go further and follow the ICJ in its decision that its sitting Members would not act as arbitrators in investor-state disputes (in this case, outside of the remit of the MIC system) or in commercial arbitration.[59] The Code of Judicial Ethics of the International Criminal Court provides for similar incompatibility requirements.[60]

56 ICSID, UNCITRAL *(n 8)*.

57 EU-Vietnam FTA *(n 10)*, Annex II.

58 'Double-hatting' refers to dispute resolution professionals accepting appointments as arbitrator and counsel on a regular basis. This practice is controversial since it is often associated with conflicts of interests. A detailed analysis of double-hatting is conducted by Giorgetti, Wahab *(n 31)*, paras 18-22.

59 Speech by H E Mr Abdulqawi A Yusuf, President of the International Court of Justice, on the Occasion of the Seventy-Third Session of The United Nations General Assembly (25 October 2018) <https:// www.icj-cij.org/public/files/press-releases/0/000-20181025-PRE-02-00-EN.pdf> accessed 13 January 2022.

60 Article 40 (2-3) ICC Code of Judicial Ethics.

While under a non-permanent system of adjudicators, a ban on double-hatting is likely to improve the perception of independence and impartiality of ISDS proceedings by reducing the concerns over conflicts of interests, it comes at a cost. Indeed, the traditional ISDS system has long accepted a certain level of conflict of interests as part of a necessary bargain in pursuit of other objectives – in particular, arbitrator competence and expertise.[61] Forbidding double-hatting entirely by requesting any adjudicator to withdraw from other cases may also erect even higher barriers to new adjudicators in the ISDS system, which in turn could stymie efforts at increasing geographical and gender diversity in investment arbitration – itself a stated goal of UNCITRAL Working Group III.[62] Furthermore, it is necessary to consider whether a ban on double-hatting would encompass only cases based on the same treaty, or whether it should address investment arbitration as a whole.[63]

If the MIC opts for a non-permanent system of adjudicators, Member States should consider not opting for a blanket ban on 'double-hatting', but see the issue as one of transparency, which can be addressed by accordingly structuring the adjudicators' duties of disclosure.

IV. Issue Conflict

A further issue of debate concerns 'issue conflicts', a conflict of interests stemming from the prior involvement of an adjudicator with a relevant legal question.[64] Such an issue conflict arises when parties are led to believe that an adjudicator may have prejudged a particular issue, owing to a previously expressed opinion – be it in a publication, an award, or

61 See Phillipe Sands, 'Conflict and Conflicts in Investment Treaty Arbitration: Ethical Standards for Counsel' in Arthur Rovine (ed), *Contemporary Issues In International Arbitration And Mediation: The Fordham Papers 28–49* (Brill 2012); Chiara Giorgetti and Jeffrey L Dunoff, 'Ex Pluribus Unum? On the Form and Shape of a Common Code of Ethics in International Litigation' (2019) 113 AJIL UNBOUND 312, 312-318.

62 See John R Crook, 'Dual Hats and Arbitrator Diversity: Goals in Tension' (2019) 113 AJIL UNBOUND 284, 284-289.

63 Giorgetti, Wahab (*n 31*), para 21.

64 Ina C Popova and Jessica L Polebaum, 'Emerging Expectations for Arbitrators: „Issue Conflict" in Investor-State Arbitration and Beyond' (2018) 41 Fordham International Law Journal 4, 937, 938.

a public statement. This in turn can lead to the impression of a lack of impartiality.[65]

The main problem lies in the fact that the most experienced adjudicators, such as those likely to populate the MIC bench, would be experts in the matter, and thus likely to have rendered awards, made speeches, or published articles in the past.[66] Interestingly, the ICSID-UNCITRAL Draft Code of Conduct takes a different approach to this issue than the IBA Guidelines, under which a published legal opinion – in writing or in speech – falls under the categories of the so-called 'Green List', meaning that disclosure is generally not warranted. However, such disclosure would be mandatory under Article 5.2(d) of the ICSID-UNCITRAL Draft Code of Conduct. Nevertheless, the practical effect might be negligible for the parties involved, since a list of publications is easily transmitted, if not already accessible online.[67] In the end, a successful MIC will need to carefully balance these impartiality-related concerns with the requirements of the selection procedure regarding competence.[68] MIC members should not be recused because of special knowledge that qualifies them as potential members in the first place.[69]

Rather than address these issues through *ex post* sanctions and annulment procedures alone, the MIC Member States should combine of variety of already existing approaches. For instance, the most natural remedy for issue conflicts is transparency and the disclosure of interests.[70] Here, the MIC Code of Conduct should give detailed guidance as to what information is required to be disclosed, so as to give a complete picture while

65 Giorgetti, Wahab (*n 31*), para 23.

66 idem, para 24.

67 Compare Sebastian Wuschka and Laura Peters, 'On ISDS Reform and the ICSID-UNCITRAL Draft Code of Conduct for Adjudicators' (17 November 2020) <https://www.luther-lawfirm.com/en/newsroom /blog/detail/on-isds-reform-and-the-icsid-uncitral-draft-code-of-conduct-for-adjudicators> accessed 13 January 2022.

68 Members of the Academic Forum point out that institutionalisation improves independence of the adjudicators from the disputing parties. However, the more independent decision makers are, the less accountable they will be and vice versa. See Malcolm Langford, Daniel Behn, and Maria Chiara Malaguti, 'The Quadrilemma: Appointing Adjudicators in Future Investor-State Dispute Settlement' (Version 2: 13 October 2019) Academic Forum on ISDS Concept Paper 2019/12, 33.

69 Kaufmann-Kohler, Potesta (*n 21*), para 102.

70 See Bungenberg, Reinisch (*n 47*), 51 (Article 8 (4) MIC Draft Statute).

avoiding unnecessary information and preserving privacy.[71] As a standing institution, the MIC would have the benefit of being able to learn from past challenges and over time develop its issue conflict 'filter'. Another possibility would be to involve ethics advisors who could consult on those matters. Finally, to avoid issue conflicts, the MIC Code of Conduct could limit the possibility of holding specific functions simultaneously or successively, such as participating in MIC proceedings as a counsel or State representative for a fixed number of years (which will be discussed below in D.VI.).[72] This could, in turn, theoretically be extended to MIC staff beyond the adjudicators.[73]

Once elected to the MIC bench, adjudicators could, through the MIC Code of Conduct, be restrained from commenting on political issues, as this could affect their perceived independence. Statements both inside and outside the court should be subjected to the greatest of restraints, lest they compromise their independence.[74]

In order to prevent issue conflicts tied to 'judicial nationalism', MIC Member States could consider nationality restrictions ensuring that adjudicators are not deciding on disputes in which their home country is involved. The fear is that in such a case, the adjudicators could be tempted to support the claim of their home State, which would leave all deciding power to the third (presiding) adjudicator.[75] However, the issue is not clear-cut. On the one hand, the involvement of judges holding the nationality of a disputing party would simplify and improve the knowledge about the national law. On the other hand, it might call into question the adjudicator's impartiality. One possible compromise would be to limit the

71 Hélène Ruiz Fabri, 'Conflicts of Interests: Navigating in the Fog' (2019) 113 AJIL UNBOUND 307, 311.

72 Compare Post-Employment Guidelines issued by the Appellate Body of the WTO, World Trade Org Appellate Body (16 April 2014), WT/AB/22.

73 Bungenberg, Reinisch (*n 47*), 51 (Article 8 (4) MIC Draft Statute); Fabri (*n 71*), 307, 311.

74 Bungenberg, Reinisch (*n 17*), para 140.

75 Gabrielle Kaufmann-Kohler and Michele Potestà, 'Can the Mauritius Convention serve as a model for the reform of investor-State arbitration in connection with the introduction of a permanent investment tribunal or an appeal mechanism?: Analysis and Roadmap' CIDS 2016, paras 171 et seqq; see also UNCITRAL, Working Group III, 'Possible reform of investor-State dispute settlement (ISDS) Standing multilateral mechanism: Selection and appointment of ISDS tribunal members and related matters, Note by the Secretariat' (8 December 2021), A/CN.9/WG.III/WP.213 (advance copy), Draft Provision 5, para 21 f.

admission of nationals of the parties as adjudicators only in case of mutual agreement.[76]

In order to reduce issue conflicts, case assignment rules should be defined in a general manner and by barring the parties from exercising influence on the outcome of a case by choosing an adjudicator. This, of course, would be complicated if parties had a say in whether or not nationals of the disputing parties could hear the dispute.[77] Nevertheless, the general possibility to challenge an adjudicator known in international law would presumably continue to exist.

V. *Duty of Disclosure*

In light of this, clarifying the disclosure obligations of adjudicators will be key to ensure that questions of ethics do not mar proceedings before the MIC. Therefore, an MIC Code of Conduct should formulate specific duties of disclosure, encompassing all facts that are likely to affect judicial independence or impartiality.[78]

The extent of the duty of disclosure should be clear in the code of conduct, both in terms of relevant matters as with regards to the temporal limits. To be effective, the duty of disclosure should continue to be effective throughout the length of the proceedings,[79] be given in writing, and communicated to all parties.[80] But what about the past – should the duty of disclosure cover all matters starting with the beginning of an adjudicator's career, or should it be limited to a certain timeframe?[81] Here, inspiration can be drawn from the ICSID-UNCITRAL Draft Code of Conduct,[82] which requires disclosure of relevant relationships five years back, and the EU Commission's proposal for the Investment Court System Code of Conduct's Article 3, which would require such disclosure reaching *at least* five years back. While making the temporal scope of disclosure

76 Bungenberg, Reinisch (*n 17*), para 173.

77 Kaufmann-Kohler, Potesta (*n 21*), paras 92 et seqq.

78 Bungenberg, Reinisch (*n 17*), para 139. See also Anne Peters, 'Managing Conflict of Interest: Lessons from Multiple Disciplines and Settings, in Conflict of Interest in Global, Public and Corporate Governance' in Anne Peters and Lukas Handschin (eds), *Conflict of Interest in Global, Public and Corporate Governance* (CUP 2012) 357, 370.

79 Rule 4.1 IBA Rules of Ethics of International Arbitrators.

80 Rule 4.3 IBA Rules of Ethics of International Arbitrators.

81 Giorgetti, Wahab (*n 31*), para 26.

82 ICSID, UNCITRAL *(n 8)*, Article 5.

duties more flexible through requiring the scrutiny to cover 'at least' a certain time-frame adds an element of uncertainty that a mathematically calculable cut-off date lacks, it would allow significant earlier relationships to be included when relevant.

The duty of disclosure should cover all circumstances that may give rise to any justifiable doubts regarding the arbitrator's independence and impartiality.[83] However, the Member States should consider whether this aim is better served with an exhaustive list of hypothetical constellations constituting problematic cases included in the code of conduct, or whether a more abstract and exemplary description – perhaps modelled after the requirements in the IBA Guidelines – should be given preference.[84] In any case, the result needs to make sure that adjudicators disclose not only any prior knowledge of the dispute, but also business relationships past and present with a party to the dispute, a party's representative, or any other party that has a potential role in the dispute, as well as their nature and duration.[85] Especially in the event of a non-permanent system of adjudicators, the duty of disclosure should also cover previous relationships with co-adjudicators as well as commitments that risk affecting the availability of the adjudicator.[86]

In order to reduce the potential for adjudicator challenges, Member States of the MIC should also consider including language clarifying the extent to disclosure of public, and, conversely, the non-public information.[87]

Importantly, the extent and importance of the disclosure obligations for day-to-day operations of the MIC will be strongly dependent on whether a full-time or part-time system of adjudicators is chosen. In case of full-time adjudicators with no other professional activities, conflicts of interests are likely to be less frequent, as the adjudicators are unlikely to exercise other and potentially conflicting professional activities in parallel. In this case, it may not be necessary to proceed to extensive disclosures for every case; a significant amount of the work would be undertaken at an earlier stage, during the selection and vetting process of the adjudicators, and

83 Giorgetti, Wahab (*n 31*), para 26.
84 See Bungenberg, Reinisch (*n 17*), para 139.
85 Giorgetti, Wahab (*n 31*), para 26.
86 ibid.
87 ibid.

case-related conflicts of interest could fall under the general obligations of adjudicators under the Statute.[88]

VI. Obligations of Former Adjudicators

Furthermore, the drafters of the MIC Code of Conduct should consider including rules determining whether and under which circumstances the adjudicators may resume their professional activities as counsel after their terms expire.[89] This could possibly include the prohibition to exercise specific duties or professions for a specified period of time after the end of their term of office.[90] Such 'cooling-off periods' could find their inspirations in the World Trade Organization (WTO) Appellate Body[91] or the Court of Justice of the European Union,[92] which impose a two-year and three-year waiting period on their members respectively, within which they are not allowed to appear as counsel before the dispute resolution body they were part of. However, they may appear in other roles, as they are merely banned from appearing 'in any manner' in cases which were pending while they were still in office or which they have dealt with directly or indirectly.[93] The European Commission's Investment Court System Proposal also incorporates such a provision.[94]

The duration of a cool-off period should, however, be well-balanced and limited, and should include an adequate compensation for loss of earnings, if the position of adjudicator is to remain attractive for the

---

88 See ICSID, UNCITRAL, 'Draft Code of Conduct Comments by State/Commenter' (14 January 2021) Comment No 11 from the European Union and its Member States on permanent adjudicators, ICSID; Article 5 Draft Code of Conduct, ICSID, UNCITRAL (*n 8*).

89 Bungenberg, Reinisch (*n 17*), para 141; Bungenberg, Reinisch (*n 47*), 25.

90 See Comment No 16 from the European Union and its Member States on permanent adjudicators, ICSID, UNCITRAL (*n 88*); Article 5 Draft Code of Conduct, ICSID, UNCITRAL (*n 8*).

91 See World Trade Org Appellate Body (*n 72*).

92 Article 9 Code of Conduct for Members and former Members of the Court of Justice of the European Union, Notices from European Union Institutions, Bodies, Offices and Agencies (23 December 2016) OJ 2016 C-483/01.

93 ibid.

94 Article 6, Chapter II-Investment, Annex II, Code of Conduct for Members of the Tribunal, the Appeal Tribunal and Mediators, Transatlantic Trade and Investment Partnership, Trade in Services, Investment and E-Commerce.

highly qualified individuals sought for these positions.[95] Finally, the code of conduct could make explicit the ongoing duty of confidentiality and moderation, even after adjudicators leave the MIC bench.[96]

VII. Remedies for Bias

While the transition from an *ad hoc* system of investment arbitration to a standing mechanism such as the MIC will lead to changes in the categories of circumstances giving rise to independence issues, 'traditional' categories of alleged conflicts will remain relevant. These include acting as a judge in his or her own cause, financial or personal interest, prior involvement in the dispute, business dealings with a party, personal or family relationship, and proven prior bias. [97] The same applies to the 'justifiable doubt' standard.[98] Depending on the final form of the MIC, the code of conduct should address circumstances relevant for both *ad hoc* arbitration and permanent adjudicators.

Clearly, ethical infractions by the adjudicators should be penalised. The MIC Member States should consider providing for the combination of challenges to the adjudicators and disciplinary action for cases of severe misconduct, provided that the principle of proportionality is complied with. In particularly serious cases – for instance, breaches of confidentiality – the code of conduct should allow for the adjudicator to be removed from offices, as is the case for CJEU judges.[99]

An element that is unlikely to change in a standing mechanism is that the right to request disqualifications will remain the main bulwark to safeguard individual independence and impartiality. However, States would need to agree on who should decide such questions. If Member States were to opt for a two-tiered MIC, it would appear logical that the second instance should have jurisdiction to rule on challenges brought against first instance judges, perhaps in a plenary setting.[100] However, in case of bias or ethical breaches in the second instance, several possibilities are open – either the decision could be taken by the MIC appeals instance itself in its plenary composition or as a special chamber, or an external

95 Bungenberg, Reinisch (*n 17*), para 141.
96 Giorgetti, Wahab (*n 31*), para 28; Bungenberg, Reinisch (*n 47*), 25.
97 Kaufmann-Kohler, Potesta (*n 21*), para 103.
98 idem, para 104.
99 Article 6 CJEU Statute (2016) OJ C202/210.
100 Bungenberg, Reinisch (*n 17*), para 159.

authority such as the PCA Secretary General, ICSID, or the ICJ, could be asked to adjudicate the matter.[101]

E. Conclusion

Overall, it appears likely that switching from an *ad hoc* to a permanent system in ISDS will achieve the aim of increasing the political accountability of adjudicators as a necessary counterpart to their judicial independence, thus limiting the risk of abuses of power and thereby respond to the critics of the current dispute resolution mechanism.[102]

In conclusion, the Member States of an MIC have a range of options in front of them to address the ethics and conduct of the MIC adjudicators, from the wholesale adoption of the ICSID-UNCITRAL Draft Code of Conduct to a tailor-made ethics regime. In particular, they will have to decide on its structure, either adopting a general code binding for adjudicators, the disputing parties and their counsels, or specific codes for each group of actors involved in the proceedings.[103] The code of conduct could reflect the procedure, comprising rules for the pre-appointment phase and provisions applicable during the actual dispute settlement.[104] It could either be an integral part of an MIC Statute, or be adopted at a separate stage, by a committee or a Plenary Body.

A code of conduct for the MIC will not, however, in itself be enough to renew public trust in ISDS if it is not accompanied by equally well-crafted selection and appointment procedures of the adjudicators themselves.

101 Kaufmann-Kohler, Potesta (*n 21*), para 104; Bungenberg, Reinisch (*n 17*), para 159.

102 Kaufmann-Kohler, Potesta (*n 21*), para 105.

103 Giorgetti, Wahab (*n 31*), paras 30-33.

104 idem, paras 28-29.

Chapter 8: Reforming ISDS Through an Opt-In Treaty – The Case of a Multilateral Investment Court

by Leonard Funk[*]

Selected Bibliography: Wolfgang Alschner, 'The OECD Multilateral Tax Instrument: A Model for Reforming The International Investment Regime?' (2019) 45.1 Brooklyn Journal of International Law, 1; Nathalie Bravo, 'The Mauritius Convention on Transparency and the Multilateral Tax Instrument: models for the modification of treaties?' (2018) 25.3 Transnational Corporations, 85; Marc Bungenberg and August Reinisch, *From Bilateral Arbitral Tribunals and Investment Courts to a Multilateral Investment Court, Options Regarding the Institutionalization of Investor-State Dispute Settlement* (SpringerOpen 2020); Gabrielle Kaufmann-Kohler and Michele Potestà, 'Can the Mauritius Convention serve as a model for the reform of investor-State arbitration in connection with the introduction of a permanent investment tribunal or an appeal mechanism? Analysis and roadmap' CIDS 2016; Anthea Roberts and Taylor St John, 'UNCITRAL and ISDS Reform: Visualising a Flexible Framework' (EJIL:Talk! 24 October 2019) <https://www.ejiltalk.org/uncitral-and-isds-reform-visualising-a-flexible-framework/> accessed 13 January 2022; Stephan W Schill and Geraldo Vidigal, 'Cutting the Gordian Knot: Investment Dispute Settlement à la Carte' (RTA Exchange 2018), Geneva: International Centre for Trade and Sustainable Development; Stephan W Schill and Geraldo Vidigal, 'Designing Investment Dispute Settlement à la Carte: Insights from Comparative Institutional Design Analysis' (2019) 18.3 The Law & Practice of International Courts and Tribunals 314.

A. Introduction

It is open to what extent the discussions of different reform options within the United Nations Commission on International Trade Law (UNCITRAL) Working Group III will ultimately lead to a multilateral re-

---

* Leonard Funk is Research Fellow at the International Investment Law Centre Cologne (IILCC).

form of investor-State dispute settlement (ISDS). Conceivable is, however, that the implementation of any structural ISDS reform(s) into the investment law framework will be a particularly challenging task considering its fragmentation into more than 3,300 international investment agreements (IIAs).[1] For practical purposes, it is therefore beneficial to anticipate how different reform options *could* eventually be implemented into the current system.[2] To that extent, discussions have emerged within UNCITRAL Working Group III about whether to develop, at least in principle, a multilateral instrument on ISDS reform (Multilateral Reform Instrument, MRI).[3] The purpose of an MRI would be to provide a framework for the incorporation of reform options (eg MIC and/or MIAM, code of conduct, rules on third party funding etc.) into the network of more than 3,300 IIAs by way of a single instrument.[4]

This chapter aims at giving a comprehensive overview of the state of discussion about how an MRI could be designed and structured. Corresponding to the core theme of this book, the emphasis will be on the implementation of a Multilateral Investment Court (MIC). This focus is appropriate insofar as an MIC is the most comprehensive and complex reform option currently at issue. Considerations on its implementation through an MRI may naturally be useful for the implementation of less ambitious reform options as well. The chapter is structured into four key questions which policy makers and academia are considering with regards to an MRI. All of these questions are closely interconnected and cannot necessarily be answered detached from each other. Nonetheless, for the purposes of this chapter they can give guidance through the multifaceted discussion about an MRI.

The first question concerns the object of implementation (B.). In principle, an MRI could implement a very specific reform option or a multitude

1 See UNCTAD, 'World Investment Report 2021, Investing in sustainable recovery' (21 June 2021), UNCTAD/WIR/2021, 123.

2 Considering the means of implementation of substantive reform options in advance could for example impact their formulation. UNCITRAL, 'Report on the work of its thirty-ninth session (Vienna, 5-9 October 2020)' (10 November 2020), A/CN.9/1044, para 104.

3 See UNCITRAL, 'Report on the work of its thirty-eighth session (Vienna, 14–18 October 2019)' (23 October 2019), A/CN.9/1004*, paras 25-27; UNCITRAL, Working Group III, 'Possible reform of investor-State dispute settlement (ISDS) – Multilateral instrument on ISDS Reform' (16 January 2020), A/CN.9/WG.III/WP.194; UNCITRAL, Report WG III, Session 39, A/CN.9/1044 (2020) (*n 2*), paras 102-111.

4 UNCITRAL WG III, Multilateral instrument on ISDS reform, WP 194 (2020) (*n 3*), para 3.

of different reform options simultaneously allowing States to choose the reform option(s) they prefer.

The second question is how the architecture of an MRI could look like (C.). An MRI could be designed as an opt-in convention, ie expressing consent to be bound to an MRI would amount to consent to apply one or more specific reform option(s) to disputes arising under IIAs. To this extent, the United Nations Convention on Transparency in Treaty-based Investor-State Arbitration[5] (Mauritius Convention) and the OECD's Multilateral Convention to Implement Tax Treaty Related Measures to Prevent Base Erosion and Profit Shifting[6] (MLI) provide useful models to consider. An MRI could also set-up a new multilateral institution which would administer the reformed mode(s) of ISDS.

The third question relates to the scope of an MRI (D.): in principle, it could encompass disputes arising under future, existing, or future and existing IIAs.

Fourth and last question is how an MRI would relate to dispute settlement provisions in existing IIAs (E.). The answer depends on whether both host and home State, only the host State, only the home State or neither host nor home State become a party to an MRI.

The chapter closes with a conclusion (F.).

B. *What is to be Implemented through an MRI?*

A very basic question in relation to the design of an MRI concerns the object of implementation: should an MRI implement a very specific reform option (eg only an MIC, see below I.) or a multitude of different reform options simultaneously (eg an MIC and a MIAM, code of conduct, rules on third party funding etc, see below II.) allowing States to choose the reform option(s) they prefer? Possibly, there may also be a middle way (see below III.).

---

5 United Nations Convention on Transparency in Treaty-based Investor-State Arbitration (Mauritius Convention) (2014) 54 ILM 751 (2015).

6 Multilateral Convention to Implement Tax Treaty Related Measures to Prevent Base Erosion and Profit Shifting (2017), available at OECD, <https://www.oecd.org/tax/treaties/multilateral-convention-to-implement-tax-treaty-related-measures-to-prevent-BEPS.pdf> accessed 6 March 2022.

I. Implementation of an MIC as a Specific Reform Option

An MIC may be implemented through an MRI which covers only an MIC. An example for such an instrument is the Draft Statute of the Multilateral Investment Court proposed by *Bungenberg/Reinisch*[7] (MIC Draft Statute). It establishes the MIC in the form of an international organisation (Article 1 MIC Draft Statute),[8] stipulates the rules concerning its organisation (particularly Part I, II, and III MIC Draft Statute), jurisdiction (Part IV MIC Draft Statute) and procedure (particularly Part V MIC Draft Statute), and contains a mechanism to extend those rules to future and existing IIAs (Article 20 (1) MIC Draft Statute)[9]. Hence, there already exists a very specific proposal which demonstrates that it is possible to create an MIC on the basis of a treaty which may streamline future discussions.[10]

II. Implementation of an MIC as Part of a Multitude of Reform Options

An MIC may also be implemented through an MRI which covers a variety of different reform options simultaneously. When expressing consent to such an instrument, States could choose 'à la carte'[11] to opt in to those reform option(s) they prefer.[12] In this case an MRI would serve as a single instrument by which the various reform options discussed in UNCITRAL Working Group III would be offered to States for implementation.[13] It could in principle cover all reform options discussed in UNCITRAL Working Group III or a selection only.[14]

---

7 See Marc Bungenberg and August Reinisch, *Draft Statute of the Multilateral Investment Court* (Nomos 2021).

8 See also Marc Bungenberg and August Reinisch, *From Bilateral Arbitral Tribunals and Investment Courts to a Multilateral Investment Court, Options Regarding the Institutionalization of Investor-State Dispute Settlement* (SpringerOpen 2020), para 546.

9 See also Bungenberg, Reinisch (*n 8*), paras 568-576.

10 Cf Bungenberg, Reinisch (*n 7*), Foreword.

11 This term was shaped by Stephan W Schill and Geraldo Vidigal, 'Cutting the Gordian Knot: Investment Dispute Settlement à la Carte', RTA Exchange 2018, Geneva: International Centre for Trade and Sustainable Development.

12 UNCITRAL WG III, Multilateral instrument on ISDS reform, WP 194 (2020) (*n 3*), para 11.

13 ibid, para 7.

14 ibid, para 13.

Quite obviously, developing an MRI bringing (all) different reform options together would be particularly complex in legal terms. Each individual reform option would require the development of specific provisions or annexes.[15] Introducing additional complexity to the already highly complex system of ISDS comes with the definite risk that a reformed system may be relatively hard to understand for both its users and the public.

On the other hand, an MRI bringing (all) different reform options together may enhance overall coherence and consistency in ISDS.[16] Without such a holistic approach bringing together the competing reform proposals, one may question whether it is at all sensible to pursue certain reform options together. For example, the implementation of an MIC and a MIAM reflect quite different philosophies: an MIC would be a fundamental systemic change of ISDS, whereas ISDS would maintain most of its basic features through the implementation of a MIAM.[17] An MRI covering a multitude of reform options can bring together such different philosophies and preferences States have regarding ISDS. However, an instrument which implements many reform options together will only find sufficient support if it comes with a high degree of flexibility for States.[18] While permitting States to flexibly implement the reform options of their choice comes with the definite advantage that it realistically allows for a wide participation of States in an ISDS reform, it also involves the risk of fragmentation of the reformed ISDS system and may furthermore result in undesirable incentives for forum shopping.[19]

III. *A Possible Middle Way?*

An alternative route towards more overall coherence and consistency may emerge if a sufficiently high number of States would be able to agree in principle – as a common denominator – upon the implementation of an

15 ibid.

16 Schill, Vidigal (*n 11*), 17-18; UNCITRAL WG III, Multilateral instrument on ISDS reform, WP 194 (2020) (*n 3*), para 12. See also Landmann, Chapter 4, Section B.I.

17 Gabrielle Kaufmann-Kohler and Michele Potestà, 'Can the Mauritius Convention serve as a model for the reform of investor-State arbitration in connection with the introduction of a permanent investment tribunal or an appeal mechanism? Analysis and roadmap' CIDS 2016, para 217.

18 See below Section C.I.2.

19 UNCITRAL, Report WG III, Session 39, A/CN.9/1044 (2020) (*n 2*), para 108.

MIC (on its own). Within a newly established basic MIC framework it could then be a subsequent step to agree upon follow-up issues in more detail which are – so far – mostly being treated as separate reform options, such as the implementation of a code of conduct for judges, an advisory centre, admissibility of third-party funding etc. For example, the MIC Draft Statute leaves it to the Plenary Body – composed of representatives of all MIC Members (Article 8 (1) MIC Draft Statute) – to inter alia adopt a code of ethics and a code of conduct for the judges of the MIC, rules of conduct and ethics for all staff members, and regulations on procedure to be followed for the registration, allocation and conduct of proceedings before the Court of First Instance and the Appellate Court, transparency, costs and Court fees (Article 8 (4) MIC Draft Statute). However, such an approach would require a prevalent political willingness to implement an MIC, if only in principle. Beyond the European Union, such willingness is so far – if at all – hardly recognisable. Against this background, the at least 40 Members striven for in the MIC Draft Statute (Article 61 (1) MIC Draft Statute)[20] seem to be quite ambitious.[21]

In conclusion, there is no obvious answer to the question whether an MIC would better be implemented on its own or as part of an "à la carte menu". There are advantages and disadvantages, or – maybe more accurate – chances and risks associated with both approaches.[22]

C. *How Could the Architecture of an MRI Look Like?*

While the UNCITRAL Secretariat maintains that the actual architecture of an MRI should be considered once there is clarity about the reform options pursued,[23] one can nevertheless examine principle options available.

---

20 The number of 40 States was chosen to avoid that the MIC constitutes just another dispute resolution mechanism of a few States alongside already existing mechanisms, Bungenberg, Reinisch (*n 8*), paras 564-565.

21 See also Stephan W Schill and Geraldo Vidigal, 'Designing Investment Dispute Settlement à la Carte: Insights from Comparative Institutional Design Analysis' (2019) 18.3 The Law & Practice of International Courts and Tribunals 314, 319-321.

22 See also Braun/Reinhold, Chapter 2, Section E.IV.

23 See UNCITRAL WG III, Multilateral instrument on ISDS reform, WP 194 (2020) (*n 3*), para 14.

I. Opt-In Convention

An MRI could be designed as a so-called 'opt-in convention'.[24] By expressing consent to be bound by a treaty,[25] States would opt in (ie consent) to apply a specific reform option or different reform options simultaneously[26] to disputes arising under (existing and/or future)[27] IIAs according to the modalities of the treaty. The reform options themselves could either be governed inside the treaty in specific provisions or annexes[28] or outside the treaty.

1. Models for an Opt-In Convention

Two models for an opt-in convention are referenced in Working Group III and in academia: The Mauritius Convention[29] and the MLI[30].

---

24 For the notion of an 'opt-in convention' see Kaufmann-Kohler, Potestà (*n 17*), paras 76-78 and 212-220.

25 According to Article 11 VCLT, the consent of a State to be bound by a treaty may be expressed by signature, exchange of instruments constituting a treaty, ratification, acceptance, approval or accession, or by any other means if so agreed.

26 See above Section B.

27 See below Section D.

28 UNCITRAL WG III, Multilateral instrument on ISDS reform, WP 194 (2020) (*n 3*), para 14.

29 See for example Nathalie Bravo, 'The Mauritius Convention on Transparency and the Multilateral Tax Instrument: models for the modification of treaties?' (2018) 25.3 Transnational Corporations 85; Bungenberg, Reinisch (*n 8*), para 577; Kaufmann-Kohler, Potestà (*n 17*); UNCITRAL WG III, Multilateral instrument on ISDS reform, WP 194 (2020) (*n 3*), paras 26-28; UNCITRAL, Report WG III, Session 38, A/CN.9/1004* (2019) (*n 3*), para 101; UNCITRAL, Working Group III, 'Possible reform of investor-State dispute settlement (ISDS), Submission from the Governments of Chile, Israel, Japan, Mexico and Peru' (2 October 2019), A/CN.9/WG.III/WP.182, 4; UNCITRAL, Working Group III, 'Possible reform of investor-State dispute settlement (ISDS), Submission from the Government of Ecuador' (17 July 2019), A/CN.9/WG.III/WP.175, para 32; UNCITRAL, Working Group III, 'Possible reform of investor-State dispute settlement (ISDS) Submission from the European Union and its Member States' (24 January 2019), A/CN.9/WG.III/WP.159/Add.1, para 36.

30 See for example Wolfgang Alschner, 'The OECD Multilateral Tax Instrument: A Model for Reforming The International Investment Regime?' (2019) 45.1 Brooklyn Journal of International Law, 1; Bravo (*n 29*); Anthea Roberts and Taylor St John, 'UNCITRAL and ISDS Reform: Visualising a Flexible Framework' (EJIL:Talk! 24 October 2019) <https://www.ejiltalk.org/uncitral-and-isds-refo

The Mauritius Convention[31] is a multilateral treaty designed to integrate the UNCITRAL Rules on Transparency in Treaty-based Investor-State Arbitration[32] (Transparency Rules) into arbitration proceedings under already existing IIAs without the need to amend the investor-State dispute settlement provisions of each individual treaty. To that end, by expressing consent to be bound by the Mauritius Convention,[33] States can express their consent to apply the Transparency Rules to investor-State arbitration under their respective IIAs concluded before 1 April 2014, ie before the Transparency Rules' automatic applicability to investor-State arbitration under UNCITRAL rules according to Article 1 (1) Transparency Rules.[34] The purpose of the Mauritius Convention is to provide States with an efficient mechanism to reach an agreement to apply the Transparency Rules to investor-State arbitration under IIAs concluded before 1 April

---

rm-visualising-a-flexible-framework/> accessed 13 January 2022; UNCITRAL WG III, Multilateral instrument on ISDS reform, WP 194 (2020) (*n 3*), paras 29-30; UNCITRAL WG III, Submission Chile, Israel, Japan, Mexico and Peru, WP 182 (2019) (*n 29*), 5; UNCITRAL WG III, Submission Ecuador, WP 175 (2019) (*n 29*), paras 30-31; UNCITRAL, Working Group III, 'Possible reform of investor-State dispute settlement (ISDS), Submission from the Government of Colombia' (14 June 2019), A/CN.9/WG.III/WP.173, paras 4 et seqq; UNCITRAL WG III, Submission European Union and its Member States, WP 159 (2019) (*n 29*), para 36.

31 See above (*n 5*).

32 UNCITRAL Rules on Transparency in Treaty-Based Investor-State Arbitration (2013) 52 ILM 1303 (2013).

33 According to Article 7 Mauritius Convention, consent to be bound by the Mauritius Convention may be expressed through ratification, acceptance, approval or accession. See also above (*n 25*).

34 Article 1 ('Scope of application') of the Transparency Rules reads:
Applicability of the Rules
1. The UNCITRAL Rules on Transparency in Treaty-based Investor-State Arbitration ('Rules on Transparency') shall apply to investor-State arbitration initiated under the UNCITRAL Arbitration Rules pursuant to a treaty providing for the protection of investments or investors ('treaty') concluded on or after 1 April 2014 unless the Parties to the treaty have agreed otherwise.
2. In investor-State arbitrations initiated under the UNCITRAL Arbitration Rules pursuant to a treaty concluded before 1 April 2014, these Rules shall apply only when:
(a) The parties to an arbitration (the 'disputing parties') agree to their application in respect of that arbitration; or
(b) The Parties to the treaty or, in the case of a multilateral treaty, the State of the claimant and the respondent State, have agreed after 1 April 2014 to their application.
(…)

2014 (cf Article 1 (2) (b) Transparency Rules).[35] This mechanism is called the *bilateral or multilateral application* of the Transparency Rules, Article 2 (1) Mauritius Convention.[36] In addition, Article 2 (2) Mauritius Convention foresees a *unilateral application* of the Transparency Rules in case that only the host State is party to the Mauritius Convention and that the investor agrees to their application in a dispute arising under an existing IIA (Unilateral Offer Mechanism).[37]

The MLI[38] is a multilateral treaty designed to modify (Article 1 MLI) tax treaties that two or more parties to the MLI have concluded with the

---

According to Article 1 (4) UNCITRAL Arbitration Rules (with new article 1, paragraph 4, as adopted in 2013), the UNCITRAL Arbitration Rules include the Transparency Rules subject to Article 1 of the Transparency Rules.

35 See UNCITRAL, 'Report of the United Nations Commission on International Trade Law, Forty-sixth session' (8-26 July 2013), A/68/17 (2013), paras 118 and 127. The concrete functioning of the Mauritius Convention is explained in more detail in Kaufmann-Kohler, Potestà (*n 17*), paras 56 et seqq. See also Lise Johnson, *The Mauritius Convention on Transparency: Comments on the treaty and its role in increasing transparency of investor-State arbitration* (CCSI Policy Paper 2014); Judith Knieper, 'The UNCITRAL Transparency Standards in ISDS as a Result of Multilateral Negotiation' (2016) 1.1 European Investment Law and Arbitration Review 155; João Ribeiro and Michael Douglas, 'Transparency in Investor-State Arbitration: The Way Forward' (2015) 11.1 Asian International Arbitration Journal 49, 61 et seqq; Stephan Schill, 'The Mauritius Convention on Transparency' (2015) 16.2 Journal of World Investment & Trade 201; Stephan Schill, 'United Nations Convention on Transparency in Treaty-based Investor-State Arbitration' in Hélène Ruiz Fabri (ed), *Max Planck Encyclopedia of International Procedural Law* (January 2019); Esmé Shirlow, 'Dawn of a new era? The UNCITRAL Rules and UN Convention on Transparency in Treaty-Based Investor-State Arbitration' (2016) 31.3 ICSID Review – Foreign Investment Law Journal 622.

36 Article 2 ('Application of the UNCITRAL Rules on Transparency') (1) reads:
Bilateral or multilateral application
1. The UNCITRAL Rules on Transparency shall apply to any investor-State arbitration, whether or not initiated under the UNCITRAL Arbitration Rules, in which the respondent is a Party that has not made a relevant reservation under article 3 (1) (a) or (b), and the claimant is of a State that is a Party that has not made a relevant reservation under article 3 (1) (a).

37 Article 2 ('Application of the UNCITRAL Rules on Transparency') (2) reads:
Unilateral offer of application
2. Where the UNCITRAL Rules on Transparency do not apply pursuant to paragraph 1, the UNCITRAL Rules on Transparency shall apply to an investor-State arbitration, whether or not initiated under the UNCITRAL Arbitration Rules, in which the respondent is a Party that has not made a reservation relevant to that investor-State arbitration under article 3 (1), and the claimant agrees to the application of the UNCITRAL Rules on Transparency.

38 See above (*n 6*).

intention of avoiding double taxation with respect to taxes on income (Article 2 (1) (a) (i) MLI); the MLI modifies such a tax treaty when each of the contracting parties has notified a specific tax treaty to the depositary as an agreement it wishes to be covered by the MLI (Article 2 (1) (a) (ii) MLI).[39] According to its preamble, the MLI's purpose is to provide an efficient mechanism for the swift and coordinated implementation of tax treaty-related measures to prevent base erosion and profit shifting (BEPS) into the network of existing tax treaties for the avoidance of double taxation without the need to bilaterally renegotiate each such agreement.[40]

Hence, both the Mauritius Convention and the MLI are designed to implement uniform rules in already existing treaty networks through a single multilateral treaty without the need to amend each individual existing treaty.[41] For this reason, both treaties are useful models for an MRI.

---

39 Article 1 ('Scope of the Convention') of the MLI reads:
'This Convention modifies all Covered Tax Agreements as defined in subparagraph a) of paragraph 1 of Article 2 (Interpretation of Terms).'
Article 2 ('Interpretation of Terms') of the MLI reads:
1. For the purpose of this Convention, the following definitions apply:
a) The term 'Covered Tax Agreement' means an agreement for the avoidance of double taxation with respect to taxes on income (whether or not other taxes are also covered):
i) that is in force between two or more:
A) Parties; and/or
B) jurisdictions or territories which are parties to an agreement described above and for whose international relations a Party is responsible; and
ii) with respect to which each such Party has made a notification to the Depositary listing the agreement as well as any amending or accompanying instruments thereto (identified by title, names of the parties, date of signature, and, if applicable at the time of the notification, date of entry into force) as an agreement which it wishes to be covered by this Convention.
(...)

40 See also OECD, 'Explanatory Statement to the Multilateral Convention to Implement Tax Treaty Related Measures to Prevent Base Erosion and Profit Shifting' (2016), paras 6 and 14. See generally on the MLI Reuven S Avi-Yonah and Haiyan Xu, 'A Global Treaty Override? The New OECD Multilateral Tax Instrument and Its Limits' (2018) 39.2 Michigan Journal of International Law, 155; Nathalie Bravo, 'A multilateral instrument for updating the tax treaty network', IBFD 2020; David Kleist, 'The Multilateral Convention to Implement Tax Treaty Related Measures to Prevent BEPS – Some Thoughts on Complexity and Uncertainty' Nordic Tax Journal 2018, 31; Michael Lang et al (eds), *The OECD Multilateral Instrument for Tax Treaties, Analysis and Effects* (Wolters Kluwer 2018).

41 Bravo (*n 29*), 86.

2. *Elements of Flexibility*

To ensure a wide participation, an MRI designed as an opt-in convention could include elements of flexibility which would allow States to tailor their individual level of involvement into the reform option(s) provided.

a) Technical Possibilities to Introduce Flexibility

Technically, there exist several possibilities to enable State parties to a multilateral treaty to customise their individual treaty obligations.[42] Inspiration for the utilisation of such elements can be drawn from the Mauritius Convention as well as from the MLI.

(1) Reservations

A means for States to unilaterally alter obligations under a multilateral treaty is to resort to reservations.[43] According to Article 2 (1) (d) Vienna Convention on the Law of Treaties (VCLT)[44], a reservation is a unilateral statement made by a State, whereby it purports to exclude or modify the legal effect of certain provisions of a treaty in their application to that State. States are permitted to formulate a reservation unless the reservation is prohibited by the treaty (Article 19 (a) and (b) VCLT) or incompatible with the object and purpose of the treaty (Article 19 (c) VCLT).

The Mauritius Convention illustrates how reservations may be used to provide for flexibility in the context of an MRI. Article 3 Mauritius Convention conclusively enumerates those reservations which the treaty makers deemed to be acceptable.[45] States may inter alia (1) carve out investor-State arbitration under a specific IIA from the Mauritius Conven-

---

42 See Thomas Giegerich, 'Treaties, Multilateral, Reservations to' in Anne Peters (ed), *Max Planck Encyclopedia of Public International Law* (September 2020), paras 6 et seq.

43 See ibid for the concept of reservations to multilateral treaties in general.

44 Vienna Convention on the Law of Treaties (VCLT) (1969) 1155 UNTS 331.

45 Article 3 ('Reservations') Mauritius Convention reads:
1. A Party may declare that:
(a) It shall not apply this Convention to investor-State arbitration under a specific investment treaty, identified by title and name of the contracting parties to that investment treaty;

tion's scope of application (Article (3) (1) (a) Mauritius Convention), (2) exclude arbitration under a specific set of arbitration rules or procedures other than the UNCITRAL Arbitration Rules (Article (3) (1) (b) Mauritius Convention) from the Mauritius Convention's scope of application, and (3) exclude the application of the Unilateral Offer Mechanism (Article (3) (1) (c) Mauritius Convention). This way of providing flexibility is described as a 'negative listing approach'.[46] If a State becomes party to the Mauritius Convention without making any of these reservations, the Transparency Rules apply to any dispute arising from an IIA concluded before 1 April 2014 if either the home State is party to the Mauritius Convention as well (Article 2 (1) Mauritius Convention) or the investor has agreed to an application (Article 2 (2) Mauritius Convention).

Following this approach, an MRI may similarly allow States to (1) exclude dispute settlement under specific IIAs from the reform option(s) provided, (2) exclude the application of specific reform options (if more than one reform option is provided), and (3) exclude an application of reform options without reciprocal consent by host and home State.[47]

(2) Declarations

States may also make use of declarations in a broader sense to unilaterally set out their individual treaty commitments, if the treaty so provides.[48] By way of an illustration, this technique is utilised in the MLI and is commonly referred to as a 'positive listing approach'.[49] In contrast to the Mauritius Convention, Article 2 (1) (a) (ii) MLI requires its parties to positively notify any tax treaty they wish to be modified to the depository.[50]

(b) Article 2 (1) and (2) shall not apply to investor-State arbitration conducted using a specific set of arbitration rules or procedures other than the UNCITRAL Arbitration Rules, and in which it is a respondent;

(c) Article 2 (2) shall not apply in investor-State arbitration in which it is a respondent.

(…)

4. No reservations are permitted except those expressly authorized in this article.

46 Bravo (*n 29*), 97.

47 UNCITRAL WG III, Multilateral instrument on ISDS reform, WP 194 (2020) (*n 3*), para 19.

48 Oliver Dörr, 'Declaration' in Anne Peters (ed), *Max Planck Encyclopedia of Public International Law* (August 2019), para 1.

49 Bravo (*n 29*), 92.

50 For the treaty text see above (*n 39*).

Similarly, an MRI could require States to positively notify all IIAs they wish to be covered by the reform option(s) provided. In line with this approach, the MIC Draft Statute allows States to flexibly choose which IIAs they wish to be subject to the exclusive jurisdiction of the MIC (Article 20 (1) MIC Draft Statute). State parties to an MRI could also be allowed to declare whether the reform option(s) implemented apply exclusively, ie entirely replace ISDS provisions in their existing IIAs, or additionally, ie supplement ISDS provisions in their existing IIAs.[51]

(3) Alternative and Optional Provisions

A treaty may furthermore provide alternative provisions, optional clauses or optional protocols for the treaty parties to modify their individual treaty obligations.[52] The MLI offers some alternative and optional provisions which parties to the MLI can choose from to address specific issues.[53]

The additional flexibility introduced through these techniques may be beneficial to an MRI as well. For example, States being respondents in disputes under their IIAs could be given a choice to resolve them before an MIC or before an arbitral tribunal with certain reform options being applicable (for example a MIAM, code of conduct, etc.).[54]

b) Desirable Degree of Flexibility

The substantive issue with regards to the presented techniques is how much flexibility is desirable considering the conflicting goals of universal participation on the one hand and integrity of the reform option(s) provided on the other hand. By their very nature, elements of flexibility pro-

---

51 Kaufmann-Kohler, Potestà (*n 17*), para 263. See also below Section E.I.

52 Giegerich (*n 42*), paras 6 et seq.

53 For example, Article 5 ('Application of Methods for Elimination of Double Taxation') MLI reads:
'1. A Party may choose to apply either paragraphs 2 and 3 (Option A), paragraphs 4 and 5 (Option B), or paragraphs 6 and 7 (Option C), or may choose to apply none of the Options.
(...)'.

54 See UNCITRAL WG III, Multilateral instrument on ISDS reform, WP 194 (2020) (*n 3*), para 16.

mote universal participation by diversifying individual treaty obligations.[55] Hence, an extensive use of such techniques in an MRI may lead to a reformed but fragmented system of ISDS.[56] Considering the different policies States have regarding ISDS,[57] however, a universally accepted MRI is not conceivable without providing significant flexibility to its parties. It will be decisive, therefore, that States manage to find the right balance between flexibility and integrity.

Within UNCITRAL Working Group III, States have just started to think about that issue. Currently under consideration is for example, whether there should be certain core provisions or minimum standards in an MRI that all its parties would have to accept.[58] The outcome of this discussion remains open for the moment. To prevent that the entire content of an MRI would be carved out, there could for example be an exhaustive list of possible reservations and declarations acceptable to all States – as was the approach adopted in the Mauritius Convention (Article 3 (4) Mauritius Convention).[59]

II. Multilateral Institution for ISDS

An MRI could also set-up a new umbrella institution which would have the task of administering different modes of ISDS, such as an MIC, a MIAM and reformed investor-State arbitration. The idea is that States can choose their preferred mode(s) of dispute settlement within a newly established institutional framework.[60] The new institution could in principle either be established on a treaty basis inside (specific provisions or annexes) or outside (separate treaty) an opt-in convention or in a separate

55 Giegerich (*n 42*), paras 6 et seq.

56 UNCITRAL, Report WG III, Session 39, A/CN.9/1044 (2020) (*n 2*), para 108. See also above Section B.II.

57 See for example Anthea Roberts, 'Incremental, Systemic, and Paradigmatic Reform of Investor-State Arbitration' (2018) 112.3 American Journal of International Law 410.

58 UNCITRAL WG III, Multilateral instrument on ISDS reform, WP 194 (2020) (*n 3*), para 39 at (i); UNCITRAL WG III, Submission Colombia, WP 173 (2019) (*n 30*), para 27; UNCITRAL, Report WG III, Session 39, A/CN.9/1044 (2020) (*n 2*), para 107.

59 Kaufmann-Kohler, Potestà (*n 17*), para 260.

60 UNCITRAL WG III, Multilateral instrument on ISDS reform, WP 194 (2020) (*n 3*), para 14. For possible institutional frameworks in more detail see also Braun/Reinhold, Chapter 2.

soft law instrument.[61] A treaty basis may, however, be more appropriate considering the material aspects to be regulated, such as setting up an institutional structure and securing its infrastructure and funding.[62] In any case and importantly, membership to the institution would be detached from consent to submit disputes under IIAs to a reformed dispute settlement option administered by the institution; consent to the settlement of disputes arising under (existing and/or future)[63] IIAs would be given through a separate opt-in mechanism.[64]

One specific proposal to this end is to set up a multilateral forum for international investment law.[65] This forum would provide States – being the masters of their treaties – a centralised place for regular meetings to discuss and shape the ISDS system as a whole despite its decentralised nature.[66] Therefore, the forum would strive for universal membership which *as such* would not necessarily mean commitment to any specific reform option.[67] However, any reform options would be docked to the forum, ie parties to the forum may flexibly opt in to specific reform options they prefer.[68] These reform options would roughly be categorised into (1) instruments (interpretive mechanisms enabling States to adopt binding interpretations of their treaty obligations, procedural rules such as a code of conduct or rules on third party funding and substantive rules), (2) dispute settlement options (domestic courts, alternative dispute resolution, State-State arbitration, investor-State arbitration, MIC, MIAM) and (3) support mechanisms for developing States (capacity building, advice and representation).[69]

This suggestion is inspired by the United Nations Framework Convention on Climate Change (UNFCCC).[70] The UNFCCC is a so-called 'framework agreement' or 'framework convention' which is a multilater-

---

61 Kaufmann-Kohler, Potestà (*n 17*), paras 76 et seq.

62 ibid, para 78. See more generally on the political and legal considerations in the context of making commitments through treaty versus soft law Alan Boyle, 'The Choice of a Treaty: hard law versus soft law' in Simon Chesterman, David M Malone, and Santiago Villalpando (eds), *The Oxford Handbook of United Nations Treaties* (OUP 2019), 101 et seqq.

63 See below Section D.

64 Kaufmann-Kohler, Potestà (*n 17*), para 77; Schill, Vidigal 2019 (*n 11*), 324-326.

65 See Roberts, St. John (*n 30*).

66 ibid.

67 ibid.

68 ibid.

69 ibid.

70 ibid; United Nations Framework Convention on Climate Change (UNFCCC) (1992) 1771 UNTS 107.

al treaty establishing broad commitments and a system of governance while leaving it to subsequent agreements between the parties to establish specific obligations.[71] With 197 parties,[72] the UNFCCC enjoys quasi universal membership. The commitments under the UNFCCC itself are limited.[73] However, the UNFCCC establishes an institutional setting – with the Conference of the Parties (COP) as the supreme body – within which more specific agreements may be concluded between the parties.[74] Prominent examples for such agreements are the Kyoto Protocol[75] and the Paris Agreement[76]. During annual United Nations Climate Change Conferences, all parties to the UNFCCC as well as the respective parties to the more specific agreements such as the Kyoto Protocol have their formal meetings.[77]

Others suggest introducing a Multilateral Investment Dispute Settlement Institution (MIDSI).[78] MIDSI would be established as a three-pillar-structure: One pillar would administer a fully-fledged two-tiered MIC, another pillar reformed investor-State arbitration and yet another pillar inter-State arbitration.[79] Hence, MIDSI would allow States to pursue different modes of dispute settlement under one institutional umbrella.[80]

Inspiration for this suggestion is drawn from the provisions on dispute settlement in the United Nations Convention on the Law of the Sea (UN-

71 Nele Matz-Lück, 'Framework Agreements' in Anne Peters (ed), *Max Planck Encyclopedia of Public International Law* (February 2011), para 1.

72 United Nations Treaty Collection, <https://treaties.un.org/pages/ViewDetailsIII.aspx?src=TREATY&mtdsg_no=XXVII-7&chapter=27&Temp=mtdsg3&clang=_en> accessed 13 January 2022.

73 Philippe J Sands and Ilona Millar, 'Climate, International Protection' in Anne Peters (ed), *Max Planck Encyclopedia of Public International Law* (January 2011), para 19.

74 ibid, paras 15-19.

75 Kyoto Protocol to the United Nations Framework Convention on Climate Change (Kyoto Protocol) (1997) 2303 UNTS 162.

76 Paris Agreement (2015) 55 ILM 743 (2016).

77 United Nations Framework Convention on Climate Change, 'What are United Nations Climate Change Conferences?' <https://unfccc.int/process-and-meetings/conferences/the-big-picture/what-are-united-nations-climate-change-conferences> accessed 13 January 2022.

78 Schill, Vidigal (*n 11*), 18-20; Schill, Vidigal (*n 21*), 318-323. See also Braun/Reinhold, Chapter 2, Section E.

79 Schill, Vidigal (*n 11*), 18; Schill, Vidigal (*n 21*), 322.

80 Schill, Vidigal (*n 11*), 18; Schill, Vidigal (*n 21*), 321.

CLOS):[81] according to Article 287 (1) UNCLOS, parties to UNCLOS shall be free to choose one or more of the means for the settlement of disputes provided, ie the International Tribunal for the Law of the Sea (ITLOS), the International Court of Justice (ICJ), or arbitration.[82] If the declarations of the parties to a dispute do not match, arbitration is the default rule (Article 287 (3) UNCLOS).[83]

Setting up a new umbrella institution which strives for universal membership and therefore allows States to flexibly choose their preferred mode(s) of dispute settlement may allow the integration of the fragmented system of international investment law into one centralised institutional setting.[84] Observers to the UNCITRAL reform process note that as a side effect States got used to regular meetings at a central hub and that there is an energy to keep meeting and talking about international investment law.[85] Hence, if States think that institutional centralisation is desirable, the end of the UNCITRAL reform process may indeed mark a good opportunity to introduce a new umbrella institution.

However, setting-up a new institutional framework raises questions concerning its relationship to existing institutions which require careful

81 Schill, Vidigal (*n 11*), 18; Schill, Vidigal (*n 21*), 326. United Nations Convention on the Law of the Sea (UNCLOS) (1982) 1833 UNTS 3.

82 Article 287 UNCLOS reads:
Choice of procedure
1. When signing, ratifying or acceding to this Convention or at any time thereafter, a State shall be free to choose, by means of a written declaration, one or more of the following means for the settlement of disputes concerning the interpretation or application of this Convention:
(a) the International Tribunal for the Law of the Sea established in accordance with Annex VI;
(b) the International Court of Justice;
(c) an arbitral tribunal constituted in accordance with Annex VII;
(d) a special arbitral tribunal constituted in accordance with Annex VIII for one or more of the categories of disputes specified therein.
(…)
3. A State Party, which is a party to a dispute not covered by a declaration in force, shall be deemed to have accepted arbitration in accordance with Annex VII.

83 See generally on the dispute settlement regime under UNCLOS Natalie Klein, *Dispute Settlement in the UN Convention on the Law of the Sea* (Cambridge University Press 2005).

84 UNCITRAL WG III, Multilateral instrument on ISDS reform, WP 194 (2020) (*n 3*), para 14; Schill, Vidigal (*n 11*), 17 et seq.

85 Roberts, St. John (*n 30*).

consideration.[86] It is to be expected that various institutions will disagree about which one takes the lead on what.[87] In order to achieve a more coherent system, such situation should be avoided as far as possible. While it remains to be awaited whether this can ultimately be accomplished, previous involvement of arbitration institutions in UNCITRAL administered ISDS reform undertakings is promising. For example, when creating the UNCITRAL Transparency Rules, arbitration institutions were invited to comment upon whether an application of the UNCITRAL Transparency Rules under their own rules could be envisaged.[88] In response, the Permanent Court of Arbitration (PCA), the International Centre for Settlement of Investment Disputes (ICSID), the London Court of International Arbitration (LCIA), the Cairo Regional Centre for International Commercial Arbitration (CRCICA), and the Arbitration Institute of the Stockholm Chamber of Commerce (SCC) provided their comments.[89] Another recent example is the Draft Code of Conduct prepared jointly by the Secretariats of ICSID and UNCITRAL.[90] Building on these experiences, it may be possible to establish a new institutional framework which integrates existing institutions with their individual legitimate institutional interests.

D. Scope of an MRI: Future, Existing, or Future And Existing IIAs?

Regarding its scope, the issue is whether an MRI applies only to disputes arising under future (I.), existing (II.), or future and existing IIAs (III.).

86 UNCITRAL WG III, Multilateral instrument on ISDS reform, WP 194 (2020) (*n 3*), para 14.

87 Roberts, St. John (*n 30*).

88 See UNCITRAL, 'Report of Working Group II (Arbitration and Conciliation) on the work of its fifty-fifth session (Vienna, 3-7 October 2011)' (17 October 2011), A/CN.9/736, para 28.

89 See UNCITRAL, Working Group II (Arbitration and Conciliation), 'Settlement of commercial disputes, Preparation of a legal standard on transparency in treaty-based investor-State arbitration, Comments of arbitral institutions on the interplay between the draft rules on transparency and their institutional rules, Note by the Secretariat' (19 July 2012), A/CN.9/WG.II/WP.173.

90 See UNCITRAL, Working Group III, 'Possible reform of investor-State dispute settlement (ISDS), Draft code of conduct, Note by the Secretariat' (9 November 2020), A/CN.9/WG.III/WP.201.

I. Only Future IIAs

An MRI could be designed to cover only disputes under future IIAs, ie IIAs which will be concluded *after* the conclusion or entry into force of the MRI. However, unless such future IIA is the renegotiation of an existing one, the network of existing IIAs in this scenario remains unaffected by the reform.[91] As the multitude of disputes in the near and mid-term future will arise from the more than 3,300 existing IIAs, the significance of a reform would be very limited in this scenario.

II. Only Existing IIAs

To the other end, an MRI could also be designed to cover only disputes arising under existing IIAs, ie IIAs which were concluded *before* the MRI.[92] If States wish to apply a specific reform option (such as the MIC) to disputes under their future IIAs, they may refer in their future IIAs to the specific instrument, rules or annexes to the MRI governing that reform option.[93] An MRI could clarify that it does not preclude States from doing so.[94]

III. Both, Existing And Future IIAs

An MRI could also cover disputes arising under both, existing and future IIAs. An example for such an approach is the MIC Draft Statute.[95]

Within Working Group III it is noted that the temporal applicability of an MRI to disputes under existing and future IIAs may facilitate the uniformity of a reformed ISDS regime.[96] This may explain why there

---

91 See UNCTAD, 'Reform of Investor-State Dispute Settlement: In Search of a Roadmap' (2013) 2 IIA Issues Note, 6.

92 Kaufmann-Kohler, Potestà (*n 17*) para 215.

93 Kaufmann-Kohler, Potestà (*n 17*) para 215; UNCITRAL WG III, Submission European Union and its Member States, WP 159 (2019) (*n 29*), para 35.

94 Kaufmann-Kohler, Potestà (*n 17*), para 216.

95 See Article 20 (1) and Article 23 (2) MIC Draft Statute (*n 7*) and Bungenberg, Reinisch 2020 (*n 8*), para 569.

96 UNCITRAL WG III, Multilateral instrument on ISDS reform, WP 194 (2020) (*n 3*), para 24.

currently is a preference within Working Group III for such an approach.[97] Other delegations argue that the whole point of an MRI is to make reform options applicable to disputes arising under existing IIAs.[98] The outcome of this discussion remains to be awaited. Strictly speaking, however, the two conceptional understandings are not inevitably mutually exclusive. While models for an MRI – the Mauritius Convention and the MLI – were indeed clearly targeted at modifying existing treaties, there seems to be no compelling reason why in the context of a broader ISDS reform a new uniform standard should not apply (at least in terms of a minimum standard) to future treaties as well.

E. How Does an MRI Relate to Existing IIAs?

If an approach is chosen that (also) covers existing IIAs, the final question is how an MRI relates to dispute settlement provisions in existing IIAs. In the absence of specific regulation in the MRI, this relationship is subject to the customary international law rules codified in Article 30 VCLT.[99] This provision governs the application of successive treaties relating to the same subject matter.[100] According to Article 30 (3) VCLT, when all the parties to the earlier treaty are parties also to the later treaty but the earlier treaty is not terminated or suspended in operation, the earlier treaty applies only to the extent that its provisions are compatible with those of the later treaty. Article 30 (4) VCLT regulates the situation that the parties to the later treaty do not include all the parties to the earlier one. In this situation, according to Article 30 (4) (a) VCLT, between parties to both treaties the same rule applies as in Article 30 (3) VCLT. In contrast, between a party to both treaties and a party to only one of the treaties, the treaty to which both States are parties governs their relations (Article 30 (4) (b) VCLT). This means that if all parties to an IIA become parties to the MRI, the dispute settlement provisions of the IIA will apply only to the extent that

97 UNCITRAL, Report WG III, Session 39, A/CN.9/1044 (2020) (*n 2*), para 109.
98 ibid.
99 Kaufmann-Kohler, Potestà (*n 17*), para 228.
100 See generally on Article 30 VCLT Alexander Orakhelashvili, 'Article 30 Convention of 1969' in Olivier Corten and Pierre Klein (eds), *The Vienna Conventions on the Law of Treaties, A Commentary, Volume I* (OUP 2011), 764; Kerstin von der Decken, 'Article 30. Application of successive treaties relating to the same subject matter' in Oliver Dörr and Kirsten Schmalenbach (eds), *Vienna Convention on the Law of Treaties, A Commentary* (Springer 2018), 539.

they are compatible with the reform options provided in the MRI.[101] In contrast, if a State party to an IIA does not become a party to the MRI, the IIA's original dispute resolution mechanism will be applicable vis-à-vis the non-party.[102]

An MRI could also address its relationship to existing IIAs by way of a compatibility clause. For example, an MRI could provide that reform options shall be deemed to be included in the provisions for investor-State dispute resolution in existing IIAs concluded by parties to the MRI, according to the modalities established within the MRI.[103]

Sunset provisions are in general of no concern when considering the relationship between existing IIAs to an MRI.[104] The reason is that an MRI would coexist with IIAs, ie it would not terminate any IIA (neither unilaterally nor reciprocally). Hence, subject to possible exceptions,[105] sunset provisions are not applicable.[106]

In application of these principles, the following possible situations can be distinguished.

I. Both Host and Home State are Parties to an MRI

In this scenario, the MRI will modify the existing IIA relationship between the two States with the result that the investor may resort to reformed ISDS (either additionally to those provided by the IIA or exclusively).[107]

II. Only the Host State is Party to an MRI

If only the host State is a party to the MRI, the existing IIA treaty relationship vis a vis the home State will not be modified through the MRI.[108] As

101 Kaufmann-Kohler, Potestà (*n 17*), para 229.
102 ibid, para 230.
103 ibid, para 234.
104 ibid, para 236.
105 *Kaufmann-Kohler, Potestà* point to some Malaysian BITs in that regard, see ibid.
106 Katharina Gatzsche, *Aufhebungen und Abänderungen von Investitionsschutzabkommen, Eine Untersuchung zur Reichweite von Survival Clauses in BITs* (Nomos 2019), para 299.
107 UNCITRAL WG III, Multilateral instrument on ISDS reform, WP 194 (2020) (*n 3*), para 33; Bungenberg, Reinisch (*n 8*), para 247; Kaufmann-Kohler, Potestà (*n 17*), para 247. See also above Section C.I.2.a) (2).
108 Kaufmann-Kohler, Potestà (*n 17*), para 250.

a result, an investor may resort to the ISDS options provided by the IIA; in principle, reformed ISDS will not apply.

However, taking the Mauritius Convention as a model, a Unilateral Offer Mechanism could be drafted into an MRI.[109] A Unilateral Offer Mechanism would enable parties to an MRI to unilaterally offer investors to resort to reformed ISDS. Hence, in this scenario an investor may – in addition to the original ISDS options provided by the IIA – resort to reformed ISDS in reliance on the unilateral offer made by the host State.

Opponents of a Unilateral Offer Mechanism note that such mechanism would grant additional procedural rights (eg the option to resort to an MIC in addition to investor-State arbitration as provided by the IIA) to nationals whose home States do not accede the MRI, which might decrease the incentive for States to join an MRI (eg in order to save costs).[110] For this reason, the MIC Draft Statute does not contain a Unilateral Offer Mechanism.[111] Despite these concerns, reform-minded States might just as well see a Unilateral Offer Mechanism as being advantageous to them as it can avoid traditional ISDS claims being initiated against them.[112] On the other hand, a Unilateral Offer Mechanism comes without any obligations for States not being reform-minded. Hence, these States have no reason to object.[113] However, one may certainly question whether investors in practice would consent to resort to an MIC or to reformed ISDS more generally if they can also resort to traditional investor-State arbitration. While it is not clear yet, which reform options will ultimately be agreed upon, in tendency it is clear that the outcome will be a more restricted or at least a more regulated mode of dispute settlement which – from investor perspective – will be less attractive.

---

109 See above Section C.I.1.

110 Bungenberg, Reinisch (*n 8*), para 202.

111 Article 19 (1) MIC Draft Statute (*n 7*) stipulates that the jurisdiction of the MIC comprises all disputes which the parties refer to it, in relation to any legal dispute arising directly out of an investment *between a Member and a national of another Member*.

112 Bungenberg, Reinisch (*n 8*), para 204.

113 Kaufmann-Kohler, Potestà (*n 17*), para 253.

III. Only the Home State is Party to the MRI

In this constellation the existing IIA treaty relationship between host and home State will not be modified as well.[114] As a result, reformed modes of ISDS in principle would not apply.

However, the issue arises whether an investor should be able to resort to reformed ISDS in reliance on an *ad hoc* consent given by the host State. Opponents argue that any incentive to accede to an MRI would be taken away if States could decide on a case-by-case basis whether they wish to apply a specific reform option or not.[115] The MIC Draft Statute does not foresee the possibility of jurisdiction through an *ad hoc* consent. If States nonetheless wish to promote the use of (one or more) specific reform options, they could insert a provision in an MRI, whereby the instrument is without prejudice to the application of the reform option(s) whenever the disputing parties agree.[116] As explained (see above, at Section II.), in the absence of incentives for investors to reach an agreement to resort to reformed modes of ISDS instead of traditional ISDS, it is questionable whether such an agreement will be reached in practice.

IV. Neither Home nor Host State are Parties to the MRI

In this constellation as well the issue arises whether an investor can – and will – resort to the MIC on the basis of an *ad hoc* agreement (see above, at Section III.).

F. Conclusion

The implementation of *any* possible structural ISDS reform will be a particularly challenging task. Difficult policy decisions will have to be taken within a given legal framework that is highly fragmented into individual obligations contained in more than 3,300 IIAs. Individual renegotiations of each of these treaties would not only be extremely laborious, but also inadequate to reform the system as a whole. Despite a recent trend to

114 ibid, para 256.

115 Bungenberg, Reinisch (*n 8*), para 206.

116 Kaufmann-Kohler, Potestà (*n 17*), para 258; UNCITRAL WG III, Multilateral instrument on ISDS reform, WP 194 (2020) (*n 3*), para 37.

regionalism, however, a truly multilateral approach to investment protection which would replace the existing system is doomed to fail.[117] As the models of the Mauritius Convention and the MLI demonstrate, an MRI designed as an opt-in convention can be a gamechanger in this field of tension as it allows for coordinated reforms through multilateral harmonisation on the one hand while maintaining existing individual treaty relationships on the other hand.[118] For successfully reforming ISDS through such an opt-in treaty, States in substance must strike the right balance between the conflicting goals of universal participation on the one hand and integrity of reform on the other hand. If a new institutional framework is to be established, existing institutions need to be sensibly integrated into the new institutional superstructure. In conclusion, no matter what the outcome of the UNCITRAL reform process will be and whether an MIC can ultimately be agreed upon, the considerations about an MRI will become relevant at some time. The 'backlash against investment arbitration'[119] calls for systemic reform which faces structural challenges, no matter which reform option will ultimately prevail.

117 For example, negotiations on a proposed Multilateral Agreement on Investment (MAI) which began at the Annual Meeting of the OECD Council at Ministerial level in May 1995 were discontinued in 1998 and will not be resumed, OECD, 'Multilateral Agreement on Investment' <https://www.oecd.org/investment/internationalinvestmentagreements/multilateralagreementoninvestment.htm> accessed 13 January 2022. See also Markus Burgstaller and Michael Waibel, 'Investment Codes' in Anne Peters (ed), *Max Planck Encyclopedia of Public International Law* (May 2011), paras 28 and 52.

118 On the challenge of 'squaring bilateralism with multilateralism' in the tax and investment law context see Alschner (*n 30*), 34-45.

119 Michael Waibel et al (eds), *The Backlash against Investment Arbitration, Perceptions and Reality* (Kluwer Law International 2010).

Chapter 9: Recognition and Enforcement of MIC Decisions – How Effective will an MIC Dispute Resolution Mechanism possibly be?

by Carla Müller[*]

Selected Bibliography: Charles N Brower and Jawad Ahmad, 'From the Two-Headed Nightingale to the Fifteen-Headed Hydra: The Many Follies of the Proposed International Investment Court' (2018) 41.4 Fordham International Law Journal 791; Marc Bungenberg and August Reinisch, *From Bilateral Arbitral Tribunals and Investment Courts to a Multilateral Investment Court: Options Regarding the Institutionalization of Investor-State Dispute Settlement* (Springer 2019); Richard Happ and Sebastian Wuschka, 'From the Jay Treaty Commissions Towards a Multilateral Investment Court: Addressing the Enforcement Dilemma' (2017) 6.1 Indian Journal of Arbitration Law 113; Gabrielle Kaufmann-Kohler and Michele Potestà, 'Can the Mauritius Convention serve as a model for the reform of investor-State arbitration in connection with the introduction of a permanent investment tribunal or an appeal mechanism? (Part1)' CIDS 2016; August Reinisch, 'Will the EU's Proposal Concerning an Investment Court System for CETA and TTIP Lead to Enforceable Awards?—The Limits of Modifying the ICSID Convention and the Nature of Investment Arbitration' (2016) 19.4 Journal of International Economic Law 761.

A. *Introduction*

The effectiveness of every dispute resolution system depends on the enforceability of its decisions. A party will only consider a decision it obtains to be valuable if its enforcement is assured. It will therefore be a crucial task for the creators of the MIC to equip it with an effective enforcement mechanism.

---

* Carla Müller is a legal trainee at the Higher Regional Court of Cologne and a PhD candidate at the University of Cologne.

In order to determine the effectiveness of an MIC enforcement system, the preliminary distinction to be made is whether MIC decisions constitute a decision of an international court or of an international arbitral tribunal.[1] The significance of this distinction lies in the enhanced systems of recognition and enforcement applicable to international arbitral awards. This holds particularly true with regard to most national legislations which do not provide a basis for the enforcement of international judgments.[2] Much can be discussed whether the MIC should be qualified as an international arbitral tribunal or as an international court. Ultimately, the MIC's classification will depend on the details of its establishment and institutional structure[3] as well as on an overall assessment of these features. There are many criteria that can be used in order to analyse whether an international adjudicatory body is an international court or an international arbitral tribunal. This contribution will address those MIC characteristics that are relevant in the context of enforcement. Among these characteristics the method of appointment of the adjudicators, the voluntary nature of the submissions and the possibility of an appeal are standing out and will be discussed in this contribution.[4]

As a general remark, *Kaufmann-Kohler/Potestà* suggest that the qualification of an MIC as arbitral body may be simplified by a certain choice of wording in the MIC Statute, eg "arbitral tribunal" instead of "court",

---

1 There are also hybrid adjudicatory bodies that represent elements of an international court and of an arbitral tribunal. The mostly referred to example therefore is the IUSCT, see eg Michele Potestà, 'Chapter IV: Investment Arbitration, Challenges And Prospects For The Establishment Of A Multilateral Investment Court: Quo Vadis Enforcement?' (2018) Austrian Yearbook on International Arbitration 157, 161.

2 ibid, 160; see for a general overview Richard F Oppong and Lisa C Niro, 'Enforcing Judgments of International Courts in National Courts' (2014) 5.2 Journal of International Dispute Settlement 344.

3 See above Braun, Reinhold Chapter 2.

4 See eg August Reinisch, 'Will the EU's Proposal Concerning an Investment Court System for CETA and TTIP Lead to Enforceable Awards?—The Limits of Modifying the ICSID Convention and the Nature of Investment Arbitration' (2016) 19.4 Journal of International Economic Law 761, 766; Richard Happ and Sebastian Wuschka, 'From the Jay Treaty Commissions Towards a Multilateral Investment Court: Addressing the Enforcement Dilemma' (2017) 6.1 Indian Journal of Arbitration Law 113, 126; see also Potestà *(n 1)* 162; Marc Bungenberg and August Reinisch, *From Bilateral Arbitral Tribunals and Investment Courts to a Multilateral Investment Court: Options Regarding the Institutionalization of Investor-State Dispute Settlement* (Springer 2019), para 502.

"arbitrator" instead of "judge", "award" instead of "judgment".[5] Such language may tip the scales in favour of an assessment of the MIC to be of arbitral rather than of judicial nature. In the end, however, language considerations will only be one aspect of the operation to distinguish between an international arbitral tribunal and an international court. It is the actual strucure and characteristics of the MIC that are determinative.[6]

This is reinforced by the fact that it is not the classification by the MIC member States which is significant but rather the qualification by the national courts of the State of enforcement.[7] The enforcement of an MIC decision falls – as any enforcement – into the jurisdiction of the national courts of the State in whose jurisdiction enforcement is sought. Only courts have the sovereign power to order the enforcement of a decision.[8]

As national courts can autonomously determine whether or not a decision falls within the scope of an international convention, these national courts have a primordial role in determining the enforcement of MIC decisions.[9] Accordingly, national law and national jurisprudence can and will have an impact on the enforceability of a decision. While carrying out these assessments, national courts regularly refer to the *lex arbitri*, the law of the seat of the tribunal, as well as to the *lex fori*, the law of the competent court, especially with regard to the determination of the scope of the New York Convention.[10]

There are several pertinent possibilities to ensure the enforcement of MIC decisions: an MIC inherent system, the enforcement mechanism provided in the ICSID Convention, or the one contained in the New York Convention. The latter options require that the MIC can be qualified as an arbitral tribunal. As already mentioned, the MIC member States cannot determine through an agreement among themselves the result of

---

5 See Gabrielle Kaufmann-Kohler and Michele Potestà, 'Can the Mauritius Convention serve as a model for the reform of investor-State arbitration in connection with the introduction of a permanent investment tribunal or an appeal mechanism? (Part1)' CIDS 2016, fn 278.

6 See ibid.

7 See for the enforcement of investment arbitration awards in general Julien Fouret, *Enforcement of investment treaty arbitration awards: A global guide* (Globe Law and Business 2021).

8 See with regard to the role of domestic courts concerning the enforcement of investment awards Gabrielle Kaufmann-Kohler and Michele Potestà, *Investor-State Dispute Settlement and National Courts* (Springer 2020), paras 146-156.

9 Kaufmann-Kohler, Potestà *(n 5)*, para 145; Potestà *(n 1)*, 170; Kaufmann-Kohler, Potestà *(n 8)*, para 146.

10 Happ, Wuschka *(n 4)*, 124-125.

the analysis of a court of a third State.[11] Therefore, the qualification of the MIC impacts especially the chances of success when enforcement is sought in a third State, ie a State that is not a member of the MIC and is therefore not bound by the MIC Convention.[12]

Additionally, legal scholars consider the implementation of a fund in order to simplify the enforcement procedure.[13] Any investor who obtains a favourable award may seek compensation from the fund which, in a next step, takes recourse to the State that was party to the proceedings. Accordingly, such a fund could be used to ensure and to streamline effective compensation of prevailing investors.

This contribution will first address whether a party may enforce an MIC decision pursuant to already existing enforcement mechanisms (B.). In a second step, the establishment of an MIC inherent enforcement mechanism will be analysed (C.). Finally, the proposition to establish a fund to complement the enforcement of an MIC decision will be discussed (D.). On this basis, a conclusion (E.) will be drawn.

B. Reliance on Existing Enforcement Mechanisms?

A party victorious in front of the MIC could rely on the already existing enforcement mechanisms. The ICISD Convention (I.) and the New York Convention (II.) are two seasoned instruments which address the enforcement of international arbitral awards. Relying on these existing instruments might be valuable from a practical perspective. These treaties are not only in force for a huge number of States but also allowed the development of a jurisprudential practice in their regard.[14]

11 See also Happ, Wuschka *(n 4)*, 124.

12 Potestà *(n 1)*, 170.

13 See for the proposition to establish a fund Bungenberg, Reinisch *(n 4)*, paras 537-540 and the discussion below at Section D.

14 As of August 2021, 164 States have ratified the ICISD Convention and 168 States the New York Convention. See for ratification status with regard to the ICSID Convention <https://icsid.worldbank. org/about/member-states/database-of-member-states> and <http://www.newyorkconvention.org/countries> with regard to the New York Convention, accessed 13 January 2022.

I. The ICSID Convention

With regard to the ICSID Convention's enforcement system, two options come into play. First, it can be discussed whether an MIC decision may be qualified as an ICSID award and is therefore eligible for enforcement under the ICSID Convention (a). Second, and in the negative, it has to be analysed whether the MIC Convention can instead be conceived as an inter-se modification of the ICSID Convention (b).[15]

First and foremost, attention needs to be drawn to the advantage of the ICSID Convention's enforcement mechanism.[16] In Article 54 (1) sentence 1 the ICSID Convention stipulates with regard to the enforcement of an ICSID award:

> Each Contracting State shall recognize an award rendered pursuant to this Convention as binding and enforce the pecuniary obligations imposed by that award within its territories as if it were a final judgment of a court in that State.

In accordance with Article 54 ICSID Convention, every ICSID member State has to treat an ICSID award as binding and must enforce a pecuniary obligation just like a final judgement of its own national courts. Even if the specific stipulation of Article 54 ICSID Convention applies only to compensation awards, this includes the kind of reparation which is most commonly attributed.

Additionally, Article 53 ICSID Convention limits the remedies against an award handed down by an ICSID tribunal. One may seek its rectification or interpretation pursuant to Articles 49 and 50, or its revision or

15 Bungenberg, Reinisch *(n 4)*, paras 495-499.

16 See for an overview over the mechanism of Article 54 ICSID Convention George A Bermann, 'Understanding ICSID Article 54' (2020) ICSID Review - Foreign Investment Law Journal 1; see also Georges R Delaume, 'ICSID Arbitration and the Courts' (1983) 7.4 The American Journal of International Law 784, 796-803; Albert Jan van den Berg, 'Some Recent Problems in the Practice of Enforcement under the New York and ICSID Conventions' (1987) 2.2 ICSID Review 439; Edward Baldwin, Mark Kantor, and Michael Nolan, 'Limits to Enforcement of ICSID Awards' (2006) 23.1 Journal of International Arbitration 1; and see the commentary to Article 54 by Christoph Schreuer et al, *The ICSID convention: A commentary* (Cambridge University Press 2009); Stefan Kröll, 'Enforcement of Awards' in Bungenberg et al (eds), *International Investment Law* (C.H. Beck, Hart, Nomos 2015), paras 40-53; J Martin Hunter and Javier Garcia Olmedo, 'Enforcement/Execution of ICSID Awards against Reluctant States' (2011) 12.3 Journal of World Investment & Trade 307.

annulment pursuant to Articles 51 and 52 ICSID Convention.[17] Apart from these remedies though – for which no national court but only an ICSID tribunal or an ICSID annulment committee is competent – an ICSID award constitutes the final decision of a dispute.[18] This systematic shows the self-contained trait of the ICSID Convention which is further reinforced by the fact that ICSID tribunals do not have a seat of arbitration.[19] Thereby a say of domestic courts in ICSID arbitrations is again excluded. Generally, the courts of the seat of an arbitral tribunal remain competent for certain disputes arising in the context of the arbitration. Since ICSID tribunals have no seat, no such power of national courts exists.[20]

As a result of this self-contained system, an ICSID award cannot be challenged or set aside on any grounds of national law.[21] Therefore, the ICSID Convention's enforcement mechanism proves to be highly effective.

1. Enforceability of MIC decisions under the ICSID Convention?

The ICSID Convention contains a very specific dispute resolution mechanism.[22] One of the particularities is the above-mentioned self-contained character; further particularities, as eg the method of constitution of panels, can also be found in the procedural rules.[23] The MIC's structure and proceedings are likely to differ from these characteristics of the ICSID

17 Van den Berg *(n 16)*, 439, 441; UNCITRAL, Working Group III, 'Appellate mechanism and enforcement issues, Draft Note by the Secretariat' (12 November 2020), A/CN.9/WG.III/WP.202, para 46.

18 See Article 53 ICSID Convention; cf also Alber Jan van den Berg *(n 16)*, 439, 441; Kröll *(n 16)*, paras 42-43, 51.

19 Van den Berg *(n 16)*, 439, 441; Frauke Nitschke and Kamel Aït-El-Hadj, 'Determining the Place of Arbitration in ICSID Additional Facility Proceedings' (2015) 30.1 ICSID Review – Foreign Investment Journal 243, 243-244.

20 Cf with a similar argument Albert Jan van den Berg, 'Appeal Mechanism for ISDS Awards: Interaction with the New York and ICSID Conventions' (2019) 34.1 ICSID Review - Foreign Investment Law Journal 156, 168.

21 Nitschke, Aït-El-Hadj *(n 19)*, 243-244; Christian Tams, 'An Appealing Option? The Debate about an ICSID Appellate Structure' (2006) Beiträge zum Transnationalen Wirtschaftsrecht 5, 8.

22 See the Convention on the Settlement of Investment Disputes between States and Nationals of Other States (ICSID Convention) (1965) 575 UNTS 159, the Rules of Procedure for Arbitration Proceedings (Arbitration Rules) and the explications above regarding the self-contained characteristics of the ICSID dispute settlement.

23 Bungenberg, Reinisch *(n 4)*, para 496

Convention.[24] Therefore, MIC decisions cannot be assimilated to ICSID awards. In consequence, MIC decisions cannot benefit from the ICSID system of recognition and enforcement.[25]

This also holds true if the MIC member States include a stipulation that an MIC decision should be qualified as an ICSID award.[26] According to general principles of international law, an agreement of any kind is only binding upon the parties of the agreement.[27] This means that the MIC Convention can only be binding for its member States.[28] Accordingly, such a stipulation would have to be considered as *res inter alios acta* in relation to all other States.[29] Again, this means that no third State would be under any obligation to consider an MIC decision as an ICSID award.[30]

On a side note, the UNCITRAL Working Group III's Secretariat furthermore refers to the possibility to amend the ICSID Convention in order to allow the enforcement of MIC decisions under its aegis.[31] According to Article 66 (1) ICSID Convention an amendment requires a consensus of all ICSID States and seems therefore unlikely. Furthermore, an amendment

---

24 Kaufmann-Kohler, Potestà *(n 5)*, para 141; Bungenberg, Reinisch *(n 4)*, para 496.

25 In particular the implementation of an appellate body would differ greatly from the ICSID Convention's system and would hinder an enforcement under its stipulations, see Reinisch *(n 4)*, 779-780; see also Kaufmann-Kohler, Potestà *(n 5)*, para 141.

26 See Article 8.41 (6) CETA for an example of such a stipulation. The provision reads: 'For greater certainty, if a claim has been submitted pursuant to Article 8.23.2 (a), a final award issued pursuant to this Section shall qualify as an award under Section 6 of the ICSID Convention.'

27 See Article 26 Vienna Convention on the Law of Treaties (VCLT); Hersch Lauterpacht, 'The Nature of International Law and General Jurisprudence' (1932) 37 Economica 301, 315-317; Christian Tomuschat, 'Pacta sunt servanda' in Andreas Fischer-Lescano et al (eds), *Frieden in Freiheit – Peace in liberty – Paix en liberté: Festschrift für Michael Bothe* (Nomos 2008), 1047-1065; Georg Dahm, Jost Delbrück, and Rüdiger Wolfrum, *Völkerrecht. Die Grundlagen. Die Völkerrechtssubjekte (I/1)* (De Gruyter 2002), 37-38, 40-43; cf with regard to the MIC Kaufmann-Kohler, Potestà *(n 5)*, paras 138-141; Bungenberg, Reinisch *(n 4)*, para 536.

28 An agreement between the member States that MIC decisions should be considered as ICSID awards would correspond to an inter-se modification of the ICSID Convention or to an establishment of an MIC inherent enforcement mechanism. Both possibilities are analysed below Sections B.I.2, C.

29 Happ, Wuschka *(n 4)*, 122; Potestà *(n 1)*, 169.

30 Reinisch *(n 4)*, 782; Happ, Wuschka *(n 4)*, 123; Potestà *(n 1)*, 169.

31 UNCITRAL WG III, Appellate mechanism and enforcement issues, WP 202 (2020) *(n 17)*, paras 48-52.

entails further risks of fragmentation[32] or of a loss of effectiveness of the ICSID enforcement regime.

2. *Inter-se Modification of the ICSID Convention?*

Yet, such kind of stipulation might be considered to be an inter-se modification of the ICSID Convention among MIC member States pursuant to Article 41[33] Vienna Convention on the Law of Treaties (VCLT).[34]

Article 41 VCLT regulates the way in which some parties of a multilateral treaty may modify this treaty among themselves.[35] If the treaty in question, such as the ICSID Convention, does not already explicitly allow or prohibit a modification between some of its signatories, an inter-se modification of the ICSID Convention by the MIC Convention is possible under two conditions. It is first required that the rights and obligations of the other members of the ICSID Convention are not impaired by the MIC Convention. Second, there must not be an incompatibility of the inter-se modification with the intention and the purpose of the ICSID Convention.

An inter-se modification should not negatively affect the rights of the other parties or the performance of their obligations. *Reinisch* suggests that reciprocal treaties respect this requirement, whereas the case might be less clear with regard to treaties containing interdependent obligations of the signatories or obligations of integral nature.[36] If the MIC Convention establishes – for a certain number of ICSID member States – a dispute settlement institution different to the one under the ICSID Convention, the new dispute settlement mechanism would only bind its signatories. It therefore seems improbable that the rights and obligations of other ICSID members would be affected.[37]

---

32 ibid, para 51.

33 The ICSID Convention is outside of the temporal scope of the VCLT. Even if it can be discussed whether Article 41 VCLT constitutes customary law, it is generally accepted to rely on the rules contained in Article 41 VCLT when assessing international instruments, see Reinisch *(n 4)*, 772.

34 Kaufmann-Kohler, Potestà *(n 5)*, para 141; Reinisch *(n 4)*, 768-776; cf Bungenberg, Reinisch *(n 4)*, 497-499.

35 See Reinisch *(n 4)*, 771-776, 781 regarding the content and extent of Article 41 VCLT.

36 ibid, 773.

37 ibid, 774.

The MIC Convention further must not modify the ICSID Convention in a manner incompatible with the effective execution of the object and the purpose of the ICSID Convention as a whole. Pursuant to Article 1 (2) its purpose and object are to provide facilities for the dispute resolution between a foreign investor and a host State in accordance with the ICSID Convention. If one were to understand this formulation as declaring any form of ISDS outside of the ICSID Convention incompatible with its objective and purpose, any inter-se modification would be impossible.[38] Therefore, it has been suggested to interpret Article 1 (2) as referring to the way in which the ICSID Convention serves the resolution of investment disputes.[39] That is to say that any promotion of an effective investment dispute resolution is compatible with the ICSID Convention.

Yet, even assuming an inter-se modification would fulfil these requirements, Article 41 VCLT limits its legal consequences. An inter-se modification obliges only the signatories of this modification, ie the MIC member States. Thus, from a practical perspective, an inter-se modification resembles an MIC inherent system[40] and has a similar level of effectiveness.[41]

3. *Interim Conclusion concerning the ICSID Convention*

In summary, it can therefore be stated that an enforcement under the ICSID Convention is unlikely.[42] Should MIC member States wish to benefit from an enforcement system as effective as the one contained in the ICSID Convention, their best option would therefore be to establish a corresponding MIC inherent enforcement system at their discretion.[43]

---

38 ibid, 776.

39 See for a detailed analysis ibid, 776-782.

40 According to the principle of *pacta sunt servanda* in international law, an MIC inherent system would also only bind its member States. This will be analysed in more detail below Section C.

41 Reinisch *(n 4)*, 781; Happ, Wuschka *(n 4)*, 123; Bungenberg, Reinisch *(n 4)*, paras 497-499.

42 Kaufmann-Kohler, Potestà *(n 5)*, para 141; Happ, Wuschka *(n 4)*, 131; see also N Jansen Calamita, 'Nus Centre for International Law Collection of Articles on an Appellate Body in ISDS: The Challenge of Establishing a Multilateral Investment Tribunal at ICSID' (2017) 23.3 ICSID Review 611, 612.

43 An MIC inherent enforcement system and its advantages will be discussed below Section C.

II. The New York Convention

The New York Convention[44] may also provide an enforcement mechanism for MIC decisions.[45] The New York Convention is an already established and seasoned international instrument that has 168 member States[46] which accordingly would recognise a foreign arbitral award in the sense of the Convention as enforceable. Thus, States that are not a member of the MIC Convention but of the New York Convention would possibly apply its regime to enforce an MIC decision. In general terms, the New York Convention allows to enforce an arbitral award if this award was not made in the territory of the State in which enforcement is sought. Its enforcement system offers the advantages of not only prohibiting a *révision au fond* of the arbitral decision but also of only allowing limited grounds to refuse recognition and enforcement.[47]

Consequently, even if the enforcement mechanism itself might not be as effective as the self-contained ICSID enforcement system, these restrictions on the reviewability render the New York Convention's enforcement mechanism very effective.[48]

In order to be enforceable under the auspices of the New York Convention, an MIC decision has to fall within the scope of application of the New York Convention pursuant to its first article.[49] The scope of application of the New York Convention centres around the existence of an arbitral award whose enforcement is sought. Even if the qualification of an MIC decision as arbitral award is pivotal, further requirements of the New York Convention leave additional room for discussion.

44 Convention on the Recognition and Enforcement of Foreign Arbitral Awards (New York Convention) (1959) 330 UNTS 3.

45 Van den Berg *(n 16)*, 439; Kröll *(n 16)*, paras 18-36.

46 <http://www.newyorkconvention.org/countries> accessed 13 January 2022.

47 See Article 5 New York Convention.

48 Calamita *(n 42)*, 614.

49 Article 1 (1) and (2) New York Convention read:
(1) This Convention shall apply to the recognition and enforcement of arbitral awards made in the territory of a State other than the State where the recognition and enforcement of such awards are sought, and arising out of differences between persons, whether physical or legal. It shall also apply to arbitral awards not considered as domestic awards in the State where their recognition and enforcement are sought.
(2) The term "arbitral awards" shall include not only awards made by arbitrators appointed for each case but also those made by permanent arbitral bodies to which the parties have submitted.'

1. *MIC as Permanent Arbitral Body?*

In order to render arbitral awards, the MIC needs to be considered as an arbitral body. This qualification is closely linked to the requirement of a voluntary submission of the dispute to the MIC.[50] According to Article I (2) New York Convention, an arbitral award cannot only be handed down by arbitrators appointed for a specific case but also by a permanent arbitral body.

Consequently, when establishing the MIC, States have to include multiple arbitral elements into the structure and the functioning of the MIC in order to allow a qualification as an arbitral body in contrast to a qualification as an international court.[51] Additionally, an analogy might be drawn to the Iran-US Claims Tribunal (IUSCT) which is frequently accepted as a permanent arbitral body by domestic courts deciding on an enforcement.[52]

a) Appointment of Adjudicators

Generally, one of the criteria to determine the potential arbitral nature of an adjudicatory body is the appointment of adjudicators by the disputing parties.[53] In this sense, *Bungenberg/Reinisch* also point out that, with regard to the MIC's arbitral nature, it might be considered problematic if MIC adjudicators were to be exclusively appointed by States and not by investors as well.[54] This is because arbitral bodies constitute a dispute resolution in

---

50 This requirement is discussed just below at Section B.II.2.

51 Kaufmann-Kohler, Potestà *(n 5)*, paras 81-89.

52 Bungenberg, Reinisch *(n 4)*, paras 528-529; cf also Van den Berg *(n 20)*, 179-180; but see Charles N Brower and Jawad Ahmad, 'From the Two-Headed Nightingale to the Fifteen-Headed Hydra: The Many Follies of the Proposed International Investment Court' (2018) 41.4 Fordham International Law Journal 791, 805-807 who reject an analogy by pointing to the very specific (political) circumstances surrounding the creation of the IUSCT. An analogy to the IUSCT can be envisaged at several instances. Whether the IUSCT is a suitable basis for an analogy is analysed in more detail just below; see for further references Kaufmann-Kohler, Potestà *(n 5)*, para 153.

53 Bungenberg, Reinisch *(n 4)*, paras 516-520; see however Kaufmann-Kohler, Potestà *(n 5)*, paras 148-152 for a presentation of the negotiation history of Article I (2) New York Convention which leads the authors to conclude that whilst the significance of the voluntary nature of arbitration was stressed, the choice of arbitrators was not granted much attention.

54 See with regard to the impact of the appointment mechanism of the adjudicators, Potestà *(n 1)*, 164-168. Potestà also suggests that 'arbitration might well "outlive"

which private adjudicators, ie not State organs, are in charge of ruling on the dispute. Additionally, an appointment of adjudicators exclusively by States could lead State courts to consider it a public policy violation if the parties cannot both participate on an equal footing in the appointment of their tribunal.[55]

Nevertheless, *Bungenberg/Reinisch* consider that – if enough private elements are introduced in the institutional structure of the MIC – it could and should still be considered an arbitral dispute resolution mechanism.[56] At the same time, the qualification of the MIC as arbitral body may be hindered if the appointment and selection of the adjudicators greatly resembles the process used with regard to international courts.[57] And even if the creators of the MIC are careful to implement it with 'private elements', this could potentially convince only some domestic courts whereas others could remain more sceptical. Hence, the risk of fragmentation of the enforcement of MIC decisions cannot be mitigated that easily.[58]

b) Analogy with the IUSCT

Legal scholars suggest an analogy with the treatment of the IUSCT. The claimants in front of the IUSCT could not take part in the appointment of the adjudicators and the courts of enforcement generally did not consider this to be problematic.[59]

Whether the IUSCT is a suitable basis for an analogy, can however be discussed. Even if there are similarities between an MIC and the IUSCT, there are differences which hinder the comparability.

---

the institution of party-appointment'; Bungenberg, Reinisch *(n 4)*, paras 512-515, 516-520; see also Brower, Ahmad *(n 52)*, 809.

55 Gloria Alvarez et al, 'Ensuring the Effective Recognition and Enforcement of MIC Decisions: Submission by the European Federation for Investment Law and Arbitration (EFILA) to the UNCITRAL Working Group III on ISDS Reforms' (7 September 2020) EFILA, para 13. See for this reasoning the French Supreme Court in *Siemens AG v BKMI and Dutco Consortium Construction Co* Cour de Cassation no 89-18708 89-18726, 7 January 1992.

56 Cf also Kaufmann-Kohler, Potestà' *(n 5)*, paras 81-99; Bungenberg, Reinisch *(n 4)*, paras 512-520.

57 See for this Happ, Wuschka *(n 4)*, 127.

58 Cf with a similar argument Alvarez et al *(n 55)*, para 25.

59 Bungenberg, Reinisch *(n 4)*, para 518; critical with regard to an analogy Happ, Wuschka *(n 4)*, 127-28 with further references.

The IUSCT has been established under particular circumstances. The Algiers Accords were concluded after a short period of negotiations in the aftermath of the conflict between the Iranian State and the United States.[60] Main objective of these negotiations was the release of the American hostages in the US Embassy in Tehran. *Brower/Ahmad* rightfully point out that the solution of an international crisis including the establishment of a specific dispute resolution system does not represent the general way of establishing an ISDS mechanism.[61] Consequently, the IUSCT has a very specific mandate to solve disputes in relation to the political and diplomatic crisis. The MIC however is supposed to be construed in a way to represent a more permanent recourse for ISDS and its establishment has not to be realised under such time-sensitive circumstances. Additionally, *EFILA* points out that the decisions recognising the IUSCT as a 'permanent arbitral body' were handed down decades ago and lack any discussion regarding the applicability of the New York Convention even though only the States appointed the adjudicators.[62]

It is therefore questionable whether the reasoning applied to IUSCT decisions can be transferred to MIC decisions. Yet, the treatment of IUSCT decisions by national courts may at least present an indication as to how these courts will assess MIC decisions. Further, jurisprudence regarding the IUSCT may serve as a guideline for the courts of enforcement.

c) Analogy with the CAS

Kaufmann-Kohler/Potestà additionally refer to the Court of Arbitration for Sport (CAS) to argue that the appointment of the adjudicators is of minor

---

60 See with this argument Brower, Ahmad *(n 52)*, 805-806; see also Alvarez et al *(n 55)*, para 14.

61 Besides the IUSCT the authors mention the Alabama arbitration which also arose following an international crisis and in which the arbitrators were only appointed by States as well, see Brower, Ahmad *(n 43)*, 806.

62 Alvarez et al (n 55), para 14 who refer to: (a) Dutch Supreme Court (*Société Européenne d'Etudes et d'Entreprises (S.E.E.E.) v Federal Republic of Yugoslavia*, Decision, 7 November 1975; (b) Court of Appeal of Rouen (*Société Européenne d'Etudes et d'Entreprises (S.E.E.E.) v République Socialiste Fédérale de Yougoslavie*, Decision, 13 November 1984); (c) Court of Appeals, Ninth Circuit, United States of America (*Ministry of Defense of the Islamic Republic of Iran v Gould Inc. Gould Marketing, Inc. Hoffman Export Corporation, and Gould International, Inc.*, Decision, 23 October 1989).

importance for the qualification as an arbitral tribunal.[63] The athletes are obliged to submit to the authority of the CAS in order to exercise their sport. The arbitrators sitting at a CAS tribunal are appointed by the President of the ad hoc Division from a preselected list but without any influence of the parties to the dispute (Article 11 Arbitration Rules for the Olympic Games of the Court of Arbitration for Sport). *Brower/Ahmad* though reject this comparison.[64] They argue that the CAS represents a regulatory and disciplinary body such as for example the Bar for lawyers. It is common that the professionals, subject to a regulatory body, do not appoint the members of the disciplinary board, at least not for their own adjudication.[65] The MIC would not constitute a regulatory or disciplinary body though, especially not regarding investors. Therefore, conclusions from the assessment of the CAS seem a little far-fetched.

d) Adjudicators as Non-State Decision Makers

A further point to be taken into account with regard to the appointment of adjudicators is their qualification as non-State decision makers. This assessment depends highly on the design of the MIC chosen by its member States. Even if the MIC would hardly be considered a public entity, its nature as private entity might also be questioned.[66] *Kaufmann-Kohler/Potestà* refer to the constitution or composition of the MIC as a decisive criterion to distinguish between public and private adjudicatory body, suggesting eg a semi-permanent roster system as indication of an arbitral body.[67] Nonetheless, *Bungenberg/Reinisch* point out that with regard to the IUSCT, whose nature cannot be clearly classified as either 'public' or 'private' but was described as an 'institution sui generis', the qualification as public or private dispute settlement institution was not brought up during enforcement proceedings under the New York Convention.[68] As argued above, comparisons with the IUSCT are however complicated.

---

63 Kaufmann-Kohler, Potestà *(n 5)*, para 96.

64 Brower, Ahmad *(n 52)*, 806-807.

65 ibid, 807.

66 Kaufmann-Kohler, Potestà *(n 5)*, paras 89-90.

67 ibid, para 90.

68 Bungenberg, Reinisch *(n 4)*, 165 who refer to the fact that neither Ministry of Defense of the Islamic *Republic of Iran v Gould*, *Flatow v Iran* nor *Dallal v Bank Mellat* touched upon the question of the institutional nature of the IUSCT.

An exclusive appointment by the States might not only question whether the MIC could be considered an arbitral tribunal but might also stir trouble with regard to the acceptance of the system by investors. Investors might be suspicious that the appointments will only serve political considerations on the part of the States and lose as a consequence their trust in the dispute resolution system and in its integrity.[69] This holds especially true because ISDS, in its current existence, provides for a say of the investors when constituting the panel.[70] Taking this power away from the investors might cause them to question the impartiality of the dispute settlement system. Even though an appointment of adjudicators only by States constitutes the general approach for international courts (eg the ECHR, the CJEU or the ICJ), it contradicts the particularities of investment arbitration. Moreover, from a psychological point of view it will seem more severe to investors if the appointment power is taken away from them than if they never had disposed of it.

e) UNCITRAL Recommendation

Finally, and for the sake of clarification, *Kaufmann-Kohler/Potestà* suggest that UNCITRAL issues a recommendation regarding the interpretation of the MIC as 'permanent arbitral body'.[71] Such a recommendation was already released by UNCITRAL with regard to the interpretation of Article II (2) and Article VII (1) New York Convention.[72] The recommendation

---

69 Brower, Ahmad *(n 52)*, 809.

70 Gloria Alvarez et al *(n 55)*, para 13.

71 Kaufmann-Kohler, Potestà *(n 5)*, para 155; Potestà *(n 1)*, 173-174; also in favour UNCITRAL WG III, Appellate mechanism and enforcement issues, WP 202 (2020) *(n 17)*, para 43.

72 See the UNCITRAL, 'Report of the United Nations Commission on International Trade Law on the work of its thirty-ninth session' (19 June - 7 July 2006), A/61/17, Annex II Recommendation regarding the interpretation of Article II (2) and Article VII (1) New York Convention, 61 f. UNCITRAL adopted this recommendation to recognise domestic legislation and case law which is more favourable than the New York Convention. UNCITRAL recommended with regard to Article II (2) New York Convention (requirement of a written agreement) that the stipulation should be considered to be non-exhaustive and with regard to Article VII (1) New York Convention that it 'should be applied to allow any interested party to avail itself of rights it may have, under the law or treaties of the country where an arbitration agreement is sought to be relied upon, to seek recognition of the validity of such an arbitration agreement'.

cannot deploy a binding effect, but it may offer guidance to national courts for their assessment of MIC decisions. Consequently, a recommendation may influence national court decisions on whether or not to allow the enforcement of an MIC decision pursuant to the New York Convention.

f) Interim Conclusion

Notwithstanding, denying one party of the proceedings the right to choose its adjudicator constitutes a rather radical departure from the general principles of arbitral proceedings.[73] In order to consider the MIC as an arbitral body, the method of appointment must be counterbalanced by 'arbitral elements'. Yet, whether such a counterweight is sufficient, can ultimately only be determined by the domestic courts of enforcement.

All in all, the assessment of the MIC as arbitral body[74] depends not only on the method of appointment[75] of the adjudicators but also on the voluntary nature of the submission of the dispute to the MIC.[76] This holds particularly true considering that the New York Convention does not determine specific requirements to be met with regard to the appointment of the arbitrators.

2. *Voluntary Submission to the MIC?*

Doubts concerning the method of appointment are closely associated with another defining element of an arbitral award: it must have been rendered after the parties' voluntary submission of the dispute to the arbitral body. In particular with regard to the New York Convention's *travaux prépara-*

73 In this sense also Alvarez et al *(n 55)*, para 14.

74 See Kaufmann-Kohler, Potestà *(n 5)*, para 154 who mention that the prerequisite of an 'arbitral body' should not only be considered fulfilled under the 'ordinary meaning' of Article I (2) but also under an 'evolutionary interpretation' of the term.

75 But see also Brower, Ahmad *(n 52)*, 808 who point out that the appointment of the adjudicators by the parties is an essential element of arbitration.

76 Kaufmann-Kohler, Potestà *(n 5)*, paras 95-98; Brower, Ahmad *(n 52)*, 807-808.

toires,[77] this element is frequently considered to be the decisive requirement in order to qualify an adjudicatory body as an arbitral tribunal.[78]

Regarding the MIC, a voluntary mechanism might be particularly questionable should the underlying MIC Convention itself provide for the MIC's jurisdiction to be compulsory. This construction is for example the one which is chosen in the MIC Draft Statute (Article 23) drafted by *Bungenberg/Reinisch*.

There are different explanations as to why the submission of a dispute to the MIC could still be considered to be voluntary. First, *Bungenberg/Reinisch* eg argue that most national courts deem that an investor's individual voluntary submission can be replaced by the consent of the investor's home State.[79] Second, another possible explanation can be found in the mechanism of arbitration without privity, which nowadays represents the most common creation of consent in investment arbitration.[80] The arbitral and voluntary nature of investment arbitration is not questioned in arbitration without privity constellations.[81] In this hypothesis, the voluntary nature of the submission ensues from the investor's choice to accept the State's offer to settle the dispute in front of an international arbitral tribunal.[82] This reasoning applies in particular should the investor

77 Kaufmann-Kohler, Potestà *(n 5)*, paras 149-152; Reinisch *(n 4)*, 767-768; Potestà *(n 1)*, 172-173.

78 Kaufmann-Kohler, Potestà *(n 5)*, paras 152-154; see also Brower, Ahmad *(n 52)*, 807-808 who point out that the parties are within their right of consensual submission to arbitration when renouncing their right to appoint the adjudicator; with doubts on this see Happ, Wuschka *(n 4)*, 128-129 who argue a distinction between arbitration among privates and arbitrations involving a State. With regard to the latter, the authors consider the voluntary acceptance of jurisdiction as no suitable criterion to determine the arbitral nature of MIC jurisdiction; Potestà *(n 1)*, 172-173; Bungenberg, Reinisch *(n 4)*, paras 503-509; cf *Vollstreckbarerklärung eines ausländischen Schiedsspruchs bei gesetzlicher Zuständigkeit des Schiedsgerichts*, Kammergericht Berlin, case ref 14 U 2979/93,7 March 1995.

79 Cf Bungenberg, Reinisch *(n 4)*, para 507.

80 Cf similarily ibid, para 505; see also Potestà *(n 1)*, 163 who points out that the investor may freely choose between the host State's domestic courts or the MIC.

81 Gabrielle Kaufmann-Kohler and Michele Potestà, 'The Composition of a Multilateral Investment Court and of an Appeal Mechanism for Investment Awards (Part 2): CIDS Supplemental Report' CIDS 2017 para 159.

82 Kaufmann-Kohler, Potestà *(n 5)*, para 88; see also Bungenberg, Reinisch *(n 4)*, para 508.

prefer the MIC to (other) arbitral tribunals. Court decisions adopting this reasoning[83] were rendered with regard to the IUSCT.[84]

This latter approach shows that – with regard to the compulsory nature of the MIC's jurisdiction[85] – several distinctions must be made. The MIC could be construed to be absolutely compulsory[86], ie excluding all other venues, including domestic courts. Moreover, it could also be compulsory only regarding other international dispute settlement mechanisms. Whilst the MIC might be more effective if the investor does not have an alternative at its disposal, this might at the same time impair its effectiveness should the compulsory nature of the MIC negatively affect the requirement of a voluntary submission.

In addition to the prerequisite of its voluntary nature, the submission needs to be expressed in an arbitration agreement in writing, see Article II (1) New York Convention.[87] The MIC would be created not by the disputing parties but through an international treaty between the member

---

83 See for further references Bungenberg, Reinisch *(n 4)*, paras 506-507.

84 As explained with regard to the qualification of the MIC as an arbitral body, the IUSCT constitutes a specific institution and has been established after and because of extraordinary circumstances. Therefore, the doubts to its comparability with the MIC, which have already been mentioned above, must be considered as well with regard to the requirement of a voluntary submission of the parties when referring to the assessment of the IUSCT. Additionally, it should be kept in mind that the political circumstances and the exceptionally high caseload surrounding the IUSCT dispute settlement system might have played a role when designing the IUSCT as competent dispute settlement institution without any alternatives. Thus, drawing conclusion from the IUSCT should be treated carefully. Furthermore, investors were not (even) allowed to bring their claim in front of the national courts of the Iranian State or the US which is – under the general investment arbitration system – usually an alternative, albeit arguably less favourable, venue for the investor. If the MIC were to still allow the investors to seek compensation in front of domestic courts, the requirement of a voluntary submission would actually be easier to argue than with regard to the IUSCT, for the investor could at least choose between a domestic and an international remedy. Indeed, even without referring to the IUSCT, there are good arguments that the submission of a dispute to the MIC can be considered a voluntary act of the investors.

85 See with regard to an MIC's jurisdiction eg the proposition in the MIC Draft Statutes, Articles 19-27.

86 This construction is eg argued for in the MIC Draft Statute, Article 23.

87 Article II (1) New York Convention: 'Each Contracting State shall recognize an agreement in writing under which the parties undertake to submit to arbitration all or any differences which have arisen or which may arise between them in respect of a defined legal relationship, whether contractual or not, concerning a subject matter capable of settlement by arbitration.'

States. As a result, the concerned investors are not privy to the arbitration agreement establishing the MIC.[88] Since *Jan Paulsson's* well-known article, investment treaty arbitration is commonly referred to as arbitration without privity.[89] Nowadays, such dispute without privity constellations and the qualification of the treaty arbitration clauses are generally considered meeting the requirement found in Article II (1) New York Convention.[90] Nonetheless and for the sake of clarity, the States establishing the MIC could consider adding an express stipulation to the MIC Convention that such an agreement should fall within the scope of the New York Convention.[91]

3. *Appeal Mechanism as Enforcement Obstacle?*

A further hurdle when seeking enforcement of an MIC decision may exist if the MIC statute implements an appeal instance.[92] Traditionally, arbitration is perceived as a fast dispute resolution mechanism and therefore does not include an appeal mechanism. Even if the New York Convention might have been designed with these traditional arbitral awards in mind,

---

88 See Reinisch *(n 4)*, 783-784 who points out the similarities with the IUSCT in this regard and mentions the national courts' original reluctance to affirm an arbitration agreement in writing when asked to enforce an IUSCT award pursuant to the New York Convention. Nonetheless, the jurisprudential practice changed over time and most courts ultimately accepted the Algiers Accords, the treaty establishing the IUSCT, as a written agreement between Iran and the US not only on their own behalf but also on behalf of their nationals.

89 Jan Paulsson, 'Arbitration Without Privity' (1995) 10.2 ICSID Review 232.

90 *Occidental Exploration & Production Company v The Republic of Ecuador* Supreme Court of Judicature - Court of Appeal case ref A3/2005/1121, 9 September 2005, para 32; Kaufmann-Kohler, Potestà *(n 5)*, paras 103, 159 with further references; Brian McGarry, 'Enforcement of Investment Court Decisions under the New York Convention: A Search for Defining Elements' in Alan Anderson and Ben Beauomt (eds), *The Investor-State Dispute Settlement System: Reform, Replace or Status Quo?* (Kluwer 2020) 12; Reinisch *(n 4)*, 784; August Reinisch, 'Enforcement of Investment Awards' in Catherine Yannaca-Small (ed), *Arbitration under international investment agreements: A guide to the key issues* (OUP 2018) 675.

91 This has eg been done in Article 26 (5) (b) Energy Charter Treaty, Article 25 (2) (b) Canada Model BIT (2014) or Article 25 (2) (b) US Model BIT (2012). See also Reinisch *(n 4)*, 784 with further references; Potestà *(n 1)*, 169-170; see also Kaufmann-Kohler, Potestà *(n 5)*, para 160.

92 See above Landmann, Chapter 4; see also eg Section 4 (Articles 46-48) MIC Draft Statute.

appeal proceedings were specifically discussed during the negotiations and the New York Convention should not be considered banning appeal instances per se.[93] Furthermore, national law and jurisprudence commonly accept two-tiered arbitration proceedings,[94] so that there is no general incompatibility between arbitration and appeal.[95]

The New York Convention explicitly excludes any enforcement if the award has not yet become binding. In order to be a genuine alternative to court proceedings, arbitration must offer a final and binding dispute resolution as well. Hence, as long as an appeal is pending or possible under the MIC Convention, an MIC decision would not fulfil the New York Convention's enforcement requirements. Accordingly, enforcement proceedings under the New York Convention would only be possible if the time limit of appeal is elapsed or if the decision to be enforced was rendered by the appellate body.[96] From this moment on though, the existence of an appellate body does not hinder the enforcement.

4. Foreign or Non-Domestic Award?

The New York Convention's requirement of a foreign or non-domestic award is less challenging. An award is of foreign nature if it has been ren-

---

93 Unlike the ICSID Convention which excludes the possibility of an appeal mechanism (cf Calamita *(n 42)*, 613), the New York Convention itself does not object to the existence of an appellate body; see also Kaufmann-Kohler, Potestà *(n 5)*, paras 162-163.

94 UNCITRAL, *Secretariat Guide on the Convention on the Recognition and Enforcement of Foreign Arbitral Awards* (New York, 1958) (United Nations 2017), paras 21-25; UNCITRAL WG III, Appellate mechanism and enforcement issues, WP 202 (2020) *(n 17)*, para 42 with further references.

95 Kaufmann-Kohler, Potestà *(n 5)*, paras 162-163; Potestà *(n 1)*, 177; cf *Mitwirkung eines juristischen Beraters im Schiedsverfahren kein Hindernis für Vollstreckbarerklärung des ausländischen Schiedsspruchs German Federal Court of Justice* (Bundesgerichtshof), case ref III ZR 169/88, 18 Janaury 1990, para 10; UNCITRAL WG III, Appellate mechanism and enforcement issues, WP 202 (2020) *(n 17)*, para 42 with further references.

96 Potestà *(n 1)*, 177-178; cf also UNCITRAL, Working Group III, 'Annotated comments from the European Union and its Member States to the UNCITRAL Secretariat*' (19 October 2020), A/CN.9/WG.III/WP., Comment No 23 from the European Union and its Member States in which it is suggested that the appeal mechanism could apply to so-called 'provisional' awards; cf for an example Article 8.41 para 3 CETA; cf also Article 48 MIC Draft Statute.

dered under the *lex arbitri* of another State than the State of enforcement.[97] An award is qualified as non-domestic, if the award is rendered in the territory of the State in which enforcement is sought but national law was not applied.[98]

Both kinds of awards have commonly been recognised by national courts as awards within the meaning of the New York Convention.[99] Legal scholars thus consider it likely that this jurisprudence will sustain and would also apply to MIC decisions.[100] The applicability of the New York Convention has been discussed with regard to a-national awards, ie awards rendered by a tribunal without a seat.[101] Yet, national courts and legal scholars assume that ICSID awards meet the requirements of the New York Convention's enforcement regime.[102] Should the MIC be construed to also issue delocalised awards, it seems probable that national courts will apply the same reasoning.[103] This prerequisite of the New York Convention should therefore not pose insurmountable problems.

5. Reservation of the New York Convention on 'Commercial Matters'?

Further, States may issue a reservation on 'commercial matters' in order to limit the applicability of the New York Convention.[104] At first sight, this might complicate the enforcement of investment arbitration awards. Yet, jurisprudential practice regularly includes investment disputes into the scope of commercial matters.[105] This appreciation is for example reinforced by the 1985 UNCITRAL Model Law on International Commercial

---

97 Bungenberg, Reinisch *(n 4)*, para 522.

98 ibid, para 524.

99 See for further references Commentary to Article I New York Convention by Hans Bagner in Herbert Kronke et al (eds), *Recognition and Enforcement of Foreign Arbitral Awards: A Global Commentary on the New York Convention* (2010), 19-36.

100 Kaufmann-Kohler, Potestà *(n 5)*, paras 156-157; Potestà *(n 1)*, 174-175; Bungenberg, Reinisch *(n 4)*, 521-528.

101 Kaufmann-Kohler, Potestà *(n 5)*, para 157 with further references; see also Alvarez et al *(n 56)*, para 15; and see also Van den Berg *(n 20)*, 180-181.

102 Christoph Schreuer et al *(n 16)*, Article 54, para 20 with further references; see also Reinisch *(n 90)*, 672-673.

103 Kaufmann-Kohler, Potestà *(n 5)*, para 157; Bungenberg, Reinisch *(n 4)*, para 525.

104 See Article I (3) sentence 2 New York Convention, cf also Kröll *(n 16)*, para 21.

105 See for references Bungenberg, Reinisch *(n 4)*, paras 530-533; see also Reinisch *(n 90)*, 674; and see Van den Berg *(n 20)*, 183.

Arbitration which specifically includes investments in the definition of commercial arbitration.[106] Moreover, treaties sometimes include an explicit stipulation that decisions rendered on the basis of the treaty are to be enforced under the New York Convention's regime, ie are deemed to be decisions in commercial matters.[107]

6. *Interim Conclusion concerning the New York Convention*

In the end, all will depend on the exact way in which the MIC is established. If arbitral elements prevail over court-like elements[108] an enforcement of MIC decisions under the New York Convention is likely.[109] Different jurisdictions may nevertheless apply the New York Convention's standards in different ways, therefore causing a fragmentation in the enforcement system.[110]

The Secretariat of the UNICTRAL Working Group III mentions the possibility to include a stipulation into the MIC Convention that the New York Convention should be applicable. The practical effect of such a stipulation is however limited as it would only bind MIC member States, but not the national courts of a third State where enforcement is sought.[111]

---

106 Article 1 (1) 1985 UNCITRAL Model Law on International Commercial Arbitration, adopted by UNICITRAL on 21 June 1985 and amended on 7 July 2006, UNCITRAL, Report of the United Nations Commission on International Trade Law on the work of its eighteenth session‘ (3-21 June 1985), A/40/17, Annex 1 and UNCITRAL, Report Trade Law, Session 39, A/61/17 (2006) *(n 72)*, Annex I.

107 Kröll *(n 16)*, paras 22-23 with reference to Article 26 (5) (b) ECT and Article 1136 (7) NAFTA; cf also Article 8.41 para 5 CETA.

108 See also McGarry *(n 90)*, 15-26 who analyses the WTO mechanism and its qualification as arbitration.

109 But see with doubts Lukasz Kulaga, 'A Brave, New, International Investment Court in Context. Towards a Paradigm Shift of the ISDS' (2018) 38 Polish Yearbook of International Law 115, 135-136.

110 Alvarez et al *(n 55)*, paras 17-19.

111 UNCITRAL WG III, Appellate mechanism and enforcement issues, WP 202 (2020) *(n 17)*, para 43; cf eg Article 26 (5) (b) ECT and Article 1136 (7) NAFTA; cf also Article 8.41 pàra 5 CETA; cf also Article 8.41-5 CETA.

C. Establishment of an MIC Inherent Enforcement System?

The best – and in the long run most likely preferable – option for enforcement constitutes an MIC inherent system of recognition and enforcement of its decisions.[112] To establish an enforcement system, the authors of the MIC will not have to start from scratch but can seek inspiration in the existing enforcement mechanisms, eg mainly the ICSID Convention.

The implementation of such an inherent enforcement system is suggested by *Bungenberg/Reinisch*[113] as well as by *Kaufmann-Kohler/Potestà*[114], the authors of the most elaborate suggestions for the establishment of an MIC published so far. It is of particular importance to have an enforcement system that obliges not only the State which is party to the dispute, but which also allows an enforcement by and in States not party to the dispute. A system coined after the ICSID Convention would benefit from the high effectiveness of this regime.[115] Yet, due to the ICSID Convention's characteristics, a mere reference to the ICSID Convention in the MIC Convention may cause problems of compatibility between the dispute resolution system of the MIC and the one created through the ICSID Convention.[116] An MIC decision was necessarily not rendered in accordance with the ICSID rules and can therefore not be treated as an ICSID award.[117] Additionally, relying on references entails usually difficulties should the frame of reference be altered and, as a consequence, it has to be determined whether the reference is dynamic or static. Therefore, it would be favourable for States to implement an entire mechanism instead of only including a mere reference to other, already existing, enforcement regimes.[118]

The member States of the MIC can establish an inherent enforcement system at their discretion. Such a system could therefore be as extensive and as effective as they wish it to be. However, an inherent enforcement system's effectiveness suffers from one main deficiency: it only binds the

112 Kaufmann-Kohler, Potestà *(n 5)*, para 140; cf Bungenberg, Reinisch *(n 4)*, paras 483, 536-540.

113 Bungenberg, Reinisch *(n 4)*, paras 483, 536.

114 Kaufmann-Kohler, Potestà (n 5), paras 140-141; see also Potestà (n 1), 168-169.

115 See above Section B.I.

116 Kaufmann-Kohler, Potestà *(n 5)*, para 141.

117 See above Section B.I. regarding the particular and self-contained dispute settlement mechanism of the ICSID Convention. In this sense also ibid, para 141.

118 ibid, para 141; see with this reasoning also Potestà *(n 1)*, 169.

MIC Convention's member States. Thus, it cannot provide a system for the enforcement of MIC decisions in third States.[119]

Consequently, the effectiveness of the MIC's enforcement mechanism depends on the number and arguably also the identity of the member States. On the one hand, the more member States the MIC has, the more States are bound by the inherent enforcement mechanism and its effectiveness increases.[120] On the other hand, even if all States are equal due to their sovereignty, they are unequal with regard to their economic strength.[121] To provide an effective enforcement mechanism, the MIC needs to also include the economically powerful States.[122]

In their MIC Draft Statute *Bungenberg/Reinisch* propose an MIC inherent system of enforcement. Article 56 sets out how an MIC decision may be enforced in member States of the MIC. Herein, the wording resembles Article 54 ICSID Convention. It therefore aims at providing the highly effective enforcement mechanism that investors may profit from under the ICSID Convention. In Article 56 (4), the MIC Draft Statute stipulates the possibility for third States to commit themselves towards the MIC Secretariat to the inherent enforcement system. According to Article 57 MIC Draft Statute the member States of the MIC will work towards creating a treaty of enforcement with third States. It remains questionable though if many States would choose this option but would at the same time refuse to adhere to the MIC Convention. It is difficult to estimate what the interest in such a commitment would be for third States.

Multiple arguments advocate in favour of the establishment of an MIC inherent enforcement mechanism. The most important advantage of an inherent system is that it renders the qualification of the MIC as an international arbitral tribunal or an international court superfluous. If, on the one hand, one comes to the conclusion that the MIC has to be qualified as an international court, the implementation of an inherent enforcement system constitutes the only possible venue of enforcement.[123] If, on the

119 Kaufmann-Kohler, Potestà *(n 5)*, para 143; Bungenberg, Reinisch *(n 4)*, para 356.

120 Cf Van den Berg *(n 20)*, 176.

121 The WTO proceedings in United States – Measures Affecting the Cross-Border Supply of Gambling and Betting Services, DS285 show two States (the United States and Antigua and Barbuda) of different economic strength facing each other in front of a dispute settlement institution and the difficulties their unequal positions may entail.

122 Alvarez et al *(n 55)*, para 23 suggest to prioritise 'pro-enforcement jurisdictions' to increase the effectiveness of an MIC enforcement mechanism.

123 See eg Potestà *(n 1)*, 160.

other hand, one comes to the conclusion that the MIC can be qualified as an international arbitral tribunal, the inherent system is applicable as well.

As the analysis regarding the ICSID Convention and the New York Convention demonstrated, their applicability to MIC decisions can be discussed as well. Regarding the first, it seems unlikely that the ICSID enforcement mechanism could be applied to MIC decisions. Regarding the second, there is a chance that domestic courts will accept to enforce MIC decision on the basis of the New York Convention. As it is upon the domestic courts to determine whether the requirements are met or not, it seems probable that an enforcement under the New York Convention would lead to a fragmented enforcement of MIC decisions. Accordingly, an MIC inherent system should be preferred over the already existing mechanisms.

The other important reason why an inherent system of enforcement seems preferable is that this allows the MIC member States to establish the regime exactly with the particularities and the extent they deem reasonable and desirable.

The inherent mechanism's greatest flaw, that its binding character is limited on the MIC member States, might decrease over time if the MIC manages to attract more members. After all, the ICSID Convention itself, which is nowadays considered to be the most efficient and most used dispute resolution mechanism in investment arbitration, entered into force when only 20 States had ratified the ICSID Convention. As the MIC project is strongly pushed by the European Commission, the MIC would probably see light with the 27 EU States as its member States and find itself therefore in a better starting position. Alternatively, a solution as envisaged by the MIC Draft Statute might provide at least an interim solution: as suggested in Article 57, the member States could aim to conclude enforcement treaties with third States in order to allow enforcement in their jurisdiction. Whilst this certainly can allow a broader enforcement than the one limited to the MIC's member States, its practicability is questionable. It might however serve as incentive for States which prefer to keep the traditional investment dispute settlement system but are poised to join in the MIC system to a certain degree and in a passive manner. The overall objective for an effective enforcement system should nevertheless remain to gain the third States as member States.

D. Fund – a Complement to the Enforcement of MIC Decisions?

Inspired by the IUSCT's enforcement fund, *Bungenberg/Reinisch* additionally suggest the establishment of a fund in order to complement an MIC inherent enforcement system.[124] For the purpose of assuring the effectiveness of enforcement under the IUSCT's dispute settlement regime, a kind of security account was established: all Iranian deposits and securities in US banking institutions in the United States are to be held in escrow by the Algerian Central Bank up to a sum of USD 1 billion. Additionally, if the balance of this fund falls below USD 500 million, the Iranian State is bound to effectuate further payments to fill the fund to a threshold of USD 500 million. This fund was meant to assure the satisfaction of US claimants.[125] As this enforcement mechanism provided a high effectiveness, recourse to other international enforcement instruments such as the New York Convention was rare.[126]

The authors propose a similarly structured fund to guarantee the effective enforcement of MIC decisions. Every MIC member State would have to pay a certain sum into the fund in order to allow an enforcement of MIC decisions via this fund.[127] Ultimately, once a successful claimant obtained compensation via the fund, its claim would be assigned to the MIC.[128]

Nonetheless, uncertainties remain regarding *how* to establish a financially sufficient fund.[129] The sum of the deposit of the member States could either be of equal value or be determined in dependence of the economic situation of each State.

Whereas an equal sum does not sufficiently take into account the economic inequality of different member States, a direct proportional connection between the volume of foreign investments and the number of investment cases can equally not be assumed.[130] Further, taking the economic strength of the member States into account neglects that the

124 Bungenberg, Reinisch *(n 4)*, paras 537-540.
125 Declaration of the Government of the Democratic and Popular Republic of Algeria (General Declaration) (1981), paras 6 and 7.
126 Bungenberg, Reinisch *(n 4)*, para 537.
127 ibid, para 538.
128 ibid, para 539.
129 ibid, para 538.
130 ibid.

defendant's economic situation has no role in determining the quantum of an MIC decision.[131]

With regard to the IUSCT only the Iranian State was obligated to effectuate payments into the fund without having itself access to the escrow account.[132] This particular arrangement was justified by the fact that the Iranian State was rarely awarded damages but mainly condemned to pay damages to US investors. In contrast, all MIC member States will be potential respondents that can be sentenced to damages. Still, it is often one specific measure by one State that entails a multitude of investment arbitration proceedings, as for example the cases brought against Argentina following its controversial laws to master its economic crisis in the early 2000s or the renewable energy cases against Spain or Italy.[133]

It can therefore be discussed if the sum owed to the fund should be contingent upon the number of cases brought against the States and their subsequent convictions. Yet, such a solution would face practical difficulties. First, it might discourage States who are concerned about frequently being the losing party from adhering to the MIC. Second, the determination of the financial contribution to the fund with regard to its amount and the frequency of this determination will prove itself challenging as well.

Beyond that, limiting the type of investors that are eligible for a refund to SMEs could be envisaged and seems appropriate in order not to

---

131 ibid.

132 ibid, para 537.

133 See with regard to Argentina Paolo Di Rosa, 'The Recent Wave of Arbitration against Argentina under Bilateral Investment Treaties: Background and Principal Legal Issues' (2004) 36.1 Inter American Law Review, 41; Esther Kentin, 'Economic Crises and Investment Arbitration: the Argentine Cases' in Philippe Kahn and Thomas W Wälde (eds), *Les aspects nouveau du droit des investissements internationaux = New Aspects of International Investment Law* (Martinus Nijhoff Publishers 2007), 629; José E Alvarez and Gustavo Topalian, 'The Paradoxical Argentina Cases' (2012) 6.3 World Arbitration & Mediation Review 491; see with regard to Spain and Italy Daniel Behn and Ole Kristian Fauchald, 'Governments under Cross-Fire: Renewable Energy and International Economic Tribunals' (2015) 12.2 Manchester Journal of International Economic Law 117; Yulia S Selivanova, 'Changes in Renewables Support Policy and Investment Protection under the Energy Charter Treaty: Analysis of Jurisprudence and Outlook for the Current Arbitration Cases' (2018) 33.2 ICSID Review 433; Igor V Timofeyev, Joseph R Profaizer and Adam J Weiss, 'Investment Disputes Involving the Renewable Energy Industry under the Energy Charter Treaty' in J William Rowley, Doak Bishop, and Gordon E Kaiser (eds), *The Guide to Energy Arbitrations* (Global Arbitration Review 2020), 45.

overstrain the financial resources of the fund.[134] Additionally, or in the alternative, one could also consider capping the damages that could be paid by the fund at a certain amount.[135]

If a fund were to be established, its coexistence with the general enforcement of MIC decisions must be regulated as well. *Bungenberg/Reinisch* argue against a mutual exclusivity but consider making enforcement via the fund subject to the substantiation that other ways of enforcement will prove to be difficult.[136] Whilst it seems certainly reasonable to avoid draining the fund with claims that could easily be enforced by resorting to other enforcement mechanisms, the requirement to establish enforcement difficulties can cause further uncertainties. Such endeavours would however undermine the initial purpose of the fund which is to ensure an uncomplicated and fast enforcement.

Accordingly, the MIC Draft Statute includes in Article 58 a provision to establish a fund for the indemnification of prevailing investors. Each MIC member State is under an obligation to pay a certain sum into this fund. If a party, after obtaining a favourable MIC decision, can demonstrate the urgency of receiving payment of the awarded sum, it may obtain satisfaction up to a certain amount out of the fund. As outlined above, the determination of the financial contributions will have to be carefully refined.

The establishment of a fund will certainly simplify for investors to seek damages, especially for SMEs. Lengthy and costly enforcement proceedings that could otherwise hinder final satisfaction could be avoided. It remains crucial though to ensure the long-term financial support of such a fund. This also entails the necessity of an effective mechanism to ensure the reimbursement of the MIC once it is subrogated in the rights of the investor.[137]

E. Conclusion

This contribution argues that the preferable enforcement mechanism is the establishment of an MIC inherent regime. This allows the member

134 ibid, para 539

135 ibid, para 539.

136 ibid, para 540.

137 See Article 58 (4) MIC Draft Statute.

States to design the enforcement mechanism to their needs.[138] Should the member States prefer to rely on the already existing mechanisms, for the reasons pointed out above especially on the New York Convention, the chances of enforcement of an MIC decision will crucially depend on its structure and its classification. If the New York Convention is to be applied, uncertainties and fragmentation may however arise if domestic courts resort to different standards.

If the MIC member States wish to establish an inherent system providing the most effective enforcement mechanism possible, they should include provisions similar to Article 54 ICSID Convention. The principles of the ICSID Convention are for example reflected in Article 56 MIC Draft Statute. Yet, the MIC member States could also follow the enforcement mechanism of the New York Convention when establishing the MIC enforcement system. Whereas the latter option would constitute – in accordance with the analysis set out above – a less effective means of enforcement in comparison with the option inspired by the ICSID Convention, it might be easier for the member States to agree on such a less invasive enforcement system.

The critical issue of enforcement is the extent to which third States participate in the enforcement mechanism. As long as the MIC has not gained enough member States to assure an effective and wide spread enforcement, gaps of enforcement might appear.[139] If one allows parallel enforcement regimes – the ones already existing in investment arbitration and the one from the MIC – there is a considerable risk of fragmentation.[140] To counter these difficulties, EFILA suggests a so-called 'phased enforcement regime'.[141] This proposition provides that the already existing ISDS mechanisms are to be applied until a certain critical number of member States is reached. Once this threshold is passed, EFILA suggests an inter-se applicability of the New York Convention only amongst the MIC member States. In the long run – and with further member States – an MIC inherent system, coined after the ICSID Convention, would come to life and replace the interim solution.[142]

138 As UNCITRAL WG III, Appellate mechanism and enforcement issues, WP 202 (2020) *(n 17)*, para 44 points out, this allows the member States to also include stipulations regarding an enforcement against the investor.

139 Alvarez et al *(n 55)*, para 24.

140 ibid, paras 24-25.

141 ibid, para 26.

142 ibid, paras 26-27.

Ultimately, even if an inherent enforcement mechanism is modelled after the ICISD Convention's regime, the MIC will have to face a difficulty that did not exist as such for ICSID: the MIC will only be one of many possible venues of investment dispute settlement and will have to compete with already functioning systems, especially the ICSID mechanism. Even if the MIC Convention includes an exclusivity stipulation – as it is done for example by the Draft Statute (see Article 23) – the MIC dispute resolution system would still have to present itself more favourable than the ICSID Convention if it aims to be accepted by many potential member States. The outcome of this competition with the existing mechanisms and most particularly the ICSID enforcement regime will be decisive for the MIC's impact and its establishment as a long-lasting means of investment dispute settlement.

The MIC should aim to be one day similarly widespread as ICSID.[143] Once such an expansion is achieved, enforcement in third States – which represents the enforcement's main predicament – becomes less and less crucial.[144] However, the way thither could turn out to be a challenging one.

143 Happ, Wuschka *(n 4)*, 131-132; Bungenberg, Reinisch *(n 4)*, para 536.
144 Happ, Wuschka *(n 4)*, 132.

Chapter 10: EU Law Requirements for the Establishment of the Multilateral Investment Court

*by Ingo Borgdorf**

Selected Bibliography: Venetia Argyropoulou, 'Chapter 2: ISDS Reform in the EU: Are We There Yet?' in Alan M Anderson and Ben Beaumont (eds), *The Investor-State Dispute Settlement System: Reform, Replace or Status Quo?* (Wolters Kluwer 2020) 50; Marc Bungenberg and Catharine Titi, 'CETA Opinion – Setting Conditions for the Future of ISDS' (EJIL: Talk!, 5 June 2019) <https://www.ejiltalk.org/ceta-opinion-setting-conditions-for-the-future-of-isds/> accessed 13 January 2022; Maria Fanou, 'The CETA ICS and the Autonomy of the EU Legal Order in Opinion 1/17 – A Compass for the Future' (2020) 22 Cambridge Yearbook of European Legal Studies 108; Andrés Eduardo Avarao Garzón, 'Designing a Multilateral Investment Court: Blueprints for a New Route in Investor-Sate Dispute Settlement' (2019) 2019.3 Zeitschrift für Europarechtliche Studien (ZEuS) 477; Catharine Titi, 'Opinion 1/17 and the Future of Investment Dispute Settlement: Implications for the Design of a Multilateral Investment Court' in Lisa E Sachs, Lise J Johnson, and Jesse Coleman (eds), *Yearbook on International Investment Law & Policy 2019* (OUP 2021).

A. Introduction

The EU plays a decisive role for the establishment of the Multilateral Investment Court (MIC). Such multilateral judicial mechanism for dispute settlement between foreign investors and their host States is at the core of the EU's agenda to reform Investor-State Dispute Settlement (ISDS). This reform agenda has been driven by the EU in two ways: First, by negotiating new-generation Investment Protection Agreements (IPAs) with third countries that provide for a court-based dispute settlement mechanism,

---

* *Ingo Borgdorf is a lawyer in an international law firm and specialised on international arbitration with a focus on Investor-State Dispute Settlement. Comments expressed in this piece are made strictly in a personal capacity.*

the Investment Court System (ICS).[1] Second, by participating in the multilateral ISDS reform process in UNCITRAL Working Group III, which considers the establishment of a standing mechanism for the settlement of international investment disputes as one possible reform option.[2] In both ways, the EU attempts to address public concerns relating to conventional investor-State arbitration by working towards the introduction of a standing multilateral dispute settlement mechanism.[3]

The Court of Justice of the European Union (CJEU) has – in principle – approved the EU's participation in such an international dispute settlement mechanism placed outside the EU judicial system. On 30 April 2019, the CJEU decided in Opinion 1/17 that the ICS of the Comprehensive Economic and Trade Agreement (CETA) concluded between Canada and the EU is compatible with the EU's constitutional framework:

> It must be recalled, at the outset, that an international agreement providing for the creation of a court responsible for the interpretation of its provisions and whose decisions are binding on the European Union, is, in principle, compatible with EU law.[4]

The approval is critical for the EU given that the MIC would be placed outside the EU judicial system. At the same time, Opinion 1/17 specifies the requirements that the MIC must meet in order to be compatible with the EU constitutional framework. Thus, when pursuing its reform agenda, the EU is bound by these requirements stemming from the fundamental principles of EU law.

This chapter addresses the role of the EU and the requirements of its legal system for the establishment of the MIC. To that end, it first retraces the EU's new approach to ISDS in its recent treaty practice, notably its shift from traditional investor-State arbitration towards a court-based dispute settlement mechanism (B.). It proceeds by showing how the EU – based on this new approach – participates in the multilateral ISDS reform

---

1 See Articles 8.27-8.29 Comprehensive Trade and Economic Agreement between Canada and the European Union (CETA) (2016).

2 UNCITRAL, Working Group III, 'Possible reform of investor-State dispute settlement (ISDS) Submission from the European Union and its Member States' (24 January 2019), A/CN.9/WG.III/WP.159/Add.1.

3 European Commission, 'Concept paper: Investment in TTIP and beyond – the path for reform' (May 2015) <http://trade.ec.europa.eu/doclib/docs/2015/may/tradoc_153408.PDF> accessed 13 January 2022, 3, 4.

4 *Opinion 1/17 pursuant to Article 218(11) TFEU*, CJEU (2019) ECLI:EU:C:2019:341, para 106.

process in UNCITRAL Working Group III (C.). Both the EU's treaty practice and its multilateral reform efforts are determined by the conditions of EU law for its participation in an international dispute settlement mechanism that stands outside the EU judicial system. These EU law conditions result from the CJEU's analysis of CETA's compatibility with EU law in Opinion 1/17, which is the centrepiece of this chapter (D.). Thereafter, the conditions of EU law are applied to the recently published MIC Draft Statute[5] with the aim of determining, whether such design of the MIC can be reconciled with the EU constitutional framework (E.). This chapter closes with conclusions on the EU law requirements for the establishment of the MIC and an outlook on its negotiation at the multilateral level (F.).

B. The EU's Approach to ISDS in Treaty Practice

The EU's new-generation IPAs reflect the EU's transition from traditional investment arbitration to institutionalised dispute settlement. The treaties break with dispute settlement by ad hoc tribunals appointed by the parties to the dispute in favour of a permanent court, the EU's ICS.[6]

The EU's ICS had its first appearance in the European Commission's concept paper on 'Investment in TTIP and beyond – the path for reform' published in May 2015.[7] Addressing concerns expressed in a preceding public consultation, the concept paper set out concrete improvements for i) the protection of the right to regulate; ii) the establishment and functioning of arbitral tribunals; iii) the review of ISDS decisions through an appellate mechanism; and iv) the relationship between domestic judicial systems and ISDS.[8] The proposed improvements were intended to feed into the negotiations of the Transatlantic Trade and Investment Partnership (TTIP), and at the same time to serve as a stepping stone towards the

5 Marc Bungenberg and August Reinisch, *Draft Statute of the Multilateral Investment Court* (Nomos 2021).

6 Catharine Titi, 'Opinion 1/17 and the Future of Investment Dispute Settlement: Implications for the Design of a Multilateral Investment Court' in Lisa E Sachs, Lise J Johnson, and Jesse Coleman (eds), *Yearbook on International Investment Law & Policy 2019* (OUP 2021), para 24.07.

7 European Commission *(n 3)*; see also Venetia Argyropoulou, 'Chapter 2: ISDS Reform in the EU: Are We There Yet?' in Alan M Anderson and Ben Beaumont (eds), *The Investor-State Dispute Settlement System: Reform, Replace or Status Quo?* (Wolters Kluwer 2020) 50, 51.

8 European Commission *(n 3)*, 3.

establishment of a permanent court.[9] The European Commission, thus, explored the establishment of a permanent investment court in bilateral relations as well as within a future multilateral framework.[10]

Consequently, the proposal for the creation of a permanent investment court entered the EU's official proposal for TTIP in the negotiations with the United States of America.[11] Section 3 of the proposal contained provisions on the resolution of investment disputes and the investment court system, which were to provide for tenured judges and an appellate mechanism.[12] Only three weeks later, the EU concluded its negotiations with Vietnam on a free trade agreement. That agreement included the EU's new approach on investment protection, in particular 'a permanent dispute resolution system with an appeal mechanism.'[13]

In February 2016, the EU and Canada agreed on a revised text of CETA, which included the main elements of the EU's new approach.[14] After significant amendments of the treaty text during its legal vetting, CETA introduced the ICS and the commitment to pursue the establishment of the MIC.[15] Likewise, the EU's IPAs with Singapore and Vietnam concluded in 2018 and 2019 foresee the creation of bilateral investment courts and contain the commitment to pursue the establishment of a two-tiered MIC.[16] Similar provisions will presumably enter into the new trade agreement between the EU and Mexico, which has been agreed in principle in April 2018.[17]

---

9 Ibid, 11.

10 Titi *(n 6)*, para 24.08.

11 European Union, 'Proposal for Transatlantic Trade and Investment Partnership, CHAPTER II – Investment' (November 2015) <https://trade.ec.europa.eu/doclib/docs/2015/november/tradoc_153955.pdf> accessed 13 January 2022.

12 ibid, Articles 9, 10.

13 European Commission, 'EU and Vietnam finalise landmark trade deal' (2 December 2015) <http://trade.ec.europa.eu/doclib/press/index.cfm?id=1409> accessed 13 January 2022.

14 European Commission, 'CETA: EU and Canada agree on new approach on investment in trade agreement' (29 February 2015) <http://trade.ec.europa.eu/doclib/press/index.cfm?id=1468> accessed 13 January 2022.

15 Articles 8.27-8.29 CETA.

16 Articles 3.9, 3.10 and 3.12 EU-Singapore IPA; Articles 3.38, 3.39 and 3.41 EU-Vietnam IPA; see also Andrés Eduardo Avarao Garzón, 'Designing a Multilateral Investment Court: Blueprints for a New Route in Investor-Sate Dispute Settlement' (2019) 2019.3 Zeitschrift für Europarechtliche Studien (ZEuS) 477, 480.

17 While the revision of the agreement is ongoing, the draft text of the EU-Mexico Global Agreement's Section on Investment Dispute Resolution published in April 2018 includes a permanent investment court and the commitment to

However, the investment court system has not yet become reality given that none of these IPAs has yet entered into force. The EU-Singapore and EU-Vietnam IPAs as well as CETA's chapter on investment protection still require ratification by the EU Member States. This is due to the fact that the competence on investment dispute settlement is shared between the EU and the Member States. In 2009, the Lisbon Treaty conferred the competence for foreign direct investment to the EU.[18] Yet, the CJEU held that the ISDS regime 'removes disputes from the jurisdiction of the courts of the Member States (...) and cannot, therefore, be established without the Member States' consent'.[19] The competence over the conclusion of international investment treaties that provide for investment dispute settlement, thus, remains shared between the EU and the Member States.[20]

Nevertheless, the ICS provided for in these agreements illustrates the EU's new approach to investment protection. This approach entails two main features turning away from traditional ISDS: first, the shift from ad hoc constitution of arbitral tribunals appointed by the disputing parties to an investment court which is composed of judges appointed for fixed terms of office and randomly selected to hear a dispute. Second, the shift from generally enforceable awards subject only to limited grounds of review to an appeal mechanism that provides for a second level of substantive review for legal correctness.[21] These features are also the basis on which the EU pursues the creation of the MIC in the negotiations at UNCITRAL Working Group III.[22]

C. *The EU's Participation in the ISDS Reform Process*

The multilateral reform of ISDS is driven by the negotiations in UNCITRAL Working Group III. As a forum for deliberations, Working Group III was mandated to identify concerns regarding ISDS, consider

---

cooperation for the establishment of a multilateral mechanism for the resolution of investment disputes, Articles 11, 12 and 14 of Section X EU-Mexico Global Agreement, <https://trade.ec.europa.eu/doclib/docs/2018/april/tradoc_156814.pdf > accessed 13 January 2022.

18 Article 206 TFEU.

19 *Opinion 2/15 pursuant to Article 218 (11) TFEU*, CJEU (2015) ECLI:EU:C:2017:376, § 292.

20 ibid, § 305.

21 Titi *(n 6)*, para 24.08; Garzón *(n 16)*, 478.

22 UNCITRAL WG III, Submission European Union and its Member States, WP 159 (2019) *(n 2)*.

whether reform is desirable and, if so, develop recommendations.[23] Its 38th session held in January 2020 was dedicated to the consideration of reform options relating to the creation of a standing multilateral investment court, a stand-alone review or appellate mechanism as well as selection and appointment of arbitrators and adjudicators.[24] These reform options were considered as a response to concerns pertaining to three main areas: first, to the perceived lack of consistency, coherence, predictability, and correctness of arbitral decisions by ISDS tribunals. Second, to the independence and diversity of arbitrators as well as the mechanisms of constituting and challenging tribunals. Third, to costs and duration of ISDS cases.[25]

The EU plays an active role in shaping this reform process in accordance with the Council's negotiating directives for a convention establishing a multilateral court for the settlement of investment disputes.[26] These negotiating directives aim at transposing the EU's new approach to investment protection into multilateral negotiations under the auspices of UNCITRAL, which could ultimately result in the creation of the MIC.[27] Notably, the submission of the EU and its Member States dated 24 January 2019 formally proposed the 'establishment of a standing mechanism for the settlement of investment disputes' as a response to concerns identified by the Working Group.[28] The standing mechanism, as envisaged by the EU, would have two levels of adjudication with an appeal that is limited to errors of law or manifest errors in the appreciation of facts, thus excluding the possibility for a *de novo* review of the facts.[29] Its adjudicators would be employed full-time for a non-renewable term of office not allowing any

23 UNCITRAL, 'Report of Working Group III (Investor-State Dispute Settlement Reform) on the work of its thirty-fourth session (Vienna, 27 November-1 December 2017), Part I' (19 December 2017), A/CN.9/930/Rev. 1, para 19.

24 UNCITRAL, 'Report of Working Group III (Investor-State Dispute Settlement Reform) on the work of its resumed thirty-eighth session' (28 January 2020), A/CN.9/1004/Add.1, para 14.

25 UNCITRAL WG III, Submission European Union and its Member States, WP 159 (2019) *(n 2)*, 2, 3.

26 Council of the EU, 'Negotiating directives for a Convention establishing a multilateral court for the settlement of investment disputes' (12981/17 ADD 1, 20 March 2018) <https://data.consilium.europa.eu/ doc/document/ST-12981-2017-ADD-1-DCL-1/en/pdf> accessed 13 January 2022.

27 ibid, 3; see also Maria Fanou, 'The CETA ICS and the Autonomy of the EU Legal Order in Opinion 1/17 – A Compass for the Future' (2020) 22 Cambridge Yearbook of European Legal Studies 108.

28 UNCITRAL WG III, Submission European Union and its Member States, WP 159 (2019) *(n 2)*, para 3.

29 ibid, paras 13, 14.

outside activities and be subject to strict ethical requirements.[30] Their independence and impartiality would be ensured by a robust and transparent appointment process.[31]

The EU is a driving force behind the reform process taking place at Working Group III. At the same time, the submission of the EU has left no doubt that – in its view – the systemic structural change brought by 'a permanent standing two-tier mechanism with full-time adjudicators [was] the only type of reform which can effectively respond to all the concerns identified.'[32] Hence, the establishment of a multilateral investment court is the only option to reform ISDS in a way that can involve the EU in future. At the same time, the EU must ensure that the multilateral negotiations result in a design of the MIC that meets the conditions identified by the CJEU.

D. The EU Law Conditions for the MIC

Opinion 1/17 dealt with Belgium's request for an opinion on the compatibility of CETA's ICS with the autonomy of the EU legal order, the general principle of equal treatment, and the right of access to an independent tribunal. Yet, while analysing its compatibility with EU law, the CJEU also identified the conditions that bind the EU in the multilateral reform negotiations.[33]

I. The CJEU's Findings in Opinion 1/17

In Opinion 1/17, the CJEU confirmed that EU law does not in principle prevent the EU from concluding 'an international agreement providing for the creation of a court responsible for the interpretation of its provisions and whose decisions are binding on the European Union.'[34] This is partic-

30 ibid, paras 16, 18.
31 ibid, para 19.
32 ibid, para 57.
33 Marc Bungenberg and Catharine Titi 'CETA Opinion – Setting Conditions for the Future of ISDS' (EJIL: Talk!, 5 June 2019) <https://www.ejiltalk.org/ceta-opinion-setting-conditions-for-the-future-of-isds/> accessed 13 January 2022; Argyropoulou *(n 7)*, 51.
34 *Opinion 2/13 pursuant to Article 218(11) TFEU*, CJEU (2014) ECLI:EU:C:2014:2454, paras 106, 182.

ularly the case where the EU Treaties, i.e. the Treaty on European Union (TEU) and the Treaty on the Functioning of the European Union (TFEU), themselves provide for the conclusion of such an agreement.[35] Indeed, the CJEU clarifies that

> the competence of the European Union in the field of international relations and its capacity to conclude international agreements necessarily entail the power to submit to the decisions of a court that is created or designated by such agreements as regards the interpretation and application of their provisions.[36]

However, where such an international agreement affects the powers of the EU, the CJEU requires that there be no adverse effect on the autonomy of the EU legal order.[37]

1. *The Autonomy of EU Law*

At the outset, the CJEU establishes the principle of autonomy of EU law stemming from the Treaties as an independent source of law, its primacy over the laws of the Member States and the direct effect of certain EU law provisions. Thus, according to the CJEU, the autonomy of EU law resides in the EU's unique constitutional framework, which comprises 'the founding values' set out in Article 2 of the TEU, the general principles of EU law, the provisions of the Charter of Fundamental Rights of the European Union (Charter) and the provisions of the Treaties.[38]

The autonomy of EU law is protected by the judicial system established by the EU Treaties that, in the interplay of domestic courts and the preliminary ruling procedure provided for by Article 267 TFEU, ensures consistency and uniformity in the interpretation of EU law.[39] Given, however, that CETA's ICS stands outside the EU judicial system, the CJEU had to be satisfied that it was compatible with the autonomy of EU law. In order to determine the compatibility, it was necessary that CETA does not confer on its court system the power to interpret and apply EU law other than the

35 ibid, para 182.
36 Opinion 1/17 *(n 4)*, para 106.
37 ibid, para 107.
38 ibid, paras 109, 110; see also Fanou *(n 27)*, 121.
39 Opinion 1/17 *(n 4)*, para 111.

provisions of CETA (a); and that its rulings do not prevent EU institutions from operating in accordance with the EU constitutional framework (b).[40]

a) No Jurisdiction to Interpret and Apply EU Law

The CJEU was satisfied that CETA did not confer on its court system the power to interpret and apply provisions of EU law. In examining a claim by an investor under Article 8.18 CETA, the Tribunal would be bound pursuant to Article 8.31 (1) CETA to apply 'this Agreement as interpreted in accordance with the [Vienna Convention], and other rules and principles of international law applicable between the Parties.' Article 8.31 (2) CETA further clarified that the Tribunal would have no jurisdiction 'to determine the legality of a measure alleged to constitute a breach of this Agreement, under the domestic law of a party.' This satisfied the CJEU that the Tribunal was confined to interpret and apply provisions of CETA.[41]

On this basis, the CJEU distinguished the provisions of CETA from the bilateral investment treaty at issue in its *Achmea* judgement. Different to CETA's investment court system, the tribunal established by the Netherlands-Slovakia investment treaty would be called upon to give rulings that might concern the interpretation or application of EU law.[42] Moreover, the CJEU held that the principle of mutual trust would not apply in relations between the Union and a non-Member State. Whereas the principle of mutual trust requires Member States to consider their respective compliance with the right to an effective remedy before an independent tribunal, the Union has no such obligation vis-à-vis Canada with regard to CETA.[43]

The fact that Article 8.31 (2) CETA allows the tribunal to 'consider, as appropriate, the domestic law of a Party as a matter of fact', does not affect its jurisdiction. According to the CJEU, the examination of the effect of a measure adopted by the host State or the Union may require taking into account the domestic law of the respondent party. Yet, that examination would not be equivalent to an interpretation of domestic law. Rather the

40 Opinion 1/17 *(n 4)*, paras 118, 156.

41 ibid, para 122.

42 ibid, para 126; *Slovak Republic v Achmea BV*, CJEU Case 284/16 (2018) ECLI:EU:C:2018:158, para 42.

43 Opinion 1/17 *(n 4)*, paras 128, 129; see also Argyropoulou *(n 7)*, 40.

Tribunal had to follow the prevailing interpretation by the courts and authorities of that Party as prescribed by 8.31 (2) sentence 2 CETA.[44]

According to the CJEU, the limitation of jurisdiction is, moreover, reflected in Article 8.21 CETA, which confers on the Union the power to determine, whether the dispute is to be brought against the Member State or the EU. This provision preserved the exclusive competence of the CJEU to rule on the division of powers between the EU and its Member States.[45]

Finally, the CJEU was satisfied that the CETA Appellate Tribunal would not be called upon to interpret or apply EU law either. When conferring upon the Appellate Tribunal the power to 'uphold, modify or reverse the Tribunal's award based on (...) errors in the application or interpretation of applicable law', Article 8.28 (2) (a) CETA made reference to the 'applicable law' under Article 8.31 (1) CETA that covers solely the provisions of CETA and the rules and principles of international law. Likewise, Article 8.28 (2) (b) CETA extending the standard of review to 'manifest errors in the appreciation of the facts, including the appreciation of relevant domestic law' would be limited to the appreciation of domestic law as a matter of fact. Thus, it is clear to the CJEU that the Parties did not intend to confer jurisdiction to the Appellate Tribunal to interpret domestic law.[46]

Therefore, the CJEU found that the powers of interpretation conferred to CETA's ICS were confined to the provisions of CETA. In light of these findings, the CJEU did neither require any provision permitting or obligating the Tribunal or Appellate Tribunal to make a reference for a preliminary ruling nor take umbrage with the absence of any procedure for the re-examination of the award by a court within the EU judicial system.[47]

b) The Level of Protection of Public Interest

The CJEU proceeded to analyse, whether the rulings of CETA's ICS might have the effect of preventing the EU institutions from operating in accordance with the EU constitutional framework. This was the case if the discretionary powers of the CETA Tribunals permitted them to call into

---

44 Opinion 1/17 *(n 4)*, paras 130, 131; see also Fanou *(n 27)*, 124.
45 ibid, para 132.
46 ibid, para 133.
47 Ibid, paras 134, 135.

question the level of protection of the public interest determined by the Union following a democratic process.[48] It, thus, addressed concerns that the CETA Tribunals might weigh the interests of investors against the public interests and thereby 'adversely affect the exclusive jurisdiction of the Court over the definitive interpretation of EU law and, accordingly the autonomy of the EU legal order.'[49]

The CJEU first observed that the CETA Tribunal cannot – where it finds that a measure is in breach with CETA protections – annul that measure or require that the domestic law of the Party should be rendered compatible with CETA. It was sufficiently clear from Article 8.39 (1) CETA that its Tribunals could 'only' order the respondent State to pay compensation to the investor for damage suffered because of that breach.[50]

Nevertheless, the CJEU considered that the Union could abandon the achievement of the level of protection of a public interest in order to avoid being repeatedly compelled by the CETA Tribunals to pay damages to an investor.[51] This situation could arise, if the treatment of a Canadian investor was incompatible with CETA because of the level of protection of a public interest established by the EU institutions. The assessment of a public interest made by a tribunal standing outside the EU judicial system could, therefore, require the Union to amend or withdraw legislation. According to the CJEU, such a situation 'undermines the capacity of the Union to operate autonomously within its unique constitutional framework.'[52]

However, the CJEU was satisfied that the parties had sufficiently ensured that the Tribunals had no jurisdiction to call into question the choices democratically made within a Party relating to, inter alia, the level

48 ibid, paras 118, 156.

49 ibid, paras 137, 138.

50 Ibid, para 144; Article 8.39.1 CETA provides: If the Tribunal makes a final award against the respondent, the Tribunal may only award, separately or in combination:
(a) monetary damages and any applicable interest;
(b) restitution of property, in which case the award shall provide that the respondent may pay
monetary damages representing the fair market value of the property at the time immediately before the expropriation, or impending expropriation became known, whichever is earlier, and any applicable interest in lieu of restitution, determined in a manner consistent with Article 8.12.

51 Opinion 1/17 *(n 4)*, para 149.

52 ibid, para 150.

of protection of public interest.[53] In order to make that assessment, the CJEU considered CETA's substantive provisions relating to the protection of the public interest and the right to regulate.

First, Article 28.3 (2) CETA provides for a general exception from the non-discrimination standard of chapter eight for measures necessary to protect public security or public morals or to maintain public order or to protect human, animal or plant life or health.[54] Subject to the requirement that the State measures are not applied in a manner that would constitute arbitrary or unjustifiable discrimination, the provision allows parties to take measures in the public interests.

Second, the CJEU relied on Article 8.9 CETA which contains clarifications on the scope of the Parties' right to regulate and the concept of legitimate expectations.[55] Section 1 explicitly reaffirms the Parties' right to regulate to achieve legitimate policy objectives including the protection of public health, safety and the environment. Section 2 further specifies that

> for greater certainty, the mere fact that a Party regulates, including through a modification to its laws, in a manner which negatively affects an investment or interferes with an investor's expectations, including its expectations of profits, does not amount to a breach of an obligation under this Section.

Third, the Parties' Joint Interpretative Instrument provides that CETA will not lower the respective standards and regulations 'related to food safety, product safety, consumer protection, health, environment or labour protection' and that it 'preserves the ability of the EU and its Member States and Canada to adopt and apply their own laws and regulations that regulate economic activity in the public interest.'[56] Taken together, these provisions sufficiently guaranteed the Parties' right to regulate by preventing CETA tribunals from calling into question 'the level of protection of public interest determined by the Union following a democratic process.'[57]

Fourth and finally, CETA contained specifications on the scope of protection afforded by the protection against expropriation and the fair and equitable treatment standard. Annex 8-A to CETA states for greater

53 ibid, para 160.
54 ibid, para 152.
55 ibid, para 154.
56 Joint Interpretative Instrument on the Comprehensive Economic and Trade Agreement (CETA) between Canada and the European Union and its Member States (14 January 2017) L 11/3, No 1 (d) and 2; ibid, para 155.
57 Opinion 1/17 *(n 4)*, para 156.

certainty that 'non-discriminatory measures of a Party that are designed and applied to protect legitimate public welfare objectives, such as health, safety and the environment, do not constitute indirect expropriations.'[58] Art 8.10 CETA lists exhaustively the situations such as abusive treatment, manifest arbitrariness and targeted discrimination, which would constitute a violation of fair and equitable treatment.

It may be argued whether these provisions do – as the CJEU repeats categorically – in fact exclude the determination of the required level of protection of a public interest from the jurisdiction of the tribunal.[59] Exceptions in IPAs should have the effect of justifying certain measures taken in the public interest but not – as a self-judging exception – to remove a tribunal's jurisdiction to determine whether a measure falls within the scope of an exception invoked. Nevertheless, the CJEU's reliance on the delimitation of substantive protection standards shows that it considers the protection of the right to regulate an essential condition for accepting the jurisdiction of a treaty-based international investment tribunal.

2. *The General Principle of Equal Treatment and the Requirement of Effectiveness*

The CJEU proceeded to consider the fact that EU investors – unlike their Canadian counterparts – would not be able to bring a dispute before the CETA Tribunal with respect to their investments within the European Union. This situation raised the question whether the mechanism complies with the principle of equal treatment guaranteed by the Charter of Fundamental Rights.[60]

The CJEU thus analysed the compatibility of CETA's ISDS mechanism with Article 20 of the Charter enshrining the guarantee of 'equality before the law' and with Article 21 (2) of the Charter, which prohibits discrimination on grounds of nationality.[61] At the outset, the CJEU denied the relevance of Article 21 (2) of the Charter to this question. It reasoned that the prohibition of discrimination on grounds of nationality contained therein corresponded to Article 18 TFEU, which in turn was not intended to apply to different treatment between nationals of Member States and

58 No 3, Annex 8-A CETA.

59 Titi *(n 6)*, paras 24.34-24.36.

60 Opinion 1/17 *(n 4)*, paras 162, 179.

61 ibid, para 51.

non-Member States.[62] Therefore, Article 21 (2) of the Charter was not relevant to potentially discriminatory treatment of EU investors as compared to their Canadian counterparts.

Subsequently, the CJEU turned to Article 20 of the Charter, which – in contrast – applied to 'all situations governed by EU law, including those falling within the scope of an international agreement entered.'[63] Equality before the law was thus available to all persons irrespective of their origin, also to EU investors.[64] The principle of equal treatment enshrined in Article 20 of the Charter required that 'comparable situations must not be treated differently and different situations must not be treated in the same way, unless such treatment is objectively justified.'[65]

Yet, the CJEU held, that the situation of Canadian investors in the EU was not comparable to that of EU investors investing within the EU. In their capacity as foreign investors, Canadian investors were to have a specific legal remedy against EU measures. In contrast, EU investors investing within the Union were not foreign investors and therefore did not require that additional protection.[66]

3. *The Right of Access to an Independent Tribunal*

Finally, the CJEU considered the compatibility of CETA'S ICS with the right of access to an independent and impartial tribunal. Article 47 of the Charter was binding on the Union when entering into international agreements and, thus, required that CETA's ICS had characteristics of an accessible and independent tribunal.[67] Despite the hybrid nature of its tribunals combining characteristics of judicial bodies with elements of traditional investment arbitration, 'those tribunals will, in essence, exercise judicial functions.'[68] Therefore, the CJEU held that CETA's ICS needed to achieve a certain level of accessibility and independence. That level had to correspond to its purpose as a mechanism, standing outside of the judicial systems of the Parties, i.e. to ensure foreign investors' confidence.[69]

---

62 Ibid, paras 168-170.
63 ibid, para 171.
64 ibid, para 172.
65 ibid, para 176.
66 ibid, paras 180-181.
67 ibid, paras 190-191.
68 ibid, para 197.
69 ibid, para 199.

a) Level of Accessibility

With respect to the guarantee of accessibility, the CJEU recalled that the possibility of any investor to bring a dispute 'can be limited solely by proportionate restrictions, including restrictions linked to the payment of court costs, that pursue a legitimate aim and do not adversely affect the very essence of the right of access to such a tribunal.'[70] However, the CJEU noted that both the costs of legal representation and costs of the proceedings which the investor may have to bear, if defeated, might constitute a financial burden on claimants who are natural persons or small and medium-sized enterprises. If these investors were effectively deterred from bringing proceedings by the financial risks involved, the ISDS mechanism might, in practice, be accessible only to investors with significant financial means.[71] Therefore, the CJEU examined whether CETA contained sufficient commitments that the level of accessibility required by Article 47 of the Charter would be put in place.[72]

Ultimately, the CJEU held that the Commission and the Council had sufficiently committed to ensure accessibility to small and medium-sized enterprises.[73] However, it made clear that CETA's provisions alone did not contain legally binding commitments to that effect. This was also true for Article 8.39 (6) CETA which provides for the CETA Joint Committee to consider supplemental rules aimed at reducing the financial burden on natural persons and small and medium-sized enterprises. Rather, it was critical for the CJEU that the Council made its approval of CETA subject to the commitment that effective access to the tribunals would be guaranteed. This connection between the financial accessibility of the ICS and the conclusion of CETA, according to the CJEU, followed from Statement No 36 on 'Investment Protection and the Investment Court System'[74]. Therein, the Commission and the Council had given a commitment to implement, rapidly and adequately, such supplemental rules, even if work within the CETA Joint Committee were to be fruitless.[75] Given that this commitment formed the basis for the conclusion of CETA, the CJEU was satisfied that the financial accessibility for all EU Investors would be

70 ibid, para 200.

71 See Nikolov, Chapter 5.

72 Opinion 1/17 *(n 4)*, para 214.

73 ibid, para 219.

74 Statement No 36 by the Commission and the Council on 'Investment Protection and the Investment Court System (ICS)', OJ 2017 L 11, 20.

75 Ibid, para 218.

ensured at the time of CETA's ratification.[76] The CJEU, thus, made its approval of CETA contingent upon a sufficient level of accessibility being achieved throughout the ratification process.[77]

b) Independence and Impartiality

With respect to the requirement of independence, the CJEU distinguished between two aspects: first, the external guarantee of independence presupposing that the judicial body exercises its functions autonomously without being subject to hierarchical constraints or external interventions. Second, the internal guarantee of impartiality requiring objectivity and neutrality with respect to the parties' interests.[78]

The CJEU held that the external aspect of independence was guaranteed by Article 8.27 providing that members of the Tribunal 'will be appointed for a fixed term and will have to possess specific expertise', and 'will receive a level of remuneration commensurate with the importance of their duties'.[79] Moreover, the CJEU specified that interpretations handed down by the CETA Joint Committee cannot produce effects on resolved or pending disputes. Albeit not expressly excluded by Article 8.31 (3) CETA, the right to an effective remedy enshrined in Article 47 of the Charter does not permit the Union to consent to interpretations with a retroactive effect.[80]

The internal aspect of independence, the CJEU held, was guaranteed by the random and unpredictable composition of the division hearing the case pursuant to Article 8.27 (6) and 8.27 (7) CETA. This is supplemented by the reference to the International Bar Association (IBA) Guidelines on Conflicts of Interest in International Arbitration and the prohibition on conflicts of interests in Article 8.30 (1) CETA.[81]

76 ibid, paras 220, 221.
77 Titi *(n 6)*, paras 24.53 et seq.
78 Opinion 1/17 *(n 4)*, paras 202-203.
79 ibid, paras 223-224.
80 ibid, para 237.
81 ibid, para 238.

II. Consequences for the Establishment of the MIC

Opinion 1/17 confirmed that CETA's ICS is principally compatible with EU law. Yet, while the scope of the opinion was limited to CETA's ICS, the CJEU indirectly drafted the conditions for negotiating the MIC.[82] The opinion thus contains the conditions for the MIC Statute in particular with regard to the applicable law, the right to regulate, access to the MIC and the independence and impartiality of adjudicators.

First, the MIC Statute needs to contain limiting provisions on the applicable law that exclude the application and interpretation of EU law or of domestic law of EU Member States. A limitation on the applicable law is necessary to guarantee that the MIC – standing outside the EU judicial system like CETA's ICS – does not have any adverse effect on the autonomy of the EU legal order.[83] Safeguarding the autonomy of the EU legal order thus requires a provision on the applicable law that confines the MIC's tribunals to interpreting and applying the provisions of the IPA at issue as well as rules of international law applicable between the parties. Along the lines of Article 8.31 (2) CETA, such provision on the applicable law must explicitly exclude the jurisdiction to determine a breach under the domestic law of the party.

In addition to that limitation of jurisdiction, the provision may further state that the domestic law of a Party may be considered as a matter of fact. An examination of the effect of a State's measure is – according to the CJEU – inevitable when the tribunal examines the compliance of that measure with the IPA at issue.[84] It needs to be clear, though, that such an examination of the measure taking into account the domestic law of a party is not equivalent to an interpretation of that law. To the CJEU, the second sentence of Article 8.31 (2) CETA sufficiently clarifies that the consideration of the domestic law as a matter of fact is not equivalent to its interpretation.[85] The provision on the applicable law may thus be complemented by a clarification that the MIC's tribunals are obliged to follow the prevailing interpretation of the domestic law by the courts of that party, who in turn are not bound by the meaning given to their domestic law by the tribunals.

82 Bungenberg, Titi *(n 33)*.
83 See Opinion 1/17 *(n 4)*, para 107.
84 See ibid, para 131.
85 See ibid, para 131.

Second, the autonomy of EU law requires that the rulings of the MIC would not have the effect of preventing the EU institutions from operating in accordance with the EU constitutional framework, i.e. that the EU had to abandon the level of protection of a public interest established by the EU.[86] Therefore, the MIC must not be in a position, where – weighing the interests of investors against the public interest – it could annul a State measure or require the domestic law of a party to be rendered compatible when in breach with the IPA at issue. Yet, a provision confining the MIC to only award monetary damages like Article 8.39 (1) CETA would, on its own, not achieve this purpose.[87] It must further be ensured that the institutions of the EU would not have to abandon the level of protection of a public interest established by the EU in order to avoid being repeatedly ordered to pay damages.

With respect to CETA, the CJEU found its substantive provisions taken together to sufficiently protect the Parties' right to regulate in the public interest. Similar substantive protections have been included in other IPAs concluded by the EU. Yet, substantive provisions are not currently being negotiated in UNICTRAL Working Group III. The negotiations are limited to the procedural aspects of the MIC, which may – as one of several possibilities – be construed as an opt-in mechanism. This means that disputes may be brought on the basis of IPAs that do not contain alike provisions on the right to regulate.[88] Given the CJEU's reliance on the right to regulate, it is therefore questionable how its conditions could be met by the MIC.

One way to address this concern may be to include – for greater certainty – a provision in the MIC Statute that requires adjudicators to take into account the level of protection of the public interest.[89] As far as the EU is concerned, however, its new-generation IPAs, which would fall under the jurisdiction of the MIC, can be expected to include similar protections of the right to regulate like CETA.

Third, access to the MIC must be guaranteed in order to meet the requirements of Article 47 of the Charter.[90] The parties to the MIC must therefore put in place mechanisms to ensure that investors are not effectively deterred from bringing proceedings by the financial risks involved, if defeated. Such mechanisms to reduce the financial burden on natural

---

86 See ibid, para 150.
87 See ibid, paras 137, 138.
88 See Funk, Chapter 08, Section C.I.
89 Titi *(n 6)*, paras 24.40 et seq.
90 See Opinion 1/17 *(n 4)*, paras 209-214.

persons and small and medium-sized enterprises may be included in the MIC Statute or take the shape of supplemental rules. In any event, more than a mere commitment to implement such rules is necessary to meet the requirements for an unconditional approval by the CJEU.[91]

Fourth, the independence and impartiality of MIC adjudicators needs to be ensured. With regard to CETA's ICS, the CJEU found its rules 'as regards the composition of the body and the appointment, length of service and grounds for abstention, rejection and dismissal of its members' sufficient.[92] Most notably, appointment of tribunal members for a fixed term and random composition of the tribunal appear to be necessary elements for the CJEU to meet the requirements of Article 47 of the Charter. Yet, Opinion 1/17 does not make a conclusive statement, whether independence and impartiality of tribunal members can be achieved by other means. The MIC Statute would, certainly, need to provide for safeguards ensuring that the tribunal exercises its functions autonomously and that its members have no personal interest in the outcome of the proceedings.[93]

In conclusion, Opinion 1/17 principally endorses the negotiating template[94] of the EU while encouraging selective amendments, eg with regard to financial accessibility to small and medium-sized enterprises.[95] Opinion 1/17 thereby continues the constitutional dialogue between the EU Commission, Parliament, Council, and the CJEU. With the conditions identified in Opinion 1/17, the CJEU establishes ground rules for the future dialogue on the establishment of the MIC.[96]

E. Are these Conditions Met by the MIC Draft Statute?

The MIC Draft Statute recently proposed by *Bungenberg/Reinisch*[97] provides a design of the MIC that may be used as a basis for further deliberations and negotiations on the ISDS reform process in UNCITRAL Working

91 See ibid, para 218.
92 ibid, para 204.
93 See ibid, paras 202-203.
94 Council of the EU, 'Negotiating directives for a Convention establishing a multilateral court for the settlement of investment disputes' (20 March 2018), 12981/17 ADD 1; see above Section C.
95 See Nikolov, Chapter 5.
96 Titi *(n 6)*, para 24.02.
97 Bungenberg, Reinisch *(n 5)*.

Group III.[98] Whether it can meet the demanding requirements established by the CJEU is the subject of the following analysis.

First, the autonomy of EU law requires a limitation of the applicable law that excludes the application and interpretation of EU law or of domestic law of EU Member States. The MIC Draft Statute does not contain a limiting provision but instead allows for parties to a dispute to agree on the applicable law. Article 31.1 sentence 1 of the MIC Draft Statute provides: 'The MIC shall decide a dispute in accordance with such rules of law as may be agreed by the parties.'

If no such agreement exists, applicable rules of international law shall be applied by the MIC pursuant to sentence 2. The provision on the applicable law neither explicitly excludes the MIC's jurisdiction to determine a breach under the domestic law of the party nor does it address the prevalence of interpretations of the domestic law given by the courts of that party. It, thus, lacks the limiting provision on the applicable law that the CJEU found to be critical with regard to CETA's ICS.[99] However, the choice of law provision creates the possibility for the EU to preclude EU law from the sources of applicable law. It may well be assumed that any new EU agreement falling under the jurisdiction of the MIC would contain language similar to 8.31 (1) CETA allowing the consideration of EU law or domestic law only as a matter of fact. Such a provision would be considered as an agreement on the applicable law under Article 31 of the MIC Draft Statute. As far as the EU is involved, the CJEU's requirements with regard to the autonomy of EU law would hence be satisfied.

Accordingly, Article 46 (g) of the MIC Draft Statute states among the grounds for appeal 'that there are manifest errors in the appreciation of the facts, including the appreciation of the relevant domestic law.' Once again, this Article underlines that – absent any agreement to the contrary – the relevant domestic law is only appreciated as a matter of fact in line with the CJEU's requirements.[100]

Moreover, Article 53 of the MIC Draft Statute requires judges of the MIC to consider internal arrangements by international organisations on the allocation of responsibility arising from a claim between the organisation and its Member States. Like Article 8.21 CETA, this provision enables the Union to determine the appropriate respondent for a claim. The possibility of such a determination preserves the exclusive competence of the

98 See above Section C.

99 Opinion 1/17 *(n 4)*, paras 128-131.

100 See ibid, para 133.

CJEU to rule on the division of powers between the EU and its Member States in conformity with the principle of autonomy of EU law.[101]

A second focus of the CJEU's requirements is the protection of the parties' right to regulate. Albeit a question of substantive law, the MIC Draft Statute addresses this matter by way of reference in Article 28. Stipulated as a general principle, Article 28.1 (e) of the MIC Draft Statute requires judges to take into account the Members' right to regulate. Admittedly, this provision by itself does not ensure that the respondent States' right to take measures in the public interest is sufficiently protected. More safeguards are necessary in the substantive law of the IPA at issue to meet the conditions set by the CJEU.

According to the CJEU, these conditions are met by the safeguards that have been included in CETA such as a the general exception from the non-discrimination standard, the reaffirmation of the Parties' right to regulate and clarifications on the concept of legitimate expectations.[102] Similar provisions have been added in the EU's most recent IPAs concluded with Singapore and Vietnam. Hence, it may be expected that future EU IPAs, potentially falling under the jurisdiction of the MIC, would contain a sufficiently high degree of protection of the Union's public interest legislation. Taken together with the reference to the right to regulate in the MIC Draft Statute as one aspect to be taken into account by judges when performing their duties, the CJEU's requirements would thus be met when the EU is involved.

Article 10 of the MIC Draft Statute addresses the (third) issue of accessibility of the MIC[103] by providing for the Advisory Centre as an organ of the MIC.[104] Pursuant to Article 10.2 (a), the Advisory Centre may upon request provide legal assistance for disputes of small and medium-sized enterprises. It is aimed at allowing access to the court irrespective of the investor's financial means. Yet, its specific duties are subject to further rules that shall be drafted by the Plenary Body pursuant to Article 10.4 of the MIC Draft Statute. Adding to this, Article 58 of the MIC Draft Statute foresees an Enforcement Fund to which Members are obliged to contribute. Pursuant to Article 58.3, the Fund shall satisfy a Member's obligation resulting from a decision of the MIC by payment of the award-

101 See ibid, para 132.
102 See ibid paras 152-161.
103 See ibid, paras 209-214.
104 See Braun/Reinhold, Chapter 3.

ed sum to a successful claimant if the immediate payment is urgently needed.[105]

Both provisions accommodate needs of small and medium-sized enterprises with regard to the costs of proceedings and immediate payment of the awarded sum after their conclusion. Thereby, they reduce the financial burden on small and medium-sized enterprises when resorting to dispute settlement by the MIC. Whether or not the MIC meets the level of accessibility required by Article 47 of the Charter will ultimately depend on whether the financial risks involved would in practice deter natural persons and small and medium-sized enterprises from initiating proceedings. This may ultimately depend on the implementation of supplemental rules that ensure the MIC's accessibility.[106]

The fourth condition of the CJEU concerning the independence and impartiality of judges is guaranteed by the provisions on the nomination and challenge of judges as well as the conditions of their service. Article 12.2 provides for parameters to determine the suitability of persons to be appointed as judges of the MIC. These parameters cover professional qualifications, ethical standards, independence and impartiality. The selection process under the observation of the Screening Committee pursuant to Article 12.2. CETA ensures the right to an independent tribunal as required by Article 47 of the Charter.[107] Article 13 of the MIC Draft Statute further specifies the conditions of service. In conformity with the CJEU's requirements[108], Article 14 of the MIC Draft Statute determines a fixed duration of appointment without the possibility of re-election. Finally, Article 15 of the MIC Draft Statute restricts a judge's removal from office to cases of substantial misconduct or failure to perform duties. These provisions secure the judges' independence from external interference, in particular by their home State.

Moreover, their independence is not questioned by the possibility of the Plenary Body's interpretative powers. Article 8.3 of the MIC Draft Statute allows the Plenary Body to adopt interpretations of the Statute by consensus, which will be binding on the other organs of the MIC. It thus represents a joint interpretation mechanism by way of which the parties may issue interpretations that are binding for the tribunals. These binding interpretations may conflict with Article 47 of the Charter[109],

105 See Müller, Chapter 9.
106 Opinion 1/17 *(n 4)*, para 218.
107 See ibid paras 202-203.
108 ibid, para 204.
109 See ibid para 237.

if they produce effects on resolved or pending disputes. The wording of Article 8.3 of the MIC Draft Statute does not expressly exclude the possibility of interpretations producing a retroactive effect. With regard to CETA, it was sufficient for the CJEU, though, that the right to an effective remedy enshrined in Article 47 of the Charter does not permit the Union to consent to interpretations with a retroactive effect.[110] The same ratio guarantees that interpretations under Article 8.3 of the MIC Draft Statute would not produce effects on resolved or ongoing cases contrary to Article 47 of the Charter.

The possibility to challenge judges in the case of conflicts of interests ensures the impartiality of judges. Article 51 of the MIC Draft Statute provides for a challenge procedure, if a disputing party considers that a judge has a conflict of interests. According to that procedure, the plenary of judges rules on a challenge by absolute majority excluding the challenged judge.

Finally, the MIC Draft Statute makes dispositions as regards the exclusion of jurisdiction of the MIC for disputes between member States. Article 19 of the MIC Draft Statute sets out the jurisdiction of the MIC as follows:

> The jurisdiction of the MIC comprises all disputes arising directly out of an investment of a national of a Member in the territory of another Member, which the parties to the dispute refer to the MIC through consent in writing.

As such, it does not explicitly preclude disputes brought by investors from one EU Member State against another EU Member State. To the contrary, Article 23.2 of the MIC Draft Statute transfers exclusive jurisdiction to the MIC to adjudicate disputes that arise out of an investment agreement between two Member States of the MIC.

Yet, it can be assumed that the EU would seek to preclude disputes based on the Energy Charter Treaty – or any potential future IPA applicable between EU Member States – from the jurisdiction of the MIC. Article 27 of the MIC Draft Statute on additional jurisdictional requirements allows to exclude such disputes by way of narrowing the definition of investor or the investment and other jurisdictional requirements in the consent-inducing instrument.[111]

---

110 ibid, para 237.

111 MIC Draft Statute, Bungenberg, Reinisch *(n 5)*, Article 27: 'The MIC does not have jurisdiction over disputes where the national of the other Member [...]

F. Conclusion and Outlook

The EU has taken significant steps towards reforming the traditional ISDS mechanism, both in the bilateral conclusion of IPAs and in multilateral negotiations in UNCITRAL Working Group III. In both ways, the EU's efforts ultimately aim at establishing the MIC for the settlement of investor-State disputes. Yet, in order for the EU to take part in dispute settlement under the MIC, its design must be reconciled with the EU's constitutional framework. In Opinion 1/17, the CJEU has confirmed that such an international court standing outside the EU judicial system is – in principle – compatible with EU law. What is more, it held that the specific design of CETA's ICS in conjunction with CETA's substantive provisions protecting the right to regulate are compatible with EU law.

At the same time, the CJEU articulated the EU law requirements with a view to the establishment of the MIC, which the parties committed to pursue in the CETA text.[112] It, thus, identified the conditions for the EU's participation in its dispute settlement mechanism: first, the MIC Statute needs to contain limiting provisions on the applicable law that exclude the application or interpretation of EU law and of domestic law of EU Member States.[113] Second, it must be ensured that the rulings of the MIC would not have the effect of undermining the capacity of EU institutions to operate in accordance with the EU constitutional framework, ie. that they had to abandon the level of protection of a public interest established by the EU.[114] Third, effective access to the MIC must be ensured also to investors who have limited financial resources, such as natural persons or small and medium-sized enterprises.[115] Fourth, the MIC Statute must guarantee the independence and impartiality of judges.[116] Both in bilateral negotiations of IPAs and in the multilateral reform process in UNCITRAL Working Group III, the EU must meet these demanding requirements.

The recently proposed MIC Draft Statute is reconcilable with the EU law requirements identified in Opinion 1/17. This being said, the procedural provisions of the Statute cannot on its own ensure that the level of protection of public interest is sufficiently guaranteed. Whether or not

---

does not fulfil other jurisdictional requirements of the underlying International Investment Agreement.'

112 Art. 8.29 CETA; Bungenberg, Titi *(n 33)*;

113 See Opinion 1/17 *(n 4)*, para 121.

114 See ibid, para 150.

115 See ibid, paras 206.

116 See ibid, paras 199.

the CJEU's requirements regarding the protection of the Parties' right to regulate are met will ultimately depend on the existence of safeguards in the substantive provisions of the IPA at issue. Moreover, the CJEU made its approval of CETA subject to the achievement of a sufficient level of accessibility. In order to meet that level, the EU and its Member States must ensure access to the MIC, in particular by providing the financial means to small and medium-sized enterprises. Nevertheless, the MIC Draft Statute provides valuable guidance on a design of the MIC that could meet the demanding requirements of EU law.

Whether the EU can achieve consensus for that design of the MIC remains to be seen. In particular, the appeal mechanism and the selection of judges may well turn out to be a 'dealbreaker' in multilateral negotiations. Moreover, the detailed requirements of EU law bear the risk to make the entire ISDS reform process 'eurocentric', which could possibly endanger its success. Indeed, if all States asserted for themselves the right to insist on their constitutional requirements as the EU does, consensus on an MIC statute could hardly be reached. At the same time, it is clear that the EU cannot participate in an ISDS mechanisms that falls short of these requirements.[117] This situation puts the EU in a difficult negotiating position at the multilateral level. It is all the more important that the EU continues these negotiations on the basis of an MIC design that would withstand scrutiny of the CJEU.

117 See also Fanou *(n 27)*, 130.

Chapter 11: Creation and Implementation of a Multilateral Investment Court: Outlook from a Practitioner Perspective

By Moritz Keller and Caroline Kittelmann[*]

Selected Bibliography: Andrea Bjorklund, Marc Bungenberg, Manjiao Chi and Catharine Titi, 'Selection and Appointment of International Adjudicators: Structural Options for ISDS Reform' (17 September 2019) Academic Forum on ISDS Concept Paper 2019/11; Charles N Brower and Jawad Ahmad, 'Why The 'Demolition Derby' That Seeks To Destroy Investor-State Arbitration?' (2018) 91 Southern California Law Review 1139; Chiara Giorgetti et al, 'Independence and Impartiality in Investment Dispute Settlement: Assessing Challenges and Reform Options' (21 January 2020) Academic Forum on ISDS Concept Paper 2020/1; Margie-Lys Jaime, 'Chapter 7: Reshaping Investor-State Dispute Settlement Through an Appellate Review Mechanism' in Alan M Anderson and Ben Beaumont (eds), *The Investor-State Dispute Settlement System: Reform, Replace or Status Quo?* (Kluwer Law International 2020), 137; Malcolm Langford, Daniel Behn, and Maria Chiara Malaguti, 'The Quadrilemma: Appointing Adjudicators in Future Investor-State Dispute Settlement' (13 October 2019) Academic Forum on ISDS Concept Paper 2019/12; Sam Luttrell, 'Testing the ICSID Framework for Arbitrator Challenges' (2016) 31.3 ICSID Review Foreign Investment Law Journal 597; Sergio Puig and Gregory Shaffer, 'Imperfect Alternatives: Institutional Choice and the Reform of Investment Law' (July 2018) 112.3 American Journal of International Law 397; Stephan W Schill and Geraldo Vidigal, 'Designing Dispute Settlement à la Carte for Investment Law: Insights from International Courts and Tribunals' (2019) 18.3 The Law and Practice of International Courts and Tribunals 314; Stephen Schwebel, 'The Proposals of the European Commission for Investment Protection and an Investment Court System' (17 May 2016) ISDS Blog <http://isdsblog.com/wp-content/uploads/sites/2/2016/05/THEPROPOSALSOFTHEEUROPEANCOMMISSION.pdf> accessed 13 January 2022.

---

* Moritz Keller is a Partner and Caroline Kittelmann is a Senior Foreign Lawyer in the International Arbitration team of Clifford Chance, Frankfurt. Comments expressed in this piece are made strictly in a personal capacity.

A. Introduction

In this concluding piece, we examine some aspects of the foregoing chapters from the perspective of a practitioner in order to offer some insights into how certain of the MIC proposals would interact with practical lawyering in the context of an ICSID-based arbitration practice.[1]

We first exclude from this piece one main aspect of our work, which is the interpretation and application of the substantive provisions of the bilateral investment treaty (BIT) applicable in a particular case. These may include typical standards such as the guarantee of fair and equitable treatment, protection from unlawful expropriation, and full protection and security, but the wording of the treaties can vary extensively.[2] The BIT, together with the applicable framework of rules, forms the basis of the investment treaty arbitration process.

It is a rather different procedure to that of a court case, in which there would be a strong emphasis on a consistent overall body of law and extensive checks and balances. Instead, the flexible, party-driven approach of investment treaty arbitration has the very different goal of resolving disputes as quickly and efficiently as possible in order to achieve a peaceful resolution of the dispute in that individual case (rather than establishing a comprehensive and infallible regime). Accordingly, lawyering in this field demands creativity and flexibility, and differs significantly from court-based dispute resolution.

The task of treaty interpretation would not be affected by an MIC, as the substantive provisions of the relevant treaty would not be displaced by the operation of an MIC. Other matters would, however, be substantially affected by some of the proposals for the implementation of an MIC.

Accordingly, in the following, we explore certain of the MIC proposals (which we address as the proposals as made by the European Union and its Member States from 12 December 2017 and 18 January 2019[3] (EU Pro-

---

1 We have limited our contribution to the ICSID framework and have not addressed other possible arbitration frameworks such as the UNCITRAL Arbitration Rules, the SCC Arbitration Rules and the ICC Arbitration Rules in any detail.

2 UNCTAD's database of bilateral investment treaties and treaties with investment provisions in force around the world (Investment Policy Hub, 'Most Recent IIAs' <https://investmentpolicy.unctad.org/inter national-investment-agreements> accessed 13 January 2022) currently shows a total of 2,298 instruments in force, with each treaty having to be interpreted and applied on its own terms.

3 UNCITRAL, Working Group III, 'Possible reform of investor-State dispute settlement (ISDS): Submission from the European Union and its Member States' (12 December 2017), A/CN.9/WG.III/WP.145; UNCITRAL, Working Group III, 'Pos-

posals), the proposals of Bungenberg and Reinisch,[4] including their 'MIC Draft Statute' of November 2020[5] (*Bungenberg/Reinisch* Proposals) and also the proposals of Kaufmann-Kohler and Potestà[6] (*Kaufmann-Kohler/Potestà* Proposals) and how these interact with two specific mechanisms as we currently know them and work with them: first, the appointment of arbitrators (or 'adjudicators') (B.) and second, avenues for review of an arbitral award (appeals) (C.). Finally, we offer some concluding remarks (D.).

B. Appointment of arbitrators

In this section we first set out the course of an ICSID appointment process as we know and work with it in its current form, in which each party is generally accorded the broad freedom to select one of the three arbitrators who will hear the dispute (with those two arbitrators then generally selecting the third arbitrator) coupled with a narrow test for challenge (I.). Then, we set out some thoughts as to how the far-reaching reforms contained in the MIC proposals – most notably the likely removal of a party choice of arbitrator, coupled with stricter conflicts rules – would impact the current ICSID appointment process (II.). We also include some remarks on the framework of diversity requirements included in the MIC proposals (III.).

---

sible reform of investor-State dispute settlement (ISDS) Submission from the European Union and its Member States' (24 January 2019), A/CN.9/WG.III/WP.159/Add.1 (together, 'EU Proposals').

4 Marc Bungenberg and August Reinisch, *From Bilateral Arbitral Tribunals and Investment Courts to a Multilateral Investment Court: Options Regarding the Institutionalization of Investor-State Dispute Settlement* (Springer 2019) (Bungenberg/Reinisch Proposals).

5 See <https://uncitral.un.org/sites/uncitral.un.org/files/media-documents/uncitral/en/bungenberg_reini sch_draft_statute_of_the_mic.pdf> accessed 13 January 2022.

6 Gabrielle Kaufmann-Kohler and Michele Potestà, 'Can the Mauritius Convention serve as a model for the reform of investor-State arbitration in connection with the introduction of a permanent investment tribunal or an appeal mechanism?: Analysis and Roadmap' (3 June 2016) and 'The Composition of a Multilateral Investment Court and of an Appeal Mechanism for Investment Awards' (15 November 2017) CIDS Supplemental Report (together, '*Kaufmann-Kohler/Potestà* Proposals').

I. Appointment of arbitrators under the current ICSID appointment process

Article 37 of the ICSID Convention addresses the constitution of an ICSID tribunal, providing that the tribunal (i) is to be constituted 'as soon as possible' after registration of the request for arbitration,[7] (ii) is to consist of 'a sole arbitrator or any uneven number of arbitrators', with such arbitrator or arbitrators to be 'appointed as the parties shall agree',[8] and (iii) shall, if the parties cannot agree on the number of arbitrators and method of appointment, 'consist of three arbitrators, one arbitrator appointed by each party and the third, who shall be the president of the Tribunal, appointed by agreement of the parties.'[9]

With regard to party agreement on the method of appointment, the relevant underlying BIT generally sets out such agreed method of appointing arbitrators. For example, the 1997 Bulgaria-Austria BIT provides:

> [...] Within three months from the receipt of the request for arbitration, each Contracting Party shall appoint one member of the tribunal. Those two members shall then select a national of a third State who on approval by the two Contracting Parties shall be appointed Chairman of the tribunal. The Chairman shall be appointed within two months from the date of appointment of the other two members.[10]

If the underlying BIT does not provide for a method of appointment, ICSID Arbitration Rule 2 sets out a default method and timetable for the parties to follow.

7 Article 37(1) ICSID Convention.
8 Article 37(2) (a) ICSID Convention.
9 Article 37(2) (b) ICSID Convention.
10 Article 8 (3) Bulgaria-Austria BIT, (1997). In Article 8 (4), the same BIT provides for a default method in the event that the necessary appointments are not made within the required timeframe: 'If within the periods specified in paragraph 3 the necessary appointments have not been made, either Contracting Party may, in the absence of any other agreement, invite the President of the International Court of Justice to make any necessary appointments. If the President is a national of either Contracting Party or if he is otherwise prevented from discharging the said function, the Vice-President shall be invited to make the necessary appointments. If the Vice-President is a national of either Contracting Party or if he too is prevented from discharging the said function, the Member of the International Court of Justice next in seniority who is not a national of either Contracting Party shall be invited to make the necessary appointments.'

The ICSID Convention and the ICSID Arbitration Rules further provide for a final default method of appointment, whereby if the arbitrators have not been appointed within 90 days of registration of the claim, either party may request that the Chairman of the ICSID Administrative Council appoint the arbitrator(s) not yet appointed.[11] These default powers effectively prevent the parties from obstructing the proceedings by failing to make the necessary appointments within the required timeframe.

The ICSID Convention and the ICSID Arbitration Rules prescribe just two basic criteria for arbitrators in relation to (i) nationality (which can be disapplied by agreement of the parties)[12] and (ii) qualifications, in which regard Article 14 (1) of the ICSID Convention provides:

> Persons designated to serve on the Panels shall be persons of high moral character and recognized competence in the fields of law, commerce, industry or finance, who may be relied upon to exercise independent judgment. Competence in the field of law shall be of particular importance in the case of persons on the Panel of Arbitrators.[13]

Beyond these matters, parties have a broad freedom to appoint their choice of arbitrator. According to ICSID Arbitration Rule 6 (2), arbitrators must sign a declaration in which they disclose any past or present relationships with the parties and any other circumstances that might cause a party to question the arbitrator's 'reliability for independent judgment'.[14]

---

11 Article 38 ICSID Convention.

12 See Article 39 ICSID Convention ('The majority of the arbitrators shall be nationals of States other than the Contracting State party to the dispute and the Contracting State whose national is a party to the dispute; provided, however, that the foregoing provisions of this Article shall not apply if the sole arbitrator or each individual member of the Tribunal has been appointed by agreement of the parties.'); Article 1 (3) ICSID Arbitration Rules ('The majority of the arbitrators shall be nationals of States other than the State party to the dispute and of the State whose national is a party to the dispute, unless the sole arbitrator or each individual member of the Tribunal is appointed by agreement of the parties. Where the Tribunal is to consist of three members, a national of either of these States may not be appointed as an arbitrator by a party without the agreement of the other party to the dispute. Where the Tribunal is to consist of five or more members, nationals of either of these States may not be appointed as arbitrators by a party if appointment by the other party of the same number of arbitrators of either of these nationalities would result in a majority of arbitrators of these nationalities').

13 Article 14 (1) ICSID Convention.

14 Within the ICSID reform process, a Draft Code of Conduct for Adjudicators is currently under consideration, which would flesh out the duties of arbitrators, see

Advising a client in the context of an ICSID arbitrator appointment process will thus typically comprise of (i) selecting the client's party-appointed arbitrator, (ii) scrutinising (and potentially challenging) the other party's party-appointed arbitrator, and (iii) participating in the joint appointment of the chairperson together with the other party.[15] Accordingly, in the following, we give some practical insights in this context into first, the process for selecting a party-appointed arbitrator (1.), and second, the scrutiny (and potential challenge) of the other side's party-appointed arbitrator (2.).

1. Selection of a party-appointed arbitrator

As described above, the ICSID process for appointing arbitrators accords broad freedom to the parties to choose the party-appointed members of their tribunal.[16] This is in line with the fundamental goal of investment treaty arbitration, which is to achieve a rapid resolution of the dispute at hand. Aside from the nationality rules (which can in any case be disapplied by party agreement) and the qualification requirements in Article 14 (1) of the ICSID Convention, the parties are free to select whomever they wish as their respective arbitrators. Although ICSID does have a roster of candidates in the form of its 'ICSID Panels',[17] in practice this is rarely used. There is currently no framework stipulating any equal representation of

---

<https://icsid.worldbank.org/news-and-events/news-releases/icsid-and-uncitral-release-draft-code-conduct-adjudicators?CID=365> accessed 13 January 2022. A first draft of the Draft Code was published in May 2020 (see <https://icsid.worldbank.org/sites/default/files/amendments/Draft_Code_Conduct_Adjudicators_ISDS.pdf> accessed 13 January 2022) and a second draft in April 2021 (see <https://icsid.worldbank. org/sites/default/files/draft_code_of_conduct_v2_en_final.pdf> accessed 13 January 2022). On the issues relating to the specifics of such a code, see Chiara Giorgetti and Jeffrey L Dunoff, 'Ex Pluribus Unum? On the Form and Shape of a Common Code of Ethics in International Litigation' (2019) 113 AJIL UNBOUND 312.

15 Absent an agreement between the parties, the chairperson would be appointed by operation of Article 38 ICSID Convention, pursuant to which the Chairman of the ICSID Administrative Council has a default power to appoint missing tribunal members.

16 Christoph Schreuer et al, *The ICSID Convention: A Commentary* (2nd edn, CUP 2009), Article 40, paras 5-7.

17 See <https://icsid.worldbank.org/about/arbitrators-conciliators/database-of-icsid-panels> accessed 13 January 2022.

States in the nationality of arbitrators who are appointed.[18] Nor are there any obligations for the parties to observe other diversity requirements (such as gender) when selecting their candidates for ICSID proceedings.

With only limited review possibilities available to parties for awards rendered in the ICSID framework (see below at C.I.), the careful selection of the arbitrators – unthinkable in a court setting – takes on great significance. The parties need to ensure they appoint someone who will do the job properly – independently and impartially, and also efficiently and professionally, and with a proper understanding of the issues at hand.

In practice, the 'best' candidate will first and foremost be someone who is experienced in the ICSID procedural setting (or at least in the conduct of large-scale disputes), who has a solid understanding of public international law and who is responsive (which means the proceedings remain efficient), reasonable (which means that there are unlikely to be any surprises) and organised, and who has the ability to make tough decisions if needed. Depending on the dispute, the background of the individual will be key in understanding the subject matter of the dispute: it might be helpful to have in-depth commercial understanding and experience, experience of negotiating contracts, financial expertise, construction knowledge, familiarity with the functioning of energy markets or the generation of renewable energy, an in-depth understanding of EU law or a particular academic specialisation.

Fundamentally, the question the practitioner will ask is whether the candidate will be able to grasp the crucial points and has the expertise and experience to fully process the issues and then understand and apply the law. In the ICSID context, particular attention should, when acting for an investor, be given to the question of whether a proposed candidate has tended to lean towards more State-friendly positions. Parties will not select a candidate who is known to take positions detrimental to their case.[19] The home jurisdiction of the individual may be a further relevant factor in connection with the intended strategy for a particular dispute. Familiarity with the legal concepts of a particular domestic legal system will likely be key. In addition, if common law style elements of proceedings (for example document production) are desired (or not desired), candidates with common law backgrounds might be preferred (or not preferred)

18 See Yarik Kryvoi, *International Centre for Settlement of Investment Disputes (ICSID)* (4th edn, Wolters Kluwer 2020), para 172, noting that 'ICSID has no explicit rules aimed at ensuring equitable representation of states among adjudicators similar to those found at the ICJ or the European Court of Human Rights'.

19 Schreuer *(n 16)*, para 24.

accordingly. The availability of the candidate's time for the purposes of the proceedings (and in particular for the relevant hearing dates, which will likely stretch over a number of days) is a further key matter to consider, as not every candidate will necessarily be available at the required times. In the context of selecting an arbitrator, bias is not generally a central issue, as it is rare to find that a candidate has for example written an article that is directly hostile to the exact position that the client intends to advance in the proceedings (bias is however a key consideration when scrutinising the other party's choice of arbitrator, see (2) below). In general, the decision on a particular candidate is much more holistic than a sifting of their previous decisions, writings and statements to glean their positions on particular matters. Indeed, the process has been described as 'more of an art than a science'.[20] It is also important that the candidate is not biased *towards* the position that will be advanced in the case: bias in this (as well as the other) direction[21] will at minimum significantly diminish that arbitrator's influence in the context of the deliberations.

If properly conducted, the procedure is perfectly capable of ensuring an appropriate level of expertise and quality. This has been confirmed by participants in the recent survey by QMUL-CCIAG[22] on investor perceptions of ISDS – the first of its kind, with the debate previously mainly focused only around the concerns of NGOs, academics and State-side stakeholders, and not of investors. Notably, investors who were surveyed praised the high quality of arbitrators in the current system and also their level of experience, given that party appointments involve considerable effort to ensure the appointee has the appropriate subject matter familiarity.[23] Even though the act of choosing one's own judge may on an instinctive level contrast sharply with the typical court procedure of random judge selection, the process does work well in practice, and also has significant upsides: parties are used to a sense of participation: they are able to exercise a degree of control (which they may also perceive as a manner of quality control), and their voices are felt to be heard. The capability to steer the jurisdictional 'flavour' of the proceedings can also be an effective tool in

---

20 Borzu Sabahi et al, *Investor-State Arbitration* (2nd edn, OUP 2019), para 6.37.

21 Sabahi et al *(n 20)*, para 6.37, noting that 'all three arbitrators must be unbiased and independent of the parties.'

22 School of International Arbitration, Centre for Commercial Law Studies, Queen Mary University of London (QMUL) and the Corporate Counsel International Arbitration Group (CCIAG).

23 See 2020 QMUL-CCIAG Survey: QMUL-CCIAG, 'Investors' Perceptions of ISDS' (May 2020), 8.

shaping the form the proceedings will take and thus further improve their efficiency and predictability.

2. *Challenging an arbitrator*

The ICSID framework contains a narrow test for the challenge of an arbitrator for an alleged lack of independence and impartiality. Under Article 57 of the ICSID Convention, '[a] party may propose to a [...] Tribunal the disqualification of any of its members on account of any fact indicating a manifest lack of' the qualities set out in Article 14 (1), which are '[...] high moral character and recognized competence in the fields of law, commerce, industry or finance, [and] independent judgment.'[24] The wording 'exercise independent judgment' has been established to consist of both (i) independence, and (ii) impartiality.[25] Unlike more lenient tests applicable in other arbitration frameworks such as the test of 'justifiable doubt' under the UNCITRAL Arbitration Rules,[26] challenges on grounds of a 'manifest' lack of independence and impartiality under the ICSID framework requires meeting a much higher threshold, making such challenges rarely successful.[27]

The interpretation of whether a fact gives rise to a 'manifest' lack of independence and impartiality has varied across tribunals. Crawford suggests that this is due to a contrast between (i) tribunals considering whether 'manifest' relates to the degree of seriousness associated with the unreliability of the arbitrator, and (ii) tribunals considering whether 'manifest'

---

24 In accordance with ICSID Arbitration Rule 6 (2), each arbitrator must sign a declaration, stating, inter alia that there is no reason they should not serve on the tribunal and that they will judge fairly between the parties without instruction or compensation, and also providing 'a statement of (a) my past and present professional, business and other relationships (if any) with the parties and (b) any other circumstance that might cause my reliability for independent judgment to be questioned by a party.'

25 Emphasis added. The ICSID Convention is equally authentic in its English, French and Spanish versions, yet only the Spanish version expressly refers to impartiality; however, a consensus has emerged that both independence and impartiality are mandatory, see Maria Nicole Cleis, *The Independence and Impartiality of ICSID Arbitrators* (Brill/Nijhoff 2017), 12-13.

26 Articles 11, 12 UNCITRAL Arbitration Rules.

27 ICSID's list of its decisions is available at <https://icsid.worldbank.org/es/node/81666> accessed 13 January 2022.

relates to the 'evident' or 'obvious' unreliability of the arbitrator.[28] Indeed, the case law demonstrates two main strands of decisions (with some variations in between[29]):

Decisions in which a distinction of the ICSID regime from commercial frameworks is upheld, whereby 'manifest' relates to the degree of seriousness and therefore requires meeting a higher threshold for a successful challenge (for example the finding in *Amco* that 'the challenging party must not only prove facts indicating the lack of independence, but also that the lack is 'manifest' or 'highly probable', and not just 'possible' or 'quasi-certain''[30]).

In more recent decisions, a standard more closely related to commercial arbitration frameworks is applied, requiring instead meeting a lower threshold of showing an 'appearance of bias' for a successful challenge.[31] This test is based on whether a third party would find on the basis of the facts raised an 'evident' or 'obvious' appearance of a lack of impartiality of the arbitrator, on a 'reasonable evaluation of the facts in the case'.[32]

The IBA Guidelines on Conflicts of Interest in International Arbitration (IBA Guidelines) incorporate the 'justifiable doubts' standard in their General Standard 2 (c), and set out a detailed framework for the disclosure of, and objection to, conflicts of interest.[33] The Orange List contained in

---

28 James Crawford, 'Challenges to Arbitrators in ICSID Arbitration' (11 October 2013) PCA Peace Palace Centenary Seminar 11, cited in Sam Luttrell, 'Chapter 11: Bias Challenges in ICSID Arbitration: Unsettled Issues' in Crina Baltag (ed), *ICSID Convention after 50 Years: Unsettled Issues* (Kluwer Law International 2016), 303-304.

29 For more detail see Luttrell *(n 28)*.

30 *Amco Asia Corporation and others v Republic of Indonesia* ICSID Case ARB/81/1 Decision on the Proposal to Disqualify an Arbitrator, 24 June 1982 (unreported), see also *Suez, InterAguas Servicios Integrales del Agua S.A., Sociedad General de Aguas de Barcelona S.A. v The Argentine Republic* ICSID Case No. ARB/03/17 Decision on the Proposal for the Disqualification of Gabrielle Kaufmann-Kohler, 22 October 2007, para 40.

31 *Blue Bank International & Trust (Barbados) Ltd v Bolivarian Republic of Venezuela* ICSID Case No. ARB/12/20 Decision of the Parties' Proposals to Disqualify a Majority of the Tribunal, 12 November 2013, para 69; *Burlington Resources Inc v Republic of Ecuador* ICSID Case No. ARB/08/5, Decision on the Proposal for Disqualification of Professor Francisco Orrego Vicuña, 13 December 2013.

32 *Blue Bank International & Trust (Barbados) Ltd v Bolivarian Republic of Venezuela (n 31)*, para 69.

33 The Guidelines contain three colour-coded lists of factual situations in relation to conflicts of interests, and set out the consequences of each: (i) the Red List, consisting of disqualifying conflicts of interest and which is divided into (i) a Non-waivable Red List, where the arbitrator must decline the appointment, and

the IBA Guidelines, which provides a non-exhaustive list of disclosable scenarios which form a basis for challenge of an arbitrator within the framework of the IBA Guidelines, including (i) previous work as counsel to one of the parties, (ii) previous repeat appointments of the arbitrator by one of the parties or their counsel, and (iii) acting as arbitrator on a related issue involving a party. However, the IBA Guidelines have no general application to ICSID arbitration and can only apply if they have been expressly agreed to by the parties to a particular proceeding.[34]

Legal advisers in ICSID proceedings (on both sides) will therefore closely scrutinise the other party's proposed candidate in order to identify any grounds for challenging and thus excluding them under Article 57 of the ICSID Convention. However, as set out above, the bar is high.[35] In particular, with the pool of ICSID arbitrators being rather small, certain individu-

---

(ii) a Waivable Red List, where the arbitrator may only accept the appointment if the parties provide informed and express consent; (ii) the Orange List, which sets out situations where a disqualifying conflict of interest may be present and the relevant circumstances should be disclosed, following which (under the Guidelines) the parties have 30 days in which to challenge the appointment; and (iii) the Green List, which is made up of situations where a disqualifying conflict of interest is not present and no disclosure is necessary.

34 *Blue Bank International & Trust (Barbados) Ltd v Bolivarian Republic of Venezuela (n 31)*, para 62 ('The Chairman notes that the Parties have referred to other sets of rules or guidelines in their arguments, such as the IBA Guidelines. While these rules or guidelines may serve as useful references, the Chairman is bound by the standard set forth in the ICSID Convention. Accordingly, this decision is made in accordance with Articles 57 and 58 of the ICSID Convention.'); followed in *Canepa Green Energy Opportunities I, S.á r.l. and Canepa Green Energy Opportunities II, S.á r.l. v Kingdom of Spain* ICSID Case No. ARB/19/4 Decision on the Second Proposal to Disqualify Mr Peter Rees QC, 10 February 2020, para 54. Also see *Repsol, S.A. and Repsol Butano, S.A. v Argentine Republic* ICSID Case No. ARB/12/38 Decision on the Proposal for Disqualification of Arbitrators Francisco Orrego Vicuña and Claus von Wobeser, 13 December 2013, para 74. Luttrell notes that the agreement of the parties to supersede Article 57 (by applying the IBA Guidelines for instance) is not necessarily enforceable, and an Article 57 analysis of a challenge might be considered inevitable, see Sam Luttrell, 'Testing the ICSID Framework for Arbitrator Challenges' (2016) 31.3 ICSID Review Foreign Investment Law Journal, 600.

35 Schreuer *(n 16)*, Article 57, para 19; Audley Sheppard, 'Arbitrator Independence in ICSID Arbitration' in Christina Binder et al (eds), *International Investment Law for the 21st Century: Essays in Honour of Christoph Schreuer* (Oxford 2009), 138. For instance, the fact that an arbitrator may have articulated an opinion on an issue relevant to the case under scrutiny does not automatically entail that the arbitrator is actually biased. Otherwise, 'no potential arbitrator of an ICSID Tribunal would ever express views on any such matter'. Citing the *Urbaser v Argentina*

als do, inevitably, appear in multiple proceedings and contexts.[36] It may be that a particular individual is repeatedly appointed by a particular side or a particular State, or even a particular law firm. Or, an individual may be engaged in parallel counsel work at the same time as acting as an arbitrator (so-called 'double-hatting').[37]

Challenges against arbitrators at ICSID have only been upheld on five occasions (publicly).[38] Of those, only three full decisions are available, but they clearly illustrate how high the bar for challenge is:

Case	Disqualified individual	Reasons
Burlington v Ecuador[39]	Professor Francisco Orrego Vicuña (investor's appointee)	Statements doubting the ethics of counsel to the respondent State – 'manifestly evidences an appearance of lack of impartiality'
Blue Bank v Venezuela[40]	Mr José María Alonso (investor's appointee)	Firm was representing same claimant in another ICSID case against Venezuela (*Longreef*); 'highly probable' that Mr. Alonso would be in a position to decide issues that were relevant in that parallel case.
Caratube v Kazakhstan (II)[41]	Mr Bruno Boesch (State's appointee)	Acting as arbitrator in parallel case with related claimant, overlap in facts and legal issues, same witnesses, resulting in 'an objective circumstance demonstrating his inability to exercise independent and impartial judgment in the present arbitration.'

Accordingly, the vast majority of challenges are dismissed – sometimes in circumstances that might in other legal frameworks lead to very different outcomes. For example, the appointment of Professor Brigitte Stern, who has acted on the side of the State in a large number of arbitrations, was challenged by the claimants in *Tidewater v Venezuela*, who argued that '[Professor Stern's] multiple appointments by the same party and the same counsel, not disclosed in her original declaration, give rise to objective and

Challenge Decision, Karel Daele, *Challenge and Disqualification of Arbitrators in International Arbitration* (Wolters Kluwer 2012), 401.

36 Luttrell *(n 28)*, 312-313.

37 Daele (*n 35*), 368-369.

38 See <https://icsid.worldbank.org/es/node/81666> accessed 13 January 2022.

39 Burlington Resources, Inc. v Republic of Ecuador *(n 31)*.

40 Blue Bank International & Trust (Barbados) Ltd. v Bolivarian Republic of Venezuela *(n 31)*.

41 *Caratube International Oil Company LLP and Devincci Salah Hourani v Republic of Kazakhstan (II)* ICSID Case No. ARB/13/13 Decision on the Proposal for Disqualification of Bruno Boesch, 20 March 2014.

justifiable doubts regarding her independence and impartiality'.[42] In the decision on the challenge, Professor Stern's position was summarised as follows:

> [i]n respect of the argument that, by being appointed multiple times by the same party she may be unduly influenced by hearing the same argument repeatedly, Professor Stern explains that she is not convinced by the number of times she hears an argument but by the intrinsic value of the argument.[43]
> As to multiple appointments by the same counsel, Professor Stern points out that she has been appointed three or more times by several law firms and does not consider this fact a professional business relationship which could endanger her independence. Professor Stern explains that she has been an academic with 'a tradition of full independence and no business relations with any specific law firm' during the length of her career.[44]

Professor Stern's co-arbitrators agreed with her position and concluded that the challenge was ill-founded[45] - an outcome that would have been extremely unlikely under for example the ICC Arbitration Rules, and would be specifically prohibited under the IBA Guidelines – not because there is necessarily actual bias (which is extremely rare, in particular among sophisticated arbitrators), but because of the *perception* of bias that such appointments (which often result in six-digit remuneration) bring with them. These issues are expressly addressed in the MIC proposals.

II. Practitioner perspective on MIC proposals on appointment of arbitrators

From a client perspective, first and foremost certainty would be needed with regard to the appointment process, including the rules for selection,

---

42 *Tidewater Inc., Tidewater Investment SRL, Tidewater Caribe, C.A., et al. v The Bolivarian Republic of Venezuela* ICSID Case No. ARB/10/5 Decision on Claimants' Proposal to Disqualify Professor Brigitte Stern, Arbitrator, 23 December 2010, para 9.

43 ibid, para 26.

44 ibid, para 28 (footnotes omitted).

45 *Tidewater Inc., Tidewater Investment SRL, Tidewater Caribe, C.A., et al. v The Bolivarian Republic of Venezuela (n 42)*, para 71, confirming that they had 'no reason to doubt Professor Stern's statement that 'the fact of whether I am convinced or not convinced by a pleading depends upon the intrinsic value of the legal arguments and not on the number of times I hear the pleading."

challenge and disqualification, as there are currently various options on the table as to the nature of the institution itself, the selection process and possibilities to challenge. It is further important to set out how any new framework would interact with any existing agreements between the parties in any applicable BIT or in any arbitration rules they have chosen to apply. After all, it is only with a clear procedural framework that practitioners can advise and guide their clients through the process of appointing the arbitrators/adjudicators and act in their best possible interests in doing so.

An analysis of the outlined reform options shows that they take a direction of travel which moves away from the general objective of a depoliticised, flexible process for the resolution of a dispute, driven by the individual factual and legal circumstances of the parties, and instead moves towards a court-style process, with arbitrators who are essentially State appointees. Such a root-and-branch change in approach[46] does not, however, appear to us to be well-grounded in empirical evidence of the consequences of the supposed shortcomings of the current system[47] that

46 For a summary of trade-offs in either direction, see Malcolm Langford, Daniel Behn, and Maria Chiara Malaguti, 'The Quadrilemma: Appointing Adjudicators in Future Investor-State Dispute Settlement' (13 October 2019) Academic Forum on ISDS Concept Paper 2019/12, 34-38 (of PDF).

47 See for example Andrea Bjorklund, Marc Bungenberg, Manjiao Chi and Catharine Titi, 'Selection and Appointment of International Adjudicators: Structural Options for ISDS Reform' (17 September 2019) Academic Forum on ISDS Concept Paper 2019/11, 7-8 ('The method of selection and appointment of arbitrators in investment arbitration has been the subject of a number of criticisms. These have included questions of independence and impartiality stemming from the fact that the arbitrators are appointed by the disputing parties themselves to hear a particular dispute, after the dispute has crystallized, and that selection might be made on the basis of a presumed predisposition in favour of the arguments that are likely to be made by the appointing party. A related critique assumes that arbitrators may have an incentive to please the party that appointed him or her in order to secure reappointment. This criticism is especially discussed in the context of arbitrators seen as state-friendly or investor-friendly, rather than as neutral. The idea that these individuals have preconceived leanings leads to a perception of lack of legitimacy. Relatedly, an assumption of lack of independence and impartiality arises from other presumed conflicts of interest, due among others to double-hatting (e.g. acting as arbitrator and counsel in different cases at the same or overlapping times).'); Sergio Puig and Gregory Shaffer, 'Imperfect Alternatives: Institutional Choice and the Reform of Investment Law' (July 2018) 112.3 American Journal of International Law 397 ('ISDS, however, involves high access costs, is removed from mass publics, and is commonly charged with failure to appropriately balance competing interests, in part because of the

are meant to be addressed by the suggested reforms.[48] The depth of proposed reform appears somewhat broad for what are, on the basis of the published Proposals, mostly perceptions. To this end, a number of commentators have favoured a more incremental approach of changes to the current system[49] to remove any negative perceptions (justified or otherwise).

Indeed, the removal of party choice of arbitrator in favour of what would essentially be State appointees has been roundly criticised, including within UNCITRAL Working Group III by arbitrator Charles Brower, who stated:

---

inability of states and other stakeholders to raise claims and counterclaims against investors. Moreover, unlike judges, arbitrators in ISDS are nominated by the parties. This selection process may shape their dispositions, reflecting different forms of bias categorized as selection, compensation, and affiliation bias. Some arbitrators represent and consult for private clients in their legal practice, and thus may face conflicts of interest. Structurally, since the ISDS system is highly remunerative for private practitioners, and since the arbitrators are paid on a case-by-case basis (and by the hour), the arbitrators have an incentive to ensure the future flow of claims. ISDS thus can lead to minoritarian bias in favor of investors, especially those that are well-organized, because they have high per capita stakes, compared to other stakeholders that are numerous but disorganized due to their low per capita stakes.' (footnotes omitted)) and 408 ('The system of appointment of arbitrators creates perverse incentives'); Chiara Giorgetti et al, 'Independence and Impartiality in Investment Dispute Settlement: Assessing Challenges and Reform Options' (21 January 2020) Academic Forum on ISDS Concept Paper 2020/1, 13-14.

48 See for example Malcolm Langford, Daniel Behn and Laura Létourneau-Tremblay, 'Empirical Perspectives On Investment Arbitration: What Do We Know? Does It Matter?' (15 March 2019) ISDS Academic Forum Working Group 7 Paper, 41 and fn 192 and fn 193, citing to two studies, one by Kapeliuk, finding that party-appointed arbitrators do not side with their appointing party, and another by Puig and Strezhnev as finding that 'while arbitrators do not completely advance their appointing party's interests, when room for discretion arises, they appear to be more likely to choose outcomes that are more favorable to the side that appointed them.'

49 See for example Stephan W Schill and Geraldo Vidigal, 'Designing Dispute Settlement à la Carte for Investment Law: Insights from International Courts and Tribunals' (2019) 18.3 The Law and Practice of International Courts and Tribunals 314-344; Stephan W Schill and Geraldo Vidigal, 'Cutting the Gordian Knot: Investment Dispute Settlement à la Carte' (RTA Exchange), Geneva: International Centre for Trade and Sustainable Development; Margie-Lys Jaime, 'Chapter 7: Reshaping Investor-State Dispute Settlement Through an Appellate Review Mechanism' in Alan M Anderson and Ben Beaumont (eds), *The Investor-State Dispute Settlement System: Reform, Replace or Status Quo?* (Kluwer Law International 2020), 137-156.

> [...] if and when [an MIC] comes into being, you will find that since states, or combinations of states, make the appointments, they will be predominantly retired civil servants of that government, retired judges, other friends of politicians in that country [...].[50]

In this vein, it cannot be assumed that if only States are permitted to select appointees, they will not wield this power with any political implication. As Judge Stephen Schwebel has stated:

> The question arises, if there is a risk, real or perceived, of bias of ad hoc arbitral tribunals, as the EU appears to insinuate, is there not a risk, real or perceived, of bias – in favor of States and against investors – in the EU Commission's proposals?[51]

With regard to the current system, there is a reason why it is said that the quality of an arbitration proceeding depends largely on the quality and skill of the arbitrators who have been chosen to hear the dispute. In particular in the ICSID context, where awards cannot be appealed in the traditional sense, it is crucial that arbitrators are appointed who will understand the dispute and who will conduct the proceedings expertly and efficiently. For these reasons, party influence in investment treaty arbitration proceedings in fact likely positively contributes to smoother proceedings and better-quality awards. There are simply no persuasive grounds for the position that giving States the power to appoint the adjudicators will

---

50 Joel Dahlquist, 'At UNCITRAL Working Group Sessions, Prominent Arbitrator Charles Brower Cautions against "Revolution" of Investor-State Arbitration System' (11 April 2019) IA Reporter <https://www.iareporter.com/articles/at-uncitral-working-group-sessions-prominent-arbitrator-charles-brower-cautions-against-revolution-of-investor-state-arbitration-system/> accessed 13 January 2022. See also Charles N Brower and Jawad Ahmad, 'Why The 'Demolition Derby' That Seeks To Destroy Investor-State Arbitration?' (2018) 91 Southern California Law Review 1139.

51 See Stephen Schwebel, 'The Proposals of the European Commission for Investment Protection and an Investment Court System' (17 May 2016) ISDS Blog <http://isdsblog.com/wp-content/uploads/sites/2/2016/05/THEPROPOSALSOFTHEEUROPEANCOMMISSION.pdf> accessed 13 January 2022. Judge Schwebel goes on to ask: 'If the fact of appointment by a party of an arbitrator is taken to import bias, is not the appointment of judges solely by States a formula for the establishment of courts biased against investors? I do not believe that it Is the intention of the EU to entrench such bias in the courts proposed by the EU Commission. But if it is to be presumed that an arbitrator appointed by an investor is biased in favor of the investor – a presumption that the record of investor/State arbitration does not sustain – is there reason to presume that judges appointed only by States will not be biased in favor of States?'

improve quality or party satisfaction: it will more likely simply result in the criticism of over-politicisation.

What is clear from all of the proposals is that free party choice of arbitrator would effectively be brought to an end.[52] It may be that the loss of this strategic device could affect claimant (investor) behaviour: they may be less willing to initiate disputes under such new conditions or may be more open to settlement than they otherwise would have been. The system of adjudication would be brought more into line with domestic court procedure, whereby the parties have no influence on the selection of the judge for their respective proceedings. Repeat appointments of arbitrators/adjudicators by sides, entities and firms would no longer be possible. What is referred to as 'double-hatting' would also be likely to be brought to an end, although in and of itself, simultaneous work as counsel and arbitrator does not appear to us to be problematic – nor was it of concern to participants in a recent key ISDS survey.[53] It should also be noted that a strict application of the IBA Guidelines (which are being used extremely successfully in the parallel world of commercial arbitration) in investment treaty arbitration proceedings would in any case likely resolve the concerns underlying the current proposed reforms. In fact, in our

---

52 See in this regard QMUL-CCIAG Survey *(n 23)*, 17 ('A number of interviewees commented that the appointment of arbitrators by the parties was an important feature of ISDS. If one eliminated that possibility, the system would lose its appeal.').

53 ibid, 15 ('A significant portion of respondents has no concerns about arbitrators taking up other roles in other proceedings, such as acting as counsel or expert witnesses. 61% of respondents said arbitrators participating in ISDS should be allowed to act as counsel in other in ISDS proceedings. 57% of respondents indicated that arbitrators should be allowed to act as an expert witness in other ISDS disputes.'); contrast the view of Philippe Sands that 'We also need to address the deplorable practice of the same individual sitting as arbitrator in one case and acting as counsel in another, giving rise to situations in which you might find yourself deliberating with your fellow arbitrators in the knowledge that one or more of them is actually litigating the very point that you are seeking to write an award on. That is unacceptable. The ends of judicialization in this context seem to be prioritising the interests of certain stakeholders. This is perhaps not a popular thing to say, but we have to address the reality of what is happening.', Philippe Sands, 'Developments in Geopolitics: The End(s) of Judicialization?' (12 September 2015) ESIL Conference Closing Speech, reprinted in EJIL Talk!, <https://www.jus .uio.no/pluricourts/english/blog/guests/2015-10-22-sands-final-lecture-esil.html> accessed 13 January 2022, with the argument that double-hatting is not a cause for concern, and is rather an overlap of roles that is necessary for career transition and is compatible with ad hoc arbitration, see Langford, Behn and Létourneau-Tremblay *(n 48)*, 43, 46.

experience arbitration institutions tend to apply even stricter standards in commercial arbitrations than those of the IBA Guidelines, with in practice any hint of an issue as to independence and impartiality resulting in a decision not to confirm the candidate as an arbitrator.

A key aspect of legitimacy and acceptance of any new regime will be a perception of balance: with the Draft Statute for example envisaging only nominations by States, this poses a significant risk of the process being overly politicised.[54] In this regard, the element of the *Kaufmann-Kohler/Potestà* Proposals that would involve multiple stakeholders in the selection process is to be welcomed as a possibility to ensure such a balance. However, even if eg business organisations are able to provide input into the process in some way, the ability of the individual investor to exercise a choice will be lost. It would remain to be seen whether adjudicators who are (wholly or partly) State appointees will necessarily do a 'better' job than those solely appointed by the individual parties.

III. Practitioner perspective on MIC proposals on diversity

The EU Proposals note that the current system of arbitrator selection as we know and work with it does not promote an increase in diversity.[55] Accordingly, the EU Proposals support the introduction of mechanisms to ensure diversity both from a geographical and gender perspective[56] (as do the *Bungenberg/Reinisch* Proposals[57]) which could be introduced in the context of a permanent institution.[58] Such changes are, as the EU Proposals and the *Kaufmann-Kohler/Potestà* Proposals note, impossible 'without moving away from the system of party-appointment'.[59]

---

54 See QMUL-CCIAG Survey *(n 23)*, 16 ('Proposals to use mandatory arbitrator lists compiled solely by states and/or have state-nominated permanent judges sitting in a standing international court were unpopular with a majority of respondents (64% and 56% respectively) saying that they would undermine confidence in the independence and impartiality of the system.').

55 UNCITRAL WG III, Submission European Union and its Member States, WP 145 (2017) *(n 3)*, para 32.

56 UNCITRAL WG III, Submission European Union and its Member States, WP 159 (2019) *(n 3)*, para 21.

57 Bungenberg, Reinisch *(n 4)*, paras 96, 167.

58 UNCITRAL WG III, Submission European Union and its Member States, WP 159 (2019) *(n 3)*, para 50.

59 UNCITRAL WG III, Submission European Union and its Member States, WP 159 (2019) *(n 3)*, para 50; see also Kaufmann-Kohler, Potestà 2017 *(n 6)*, para 52.

It is a fact that the pool of arbitrator candidates contains more men than women.[60] But although party appointments do not allow for any direct impetus for change, things are changing, albeit slowly. The arbitral institutions are making strong efforts to bring the genders more into balance in the appointment process, and the trend is towards equality, although this will take a long time.

In the proposals, there appears to be a much greater focus on legal systems and geography than gender. The UNCITRAL Secretariat states in its Note with regard to gender diversity that 'The Arbitration Pledge for diversity, addressing gender diversity, can also be mentioned as an effort to pursue this goal in the field of international arbitration'.[61] The European Commission is a signatory of the Pledge.

From a practitioner perspective, clients appear to be ahead of the curve on gender equality. Some clients (notably on the investor side) will for example actively reject a list of proposed arbitrators if it does not contain any female candidates. On the State side, progress appears to be somewhat slower. Hence, a framework that removes party control over diversity and instead enshrines it in the applicable rules will likely be more effective in improving diversity than taking control from the parties and handing it to States.

C. *Appeals*

In this section we first set out the course of an ICSID annulment as we know and work with it (I.) and then provide some thoughts as to how the MIC proposals would impact the current ICSID process (II.).

I. *'Appeals' within the current ICSID framework*

ICSID awards are subject to only a very limited review process once the award has been handed down – there is no general possibility to appeal against an award in the manner of a court-style appeal procedure. Nor do

60 See Langford, Behn, and Létourneau-Tremblay *(n 48)*, 32-39.

61 See UNCITRAL, Working Group III, 'Possible reform of investor-State dispute settlement (ISDS) Selection and appointment of ISDS tribunal members' (16 November 2020), A/CN.9/WG.III/WP.203, para 13.

domestic courts have any power to review an ICSID award[62] – they must enforce it as though it were a final decision of their domestic court system. This is in line with the objectives of investment treaty arbitration of a fast and efficient final outcome to a dispute.

There are limited avenues for fixing perceived shortcomings of an award, under two sets of circumstances:[63]

First, a party can request an interpretation of the award in the event that there is a dispute between the parties as to its scope or meaning.[64]

Second, if a party comes to know a new fact that could have a decisive effect on the award, that party may apply for revision of the award.[65] Such new fact must not have been known to the Tribunal or the applicant when the award was rendered, and the applicant must not have negligently ignored the new fact.[66]

In addition to these avenues for interpretation and revision of an award, there is a very limited framework for the 'annulment' of an award based on the most fundamental procedural principles.[67] Ad hoc committees hear ICSID annulment proceedings, with their Members appointed by the Chairman of the ICSID Administrative Council from the Panel of Arbitrators.[68] The Panel of Arbitrators consists only of State nominees.[69]

---

62 See Article 53 (1) ICSID Convention, which expressly excludes any appeal, or review by national courts of ICSID awards ('The award shall be binding on the parties and shall not be subject to any appeal or to any other remedy except those provided for in this Convention. Each party shall abide by and comply with the terms of the award except to the extent that enforcement shall have been stayed pursuant to the relevant provisions of this Convention.'). Note that this excludes awards rendered under the ICSID Additional Facility.

63 In addition to the circumstances where a party is of the view that a tribunal has failed to decide on a particular question in the award or the award contains a clerical or arithmetic error, whereupon it can request rectification of the award by the tribunal in the form of a supplementary decision, see Article 49 (2) ICSID Convention and ICSID Arbitration Rule 49.

64 Article 50 ICSID Convention and ICSID Arbitration Rules 50-54.

65 Article 51 ICSID Convention and ICSID Arbitration Rules 50-54.

66 Article 51 (1) ICSID Convention and ICSID Arbitration Rule 50 (1) (c) (ii).

67 Article 52 ICSID Convention and ICSID Arbitration Rules 50 and 52-55.

68 Article 52 (3) ICSID Convention and ICSID Arbitration Rule 52 (1).

69 See Database of ICSID Panels <https://icsid.worldbank.org/about/arbitrators-conciliators/database-of-icsid-panels> accessed 13 January 2022.

The focus of the annulment process is not on legal or factual error, and consequently not on the correctness of the outcome, but rather strictly on the 'process of arbitral decisionmaking'.[70]

II. Practitioner perspective on MIC proposals on appeals

Although the EU Proposals state that the 'key problem' of the current framework is that '[p]redictability and consistency can only be effectively developed through the establishment of a standing mechanism with permanent, full-time adjudicators' and 'stakeholders cannot have reasonable expectations that a ruling in one dispute will be followed in another due to the ad hoc nature of the tribunals',[71] there does not appear to be convincing empirical evidence of inconsistency. As such, there do not appear to be grounds for the position that a mechanism for appeals 'will ensure correctness' by eliminating legal errors in first instance decisions, ensuring a 'check on those who would otherwise be independent decision-makers' and 'will gradually bring about greater consistency'.[72]

To resolve the alleged problem of inconsistency, the *Bungenberg/Reinisch* Proposals suggest either (i) a separate appellate body, based on the WTO Dispute Settlement Mechanism (which has a first instance and an appellate body),[73] with competence including the grounds for annulment listed in Article 52 of the ICSID Convention as well as the substantial scrutiny of the award regarding errors in the application or interpretation of the applicable law and manifest errors of fact,[74] or (ii) the establishment of a Multilateral Investment Appeals Mechanism (MIAM) to serve as the second instance in *ad hoc* arbitration proceedings, which would otherwise continue to be practiced as now.[75] With regard to the MIAM grounds for appeal, these should include (i) 'compliance with the procedural principles by the arbitral tribunal in the first instance proceedings', (ii) 'whether fact-finding was properly carried out', (iii) 'whether an objective appreciation

70 Frédéric G Sourgens et al, *Evidence in International Investment Arbitration* (OUP 2018), para 12.04.
71 UNCITRAL WG III, Submission European Union and its Member States, WP 159 (2019) *(n 3)*, para 41.
72 UNCITRAL WG III, Submission European Union and its Member States, WP 159 (2019) *(n 3)*, para 43.
73 Bungenberg, Reinisch *(n 4)*, para 176.
74 ibid, paras 356-358.
75 ibid, para 607.

of the facts was carried out', and (iv) 'whether there were 'serious errors of fact''.[76] It remains in their view to be clarified whether reference to Article 52 of the ICSID Convention should be made.[77]

There is much discussion, both in the Proposals and in the arbitration community, of a supposed lack of consistency in investment treaty arbitration awards that is driving proposals for reform in the direction of an appeals instance. However, the only empirical evidence of inconsistency[78] provided directly in the Proposals (apart from the reference in the EU Proposals to the *CMS* case[79]) seems to be the statement that:

> Awards issued by investment tribunals are inconsistent or sometimes even contradictory, and there is no appropriate mechanism in place to remedy or limit such inconsistencies. For example, tribunals have reached inconsistent or conflicting conclusions on core matters such as the effect of so-called 'umbrella clauses' or of 'most-favored-nation clauses'.[80]

Such examples, which would seem to take the form of different 'strands' of case law (as also typically found in the jurisprudence of all national and international courts), do not appear to us to be so serious such as to warrant wholesale reform in the form of an appellate instance. Concerns as to consistency and quality control seem to be based on a handful of decisions[81] rather than any pervasive tendency, and simply do not seem to constitute convincing grounds for change.

Investment treaty arbitration disputes do not arise in a single legal framework, but rather under one of several thousand different BITs, with

---

76 ibid, para 633.

77 ibid, para 634; Article 46 MIC Draft Statute.

78 See also for example Puig, Shaffer *(n 47)*, 408 ('...there is no appeal mechanism to provide for consistency and a check on poor decisions; and inconsistent decisions made by ad hoc tribunals limit the law's expressive value. A multilateral investment court system seems better on many counts.').

79 UNCITRAL WG III, Submission European Union and its Member States, WP 145 (2017) *(n 3)*, para 29 (citing *CMS Gas Transmission Company v The Republic of Argentina* ICSID Case No. ARB/01/8 Decision of the ad hoc Committee on the Application for Annulment of the Argentine Republic, 25 September 2007, para 158).

80 Kaufmann-Kohler, Potestà (2016) *(n 6)*, para 22. See also Jaemin Lee, 'Introduction of an Appellate Review Mechanism for International Investment Disputes - Expected Benefits and Remaining Tasks' (2014) TDM 1, Fn 6, listing the issues of the definition of 'investment', and the application of MFN provisions.

81 Lee *(n 80)*, Fn 6.

myriad variations in wording, and in a highly individual (as well as highly complex) facts scenario. Currently, each tribunal has jurisdiction to hear one dispute, under one set of rules and standards. Any hope of achieving consistency would be inherently problematic also in an MIC environment, where the legal basis of the different disputes can vary so much. As such, it could in the present context only ever be a very long-term goal. Quality control also only seems to be an argument in favour of an appeals instance at first glance, since there is no objective indication that a decision made by an appeals instance would be any better in quality than the first instance decision.

The current ICSID annulment framework represents, in our view, a fair compromise. If an appeals instance were to be introduced, ICSID disputes which already take a significant time to resolve, would take even longer to conclude. The relative finality of an ICSID award in terms of time from award to enforcement, and also duration and costs of the proceedings, would therefore be significantly diminished. Introducing an appeals instance would, similarly as with the doing away with of arbitrator selection, mean a shift away from the ideals of investment treaty arbitration towards a process that more closely resembles a court proceeding.

Furthermore, the often-cited example in the Proposals of the WTO Appellate Body as a role model for a future MIC[82] is unconvincing[83]: with the WTO Appellate Body currently hamstrung as a result of its own internal conflict, it in fact shows only too well the conflicts of a clash of interests between its members – along the same fault line between those favouring a rapid, final dispute resolution mechanism versus those favouring the development of a comprehensive legal framework. It is another reminder that it cannot be assumed that States will not put forward political appointees to any future MIC or MIAM.

Finally, an open issue is how an appeals instance before an MIC in proceedings where the ICSID Convention is applied would interact with Article 53 of the ICSID Convention (which precludes any appeal of an award). Without far-reaching change (inter se modification of the ICSID

82 See for example UNCITRAL WG III, Submission European Union and its Member States, WP 159 (2019) *(n 3)*, para 46.

83 See Puig, Shaffer *(n 47)*, 361-409, 400 ('Permitting investors to take disputes directly could depoliticize them as compared to having them resolved through diplomatic confrontation. Yet, because states control the appointment of the judges, the process could become politicized, as seen in the crisis besetting the WTO's Appellate Body. Members of the international investment law community fear a similar attack on a potential investment court.' (footnote omitted).

Convention or adoption of the proposed Mauritius-style treaty framework, for example), ICSID MIC proceedings would in any case be limited to the application of the ICSID Additional Facility framework.

D. Concluding Remarks on the Broader Context

Investment treaty arbitration has had a somewhat unexpected trajectory – from its roots in the aims and concerns of the practitioners and politicians who developed its framework, driven by the need for the depoliticisation of foreign investment disputes, to its current circumstances: with more than 1,000 treaty-based disputes listed in UNCTAD's database,[84] not even including the likely large number of confidential cases that are not publicly reported (eg cases under the UNCITRAL Arbitration Rules). In the course of this rapid expansion, public international lawyers (and therefore also States) have assumed an increasingly central role in both the proceedings themselves as well as the evolution of the principles and frameworks utilised thereby, citing to the public law element of investment treaty disputes. At the same time, public interest has also increased, with calls for greater transparency in order to, it is claimed, enhance legitimacy. As a result, we are seeing a shift in the reform discussions from the more business-based approach of investment treaty arbitration, whereby the main priority is a quick and decent outcome, to something that much more resembles a court process. This shift is clearly discernible in the EU Proposals, the *Bungenberg/Reinisch* Proposals and the Draft Statute, and the *Kaufmann-Kohler/Potestà* Proposals.

Any consideration of these various options for reform necessitates a parallel consideration as to what is the goal of the reforms – what is the nature of the process that should be the outcome? It is our experience that parties want their dispute resolved, quickly and efficiently. If speed and efficiency are the main drivers, then inherent in that approach is that in a system without precedent, with more than 3,000 different investment treaties, homogeneity will not be possible to achieve. The current system would appear to function on this premise: cases are disposed of relatively quickly and efficiently, with an emphasis on finality of the award, but for that, the homogeneity of a type normally associated with a domestic legal

84 Investment Dispute Settlement Navigator, Investment Policy Hub (UNCTAD), <https://investment policy.unctad.org/investment-dispute-settlement> accessed 13 January 2022.

system may simply not be possible. If, rather than a rapid and efficient resolution of a dispute, instead the emphasis is on developing a legal process that more closely resembles a court proceeding, this would be a marked departure for investment treaty arbitration from its roots. In that case, practitioner work in investor-State dispute resolution will take on a very different shape – selection procedures for arbitrators will be either non-existent or very narrow in scope, and if the avenues for appeals are broadened, it can only be expected that as now, both parties will, similarly, use all possibilities available to them to try to achieve their desired outcome.

In the meantime, the question posed by Lee in 2014 will continue to be hotly debated:

Should the basic 'traditional traits of arbitration' based on the parties' discretion and control be preserved as much as feasible, or should the proceeding become more 'judicialized' or 'institutionalized' in the future in a way that resembles court proceedings so as to better address the concern over the legitimacy of arbitral decisions affecting national sovereignty or regulator authority of a state involved?[85]

---

85 Lee *(n 80)*, 5-6.